THE DOG LOVER'S COMPANION TO

NEW YORK CITY

JoAnna Downey with Christian J. Lau

D0968041

AVALON
TRAVEL

THE DOG LOVER'S COMPANION TO NEW YORK CITY
The Inside Scoop on Where to Take Your Dog
First Edition
JoAnna Downey with Christian J. Lau

Published by
Avalon Travel Publishing
1400 65th Street, Suite 250
Emeryville, CA 94608, USA

Printing History
1st edition—November, 2002
5 4 3 2 1

ISBN: 1-56691-428-0
ISSN: 1538-5027

Editor: Kevin McLain
Series Manager: Angelique S. Clarke
Copy Editor: Jeannie Trizzino
Graphics: Laura VanderPloeg, Melissa Sherowski
Production: Jacob Goolkasian
Map Editor: Naomi Adler Dancis
Cartography: Kat Kalamaras
Index: Laura Welcome

Cover and Interior Illustrations: Phil Frank

Distributed by Publishers Group West

Printed in the United States by Worzalla

KEEPING CURRENT

Note to All Dog Lovers:

While our information is as current as possible, changes to fees, regulations, parks, roads, and trails sometimes are made after we go to press. Businesses can close, change their ownership, or change their rules. Earthquakes, fires, rainstorms, and other natural phenomena can radically change the condition of parks, hiking trails, and wilderness areas. Before you and your dog begin your travels, please be certain to call the phone numbers for each listing for updated information.

Attention Dogs of New York City:

Our readers mean everything to us. We explore New York City and the surrounding areas so that you and your people can spend true quality time together. Your input to this book is very important. In the last few years, we've heard from many wonderful dogs and their humans about new dog-friendly places, or old dog-friendly places we didn't know about. If we've missed your favorite park, beach, outdoor restaurant, hotel, or dog-friendly activity, please let us know. We'll check out the tip and if it turns out to be a good one, include it in the next edition, giving a thank-you to the dog and/or person who sent in the suggestion. Please write us—we always welcome comments and suggestions.

The Dog Lover's Companion to New York City
Avalon Travel Publishing
1400 65th Street, Suite 250
Emerville, CA 94608, USA
email: atpfeedback@avalonpub.com

To my mother, Ilma Cunningham, for teaching me how to listen to the wisdom of dogs; and to all the dogs who have passed through my life: Freckles, Charlie, Spooky, Penny, Hildy, Sarai, Pete, Mac, Ginger, Tasha, George, and Inu.

ACKNOWLEDGEMENTS

No book would ever be written without the assistance of a great many people. It may or may not take a village to raise a child, but it most certainly took a whole city to write this book. I want to thank all the park administrators, town clerks, hotel concierges, restaurant owners, animal control officers, and state recreation supervisors for their patience as I asked my endless questions. In addition, my appreciation goes out to Ed Benson of the Central Park Conservancy, Susan Buckley and her dog William of PAWS, Scott Schimmel and his dog Clementine, the editors of Urbanhound, and the various heads of the dog runs and parks who were invaluable in their assistance.

CONTENTS

Highland Park
Marine Park
Northside
Park Slope
Red Hook

Sheepshead Bay
Southside
Sunset Park
Williamsburg

Astoria
Bayside
Bayswater
Breezy Point
Brookville
College Point
Douglaston
East Elmhurst
Edgemere
Flushing
Forest Hills
Fresh Meadows

Glendale
Howard Beach
Jamaica
Kew Gardens
Long Island City
Middle Village
Murray Hill
Rockaway Park
Springfield Gardens
Whitestone
Woodside

Bulls Head
Donegan Hills
Egbertville
Great Kills
Huguenot Park
Midland Beach
Mount Loretto
New Dorp Beach
Prince's Bay
Richmond

Rosebank
Saint George
Shore Acre
South Beach
Stapleton
Sunnyside
Tottenville
Travis
Woodrow

Amagansett (East Hampton
   Township)
Aquebogue (Riverhead Township)
Babylon (Babylon Township)
Bay Park (Hempstead Township)
Bethpage (Oyster Bay Township)
Bridgehampton (Southampton
   Township)

Copiague (Babylon Township)
East Hampton (East Hampton
   Township)
East Marion (Riverhead Township)
East Meadow (Hempstead
   Township)
East Moriches (Brookhaven
   Township)

Farmingville (Brookhaven Township)
Fire Island
Flanders (Southampton Township)
Garden City (Hempstead Township)
Grace Estate (East Hampton Township)
Great Neck (North Hempstead Township)
Greenport (Southold Township)
Hampton Bays (Southampton Township)
Hauppauge (Islip Township)
Huntington Station (Huntington Township)
Lido Beach (Hempstead Township)
Manorville (Brookhaven Township)
Mastic Beach (Brookhaven Township)
Middle Island (Brookhaven Township)
Montauk (East Hampton Township)
Nesconset (Smithtown Township)
Old Westbury (North Hempstead Township)

Plainview (Oyster Bay Township)
Port Jefferson (Brookhaven Township)
Quogue (Southampton Township)
Riverhead (Riverhead Township)
Riverside (Southampton Township)
Rockville (Hempstead Township)
Rocky Point (Brookhaven Township)
Roslyn (North Hempstead Township)
Saint James (Smithtown Township)
Seaford (Hempstead Township)
Shelter Island
Smithtown (Smithtown Township)
Southampton
South Haven (Brookhaven Township)
Stony Brook (Brookhaven Township)
Uniondale (Hempstead Township)
Wainscott (East Hampton Township)
West Bay Shore (Islip Township)
Westhampton Beach (Southampton Township)
West Hills (Huntington Township)
Woodbury (Oyster Bay Township)

Ardsley
Armonk
Cortlandt
Croton-On-Hudson
Dobbs Ferry
Elmsford
Harrison
Hartsdale
Hastings-On-Hudson
Katonah
Larchmont
Mamaroneck

Mount Pleasant
New Rochelle
North Castle
North Salem
Peekskill
Pound Ridge
Rye
Scarsdale
Tarrytown
White Plains
Yonkers
Yorktown

Bear Mountain
Blauvelt
Congers

Mount Ivy
New City
Nyack

RESOURCES

NEW YORK CITY

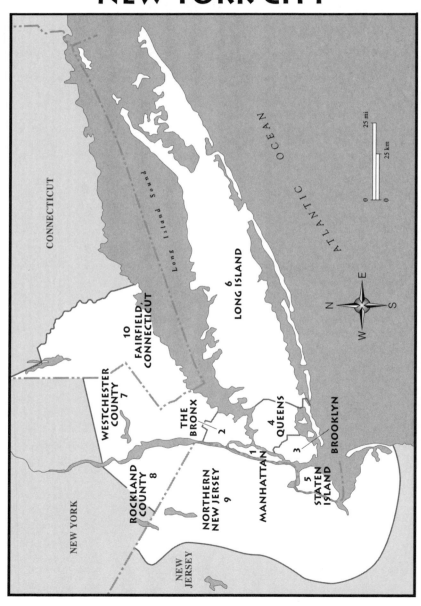

MAPS

INTRODUCTION

INTRODUCTION

A dog's curiosity is wholesome; it is essentially selfish and purposeful and therefore harmless. It relates to the chase or to some priceless bit of local mischief... .A man's curiosity, on the other hand, is untinged with imme- diate mischief; it is pure, and therefore very dangerous. The excuse you men give is that you must continually add to the store of human knowl- edge—a store that already resembles a supermarket and is beginning to hypnotize the customers. No dog would fritter away his time on earth with such tiresome tricks. A dog's curiosity leads him into pretty country and toward predictable trouble, such as a porcupine quill in the nose. Man's curiosity has led to outer space where rabbits are as scarce as grav- ity. Well, you fellows can have outer space. You may eventually get a quill in the nose from some hedgehog of your own manufacture, but I don't envy you the chase.

— From *Fred on Space*, by E.B. White

There is no city in the world where man's curiosity is keener than in New York City. Fast paced, undeniably exciting, and at times, exhausting beyond belief, life in New York is never easy, far from simple, and, most importantly, never dull. Most of us spend our days in the never-ending demand of shopping at that store of human knowledge, dining at the table of plenty, listening for the sound of continual applause, competing in a race that may never be won, only to fall asleep every night in the bed of material excess with a distant, but ceaseless, gnawing deep in the gut, a never-ending case of indigestion, the vague suspicion that maybe, *just maybe,* we're falling behind in the game. And in an increasingly hectic world of cell phones, beepers, email, and voice mail, where everyone wants a piece of you and wants it NOW! who can blame us if blasting off for some new and different planet seems just the right ticket?

Fortunately, our dogs are always ready to provide us with a much-needed and daily dose of reality. Open the door of your apartment after a long day and there's your faithful friend, thrilled to see you, happy to hear all your tales of the city, and determined to remind you that no matter how crazy things get, you are never very far from a walk around the block, the excitement of meeting a new friend, or even the pleasure of a good nap. All they ask in return is that they get to share it all with you.

Many people think living with a dog in the city is some form of cruelty, but in our experience the exact opposite is true. Dogs are among the most social creatures in the animal kingdom; the worst kind of torture to them is being left out and behind. All they really want in life is to be with us, a part of the pack and the rhythm of our lives. City dogs are never left in the backyard all day long with nothing more than the mail carrier and the meter reader for company. And because they must be walked several times a day, they get to be out and about in the world on a regular basis. Ready to go at the drop of the leash, our city dogs can't imagine what their suburban cousins do in those tract homes with the big backyards and nobody else to play with. And frankly, neither can we. Our dogs are much more than a token symbol of the American family; because they share such close quarters with us, we have learned their likes and dislikes, their passions and peeves, and in turn, they know our every mood and tone of voice. And where else could you find a roommate who, in the words of humorist Josh Billings, "is the only thing on this earth that loves you more than he loves himself?"

In fact, in all our years of living with dogs, we have never once been turned down when asked the question, "You want to come?" Put it like that, and our dogs will jump up, wag their tails eagerly, and be out the door in a flash. Never once have they asked suspiciously, "So where are you going?" before making their decision. Never once have they answered, "Naw, I think I'll stay here and take a nap." No, even if you asked your faithful friend to go to hell and back with you, the answer would be the same: "Can we go *now?*"

But that isn't to say we don't have to find creative ways to find them a little green space—especially in a city as large as New York. With over eight million residents, it is the most populous city in the country and with an estimated one million dogs living in apartments and homes all over the city, and tens of thousands more destroyed in animal shelters each year, few cities are in greater need of outlets to help make their pets' lives a little easier.

Unfortunately, as the world gets more crowded and patience grows thinner, it becomes harder to take your dog even when your schedule allows. Parks have become a turf battle between dog owners and those who think canines occupy a place only slightly above beetles. Hotel desk clerks and restaurateurs raise a horrified eyebrow when you ask if your dog can come in. As deep as the human-dog bond goes, you just stop expecting your dog to be welcome and, instead, leave her behind watching reruns of *Home Alone.*

Of course our dogs, George and Inu, don't let us off that easily. In fact, they are master guilt-meisters. Convinced that every time we walk out the door we are off to chase squirrels or roll in something stinky, our dogs pull out all the stops to get us to bring them along. When George, a shaggy, 30-pound bearded collie-terrier mix, gets the bad news that he has to stay at home, he tortures JoAnna by hiding behind the potted plant in the front hall. He slinks into the corner right by the front door, looking oh-so-pitiful, but refusing to disappear into the bedroom, thereby forcing JoAnna to pass him on her way out. And there he sits, peering pathetically between the scrawny branches, ears down and eyes mournful, silently pleading with her to change her mind. Inu, a golden retriever, uses a different tactic. He curls into a tight little ball and sinks way down onto the floor so that only his sad puppy-dog eyes can be seen. The message is clear: "How can you go out and have all that fun without me?"

To avoid this doggy guilt, we've adapted our lifestyles to include our dogs whenever possible. We tend to rent videos instead of going to the movies. We often order take-out food instead of eating in restaurants. We take our dogs to the bookstore, the grocery store, the hardware store, and wherever else we can get away with it. We set out to learn which places in our neighborhood are dog friendly, and with this book we've taken things even further.

With *The Dog Lover's Companion to New York City,* we've tried to discover the best of everything you can do with your dog in the Greater New York area, including all five boroughs, Westchester and Rockland Counties, across state lines into northern New Jersey and southern Connecticut, all the way out to the tip of Long Island, and everything in between. Along the way we've met people and dogs we never would have known, talked to folks in jobs we never knew existed, discovered trails and towns that were once only names on a map, and best of all, allowed our dogs to lead us, instead of the other way around. George and Inu always seemed to know that whether we were checking out a dog run or a hotel, a restaurant or a doggy excursion, out on the road or trail it was their job to show us the hidden joys a particular park or place had to offer. We would never have experienced these places in the same way without them.

We discovered that New York City has more dog runs than any other city in the country, more dedicated dog groups and owners actively working to make life in New York City a little bit better for both dogs and their human companions, and more spas, gyms, holistic healers, and stores all dedicated to making every pup as buff and beautiful as a New York dog should be. We found parks and beaches within the city boundaries that offer an escape from the urban jungle and, just outside the five boroughs, plenty of parks and conservation lands that provide a slice of doggy bliss.

And you'll find dozens of diversions where your canine pal can join you. Your dog can go on a harbor cruise, bone up on a little history, ride in a horse-drawn carriage or a chauffeured limousine, march in a pets-only parade, and make a lot of new friends, all with you tagging along. Best of all, you and your pooch can travel in style at the many hotels, restaurants, and outdoor cafés that welcome you and your dog. Our hope is that after reading this book you'll find it even harder to close your door on that lovable little mug of hers; we also expect your dog's tail will be wagging on a regular basis. Maybe you'll even learn things about New York you never knew. We know we did!

To help you locate all those great parks, restaurants, hotels, and diversions, we've organized each borough into neighborhoods—which is how most New Yorkers think of the city anyway. If you want to find a dog-friendly restaurant in Greenwich Village, for example, simply look under that neighborhood name in the Manhattan chapter. If you are looking for a dog park in Brooklyn Heights, you'll find it listed under that neighborhood heading in the Brooklyn chapter. In the other chapters, which are organized by county, you'll find the information arranged by city or town. Of course, our helpful maps at the beginning of each chapter will always point you in the right direction. Trust us, follow our lead, and you won't miss a thing!

THE PAWS SCALE

At some point we've got to face the facts: Humans and dogs have different tastes. We like eating oranges and smelling lilacs and covering our bodies with soft clothes. They like eating road kill and smelling each other's unmentionables and covering their bodies with horse manure.

The parks, beaches, and recreation areas in this book are rated with a dog in mind. Maybe your favorite park has lush gardens, a duck pond, a few acres of perfectly manicured lawns, and sweeping views of a nearby skyline. But unless your dog can run leash-free, swim in the pond, and roll in the grass, that park doesn't deserve a very high rating.

The very lowest rating you'll come across in this book is the fire hydrant symbol 🐾. When you see it that means the park is merely "worth a squat." Visit one of these parks only if your dog just can't hold it any longer. These parks have virtually no other redeeming qualities for canines.

Beyond that, the paws scale starts at one paw 🐾 and goes up to four paws 🐾 🐾 🐾 🐾. A one-paw park isn't a dog's idea of a great time. Maybe it's a tiny park with few trees and too many kids running around. Or perhaps it's a magnificent-for-people park that bans dogs from every inch of land except paved roads and a few campsites.

Four-paw parks, on the other hand, are places your dog will drag you to visit. Some of these areas come as close to dog heaven as you can get on this planet. Many have water for swimming or zillions of acres for hiking. Some four-paw parks give you the option of letting your dog go leash-free. Others have restrictions, which we'll detail in the descriptions.

You will also notice a foot symbol 👣 every so often. The foot means the park offers something extra special for humans in the crowd. You deserve something for being such a good chauffeur.

This book is not a comprehensive guide to all of the parks in the metropolitan New York area. We've tried to find the best, largest, and most convenient parks. Some areas have so many wonderful parks that we found ourselves getting jaded. What would have been a four-paw park in one area looked like a mere two- or three-paw place after seeing so many great spots in another area. Other spots had such a limited supply of parks that for the sake of dogs living and visiting there, we ended up listing parks that wouldn't be worth mentioning otherwise.

Since driving in New York can sometimes feel like driving the course at the Indy 500, we've given specific directions to all the parks. When you ask a New Yorker how to get somewhere, you'll most often get a look that says, "If you have to ask, you shouldn't be going there." Or you'll get scrambled and vague directions that result in your becoming hopelessly lost. Although we've tried to make it as easy as possible for you, we highly recommend picking up a detailed street map before you and your dog set out on your adventures.

TO LEASH OR NOT TO LEASH

That is not a question that plagues dogs' minds. Ask just about any normal, red-blooded American dog if she'd prefer to visit a park and be on leash or off, and she'll say, "Arf!" (Translation: Is this a trick question?) No doubt about it, most dogs would give their canine teeth to be able to frolic without that dreaded leash.

The official leash law for dogs in all five boroughs of New York City is that pups must be on a leash in all city parks, with the exception of designated dog runs. Parks without dog runs, however, operate under an unofficial rule that allows dogs to be leash-free before 9 A.M. and after 9 P.M. What this means, however, is that the off-leash hours often depend on the good graces of the official enforcing them; they aren't really part of the law, just a courtesy that dog owners have enjoyed with the park officials. Leaders of the canine community in New York have repeatedly asked the Parks Department to make the off-leash courtesy hours official and, therefore, legal. But as we go to press, the Parks Department has not yet made a decision on this request. Think of it this way—the leash law is a little like the seat belt law. Ninety percent of the time, you will not be stopped for having your dog off-leash during the courtesy hours. But if your dog is acting up in other inappropriate ways, you could get ticketed.

The full running dog symbol (🐕) means that, in designated areas, your dog is allowed off leash during all hours. When you see the clock superimposed on the running dog symbol (🐕), you'll know that the courtesy rules are in effect. The rest of the parks demand leashes. We wish we could write about the places where dogs get away with being scofflaws, but those would be the first parks the animal-control patrols would hit. We can't advocate breaking the law, but if you're going to, please follow your conscience and use common sense.

And just because dogs are permitted to be off-leash in certain areas, that doesn't necessarily mean you should let your dog run free. In state forests and large tracts of land, unless you're sure your dog will come back to you when you call or will never stray more than a few yards from your side, you should keep her leashed—for her sake. A deer or rabbit that crosses your path could mean hours of searching for your stray dog. And an otherwise docile homebody can turn into a savage hunter if the right prey is near. In pursuit of a strange scent, your dog could easily get lost in an unfamiliar area.

Be careful out there. If your dog really needs leash-free exercise but can't be trusted in remote areas, she'll be happy to know that several beaches permit well-behaved, leashless pooches, as do the ever-growing number of enclosed dog parks.

THERE'S NO BUSINESS LIKE DOG BUSINESS

There's nothing appealing about bending down with a plastic bag or a piece of newspaper on a chilly morning and grabbing the steaming remnants of what your dog ate for dinner the night before. It's disgusting. Worse yet, you have to hang on to it until you can find a trash can. And how about when the newspaper doesn't endure before you're able to dispose of it? Yuk! It's enough to make you wish your dog were a cat.

But as gross as it can be to scoop the poop, it's even worse to step in it. It's really bad if a child falls in it, or—*gasp!*—starts eating it. And have you ever walked into a park where few people clean up after their dog? The stench could make a hog want to hibernate.

Unscooped poop is one of a dog's worst enemies. Public policies banning dogs from parks are enacted because of it. At present one of the biggest obstacles to making the courtesy leash hours into law is the negligent behavior of a few owners. A worst-case scenario is already in place in several communities on Long Island—dogs are banned from all parks. Their only exercise is a leashed sidewalk stroll. That's no way to live.

If we had a nickel for every dog constable that listed violations of the pooper-scooper laws as the thing that made their job most difficult, let's just say we could quit our day jobs. Almost everyone we spoke to named unscooped poop as their number one headache—and the thing most likely to make their towns ban dogs from public parks. Several officials told us the biggest pressure they have right now is what to do about the "dog problem" complaints they receive from residents.

Just be responsible and clean up after your dog *everywhere* you go. Stuff plastic bags in your jackets, your purse, your car, your pants pockets—anywhere you might be able to pull one out when needed. Or if plastic isn't your bag, newspapers do the trick. If it makes it more palatable, bring along a paper bag, too, and put the used newspaper or plastic bag in it. That way you don't have to walk around with dripping paper or a plastic bag whose contents are visible to the world.

If you don't enjoy the squishy sensation, try one of those cardboard or plastic bag pooper-scoopers sold at pet stores. If you don't feel like bending down, buy a long-handled scooper. There's a scooper for every taste.

We've tried to not lecture about scooping throughout the book, but it does tend to be JoAnna's pet peeve. To help keep parks alive, we should harp on it in every park description, but that would take another 100 pages, and you'd start to ignore it anyway. And if we mentioned it in some parks and not others, it might convey that you don't have to clean up after your dog in the descriptions where it's not mentioned. Trust us.

Every park has a pooper-scooper law!

ETIQUETTE REX: THE WELL-MANNERED MUTT

While cleaning up after your dog is your responsibility, a dog in a public place has his own responsibilities. Of course, it really boils down to your responsibility again, but the burden of action is on your dog.

Etiquette for restaurants and hotels is covered in other sections of the introduction. What follows is some very basic dog etiquette. We'll go through it quickly, but if your dog's a slow reader, he can go over it again: No vicious dogs; no jumping on people; no incessant barking; dogs should come when they're called; dogs should stay on command; no leg lifts on backpacks, human legs, or any other personal objects hanging around beaches and parks.

Everyone, including dogs, makes mistakes, but you should do your best to remedy any consistent problems. It takes patience, and it's not always easy. For instance, George considers it his doggy duty to bark at weird people—at least those he thinks are weird (and we hate to say it, but he's usually right). But that's no excuse. Strange folk or not, your dog shouldn't be allowed to bark at others unless they're threatening you or breaking into your house.

And Inu has this selective hearing problem. He only pays attention to commands when the wind is blowing a certain way (at least that's his explanation). Tell him to come one day, and he's right there. But when the breeze is blowing toward a certain great smell. . .well, it seems to cloud his usual good hearing. But "under voice control" means *all* the time. If your dog won't obey you, fix the problem or put him on a leash. There are certain public behaviors that should not be tolerated in a dog. George and Inu are constantly learning their boundaries the hard way, and we're constantly learning to avoid situations that might make our sweet dogs look like canine delinquents. There's a limit to the "dogs will be dogs" adage.

SAFETY FIRST

A few essentials will keep your traveling dog happy and healthy. When planning a trip with your dog, know his limitations. Some dogs are perfectly fine in a car; others get motion sickness. Some dogs happily hop in their carriers for airline flights; others are traumatized for hours. Only you know your dog's temperament. Here are some guidelines to consider before you hit the road:

Heat: If you must leave your dog alone in the car for a few minutes, do so only if it's cool out and if you can park in the shade. Never, *ever*, leave a dog in a car with the windows rolled up all the way. Even if it seems cool, the sun's heat passing through the window can kill a dog in minutes. Roll down the window just enough for your dog to get air, but so there's no danger of him getting out or someone breaking in. Make sure he has plenty of water.

You also have to watch out for heat exposure when your car is in motion. Certain cars, such as hatchbacks, can make a dog in the backseat extra hot, even while you feel okay in the driver's seat.

Try to take your vacation so you don't visit a place when it's extremely warm. Dogs and heat don't get along, especially if the dog isn't used to heat.

The opposite is also true. If a dog lives in a hot climate and you take him to a freezing place, it may not be a healthy shift. Check with your vet if you have any doubts. Spring and fall are usually the best times to travel.

Water: Water your dog frequently. Dogs on the road may drink even more than they do at home. Take regular water breaks, or bring a heavy bowl (the thick clay ones do nicely) and set it on the floor so your dog always has access to water. When hiking, be sure to carry enough for yourself and a thirsty dog.

Rest stops: Stop and unwater your dog. There's nothing more miserable than being stuck in a car when you can't find a rest stop. No matter how tightly you cross your legs and try to think of the desert, you're certain you'll burst within the next minute. But think of how a dog feels when the urge strikes, and he can't tell you the problem. There are plenty of places listed in our book for you to allow your dog to relieve herself.

How frequently you stop depends on your dog's bladder. If your dog is constantly running out the doggy door at home to relieve himself, you may want to stop every hour. Others can go for significantly longer without being uncomfortable. Watch for any signs of restlessness and gauge it for yourself.

Car safety: Even the experts differ about how a dog should travel in a car. Some suggest doggy safety belts, available at pet supply stores. Others firmly believe in keeping a dog kenneled. They say it's safer for the dog if there's an accident, and it's safer for the driver because there's no dog underfoot. Still others say you should just let your dog hang out without straps and boxes. They believe that if there's an accident, at least the dog isn't trapped in a cage. They say that dogs enjoy this more anyway.

We tend to agree with the latter school of thought. Inu and George travel very politely in the backseat and occasionally love sticking their snouts out of the windows to smell the world go by. The danger is that if the car kicks up a pebble or annoys a bee, their noses and eyes could be injured. So we usually open the window just enough so our dogs can't stick out much snout.

Whichever way you choose, your pet will be more comfortable if he has his own blanket with him for the duration of your trip. A veterinarian acquaintance uses a faux-sheepskin blanket for his dogs. At night in the hotel, the sheepskin doubles as the dog's bed.

Planes: Air travel is even more controversial. Many people feel it's tantamount to cruel and unusual punishment to force a dog to fly in the cargo hold like a piece of luggage. And there are dangers to flying that are somewhat beyond your control, such as runway delays (the cabin is not temperature-controlled when on the ground) and connecting flights that tempt wrong-way fates.

Lately the airlines have made it increasingly difficult to fly with your pet. Since 2000 most of the major airlines have declared blackout periods for your pet—these usually fall at the peak flying times like summer and during holidays. And with increased airline security at airports, it is only a matter of time before the only way to travel with your pet is with a travel service. In the meantime, make sure when you book your reservation that you tell the travel agent or airline representative you will be traveling with your pet, and be doubly certain the airline will allow your pet on board.

If you must fly, there are some very specific rules you can follow to ensure your dog's safety. For example, always book nonstop flights. Don't take the chance that your dog could be misdirected while changing planes. And always inform the flight crew you are traveling with your pet. That way they can inform you when your dog has boarded the plane safely and will take extra precautions when on the runway. Also, make sure you schedule takeoff and arrival times when the temperature is below 80° F and above 35° F. And don't forget to consult the airline about its regulations and required certificates. Most airlines will ask you to show a health certificate and possibly proof of a rabies vaccination.

The question of tranquilizing a dog for a plane journey is difficult. Some vets think it's insane to give a dog a sedative before flying. They say a dog will be calmer and less fearful without taking a disorienting drug. Others think it's crazy not to afford your dog the little relaxation he might not otherwise get without a tranquilizer. We suggest discussing the tranquilizer issue with your vet, who will take the trip's length and your dog's personality into account. On their first flight together, JoAnna gave George a very mild sedative. He was very dehydrated afterward, so on the return leg he went without the drug. He was just fine and has not been sedated since. Flying is not his favorite activity, but it's better than being left at home, so he trusts JoAnna to make sure he's treated okay.

Medical Emergencies: Unfortunately, some pet emergencies are unavoidable. The last thing you need if your pet requires immediate assistance is to be groping for the Yellow Pages, trying to locate the nearest emergency room. Our advice: know the location closest to you before you need it. A listing of the 24-hour animal hospitals in and around the New York City area is included in the Resources section at the back of this book for quick reference.

THE ULTIMATE DOGGY BAG

Your dog can't pack her own bags, and even if she could, she'd probably fill them with dog biscuits and chew toys. It's important to stash some of those in your dog's vacation kit, but here are some other items to bring along: bowls, bedding, brush, towels (for those muddy days), first-aid kit, pooper-scoopers, water, food, prescription drugs, tags, treats, toys, and, of course, this book.

Be sure your dog wears her license, identification tag, and rabies tag. On a long trip you may even want to bring along your dog's rabies certificate. Some parks and campgrounds require rabies and licensing information. You never know how picky they'll be.

It's a good idea to snap one of those barrel-type IDs on your dog's collar, too, showing the name, address, and phone number of where you'll be vacationing. That way if she should get lost, at least the finder won't be calling your empty house. Carrying a picture of your dog, in case the two of you become separated, is also not a bad idea.

Some people think dogs should drink only water brought from home so their bodies don't have to get used to too many new things. We've never had a problem giving our dogs tap water from other parts of the state, nor has anyone else we know. Most vets think your dog will be fine drinking tap water in most other U.S. cities.

BONE APPÉTIT

In Europe dogs enter restaurants and dine alongside their folks as if they were people, too. (Or at least they sit and watch and drool while their people dine.) Not so in America. Rightly or wrongly, dogs are considered a health threat. But many health inspectors will say they see no reason why clean, well-behaved dogs shouldn't be permitted inside a restaurant.

Ernest Hemingway made an expatriate of his dog, Black Dog (a.k.a. Blackie), partly because of America's restrictive views on dogs in dining establishments. In "The Christmas Gift," a story published in *Look* magazine in 1954, he describes how he made the decision to take Black Dog to Cuba rather than leave him behind in Ketchum, Idaho:

> *This was a town where a man was once not regarded as respectable unless he was accompanied by his dog. But a reform movement had set in, led by several local religionists, and gambling had been abolished and there was even a movement on foot to forbid a dog from entering a public eating place with his master. Blackie had always tugged me by the trouser leg as we passed a combination gambling and eating place called the Alpine where they served the finest sizzling steak in the West. Blackie wanted me to order the giant sizzling steak and it was difficult to pass the Alpine.... We decided to make a command decision and take Blackie to Cuba.*

Fortunately, you don't have to take your dog to a foreign country in order to eat together at a restaurant. New York has many restaurants with outdoor tables, and these establishments welcome dogs to join their people for an alfresco experience.

The law on patio-dining dogs is somewhat vague, and you'll discover different versions of it. But in general, as long as your dog doesn't go inside a restaurant (even to get to outdoor tables in the back) and isn't near the food preparation areas, it's probably legal. The decision is then up to the restaurant proprietor.

The restaurants listed in this book have given us permission to tout them as dog-friendly eateries. But keep in mind that rules can change and restaurants can close, so we highly recommend phoning before you get your stomach set on a particular kind of cuisine. Also, even if they are listed here as allowing dogs, as a courtesy you should politely ask the manager if your dog may join you on that particular day. Remember, it's the restaurant owner, not you, who will be in trouble if someone complains.

Some basic restaurant etiquette: Dogs shouldn't beg from other diners, no matter how delicious that steak looks. They should not attempt to get their snouts (or their entire bodies) up on the table. They should be clean, quiet, and as unobtrusive as possible. If your dog leaves a good impression with the management and other customers, it will help pave the way for all the other dogs who want to dine alongside their best friends in the future.

A ROOM AT THE INN

Good dogs make great hotel guests. They don't steal towels, and they don't get drunk and keep the neighbors up all night. This book lists dog-friendly accommodations of all types, from motels to bed-and-breakfast inns to elegant hotels. But the basic dog etiquette rules are the same.

Dogs should *never* be left alone in your room. Leaving a dog alone in a strange place is inviting serious trouble. Scared, nervous dogs can tear apart drapes, carpeting, and furniture, or injure themselves. They can also bark nonstop and scare the daylights out of the housekeeper. Just don't do it.

Only bring a house-trained dog to a lodging.

Of course we assume if you travel with your pet, she has been de-fleaed. With the advent of so many fast-acting topical treatments such as Advantage, Frontline or Program, keeping your pup flea-free is now a cinch. We haven't seen a flea around our homes for ages and we would certainly never consider traveling with a pet who brought his own pets. Yikes! Often the hotel pet fee goes toward de-fleaing your room after a pet has stayed there, but we recommend you arrive with a pet who doesn't have any tiny hitchhikers along for the ride. We really can't think of anything more rude than leaving behind two or twenty critters for the kind innkeeper who took you in.

It helps if you bring your dog's bed or his blanket. He'll feel more at home and won't be tempted to jump on the bed. If your dog sleeps on the bed with you at home, bring a sheet and put it on top of the bed so the hotel's bedspread won't get furry or dirty.

After a few days in a hotel, some dogs come to think of it as home. They get territorial. When another hotel guest walks by, it's *"Bark! Bark!"* When the housekeeper knocks, it's *"Bark! Snarl! Bark! Gnash!"* Keep your dog quiet or you'll both find yourselves looking for a new home away from home.

For some strange reason, many lodgings prefer small dogs as guests. All we can say is, *"Yip! Yap!"* It's really ridiculous. Large dogs are often much calmer and quieter than their tiny, high-energy cousins. (Some hotel managers must think small dogs are more like cats. Wrong.) If you're in a location where you can't find a hotel that will accept you and your big brute, it's time to try a sell job. Let the manager know how good and quiet your dog is (if he is). Promise he won't eat the bathtub or run around and shake the hotel. Offer a deposit or sign a waiver, even if they're not required for small dogs. It helps if your sweet, soppy-eyed dog is at your side to convince the decision-maker.

You could always sneak dogs into hotels, but we don't recommend that you attempt to do so. The lodging might have a good reason for its rules. Besides, you'll always feel as if you're going to be caught and tossed out on your tail. You race in and out of your room with your dog as if ducking sniper fire. It's better to avoid feeling like a criminal and move on to a more dog-friendly location. For a sure bet, try a Motel 6, a Red Roof Inn, or, for the ultimate in doggy lodging, any Loew's Hotel, all of which have doggy patron programs. Most of these establishments allow you to bring your dog with you. Some have more lenient pet rules than others.

The lodgings described in this book are for dogs who obey all the rules. Rates listed are for double rooms, unless otherwise noted. Although camping is not a highlight in this book, we do list some sites in the New york area where you and your pooch can enjoy a night under the stars (or snuggled in your tent, if you prefer). In all the state and county campgrounds you must show proof of a current rabies vaccination for your pet and dogs must be on-leash at all times. This means your pup must be leashed when you are walking through the grounds, on your way to the facilities and even when your pup is relaxing at your own campsite. Rover should not rove into your neighbor's site in search of a hot dog or two and, when children are around, you must be extra vigilant to mind your pet. Dogs are notoriously territorial and may not take kindly to a child or adult wandering by your tent. Finally, to insure that everyone is a happy camper, curb your dog's barking. Nothing will land you on the "no dogs allowed" list faster than a dog who bays at the moon after lights out.

TRANSPORTATION

Getting around New York without a car is simple if you're a human. Simply hop on a bus, the subway, a cab, or call a car service, and you're there. If you're a person with a dog, however, life becomes a little more challenging. On a daily basis, the need for a car is minimal. No doubt you frequent the nearest park, dog run, vet's office, and pet store. But what do you do if your dog needs emergency care or you need to go to another area of the city with your pup? And let's face it, all of us need to get out of town every once in a while. Many of the really great spots listed in this book require a car to reach them.

By law, taxi drivers are not required to transport your pup, but some of them will. We find if our dog is leashed, quiet, and well behaved, and doesn't have a spiked collar around his neck, the odds are much better a driver will stop and let us ride. Also, to ensure future success, we suggest bringing a blanket for the seat if your dog sheds and tipping the driver really well.

As far as subways and buses are concerned well, size really *does* matter, only this time, the smaller the better. If your dog can fit into a container (that you can actually carry) or your bag, she is welcome to ride. The same rules apply on the Long Island Railroad, the PATH trains and the Hampton Jitney. Larger dogs have been known to circumvent the small dogs–only rule, but we can't ensure your success, so you're on your own with each respective driver, conductor, and operator. The Metro-North Railroad will allow well-behaved dogs on board at the discretion of the conductor. This means they also have the right to refuse you, so be forewarned. But for any dog bigger than a breadbox, it seems, riding the public transportation system is not your best bet.

Now that we've told you the bad news, here's the good news. There are pet transport services springing up all over the city that will take you and your pup anywhere in the Tri-State area. These include taxis just for pets, vans that will transport you to the Hamptons and even limousine services to squire you and Fido around town. A list of transportation services is included in the Resources section at the back of this book for easy reference.

NATURAL TROUBLES

Chances are that your adventuring will go without a hitch, but you should always be prepared to deal with trouble. Make sure you know the basics of animal first aid before you embark on a long journey with your dog.

The more common woes—ticks, burrs, poison ivy, and skunks—can make life with a traveling dog a somewhat trying experience.

Ticks are hard to avoid in the areas just outside New York City. They can carry Lyme disease, so you should always check yourself and your dog thoroughly after a day in tick country. In fact, it's a good idea to keep checking for a day or two after you've been out. Ticks are crafty little critters, and it's not unusual to find ticks on your dog two, three, and four days after your walk in the woods. Don't forget to check ears and between the toes.

If you find a tick that is unattached, you can remove it from your dog with your hands, but tweezers are best. If you find an attached tick (it's usually swollen and looks like a dark corn kernel), use tweezers to grasp it as close to your dog's skin as possible and pull it straight out. If you are unable to grasp the tick close to the skin, try twisting it counterclockwise, "unscrewing" the tick's head. Frequently they will let go. Avoid leaving any tick mouthparts embedded under your dog's skin. Disinfect the area before and after removing the pest.

The tiny deer ticks that carry Lyme disease are difficult to find. Consult your veterinarian if your dog is lethargic for a few days, has a fever, loses her appetite, or becomes lame. These symptoms could indicate Lyme disease. If you spend a lot of time on Long Island, or any of the woodlands we recommend, we suggest you have your dog vaccinated.

Poison ivy is also a common menace. Dogs don't react to poison ivy, but they can easily pass its oils on to people. If you think your dog has made contact with poison ivy, avoid petting her until you can get home and bathe her (preferably while wearing rubber gloves). If you do pet her before washing her, make sure you wash your hands immediately and don't touch your eyes.

If your dog loses a contest with a skunk (and she always will), rinse her eyes first with plain warm water, then bathe her with dog shampoo. Towel her off, then apply tomato juice. If you can't get tomato juice, you can also use a solution of one pint of vinegar per gallon of water to cut through the stink.

HE, SHE, IT

In this book, whether neutered, spayed, or *au naturel,* dogs are never referred to as "it." They are either "he" or "she." We alternate pronouns so no dog reading this book will feel left out.

BEYOND THE BORDERS

There may be times when you and your dog actually find yourselves leaving New York to visit other parts of the United States. Avalon Travel Publishing offers The Dog Lover's Companion series of books for different parts of the country, including Atlanta, Boston, Florida, New England, Pacific Northwest, Seattle, Texas, and Washington, D.C. All of the authors are experts in their areas and have adventurous dogs who help them explore and rate various attractions. Keep your eyes peeled for upcoming books or log on to www.dogloverscompanion.com to order yours.

If you're interested in more dog news in New York City, check out Urbanhound. This resource website details doggy day care centers, pet stores, current dog events; answers your health and behavior questions; and helps you find just about any service you need for your pup in the five boroughs. You can find this helpful guide at the website: www.urbanhound.com.

A DOG IN NEED

If you don't currently have a dog but could provide a good home for one, we'd like to make a plea on behalf of all the unwanted dogs who will be euthanized tomorrow and the day after that and the day after that. JoAnna adopted George from an animal shelter, and Chris saved Inu from inattention at the hands of his previous owners. We believe and support all efforts to control the existing dog population (spay or neuter your dogs!) and to assist the ones who currently and desperately need homes. Animal shelters and humane organizations are overflowing with dogs who would devote their lives to being your best buddy, your faithful traveling companion, and a dedicated listener to all your tales of bliss and woe.

For information contact your local shelter or the National Humane Education Society (521-A East Market Street, Leesburg, VA 20176), a nonprofit organization that teaches people about the importance of being kind to animals and maintains the Peace Plantation Animal Sanctuary for dogs and cats.

Need a nudge? Remember these words by writer Lloyd Alexander: "I had no particular breed in mind, no unusual requirements. Except the special sense of mutual recognition that tells dog and human they have both come to the right place."

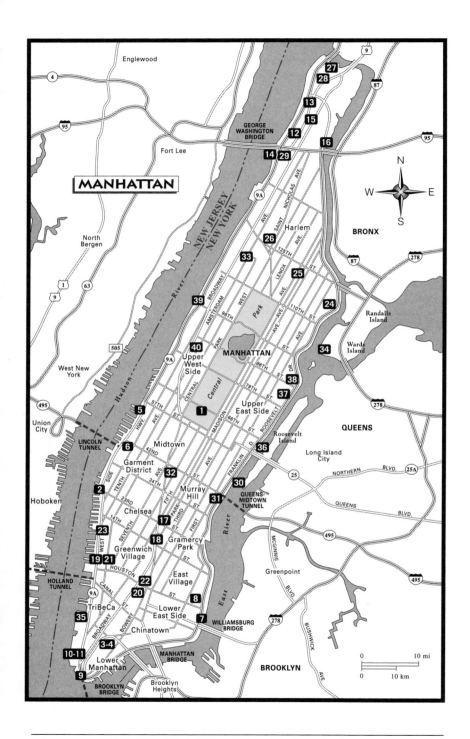

MANHATTAN

1 MANHATTAN

God...sat down for a moment when the dog was finished in order to watch it...and to know that it was good, that nothing was lacking, that it could not have been made better.

—Rainer Maria Rilke

Although New Yorkers like to think of themselves as the cosmopolitan elite, there is an undeniable provincialism that permeates the borough of Manhattan. Forget about the rest of New York City. (What do you mean, the *rest* of New York City?) The world begins at the East River, ends at the Hudson River, and in between lies the center of the universe. Try asking a Manhattan resident to come visit Brooklyn, Queens, or Staten Island, and you'll know what we mean. They look as dumbfounded as if you had just asked them to get in their spaceship and fly to Mars. Of course, we have no doubt that when spaceships are available to Mars, it will be a New Yorker who is the first to hop on board. They just won't be landing in the other boroughs first.

PICK OF THE LITTER– MANHATTAN HIGHLIGHTS

BEST CITY PARKS

Central Park

Fort Tryon Park & Dog Run, Fort George

Inwood Hill Park & Dog Run, Inwood

Riverside Park, Upper West Side

BEST DOG PARKS

Madison Square Park & James' Dog Run, Gramercy

Riverside Park, Upper West Side

Washington Square Park & George's Dog Run, Greenwich Village

BEST EVENTS

Bark Breakfast, Midtown East

Blessing of the Animals, Morningside

Corner Book Store Canine Buffet, Upper East Side

Great American Mutt Show, Clinton

New York Pet Show, Midtown West

BEST RESTAURANTS

Barking Dog Luncheonette, Upper East Side

Barney Macs, Greenwich Village

Dawgs on Park, East Village

DBA, East Village

Empire Diner, Chelsea

New Leaf Café, Fort George

BEST PLACES TO STAY

The Four Seasons, Midtown East

Metropolitan Hotel, Midtown East

The Muse Hotel, Midtown West

Regency Hotel, Midtown East

SoHo Grand, Soho

Simply put, there is little reason to leave this island if you are a Manhattan resident. To mangle the lyrics of that famous song, "If you can't get it here, you can't get it anywhere." And that goes for dogs, too. Whatever a dog might desire, be it a taxi, an astrologer, a holistic healer, a masseuse, a party planner, a gym, or a personal trainer, you'll find it in Manhattan. There are dog groups, dog events, dog spas, dog pools, dog hotels, dog parties, and more dog runs here than in any other borough in the city—or any city in the country, for that matter.

Since the first dog run was built in Tompkins Square Park in 1990, dogs and their owners have seen an explosion of runs (25 in Manhattan alone and counting), providing a place not only for off-leash recreation, but also for owners to congregate, share stories, and connect with their neighbors in ways they never imagined. The dog runs provide a social outlet that makes this city seem a little more friendly, a little less scary, a little more manageable—not to mention what it does for us! The success of the dog parks in Manhattan has demonstrated a model for the other boroughs to follow.

In this chapter, we organize the material by neighborhood. We'll tell you about places you may know about, and hopefully introduce you to many more that you don't. You probably know where to eat, where to walk, where to socialize, and where to buy doggy treats within the confines of your own immediate neighborhood. What you may not know is how much more is out there beyond your view. So hop in that spaceship and fly a little — we promise we won't make you stray too far from the center of the universe.

CENTRAL PARK

There can never be too many superlatives to describe this granddaddy of all city parks. Although not technically a "neighborhood," Central Park is, undoubtedly, a world unto itself. Spanning both the Upper West and East Sides, the park runs from 59th Street all the way to 110th Street. Long the center of New York life, there is simply no other way to start this book than with the many diverse sections in this park of parks.

Parks, Beaches, and Recreation Areas

1 Central Park 🐾 🐾 🐾 🐾 🏊

In the mid-1800s, A. J. Downing, one of the first environmentalists in this country, recognized that the population growth in New York City would soon overwhelm every bit of open space on the island of Manhattan. Much of the waterfront had already been developed for industry so civic leaders looked inward, or rather toward the center of the city, and found that the 843 acres that are now Central Park were too hilly, rocky, and swampy—in other words, geologically undesirable—for development. In 1853, the land was deemed suitable for New York's first public park, and the rest, they say, is history.

THINK GLOBALLY, BARK LOCALLY

As might be expected, New Yorkers have a long history of activism, and dog owners are no different. There are several very active dog groups in Manhattan that have worked, and continue to work, to improve the quality of life for their pets. Almost all dog runs in New York City are privately funded and have originated through the efforts of local dog owners. Below is a list of large groups that manage more than one run, although almost every dog run has its own group which are detailed within each respective neighborhood.

Friends and Lovers of Riverside Area Life (FLORAL): This organization is dedicated to improving the lives of dogs in the Upper West Side. Responsible for the three dog runs currently in Riverside Park, this organization has been waging a campaign to build an even bigger run at 73rd Street. These efforts have thus been thwarted by the city (if you're interested in the chronology of events, it is detailed on their website) but hope springs eternal, so the fundraising efforts continue. If you wish to contribute or learn more about this group, contact them at P.O. Box 330, Planetarium Station, New York, NY 10024; 212/580-6932; website: www.rspfloral.org.

New York Council of Dog Owner Groups (NYCDOG): This umbrella group represents over 21 dog groups throughout Manhattan. With over 15,000 members, this growing organization is dedicated to promoting "off-leash recreation, responsible dog ownership, and respectful park stewardship" throughout the city. They organize fund-raising events, help smaller groups open new dog runs, literally fight City Hall, and even inform their members about where their local city officials stand on the dog issues. To learn more or contribute to this invaluable organization contact NYCDOG at P.O. Box 330, Planetarium Station, New York, NY 10024; 212/580-6932; website: www.nycdog.org.

PAWS: This wonderful organization is dedicated to improving the lives of dogs who visit Central Park. It has put together a dog-owner's guide to Central Park that lists the areas of the park where dogs are welcome. PAWS also issues a monthly newsletter and works with the Central Park Conservancy to avoid misunderstandings between dog owners and park officials. PAWS is run by Susan Buckley; for more information, contact her at 212/988-2811. To receive a copy of the dog owners guide and get on the mailing list for *The Central Barker*, the monthly PAWS newsletter, call Ed Benson at the Central Park Conservancy at 212/360-1422.

In 1857, the design plan submitted by Parks Commissioner Franklin Law Olmsted and Calvert Vaux, an English landscape architect, was accepted by the city. Over 20,000 laborers went to work reshaping the original area into the pastoral space you see today. No one could have dreamed how popular this park would become. By 1865 over seven million visitors a year came to Central Park and, despite many rises and falls, this park has been the main recreation and leisure center in New York ever since.

In one of those "fallen periods," the early 1980s, Central Park had become a shell of its former self. The city's budget was simply too stretched to properly care for this legacy. Thanks to the tireless efforts of local residents, however, the Central Park Conservancy was born and is now a leader in park conservation all over the country. A thriving organization that raises private monies for maintaining the park's infrastructure, the Conservancy is responsible for maintaining the beauty of this magnificent park and for "conserving" Olmsted and Vaux's original vision.

It is this vision that has also, at times, been the bane of many a dog here. Over the years, various groups have tried to establish dog runs in Central Park, but both the Parks Department and the Central Park Conservancy oppose the runs because they are not in keeping with the original design for the park. Like the Constitution, this interpretation is open for debate, but, fortunately, there are plenty of trails, woods, meadows, and lakes, plus an abundance of space, where you can take your leashed dog. And until that day comes that we get an off-leash space, don't forget that dogs are allowed to romp leash-free before 9 A.M. and after 9 P.M.

For dogs who are part hound and part social butterfly, a good place to start exploring is at the ever-popular "Dog Hill," which is located behind the Metropolitan Museum of Art just above 79th Street. During the morning rush hour and after work, dogs of all shapes and sizes can be found cavorting with their pals here. Occasionally, park officials come by and break up the revelry, but most days you will be left to your fun. On the West Side, the place for dogs in the know is around the Great Lawn. Yes, it's true the Great Lawn is off-limits to pups, but there are plenty of dog-friendly areas all around the boundaries of the Great Lawn. The Great Lawn Oval is a popular promenade for Upper West Side canines.

In the northern part of the park, at the Great Hill, which is located near West 106th Street, you'll find an equally popular doggy gathering spot; from here you can also splash in the mud and streams of the Loch. Throughout the rest of the park, any time you come across an open, grassy area, you'll almost always find a happy group of dog owners and their merry crew of canines meeting and greeting. Some of our other favorite places include the Hecksher ball fields (except during baseball season), the meadow on the northwestern side of the Reservoir, the lawn south of Tavern on the Green and the lawns north of the Alice in Wonderland statue near Conservatory Water.

For dogs who can't imagine a day without woods, mud, and the smells of the forest, the Ramble is George's favorite place for a walk. This maze of twisting hidden trails, located in the middle of the park between 73rd and 79th Streets, is a great place to get lost. Sculpted out of a wooded hillside and molded into a wild, rocky place, the Ramble, ironically, is completely artificial. But don't tell your dog. She'll definitely think this wild jungle is the real deal. (Of course, she lives in the city—what does she know about nature?)

The Harlem Meer and Landscape is another great area to help a city dog forget he's in the city. Located on the East Side between 106th and 110th Streets and constructed after the rest of the park was completed, this area is the most rugged and rustic section of Central Park. The 11-acre lake and its 65 acres of surrounding woods offer your happy camper a paradise of water, grass, trees, and enough mud to ensure a bath before he gets back into your apartment.

The six-mile loop road that circles the entire park is closed to vehicles Monday–Friday, from 10 A.M.–3 P.M. and again from 7–10 P.M. and all weekend long. You still have to watch out for cyclists, runners, in-line skaters, and who knows what else, but without the car traffic racing by, the sidewalks provide a safe haven for an easy stroll.

History hounds will be happy to know they have a landmark commemorating one of their own. One of the most beloved statues in Central Park is of Balto, the sled dog who made the trip from Anchorage to Nome, Alaska, through a blizzard in 1925 providing a supply of emergency medicine during a severe diphtheria epidemic. Balto's bronzed likeness can be found on the eastern side of the park near 67th Street.

There are three dog fountains in Central Park—all funded by the generosity of various dog owners and the ASPCA. On the East Side, there is

EARMARK YOUR CALENDAR

You'll see dozens of dog walkers every day in Central Park, but on certain days, all of that walking raises money for worthy causes.

Pause for Paws: Join the annual **Pooch Picnic and Dog Walkathon** held in the Eastern Meadow of Central Park. This fundraiser, sponsored by local dog organizations, helps local animal shelters provide aid to dogs and their owners unable to pay for veterinary care. Events are held throughout the five boroughs. Agility courses, costume parades, competitions, and races are just a small part of this fun-filled day. Held the first weekend in June. For more information, call 212/246-3097 or visit the website: www.pawsacrossamerica.com.

Walk a Mile in My Shoes: The ASPCA Dog Walk, known locally as "Woofstock," raises money for the Big Doggy of all humane societies—the American Society for the Prevention of Cruelty to Animals. In addition to the walk, there is food (both the people and canine versions), music, Frisbee contests, and more. Held in late October. For details, call 212/876-7700.

a fountain located at the 90th street entrance next to the people fountains. Another fountain can be found along Central Park South at the Avenue of the Americas entrance to the park, and yet another on the western outskirts of the Great Lawn.

Central Park PAWS, an organization formed in early 1999 that is dedicated to improving the lives of Central Park dogs, has put together a dog-owner's guide to Central Park listing all of the areas of the park where dogs are allowed. You can get your copy of this helpful guide and park map by calling the Central Park Conservancy at 212/360-1422 or downloading them from the website: www.centralparknyc.org.

The Visitor Information Center is in the Dairy at 65th Street by the Central Park Zoo and Carousel. Additional maps and other information are available here.

Dogs are not allowed in the Sheep Meadow, Strawberry Fields, Great Lawn, East Meadow (during its current renovation), North Meadow, or in any playgrounds, ball fields or public facilities. He must be leashed at all times in the Ramble, North Woods, and public meeting grounds—like the Kerbs Boathouse and Bethesda Terrace. In the other areas, the "before 9 A.M. and after 9 P.M." rule applies. Located between Central Park South and Central Park North (59th and 110th Streets) and Central Park West (8th Avenue) and 5th Avenue. Open 24 hours a day; 212/360-3444.

Restaurants

Ice Cream Café: The name says it all. We treat our ice cream–loving pups to a cup of vanilla Häagen-Dazs at this sweet shop in Central Park; we save the Belgium chocolate for ourselves. There are plenty of other sweet temptations to choose from, too. And we aren't just talking about the great view of the model boats on Conservatory Water. Central Park at 72nd Street and 5th Avenue; 212/289-0997.

Park View at the Boathouse: Dogs love to stop and say hello to the bartenders at the Boathouse in Central Park. That's because, although they aren't allowed in the restaurant, they know they're allowed at the outdoor tables in the bar. George and Inu don't mind if there's no room at the inn because they can eat their fill of appetizers here. It's a nice way to unwind after a day exploring the park. Central Park at 72nd Street and East Park Drive North; 212/517-2233.

CHELSEA

The neighborhood of Chelsea is located on the West Side between 14th and 30th Streets and includes the historic Flatiron District, a 19th century commercial area that has now been converted into artist lofts and shops. Popular with dogs and artistic folk alike, this neighborhood doesn't have a lot of park choices for pups, but what it lacks in essentials, it makes up for in enthusiasm.

Parks, Beaches, and Recreation Areas

❷ Chelsea Waterside Park & Dog Run 🐾 🐾 🐾 🐕

Yes, it's true that the dog owners in Chelsea don't have a lot of choice where they let their dogs exercise. Fortunately, with the opening of a new dog run along West Side Highway, you don't need quantity if you've got quality. This new dog park, which takes the place of the old Tom's Dog Run at West 22nd Street and 11th Avenue, is located in a triangle bordered by 11th Avenue, 24th Street, and the West Side Highway. And it's a delight. One of the few dog runs

DIVERSION

Day of Beauty: Only in New York could you expect to find a spa dedicated to the needs of your canine. Now she never need have a bad hair day again. The staff at **New York Dog Spa and Hotel Boutique** in Chelsea will pamper your pooch with hot oil treatments, massage, and special grooming techniques. Your pup may never be content with a simple nail-clipping again. 145 West 18th Street; 212/243-1199; website: www.nydogspa.com.

co-maintained by the state and the West Chelsea Dog Owners Association, this is about as high-tech as dog runs get. There's a running fountain, rocks for climbing, a faux-log for shade and hiding under, benches, mutt mitts, and light-colored asphalt flooring, which stays cooler on sizzling summer days. The run itself isn't large, but it's so well designed that this small space actually feels bigger than it is. Dogs are not allowed in any other section of the park. Located at 23rd Street and 11th Avenue. Open dawn–1 A.M. 212/408-0234.

Restaurants

Cafeteria: Well, with a name like this, what else can you expect but the blue plate special and some spaghetti and meat balls? You won't be disappointed. They even serve a meatloaf special. There's plenty of other comfort food on the menu to satisfy most finicky Fidos, and the outdoor tables make dining here both comfortable and convenient. 119 7th Avenue; 212/414-1717.

Chelsea Grill: New York dogs stop, sit, and shake when dining at this Manhattan mainstay. That's because they get to dine on the continental cuisine of their choice at the sidewalk tables outside. Be on your best behavior and you might even talk the proprietors into letting you sneak into the rear garden. 135 8th Avenue; 212/242-5336.

Empire Diner: This nifty little diner is a landmark and mainstay of Chelsea. There are plenty of tables outside for you and your dog, and they will even bring your pup some water on request. Standard diner fare, but the grub is good. Check out their annual Halloween dog party (see the Diversions in the Fort George section). 210 10th Avenue; 212/243-2736.

Markt: That's right; you read right. X "markt" the spot, and Spot is happy it did. This is one of the few places in Chelsea's oh-so-trendy meat packing district where dogs can enjoy seafood instead of filet mignon. The tables outside are open to you and your fish-loving fox terrier. 401 West 14th Street; 212/727-3314.

CHINATOWN/LITTLE ITALY

Somehow these two diverse communities, located below Canal Street in Lower Manhattan, always seem to end up smack dab in the middle of one another's business—and what a business it is. San Francisco's Chinatown may get the movies and the press, but New York City's Chinatown boasts of the largest Chinese population outside of China. And Little Italy has long been a fertile, and tasty, tourist attraction. Its many restaurants along Mulberry Street satisfy any carbo craving imaginable. Although there are no parks for dogs in this district, if you and your pup just want to take in the sights and smells, this is the place for plenty of both.

Restaurants

Ferrara's: For those with a sweet tooth, you'll be wagging your tail with pleasure after a visit to this famous bakery and café in the heart of Little Italy. Gelati, cannoli, tiramisu, and sweet cream pastries are just a small sampling of the many scrumptious desserts waiting for you here. There are outdoor tables and benches along the street where you can enjoy your treat. Just make sure you get enough to share because your pup will be sure to want a bite. 195 Grand Street; 212/226-6150.

Il Fornaio: Just about all the outdoor restaurants along Mulberry Street allow dogs—and there are so many, it's hard to choose just one. We like this one because of the divine focaccia it serves with all its entrées. With a full

EARMARK YOUR CALENDAR

Chinese New Year: Don't wait for the Year of the Dog, come out every year for a New Year celebration you'll never forget. Join the fun on Mott Street in Chinatown on the first full moon after January 21 and before February 19. Simple, right? Don't worry, you'll know when it is because this is one celebration that no one can miss. There are dragons, drums, colorful costumes, firecrackers, and lots of family fun. As long as your dog isn't frightened of loud noises, bring her along. For dates and information, call 212/431-9740.

Feast of San Genarro: This festival to beat all festivals has been held each September since 1926 in Little Italy. Over a million people each year attend this 11-day carnival and food-fest honoring Saint Genarro, martyred in Naples some 1700 years ago. Legend has it that if two vials of San Genarro's blood liquefy on feast days, Neapolitans (and New Yorkers) will have good luck. Since many of the activities are held outdoors, you and your canine friend are welcome to attend. Street entertainers and over 300 vendors selling food, crafts, and Italian specialty items line up along Mulberry Street and adjoining areas in Little Italy. As long as your dog doesn't mind crowds, come on down and join the fun. 212/484-1222.

range of pasta, veal, and antipasto dishes to choose from, our pups lie at our feet and simply say *Mangia!* 132A Mulberry Street; 212/226-8306.

The Original Vincents: Established in 1904, this Italian mainstay has anchored the action on Hester and Mott Streets since the turn of the last century. You and your dog may not remember the opening, but you'll enjoy years of tradition as you lap up your linguine or munch on the manicotti. 119 Mott Street; 212/226-8133.

Umberto's Clam House: In the summertime, this seafood restaurant has a large outdoor seating area where you and Muttley can take in all the festivals, parades, and hectic street scene from your comfortable seat on the corner of busy Mulberry Street. Well-behaved dogs are welcome on the sidewalk beside your table. 386 Broome Street; 212/431-7545.

CIVIC CENTER

This neighborhood encompasses the area between City Hall and the historic South Street Seaport, which nestles comfortably in the shadow of the Brooklyn Bridge. Long a historic, civic and tourist area, this community is proud of its early Manhattan landmarks like New York's first "tallest building in the world" (the Woolworth Building) and City Hall itself, has seen more than a hundred mayors come and go since its first inauguration in 1816.

Parks, Beaches, and Recreation Areas

3 City Hall Park 🐾 🐾

We can't call this a great park, but it certainly gets a lot of traffic and since it is one of the only green spaces in Lower Manhattan where you can take your dog, it gets a higher rating than it probably deserves. There are plenty of benches and criss-crossing trails running along a four-block area in front of

DIVERSIONS

Ferries for Fidos: New York Waterway offers the largest ferry and sightseeing fleet in New York Harbor, happily transporting you and your pup across the waters around Manhattan and between Seaport and New Jersey. Two- and three-hour cruises around Manhattan depart from Pier 83 in Midtown. Fares for adults are $24. New Jersey–bound feries leave Pier 11 at the South Street Seaport for Port Imperial Park in Weehawken ($6), Hoboken ($2), and Liberty State Park in Jersey City ($5). Adult fares are priced as one-way tickets. Dogs get a free ride but must be on a leash at all times. 800/533-3779; website: www.nywaterway.com.

One-hour Liberty cruises on **Circle Line Tours** leave from Pier 16 at the Seaport from March to September. This tour takes you around the tip of Manhattan, including spectacular views of lower Manhattan, Ellis Island, and the Statue of Liberty. Fares are $12 for adults. Dogs travel free, but they must be leashed and stay on the outer decks. Longer cruises are available from Pier 83 in Midtown. 212/563-3200; website: www.circleline.com.

City Hall; your dog can enjoy a short jaunt amidst the surrounding concrete jungle. Dogs are not, unfortunately, allowed on the grass and must be leashed at all times. The park is roughly bordered by Broadway, Chambers Street, and Park Row. Open 6–1 A.M. 212/408-0234.

4 Fishbridge Park & Pearl Street Dog Run 🐾 🐾 🐾 🐕

Fishbridge Park is home to the tiny Pearl Street Dog Run, tucked under the towering hulk of the Brooklyn Bridge. The park doesn't offer your dog many exercise options, but it is a great neighborhood hangout. One of the few off-leash sections in this area, you'll find this a great spot to meet up with other local dog owners; the run is well-maintained with donations from local residents. A community garden decorates the space next door to the run.

In the run there is a dirt floor, single bench, trash can, plastic bag dispenser, and hose to wash down your dog's waste. Members are asked to donate $20 a year or more for the upkeep of the run. Checks can be mailed to the South Waterfront Neighborhood Association, PO Box 279, Peck Slip Station, New York NY 10272. Located at Dover and Pearl Streets. The run is open 24 hours. 212/267-5316 (dog run), 212/408-0234 (parks department).

Nature Hikes and Urban Walks

Brooklyn Bridge: For an exhilarating and unusual walk over one of the great New York landmarks, take a stroll across the Brooklyn Bridge. On opening day, May 24, 1883, over 150,000 people crossed the bridge. Today you and

---

Summer Jammin': Throughout the summer, you and your dog can join the fun at Pier 17 for a boatload of **free summer concerts.** There are lunchtime concerts from noon to 2 P.M. on Tuesday and Thursday, and evening concerts from 6 P.M. to 8 P.M. on Friday and Saturday. For more information and times, call 212/SEA-PORT (212/732-7678); website: www.southstreetseaport.com.

your pup can add your paw prints to the millions of others who have walked across this beautiful bridge since its opening.

Built between 1870 and 1883, the bridge spans 1,596 feet across the East River and was, at the time it was completed, 50 feet longer than any other bridge built in the world. This great feat of engineering was beset by many disasters during its push to completion, including the death of the original architect, John A. Roebling, and the debilitating illness of Roebling's son, Washington, who had taken over the construction after his father's death. Fortunately the bridge, like New York City itself, was bigger than any disaster thrown in its path and today it stands as one of New York City's life arteries.

The wood-planked pedestrian and bike path runs directly down the middle of the bridge and, although dogs must be leashed, you won't feel you are walking in the middle of New York traffic (even though you are!). The views are spectacular and you are well shielded from the cars rushing by on either side.

To reach the bridge walkway, start at City Hall Park in Manhattan (see above) and end your 30-minute walk at Cadman Plaza Park in Brooklyn Heights (see the Brooklyn chapter). Watch out for joggers and cyclists and stay to the outside of the walkway in the pedestrian lane. 212/360-3000.

Restaurants

South Street Seaport: Just about all the restaurants here will allow you and your well-behaved dog to sit in their outdoor areas on approval. Some establishments will allow your dog to sit by your side; others insist that you keep your dog confined to the outer tables only. We've never had a bad experience here as we wind down on a warm summer's day. To guide you, we've listed a few of our favorites, but that doesn't mean they are the only restaurants that allow dogs.

Of course, you can also always get something to-go from the food court inside the Seaport and sit out on Pier 17. There is plenty of seating available.

Bridge Café: A tavern has stood on this spot since 1794 and, although the times and names have changed, this historic tavern still offers up good food, plain and simple. Although there aren't any tables for you and your dog to sit at, they have a to-go menu and it's right across the street from Fishbridge Park and the Pearl Street Dog Run. We suggest you pick up a quick snack to go and enjoy it on one of the benches in the dog run while your pal plays with his mates. 279 Water Street at Dover; 212/227-3344.

Il Porto: If you're longing for some great seafood (I mean, you *are* at the Seaport!) try this fresh fish restaurant. With a full menu of the freshest grilled fish, your only problem will be deciding which to choose. There are plenty of tables outside where you and Rover can try a little sole food. 11 Fulton Street; 212/791-2181.

J. P. Mustard: This café offers sandwiches to-go or full table service for you and Fido. Even though they advertise themselves as an old-fashioned deli, with appetizers like smoked salmon and stuffed grape leaves, or triple-decker sandwiches with brisket of beef and Bermuda onion, this is not your father's delicatessen. Best of all are the outdoor tables where you can sit and enjoy your meal. They even deliver. 199 Water Street at the Seaport; 212/785-0612.

Red: This Mexican restaurant serves up a full plate of Tex-Mex and Southwest cuisine. There are plenty of tables outside where you and your dog can get a taste of the New York version of margaritas and chicken fajitas. 19 Fulton Street; 212/571-5905.

Seaport Café: This simple little café offers your usual fare of burgers and salads. The outdoor tables are casually situated, so you'll find this a comfortable setting to catch the busy seaport action with your pup. 89 South Street Seaport along Pier 17; 212/964-1120.

CLINTON/HELL'S KITCHEN

Don't ever refer to this neighborhood, located loosely from 8th Avenue to the Hudson River between 34th and 59th Streets, as part of Midtown West. Residents will tolerate being called the gentler "Clinton," but really prefer Hell's Kitchen—a name that comes from a notorious gang that roamed this area after the Civil War. With a rebel history of crime, corruption, and bootleg whisky joints during Prohibition, this community has tamed its wild ways, but it will always be as colorful as it is proud.

Parks, Beaches, and Recreation Areas

5 DeWitt Clinton Park & Dog Run 🐾 🐾 🐕

This six-acre park is named for the state senator who championed the Erie Canal in the 19th century. While the park doesn't exactly measure up to the technological wonder of the canal, it gets the job done. Most of the park is covered by recreational areas where your dog can't go, but you can walk on the cement walkways around the ball courts. Best of all, part of the concrete area has now been sectioned off for a leash-free space for dogs. The dog run is located on the southern side, along 52nd Street, and offers a fairly substantial space for leash-free cavorting.

Although the surface is merely concrete, there are several benches, plenty of shade, and enough room to chase a ball. There is also a hose, water bowl, bulletin board for monthly updates, and an occasional newsletter published by Friends of Dewitt Dog Run. To contribute to the maintenance of the run contact: www.dogrun.org. Located between 52nd and 54th Streets, and 11th and 12th Avenues. Open 6 A.M.–10 P.M. 212/360-3401 (dog run), 212/408-0234 (parks department).

6 Hell's Kitchen–Clinton Dog Run 🐾 🐾 🐕

This members-only dog run, located at the entrance to the Lincoln Tunnel, does the best it can with scant material. Long, narrow, and scrunched up against the concrete wall of the tunnel, it offers wood-chip flooring, a shade umbrella, a small plastic pool (in the summer months), and lights for nighttime visitors. Membership costs $15 a year and you'll need to pay up in order to receive a key to unlock the gate. To become a member, contact the Hell's Kitchen Neighborhood Association. Located on the southeast corner of West 39th Street at 10th Avenue. Open 24 hours a day. 212/736-4536.

EAST VILLAGE

Long the hotbed of counter-culture and political protest, the East Village lies between 14th and Houston Streets on Manhattan's Lower East Side. Although still a spot for great food and jazz, as well as tattoos and piercings of many kinds, its shaggy days have long since been tempered by rising real estate and gentrification. But even if the East Village has been de-fanged a bit, we will always love this neighborhood for being the site of the city's first dog run, located in Tompkins Square Park.

EARMARK YOUR CALENDAR

Best in Show — Finally! A show that mutts can call their own! In the spring of 2001, the first annual **Great American Mutt Show** was held and it has all the makings of an annual event. Mixed Breed mongrels competed in over 30 classes like Mostly Hound, Mostly Shepherd, Mostly Collie, Most Musical, Best Lap Dog, Longest Tail, and a whole slew of other categories. An all-day event at Pier 92, mutts from all over got to strut their stuff and showed that you don't have to be pedigreed to be a winner. Sponsored by Tails in Need (TIN), it was created to raise funds for organizations that support animals in need. For this year's date, call 212/327-3164.

Parks, Beaches, and Recreation Areas

7 East River Park 🐾 🐾 🐾 🌊

This is one of the larger parks in New York City, and although much of it is covered by recreation areas where your dog can't go, the sheer size of this park means you and your dog will get in a good workout. Located along the East River between 14th and Jackson Streets, there are great views of Brooklyn and the bridges along the promenade that runs by the water. Mingled in among the many ball fields and recreation areas are open grassy areas where your dog can run, fetch a ball, or chase his tail. The park is separated from the city by FDR Drive, but you can access the park via the pedestrian walkways available at 10th, 14th, 16th, and Houston Streets. Open 6–1 A.M.; dogs must be leashed before 9 A.M. and after 9 P.M. 212/408-0234.

8 Tompkins Square Park & Dog Run 🐾 🐾 🐾 🌊

As parks go, Tompkins Square Park gets only average ratings. There is a bench-lined pedestrian walkway under plenty of shade trees, but dogs are not allowed on the lawns—the situation is a little like "grass, grass everywhere and ne'er a blade to sniff." Fortunately, East Village dog owners, following their activist tradition, took matters into their own paws in 1990 and established New York City's first dog run here. It's been going gangbusters ever since. The run is fairly small, but it is well maintained and you'll meet lots of local dogs and their owners here. There is a bulletin board to keep you up-to-date on all the local happenings from monthly cleanups to Halloween parties. The park is bordered by 7th and 10th Streets, and Avenues A and B. Open 6 A.M.–midnight 212/522-3298 (dog run), 212/408-0234 (parks department).

Restaurants

Aunt B's on B: If you're longing for a little home cooking, just like your favorite Auntie used to make, you've come to the right place. That's because you and your chow can chow down on decadent breakfasts of French toast filled with cream cheese, homemade biscuits with berry butter, and banana walnut pancakes. Top it off with tea or an espresso in B's outdoor garden. You'll B a busy eater at B's. 186 Avenue B; 212/505-2701.

Dawgs on Park: This newly opened specialty hot dog stand is a welcome addition to colorful Tompkins Square Park. Serving "healthy" fast food such as beef, turkey, or tofu pups, you have a choice of taking yours fried, grilled, or steamed. You can even smother your "dawg" in veggie chili or corn salsa. Facing the eastern side of the park right near the dog run, we can't think of a better way to end a good romp with your canine pals than ordering, "one dog to walk!" 178 East 7th Avenue; 212/598-0667.

DBA: This bar serves some of the best single malt scotch in the city. Choose from countless brands. If that isn't enough to draw you, maybe discovering that this dog-friendly bar welcomes all canine customers will. Join the happy hour where everyone knows your name (or at least your dog's name) with as many dogs as there is scotch. 41 1st Avenue; 212/475-5097.

Frank: This lively bar and café has charm and a great location to go along with its good food. Sit outside at the quaint tables with your dog as you nosh on fish, vegetarian fare, and great appetizers. George likes the spiced meatloaf with mashed potatoes. 88 2nd Avenue; 212/420-0106.

Ovo: For a pizza place with attitude, trot on over to this eatery on trendy 2nd Avenue in the East Village. If crusted sea bass or linguine with shrimp doesn't get your mouth watering, then maybe over 20 kinds of wood-oven pizza will. There are plenty of tables outside to welcome you and your dog on summer days. Make sure you try the tiramisu for dessert. 65 2nd Avenue; 212/353-1444.

Pierrot Bistro: This Parisian-style restaurant offers a fabulous *prix fixe* dinner and Sunday jazz brunch. With name jazz artists serenading you while you dine, this is one hot spot for Spot. Lap dogs may join their owners inside, while larger pups have to make do with the outdoor tables. 28 Avenue B; 212/673-1999.

Veselka: This 24-hour haunt is home to what can only be described as Russian/Ukrainian comfort food. Stop by for borscht and blintzes with your borzoi as you hang with the cool crowd of the East Village. There are outdoor tables in the summer for people watching at all hours. 144 2nd Avenue; 212/228-9682.

FINANCIAL DISTRICT/ BATTERY PARK CITY

This neighborhood encompasses the lower tip of Manhattan and includes the Wall Street District and the historic sections surrounding the famous landmark, Trinity Church. It is also home to Ground Zero, the remains of the World Financial Center, so life for neighborhood dogs and their owners here is still

DIVERSION

A Ferry for Fluffy: One of the most visible, and mobile, land-marks in New York City is the **Staten Island Ferry.** It also holds the unique distinction of being the only mode of tourist transportation to go down in price instead of up. That's because it used to cost a quarter to cross New York Harbor to Staten Island, but now it's free. That's right. Passengers (and dogs) are free; cars cost $3.50. The official rule for dogs is as follows: only small dogs in carrying cases allowed. However, the unofficial rule seems to be "whatever the officials decide." Our advice? Go during off-peak hours and make sure your dog is really, really well-behaved when you ask if you can bring him aboard. Usually they'll say yes. 718/815-BOAT (718/815-2628).

disrupted, to say the least. Plans for a new dog park in Battery Park City have been put off as we go to press, but we are optimistic that this neighborhood will bounce back as it has so many times before. Visitors can wander by the New York Stock Exchange, catch a ferry to Staten Island or New Jersey, see the Statue of Liberty or take a boat trip around the island of Manhattan.

Parks, Beaches, and Recreation Areas

9 Battery Park 🐾 🐾 🐾

This 22-acre park offers local dogs more green space than any other park in the Financial District. It is also the most frequented by dogs and people alike. On weekends, the crowds can get very thick. It is from this tip of Manhattan that visitors can take the trip out to the Statue of Liberty and Ellis Island, so dogs must be leashed as you make your way through the throngs. Dogs are allowed along the promenade and on the walkways, but not on the grassy areas, so sniffing the shrubs is as good as it gets. There are plenty of shade trees and benches, however, and if your pooch likes the view across New York Harbor, well, it doesn't get much better than this. Located at the intersection of Battery Place, Broadway, and State Street. Open 6–1 A.M. 212/408-0234.

10 Battery Park City & Little West Dog Run 🐾 🐾 🐕

There were high hopes in fall 2000 that not only were improvements going to be made to the two existing dog runs in Battery Park City, but that a third dog run was to be added near Gateway Plaza. My, what a difference a year makes. As of summer 2001, the plans for a third dog run had been scuttled and the run at River Terrace was bulldozed to make room for a new office building. The run at Little West and West Thames Streets has been temporarily relocated to an asphalt parking lot at Little West Street and 3rd Place. On hot summer days this black asphalt can really get hot, but this hasn't stopped the local

Little Red Lighthouse Swim: Each September the Little Red Lighthouse Festival brings hundreds of lovers of children's literature and nautical history to Fort Washington Park and its most famous landmark, which lies in the shadow of the "Great Gray Bridge." Watch the participants plunge into the city waters for an eight-mile swim down the Hudson River or just enjoy the festivities commemorating the history of this special site. 856/757-1337.

dogs from enjoying their leash-free freedom. There are several benches and the run is well-maintained by the Battery Park City Parks Conservancy, a group of 500 local dog owners who also fund the dog run. Located at Little West Street and 3rd Place. Open 24 hours. 212/267-9700.

11 Rector Park 🐾

This tiny park offers a bit of shade in the midst of concrete. You'll have to be content with looking at the well-groomed lawn, however, because dogs are not allowed to set paw on the grass. Dogs must be leashed. Located at the intersection of Rector Place and South End Avenue. Open 6 A.M.–9 P.M. 212/408-0234.

Nature Hikes and Urban Walks

Battery Park City Esplanade: This lovely promenade offers world-class views of New York Harbor and beyond. You and your hound will enjoy walking along the well-tended walkway, but you're not allowed to step on any of the park areas along the way. Dog-Free Park signs are posted along the way, so you won't have to do any guesswork about where you are allowed. We're a little disappointed that dogs can't have at least one of these grassy parks to enjoy. 212/408-0234.

Restaurants

In addition to the neighborhood restaurants listed below, you'll find many outdoor restaurants to satisfy all palates in North Cove Harbor along the Battery Park City Esplanade. Most of these outdoor seating areas are roped off, which means you can only sit at the outer tables with your dog. There are, however, many public tables along the way and you are welcome to order food at any of the cafés, coffeehouses, and restaurants and enjoy them in the open areas with your dog.

Garden Café: With a large menu that includes breakfast, lunch, and full-course dinners, this small café gives you a choice of take-out, delivery, or in the summer a few tables outside where you can sit with your dog. 301 South End Avenue; 212/488-8444.

DIVERSION

Venture on the *Ventura*: Take a trip into the past on the *Ventura*, a historic sailing ship that first set sail in 1921. Dogs may hop aboard for the Friday evening sunset cruises or the Sunday "Bring Your Own Brunch" cruise around the harbor. The evening cruise sets sail at 5:45 P.M.; the brunch cruise sets out at 11:45 A.M. The departure dock used to be at the North Cove Marina, but due to the events at the World Trade Center, it is currently looking for a new home as we go to press. Call for current details. 212/786-1204; website: www.sailnewyork.com.

Steamers Landing: This lovely seafood restaurant has one of the best water views in Manhattan. Fortunately for your dog, the outdoor patio runs along the promenade, which means she can join you for the view. Just enter through the regular front door without your pooch and once you've secured a table, you can bring your dog in from the promenade. Café-on-the-Hudson between Liberty and Albany Streets; 212/432-1451.

Places to Stay

Holiday Inn: This Financial Center location offers luxurious rooms with views of the New York Harbor. Your dog probably won't care about that, but she will definitely enjoy being included in your next stay here. Rates are $149–259. 138 Lafayette Street, New York, NY 10013; 212/966-8898 or 800/HOLIDAY (800/465-4329); website: www.holiday-inn.com.

Holiday Inn Wall Street: If you want to be in the heart of Wall Street, this reasonably priced hotel is a good option. Located near Trinity Church, Battery Park, and the Seaport, this makes an ideal place for exploring Lower Manhattan. Dogs are welcome on approval, but only in certain rooms. Rates are $189–289. 15 Gold Street, New York, NY 10038; 212/232-7700; website: www.holiday-inn.com.

Regent Hotel: This hotel has recently upped their size limit—by five pounds! This means pups who weigh in at 25 pounds or less are allowed. So if yours makes the cut, you'll both enjoy this clean and comfortable full-service hotel. If not, all we can say is, better wait until next year. Maybe it'll go up another five pounds! Rates are $149–289. 55 Wall Street, New York, NY 10005; 212/845-8600.

FORT GEORGE

This upper Manhattan neighborhood is just coming into its own. Long a source of community pride, this district has seen a flood of restaurants, stores, and families move in recently, all seeking larger dwellings and more space than is possible in other parts of Manhattan. With roomy Fort Tryon Park nearby and a planned renovation for Fort Washington Park, we hear the list is long for pups wanting to become "Uptown Dogs."

Parks, Beaches, and Recreation Areas

12 Bennett Park 🐾 🐕

This little two-block square park is well-maintained, but it doesn't offer a lot for dogs who need exercise. You can walk your dog along the concrete walkways and sit a spell on the benches under a shade tree. That's about it. Small dogs may be content here, but energetic canines will need more leg room. Located between 183rd and 185th Streets and Fort Washington and Pine Hurst Avenues. Open 6 A.M.–10 P.M. 212/408-0234.

13 Fort Tryon Park & Dog Run 🐾 🐾 🐾 🐾 🐕

This 62-acre park is one a gem among New York City parks. Located high on a crest overlooking the Hudson River, it was once a protective fortification along the river and now is home to the lovely Saint William's Dog Run. Old Fort Tryon was built to protect New York from the invading British in 1776 and fell that very same year to the Hessians. You can still see the remains of the fortifications at the southern end of the park near Fort Washington Avenue.

The rest of the grounds were once the estate of C. K. G. Billings, a wealthy industrialist. John D. Rockefeller bought the property in 1909 and gave it to the city in 1930. Today the park is home to The Cloisters, which is home to the Metropolitan Museum of Art's world-class collection of illuminated manuscripts and 14th century art. Needless to say, you can't take your dog inside the museum or on the immediate grounds, but fortunately there is plenty of park left over to satisfy every canine desire.

There are lovely winding trails along the cliffs overlooking the Hudson River, lookout points where you and your dog can take in the view, and trees and open grassy areas for lounging on lazy summer days or for chasing sticks and balls in every season. On the western side of the park, on a hillside below the parking area across from the New Leaf Café, locals have long gathered with their dogs. As of November 2001, this hillside was designated a new off-leash area. Called Saint William's Run, this one-acre area is a triangle-shaped hillside separate from the rest of the park and affording great views, an open area for running and lounging, and plenty of shade trees in the summer. Dogs are allowed to go leash-free in the rest of the park before 9 A.M. and after 9 P.M. but must be leashed the rest of the time. The park is bordered by Dyckman

EARMARK YOUR CALENDAR–OCTOBER

Howling Halloween: Poodles dressed as pumpkins and grey-hounds in goblin suits? It must be Halloween in Manhattan.

Central Park: Join the fun at Rumsey Playfield the Saturday before Halloween for the annual **Dress Your Pet Great Halloween Party.** Madness reigns from 11 A.M. to 3 P.M. as canines and their owners gather for a raffle, prizes, free hayrides, a haunted house, and entertainers. 212/360-1319; website: www.nyc.gov/parks.

Chelsea: You and your pup are invited to the **Empire Diner's Annual Canine Halloween Costume Contest** the Saturday before Halloween. Local restaurants and pet stores provide the prizes. 210 10th Avenue; 212/243-2736.

Gramercy: To avoid hurting any doggy feelings, organizers claim that all contestants who show up in costume at this annual **Halloween Bash** will get a goody bag. It all happens the Saturday before Halloween at the Union Square Dog Run between 1 P.M. and 4 P.M. 212/242-1414.

Greenwich Village: The famous **Village Halloween Parade** is the biggest holiday bash in the city. Not only are participants invited to dress up, but you can also enjoy watching the giant puppets and other crazily-clad marchers who decorate the city streets. The parade runs along 6th Avenue from Houston Street to 23rd Street. The fun begins around 6 P.M. on October 31 and officially ends around 9 P.M., but the party goes on all night. Costumed dogs can also trot over to the Washington Square Dog Run for a special Halloween Parade all their own. 914/758-5519; website: www.Halloween-NYC.com.

Midtown East: Spacious doggy day care center Biscuits and Bath's Doggy Village pulls out all the stops for its annual **Halloween Party** the last Sunday before Halloween. Compete for prizes, bob for biscuits, and get photographed in the pumpkin patch. Admission is $10. 227 East 44th Street; 212/692-2323.

Upper Westside: Held at O'Neal's Boat Basin on 79th Street and the Hudson River, FLORAL's annual **Halloween Extravaganza** includes all sorts of fun for canines—costume contests, a raffle, live music, and even a cash bar (for their human escorts). Held the last Sunday before Halloween, 11 A.M.–3 P.M.. Your $5 admission supports the dog runs in Riverside Park; website: www.rspfloral.org.

and 192nd Streets, Broadway and Riverside Drive. Open 6 A.M.–midnight. 212/408-0234.

14 Fort Washington Park 🐾 🐾 🏊

This 158-acre park has a more exciting past than it does a present. On June 20, 1776, the Continental Army began a hastily constructed fort for General George Washington at the intersection of present-day Fort Washington Avenue and 183rd Street. Unfortunately, Fort Washington's prime position did not spare it from the British bombardiers who captured this last American stronghold in Manhattan on November 16, 1776, as General Washington watched helplessly from Fort Lee on the New Jersey side of the Hudson.

The present-day park opened in 1925 and quickly became a favorite of Hudson River tourists, who flocked here for the view and the promenade. The glory was short-lived, however, for in 1927 the construction of the George Washington Bridge marked the eventual demise of this once lovely park.

Located in the shadow of the great bridge, this park soon became a weedy, neglected area. Today the West 181st Street Beautification Project and the New York Restoration Project are trying to restore the park to its former glory. They have put in new benches and walkways and have cleaned up the park. It still has a way to go before it can rival nearby Fort Tryon Park, but we applaud the efforts of these groups and feel certain this park will soon be a place you will want to come with your dog. Dogs must be leashed. The park is bordered by 178th and Dyckman Streets, and Riverside Drive and the Hudson River. Open 6–1 A.M. 212/408-0234.

15 Gorman Memorial Park 🐾 🐾 🏊

This two-block-long park is carved on top of a rocky hilltop, and although you can wander along the concrete paths, dogs are banned from the grassy areas. This is a pleasant neighborhood park, so if you live in the neighborhood and are looking for a spot to while away an afternoon, this might suffice—but don't make a special trip. Located at the intersection of 189th Street and Broadway. Open dawn–dusk. 212/408-0234.

16 High Bridge Park 🐾 🏊

This long, narrow park takes its name from the High Bridge, which was built to carry the Old Croton Aqueduct (see the Westchester chapter) over the Harlem River and supply clean water to disease-ridden Manhattan in the 1840s. In the 20th century, it was the site of Coogan's Bluff, which once overlooked the famous Polo Grounds where the New York Giants played.

Today, this park is less stellar than its origins. Located high on a ridge looking out over the Harlem River, the view is now obstructed by the large housing projects that were built after the Polo Grounds were leveled in 1964.

The park is mostly playgrounds with a few scruffy trails that lead around them for dogs. The park is bordered by Dyckman and 155th Streets and Amsterdam Avenue. Open dawn–dusk. 212/408-0234.

Nature Hikes and Urban Walks

Little Red Lighthouse: Originally built in 1880 at Sandy Hook, New Jersey, this charming little light was relocated to its present location on Jeffrey's Hook in 1921. In 1942, the children's book, *The Little Red Lighthouse and the Great Gray Bridge* by Hildegarde H. Swift and Lynd Ward, popularized the lighthouse with the message that small things matter in a big world. When the city sought to destroy the lighthouse in 1951, lovers of the book rallied in outrage and their protests resulted in the lighthouse being designated a historical landmark. Today it is managed by the Parks and Recreation Department. For those who can find it, the view across the Hudson is truly spectacular.

Although the route is not well marked, the easiest way to reach the lighthouse is from West 181st Street just north of the George Washington Bridge. Take the footbridge over the Henry Hudson Parkway into Fort Washington Park and follow the bike path south. (As we go to press in the aftermath of the September 11 attacks, pedestrians were not being allowed all the way down to the lighthouse for security purposes, but we trust that will eventually change.) 212/408-0234.

Restaurants

New Leaf Café: Stop by this café/restaurant for a cup of espresso, baked goods, or great salads and sandwiches. The best thing is the location—right in the heart of Fort Tryon Park and just across from the park's new off-leash area (Saint William's Run). Dogs are allowed at the outdoor tables and on any given summer day, the four-legged patrons may outnumber the two-legged ones. Just our kind of place. 1 Margaret Corbin Drive at Fort Tryon Park; 212/568-5323.

GRAMERCY

This lovely residential area was first built in the 1840s and 1850s and quickly became one of the most fashionable neighborhoods in the city. With its lovely homes and row houses facing elegant Gramercy Park, it was one of the first planned communities in the country. Today it is a designated historical district, and although non-residents still can't take their pups to Gramercy Park (the only privately owned park left in the city), there are several good dog runs close by to ease the snub.

EARMARK YOUR CALENDAR–SEPTEMBER

Dog Day Afternoon: To highlight the American Kennel Club's (AKC) **National Dog Week,** held during the second week of September, the AKC hosts its annual canine extravaganza Dog Day Afternoon at Madison Square Park. Canine experts are on hand to answer your questions, introduce you to different dog breeds, and conduct agility and obedience demonstrations. Booths are set up with information and samples for your pup. There are activities for kids, live entertainment, and the first 500 attendees will receive a special goody bag for their pet. For exact dates and information, call 919/233-9767.

Parks, Beaches, and Recreation Areas

17 Madison Square Park & James' Dog Run 🐾 🐾 🐾 🐾 🐕

James' Dog Run is one of the best in the city. It was renovated in 2000 and is clean and spacious with plenty of room for your dog to exercise, socialize, or do her own thing. The run is covered with pea gravel, and there are benches, shade trees, and mutt mitts available. It is well-maintained by the Friends of James' Dog Run; frequent users are expected to make a donation. Be prepared for group clean-up days, which are scheduled periodically. The results of these group efforts make a big difference in your pup's enjoyment of this run.

Leashed dogs are allowed in the rest of Madison Square Park, but not on the grass. James' Dog Run is on the western side of the square along 5th Avenue between 24th and 25th Streets. To make a contribution send a check to the Friends of James' Dog Run at P.O. Box 1119, Madison Square Station, New York, NY 10159. The park is located at the intersection of 23rd Street, Broadway and 5th Avenue. Open 6 A.M.–midnight. 212/408-0234 (parks department).

18 Union Square Park & Dog Run 🐾 🐾 🐾 🐕

This three-block-wide square is one busy place. Fortunately for you and your pup, there is a designated dog run here to help you and your pup find a small corner of your own amidst the crowds. Although this isn't the spiffiest dog run in the city, it gets a lot of use and offers enough room for your dog to chase a ball and get in some serious playtime.

There are picnic tables and benches, shade trees, several dog bowls, water, and crushed gravel flooring.

The Friends of Union Square Dog Run are currently raising money to renovate the run; if you'd like to make a donation, there are envelopes provided at the dog run.

Leashed dogs are allowed in Union Square Park, but can go leashless in the run only. The run is located on the southwestern side of the park between 14th and 15th Streets. The park is bordered by 14th Street, Broadway and Park

Avenue. Open dawn–dusk. 212/242-1414 (dog run), 212/408-0234 (parks department).

Restaurants

Luna Park: The best thing about this Mediterranean outdoor café is that it's located in Union Square Park. Take your pal to the dog run here and then sit down and enjoy brunch, lunch, or dinner in style. Luna serves a full menu of pasta, fish, gourmet salads, and desserts. 17th Street at Union Park; 212/475-8464.

GREENWICH VILLAGE

For over a century, this area below West 14th Street and above Houston Street has attracted artists and bohemians from all over the country. One of the few areas in Manhattan not on a grid, the streets criss-cross wildly and reflect the reckless devil-may-care attitude that defines the Village. Although no starving artist could ever afford to live here anymore, the atmosphere is still one of excitement and stimulation. Dogs are popular in the Village, and although there is little green space to be found, canine owners are vocal and active in opening and maintaining off-leash areas for their companions.

Parks, Beaches, and Recreation Areas

19 Hudson River Park 🐾 🐾

This promenade along the Hudson River is currently in the second phase of a four-phase development project. By 2006 there will be 550 acres of parkland here along the waterfront of west Manhattan. The proposed park will run from Battery Park to 59th Street.

Currently the park runs along the river between Houston and Bank Streets and you and your dog can walk along the gravel paths overlooking New Jersey, but dogs are not allowed on the lawns. Here's hoping West Village D.O.G. will

EARMARK YOUR CALENDAR–MAY AND SEPTEMBER

Art Squared: Twice yearly, at the end of May and again at the beginning of September, New York City artists bookend summer with the **Washington Square Outdoor Arts Festival** in Washington Square Park. On Memorial Day and Labor Day weekends, hundreds of artists descend upon the Village, and you and your dog are invited, too. We can hardly drag George away from the watercolors, while Inu thinks edible art definitely takes the cake. For exact dates and information, call 212/982-6255.

On the Waterfront: Be there for **Riverflicks,** the summer movie series at Pier 54 (every Wednesday evening) and Pier 25 (on Friday nights) in Hudson River Park from July through September. You and your dog can join the pup-arazzi for the outdoor movie series. Shows are rated R on Wednesday; PG or G on Friday. All movies start at 8:30 P.M.; admission is free. 212/533-PARK (212/533-7275).

prove successful in getting a new dog run here when the park is expanded to Gansevoort Street. Dogs must be leashed. Located on the West Side Highway between Houston and Bank Street. Open dawn–1 A.M. 212/791-2530

20 Mercer-Houston Dog Run 🐾 🐾 🐕

This small asphalt-covered dog run is well-used and well-maintained. We think George's Dog Run in Washington Square Park (only a few blocks from here) offers a lot more, but the dogs and their members-only owners who frequent this run are fiercely loyal to this place, and it shows. There are four benches, a hose, a dog bowl and, in the summer, a small wading pool for dogs who long for a quick dip. There is a bulletin board with photos of the many dogs who frequent this run, but there is little shade for hot summer days. To become a member and receive a key to the run, send a letter to the Mercer-Houston Dog Run Association at P.O. Box 101, New York, NY 10012. A $50 annual dues are also required. Located at the corner of Mercer and Houston Streets. Open 24 hours. No phone.

21 James J. Walker Park 🐾

Although dogs are allowed here on the concrete walkways, this park is mostly composed of ball fields, a playground, and a pool (where dogs can't go), so we can't recommend this unless your dog just needs to get out now. Dogs must be leashed. The park is bordered by Clarkson and Hudson Streets and Saint Luke's Place. Open dawn–9 P.M. 212/408-0234.

22 Washington Square Park & George's Dog Run 🐾 🐾 🐾 🐾 🐕

First established as a public park in 1827, Washington Square Park is one of New York City's most famous landmarks. This 10-acre park has been the scene of countless movies, books, plays, and poems. Home to novelist Henry James (who memorialized the square in his novel of the same name), and current artists such as playwright John Guare and actress Susan Sarandon, this elegant historic park and neighborhood was named for the first president named George and reflects New York in a time that has long since past. The park itself offers tree-lined walkways, the famous Washington Arch designed by Sanford White, a large fountain (where your dog will be tempted to go, but is not allowed), and many benches to watch the thousands of people who parade by every day.

Fortunately for dogs, there is also a dog run here, and it is one of the largest and well-used dog runs in the city. Located at the Thompson Street entrance on the southern side of the park, George's Run (we, of course, think this is an exceptional name) offers more running room than almost any other dog run in Manhattan. Shaded by large trees, the run has a dirt floor, several benches, enough room to throw a ball, and plenty of playmates for your pup. There is also a water hose, water bowls, and mutt mitts to pick up after your pet.

This run gets a *lot* of use—so much that on hot summer days, the smell of dog urine flattens you like a truck barreling down 7th Avenue. The dog owners here do their best to keep the park clean and the crowds down. Maintained by the Washington Square Dog Run Association, this organization conducts fund-raisers, solicits money from local businesses, and publishes a yearly dog calendar and newsletter called *Dog Run.*

For more information contact Washington Square Dog Run Association, c/o Wayne Amendola, 360 West 15th Street, Apt. A, New York, NY 10011. Located between MacDougal and 4th Streets and University and Waverly Place. Open 6–12 A.M. 212/989-1448 (dog run), 212/408-0234 (parks department).

23 West Village Dog Run 😺 🐾 🐕

Consisting of little more than asphalt, benches, a water hose, drinking bowl, and some shade awnings, this out-of-the-way run is, nevertheless, clean and well-maintained. Membership costs $40 a year and is open to anyone, but space is limited to 300 families, so expect to wait a while if you're new in the area. There is hope that when the new Hudson River Park is completed, there will be space for a new, larger dog run to take the place of this one, but at press time, nothing had been decided. To inquire about membership contact the West Village Dog Owners Group (WVDOG), 41 Bethune Street, New York, NY 10014. Located on Little West 12th Street between Washington Street and 10th Avenue. Open 24 hours a day; 212/807-0093.

A Biscuit a Day Keeps the Blues Away: At least that's true when your dog stops by for a visit to Shelly Davis' **Bed and Biscuit.** This unusual day care is really a home away from home. That's because it's in Shelly's home. Specially screened dogs are welcome to spend the day with Shelly in a cage-free environment. Included are several walks a day, plenty of stimulation, and loving care and attention. Shelly also offers nutritional advice and homeopathic treatments for elderly and chronically ill dogs. Each weekend several dogs get to go away for a retreat to Shelly's home in Woodstock (see the Beyond the Skyline chapter). For more information, call 212/475-6064; website: www.bednbiscuit.com.

Restaurants

Barney Macs: This neighborhood favorite is a late-night hangout. Open until 4 A.M., you'll be able to soothe the savage beast at most any hour. Named for the black Labrador who, from his vantage point atop the store sign, is the "watchdog of the neighborhood." This café welcomes you and your dog at its outdoor tables, where you can be your own watchdogs. Artists, service people, firefighters, and the men and women in blue get 2 for 1 drinks during the 911 Happy Hour from 4–7 P.M. daily. Look for the sign with the big black dog on it. 190 West 4th Street; 212/206-7526.

Bruno Bakery: For divine bakery items like chocolate cream puffs and apple tarts, stop by this yummy sweet shop and pick up a calorie-laden dessert to take to the park. There are even chairs and tables outside, just in case you can't wait to dive into your treat. 506 La Guardia Place; 212/982-5854.

Chez Jacqueline: For great French cooking that will make you homesick for Paris, we recommend this trendy little bistro in the Village. And although the food is delicious, your dog will agree that the best thing about it is the decidedly French attitude towards dogs. They're welcome to sit with you whether you're whiling the day away with a cappuccino or dining alfresco at the outdoor patio. 72 MacDougal Street; 212/505-0727.

Chez Ma Tante: This wonderful French restaurant has long been a favorite of ours. Serving exceptional Provençal-style French cuisine, your dog will enjoy sitting beside you at the open French doors or sidewalk café tables. See and be seen at this busy crossroads between Bleecker Street and 7th Avenue. 189 West 10th Street; 212/620-0223.

Chumley's: This dog-friendly bar welcomes both four-footed and two-legged patrons. Originally a speakeasy in the 1920s, this Village mainstay has always been on the cutting edge. You and your dog will feel right at home as you go tail-to-tail with the many pups nosing their way between the tables. So next time you stop by for a pint, make sure your mate is with you. 85 Bedford Street; 212/675-4449.

Cornelia Street Café: For a relaxed atmosphere and reasonably priced food, this French-American café is a great place to people watch on a summer day. Your dog is welcome at the sidewalk tables outside. 29 Cornelia Street; 212/989-9319.

Grey Dog's Coffee: How can you go wrong with a name like this? This local coffeehouse has a dog's welcome mat spread out in every season. Water bowls and dog biscuits are available on request—as well as smoothies, cappuccino, and desserts for you. 33 Carmine Street; 212/462-0041.

Peanut Butter & Co.: This novelty sandwich store is a delightful alternative to the usual deli fare in New York City. Although there is little more offered here beyond unusual peanut butter concoctions, the idea is so delightful we just had to include it in this book. There are two benches outside where you can enjoy your Fluffernutter, Peanut Butter BLT, or Ants on a Log (PB and raisins on a celery stalk). Or, take your retro sandwich to Washington Square Park a few blocks away. 240 Sullivan Street; 212/677-3995.

Señor Swanky's: This outdoor eatery touts itself as a Mexican Café and Celebrity Hangout. Although we've never seen any celebrities (and wonder why any celebrity would hang out in a place designated for them), George and Inu think this place is cool merely because dogs are allowed to sit outside at the café tables here. The menu is standard Mexican fare, but the people watching from the corner of trendy Bleecker Street is worth the trip. 142 Bleecker Street; 212/979-9800.

HARLEM/SPANISH HARLEM

During the 1920s, Harlem was at the center of the wildly exciting Harlem Renaissance, an African-American artistic and cultural movement featuring an explosion of jazz, dance, and creativity the likes of which America had not seen before nor has since. Home of the famous Cotton Club and the Apollo Theatre, Harlem takes a fierce pride in its African-American heritage—as a walk through this community from East 96th Street to East 125th Street will demonstrate.

Parks, Beaches, and Recreation Areas
🔟 Jefferson Park & Tom's Dog Run 🐾 🐾 🐕

Although you won't be rushing to this park if you don't already live in this neighborhood, for those who do walk here daily, it is a surprisingly pleasant two-block recreation area. Best of all, there's an off-leash dog run known as Tom's Dog Run located in the far eastern corner next to the FDR Drive. Dogs are not allowed on the ball field or playground, but you can walk along the grassy areas as you head for the leash-free area.

Tom's Dog Run is an oval, dirt-covered area with a few benches, some shade, plastic bags, and enough room to toss a ball. This isn't one of the more popular dog runs in the city, but you will find some other dogs to socialize with during prime hours. There is no formal group that operates this run, but there's a small bulletin board so you can "bone" up on all the latest news. The park is bordered by 111th and 114th Streets and 1st Avenue. Park and run open from 6 A.M.–10 P.M. 212/828-9778.

DIVERSIONS

Farmer Fidos: City-dwellers longing for fresh air and fresh produce can find it at any of Manhattan's farmer's markets.

Greenwich Village: This is one market that allows dogs! Bring your pup with you on your weekly trip to the Tompkins Square or the Saint Mark's Greenmarkets. Leashed dogs are welcome, and we think it's a lot more fun to shop with our dogs along. We can always rely on them to give us an opinion about everything from the produce to the bakery items. Shop on Tuesday, 8 A.M.–1 P.M. at Saint Mark's Church on 10th Street and 2nd Avenue, or Sunday at Tompkins Square Park, 10 A.M.– 6 P.M. 212/477-3220.

Battery Park: Take Fido to the Bowling Green Greenmarket for your weekly shopping spree. Held on Thursday at Broadway and Battery Park Place, this weekly farmer's market promises a fun and "fruitful" outing for you both. 8 A.M.–3 P.M. 212/477-3220.

Gramercy: Bring your guys, dolls, and dogs to the weekly Union Square Greenmarket—the granddaddy of them all. Arguably the most popular and plentiful greenmarket in the city, this large farmer's market has something for every taste. You and your dog will feel right at home as you wander among the more than 80 stalls, choosing between cheeses, produce, candles, honey, seafood, and countless other food and goodies. For a perfect day, top it all off with a visit to the dog run at Union Square Park. At Broadway and 14th Street Monday, Wednesday, Friday, and Saturday from 8 A.M.to 6 P.M. 212/477-3220.

Harlem: From July through October, bring your dog to 144th Street and Lenox Avenue for the weekly greenmarket. With a bounty of produce, crafts, and ethnic foods available, you and your pup will have a hard time choosing which to haul home. Our dogs always volunteer to take a taste test when we take too long to make up our minds. Held on Tuesday from 8 A.M. to 3 P.M. 212/477-3220.

25 Marcus Garvey Park 🐾 🐾 🐢

This historic park in the heart of Harlem is also known as Mount Morris Park. That's for the Mount Morris Watchtower, completed in 1857, which stands at its center. In the early and middle 19th century, there were many watchtowers built on the hills of upper Manhattan to alert the city to a fire before it could spread. The only problem was, most of the structures were built of wood and succumbed to the very fires they were built to guard against. In the 1850s a new steel structure was perfected and the Mount Morris Watchtower is the last surviving example of this construction.

To reach the tower, you'll climb the wide staircase in the center of the park. The tower is off-limits to visitors, but there is a large square at the top for those who hanker for a view through the trees. Down below, you can wander around the stone fortress that houses the tower, but watch out for broken glass on your climb. There is a new active conservancy group here that has restored the park from the trash-strewn mess it was only a few years ago. We applaud their efforts but, in all honesty, the park still has a way to go.

Dogs allowed to shed their leashes before 9 A.M. The park is bordered by 120th and 124th Streets and Madison Avenue. The park opens at 6 A.M. and closes at dusk. 212/408-0234.

26 Saint Nicholas Park 🐾 🐾 🐢

Skinny is definitely good at this long narrow park in Harlem. At 15 blocks north to south, but barely a block wide, you and your dog will enjoy exploring the nooks and crannies here. Set on a hillside, this park hearkens back to the time when upper Manhattan was covered with hills and cliffs. Manhattan's crags have been covered with concrete and buildings, but in this park you can still find some grass, winding trails, and trees. This isn't a must-see park, and you do have to watch for broken glass, but if you live here, your dog will consider this place his own. Entrances are located at 128th, 133rd, 130th, and 135th Streets along Saint Nicholas Terrace. Dogs are allowed off-leash romping before 9 A.M. and after 9 P.M.

Located between 127th and 141st Streets, Nicholas Avenue and Nicholas Terrace. Open dawn–10 P.M. 212/408-1234.

INWOOD/WASHINGTON HEIGHTS

Located at the tip-top of Manhattan, these neighborhoods run from 165th to 220th Streets. Featuring the last remnants of the Dutch occupation, this district also marks the landmark spot where the Dutch told the Delaware Native Americans, "We'll take Manhattan," and then did—for 60 guilders. Considering current real estate prices, even jaded Wall Street dogs have got to agree that ranks as the best investment deal in history.

EARMARK YOUR CALENDAR

Breakfast at. . . No, it's not Tiffany's—it's better. If your dog has been clamoring to come to your next power breakfast, you'll finally able to say "Yes!" That's because the Regency Hotel in Midtown East sponsors an annual **Bark Breakfast** at its Five-Forty Restaurant. Offering a special pet menu for that day only, hotel guests and local residents are invited to bring their pup along on this special day. Canine Styles provides a special goody bag for your pup. Dates vary each year, so call for information. 540 Park Avenue; 212/759-4100.

Parks, Beaches, and Recreation Areas

27 Inwood Hill Park & Dog Run 🐾 🐾 🐾 🐾 🐕

Although we always applaud off-leash areas, this is one park where having a dog run is almost unnecessary. Simply put, this large park is one of the best places for dogs in Manhattan. It's not nearly as congested as the other large parks nearby—Central Park or Van Cortlandt Park in the Bronx. Developed in 1916, this park has 196 acres of the last remaining natural forested land left in Manhattan. You can also visit the spot where Dutchman Peter Minuit made his historic 60 guilder real-estate deal at the expense of the Delaware Native Americans. The monument is located near the dog run near West 207th Street

You'll find plenty of forested trails that traverse the hill itself, open grassy areas, and even two large estuaries on the Harlem River, which runs along the park's northern boundary. There is enough room to forget you're still in the city. The parks department does a great job keeping this park clean, safe, and even a little rustic. Don't tell anyone we told you, but there are plenty of places to let your dog go leash-free here so, understandably, you may not use the leash-free area as often as you might in other parks.

If you wish to use the dog run, it's located behind the baseball diamond against the hill near the Seaman Avenue entrance. Covered with pea gravel, there is plenty of shade, a water hose and bowl, and although not large, there is still ample room to toss a ball. A separate area for smaller dogs is being planned nearby. To contribute to the run, contact Inwood Hill Dog Run, 25 Indian Road, New York, NY 10034-1017.

Separate trails can be accessed from the western side of the hill via Dyckman Fields near Dyckman Marina. Located between Dyckman Street, Payson and Seaman Avenues and the Harlem and Hudson Rivers. The dog run is open 24 hours; the park is open 6–1 A.M. 212/569-7721.

28 Isham Park 🐾 🐾 🐾

With Inwood Hill Park right across the street, it's hard to work up any enthusiasm for this small, hilltop park, but locals like it for the quiet and relative solitude compared with its bigger brother next door. Divided in two sections, the larger and more tranquil space is between Park Terrace and Broadway. There are trees, plenty of grass, and bench-lined walkways. The park is bordered by Cooper Avenue, Park Terrace, and Broadway. Open 6 A.M.–10 P.M. 212/408-0234.

29 J. H. Wright Park & Dog Run 🐾 🐾 🐕

This seven-acre park in Washington Heights is novel only for the fact that it houses a dog run in a neighborhood where there are few (okay, none, unless you want to hike the 30 plus blocks to Inwood Park). The park is named for J. Hood Wright, a wealthy 19th century financier who built a mansion on this site. Now your pup can cavort leash-free in the small gravel run located along 173rd Street. There are few amenities here, just a few benches and little shade. But it provides a leash-free space, and that has to be a step in the right direction. The parks department runs this space, because at this time there is no active group of dog owners to do so. Dogs must be leashed in the rest of the park. Located between 173rd Street and Haven and Fort Washington Avenues. Open 6 A.M. until 10 P.M. 212/795-1388 (dog run), 212/408-0234 (parks department).

Restaurants

Tubby Hook Café: This obscure little café/restaurant offers one of the best views in Manhattan. Located at the Dyckman Avenue Marina, the outdoor tables are situated on a bluff overlooking the Hudson River and the George Washington Bridge. During the day, there is a large grassy area with open seating; order your burgers, ice cream, or sandwiches from the take-out window and enjoy sitting outside with your pal at your feet. At night there is a full menu with bar and table service. Dogs are allowed to join you at the outer tables. 348 Dyckman Avenue. No phone.

LINCOLN CENTER

Although there are no parks in this neighborhood, both Riverside Park and Central Park are close by, so your pup won't feel starved for green space. With theater, opera, ballet, and the prestigious Juilliard School all feeding the arts scene at Lincoln Center, and countless restaurants lining the streets, you won't feel starved for much else either. The following restaurants are only a tiny sampling of the many you can choose from.

DIVERSIONS

I know that dogs are pack animals, but it is difficult to imagine a pack of standard poodles...and if there was such a thing as a pack of standard poodles, where would they rove to? Bloomingdale's?

—Yvonne Clifford, American actress

Noses on the Glass: From Thanksgiving through New Year's, you'll bring new meaning to window shopping when you visit New York department stores for their annual holiday window decorations. Each store offers unique window dressing that is always worth a visit. The following is a listing of all the stores that do it up right. Our advice? Don't attempt a visit on the day after Thanksgiving.

Barney's 212/826-8900
Bergdorf Goodman 212/753-7300
Bloomingdales 212/705-2000
Bendel's 212/247-1100
Lord & Taylor 212/391-3344
Macy's 212/494-4495
Sak's Fifth Avenue 212/753-4000

Restaurants

Fountain Café: Enjoy a summer meal surrounded by the arts of Lincoln Center. Grab a bite, watch theatergoers and opera lovers come and go, and listen to street musicians serenade you and your pup under the stars. Cappuccino, cocktails, and desserts are also on the menu. Lincoln Center at 65th Street and Columbus; 212/874-7000.

Opera Espresso Café: Long an after-theater and opera mainstay, this tiny café offers great desserts, coffee drinks, and light summer fare for the hungry late night crowd. The café also serves lunch, but our dogs like it better during our evening walk. 1928 Broadway; 212/799-3050.

The Saloon: This Lincoln Center establishment survived the excesses of the 1980s and the opulence of the 1990s and now, in the words of Sondheim's anthem to aging, "is still here" as we enter the 21st century. Although we can't get too excited about the rather pedestrian menu of brie omelettes, focaccia sandwiches, and fettucine alfredo, they do have a menu that goes on for days, so you needn't worry about finding something you'll like. The premiere attraction here has always been the street scene, so grab an outdoor table for a catbird's seat to all the action on Broadway. 1920 Broadway; 212/874-1500.

Places to Stay

Phillips Club: This modern all-suite hotel is located near Lincoln Center and caters to guests for long-term as well as short-term stays. You are welcome here for a night up to a year. All suites, from a studio to a three-bedroom apartment, are luxuriously furnished with kitchens, dishwashers, microwaves, and full amenities. One pet per suite is allowed and a refundable deposit is required. Rates are $310–2,000 per night; weekly and monthly rates available. 155 West 66th Street, New York, NY 10023; 212/835-8820 or 877/854-8800; website: www.phillipsclub.com.

MIDTOWN EAST

The heart of Manhattan is, undoubtedly, the section referred to as Midtown. Separated from the west side by 5th Avenue, Midtown East covers the area from 34th Street all the way up to Central Park. Landmarks include Rockefeller Center, the Empire State Building, the New York Public Library, the shops of 5th Avenue, and the United Nations. Although a little more staid and a little less funky than its western counterpart, this neighborhood features some of the most expensive real estate in Manhattan; step one paw in any shop or hotel and you'll know what we mean.

Parks, Beaches, and Recreation Areas

30 Peter Detmoldt Park & Dog Run 🐾 🐾 🐾 🐕

This park is a well-planned concrete recreation area located in a hidden corridor between the FDR Drive and Beekman Place. You might live here for years and never know this place existed—if you didn't have a dog. Dogs in the know understand that this is one popular dog run. Dog walkers bring their "clients" here and locals gather to catch up on all the gossip. The park is only three blocks long, but lucky for you, the run takes up about a third of that. There are plenty of trees, benches, lamps (for those dark winter evenings), and enough room to chat or chase your tail. The only drawback is the concrete tile underfoot.

The run is supported by donations and maintained by PDP-ARF, Inc. (Peter Detmold Park—Animals Run Free), c/o Maranyc, 120 East 56th Street, New York, NY 10022.

Dogs are allowed to go leashless in the dog run but must be leashed in the park. The entrance to the park is off 51st Street. The park is bordered by 49th and 51st Streets and the FDR Drive. Open dawn–8 P.M., except in the winter, when it is open until 7 P.M. and in the summer months when it is open until 9 P.M. 212/408-0234.

31 Robert Moses Park & Dog Run 🐾 🐾 🐕

Named for the powerful and controversial Robert Moses, Parks Commissioner

I Love a Parade, or Two, or Three or... Stand long enough on 5th Avenue and before you know it, a parade will go by. In fact, there are far too many 5th Avenue parades for us to list them all here. Suffice it to say that on any given day, week, month, or season, you'll be able to find *someone* celebrating *something* down 5th Avenue. One of our favorites is the annual **Easter Promenade,** held on Easter Sunday, whenever that may fall. The revelers make their way down 5th Avenue from 57th to 44th Streets. Watch the participants dress up in outrageous Easter bonnets as they celebrate the first rite of Spring. For more information on all the parades, go to the website: www .carnaval.com/cityguides/newyork/parades.htm.

of the 1930s to the 1950s, the only thing this tiny concrete strip has going for it is that it's leash-free. That, and the fraternity of friendly dogs and owners who congregate here. Admittedly, that's the main reason we hang out in dog runs, but if your dog needs exercise, you might be disappointed. Located along busy 41st Street on a paved lot, there are few amenities: a little shade, a few benches, and one trash can. Be sure to bring your own water in the summer. Located on East 41st Street at 1st Avenue. Open dawn–10 P.M. 212/408-0234.

Nature Hikes and Urban Walks

East River Esplanade: Although we wouldn't call this a great walk in the park for your pup, it fits the bill when you need to get away from the concrete of the city. You can look across the East River and take in the 59th Street Bridge uptown, the skyscrapers downtown, and the famous Pepsi sign across the water in Long Island City. So if you're just hankering for a glimpse of water and a respite from the hectic city surrounding you, take a break with your pal and take in the sights. To reach the Esplanade, enter through a tunnel under the busy FDR Drive at 37th Street. 212/408-0234.

Restaurants

Café Blue at the Greenhouse: This outdoor eatery is really just a little gourmet to-go stand with tables outside. But the food is great and your dog is welcome, so in our book, it may as well be the finest French restaurant. Dine on lavish salads, gelati, espresso, and unusual sandwiches. 342 East 47th Street. No phone.

Café Saint Bart's: Join the hip and holy crowd at this trendy terrace café located at Saint Bartholomew's Church. At night the terrace is magically decorated with small twinkling lights and the voltage generated by the energetic crowd lights up the night. The food is standard and on the expensive side, but

DIVERSIONS

Swim the Concrete Jungle: Take your dog for a swim and never leave the city. That's right. At **Bonnie's K9 Corp,** your dog can swim in a specially designed dog pool, work with a personal trainer, and even have a puppy massage. So when the beaches are shutting out your pup on those hot summer days, join the K9 Corp. A 25-minute swim is $35 with a trainer, $25 to go it alone. 133 East 39th Street; 212/414-2500; website: www.K9-swimtherapy.com.

Water dogs who just can't get enough of a good thing can also visit Biscuits and Bath's **Doggy Village,** 227 East 44th Street; 212/692-2323, for a dip in the special basement dog pool. An annual swim membership costs $100, and each 30-minute swim is $30.

they do serve Inu's favorite—free dog biscuits—on request. Dogs are welcome at the outdoor tables. 109 East 50th Street at Park Avenue; 212/888-2664.

Silver Swan: Our dogs expect a little wienerschnitzel every once in awhile and when they get the craving, we head for this friendly German restaurant. The Swan serves genuine German dishes and has one of the largest selections of German beers in the city, so your dachshund will feel like she's come home on a visit here. Dogs are welcome at the sidewalk tables along Park Avenue. 41 East 20th Street; 212/254-3611.

Verbana: The Verbana staff really roll out the red carpet for their four-legged guests. You'll never feel unwelcome or see the curl of an upper lip when you ask if your dog may join you here. Serving great Italian food for you, and dog biscuits and water for your Italian greyhound, this restaurant is likely to become a favorite stop for you and Spot. 54 Irving Place; 212/260-5454.

Places to Stay

Drake Hotel: This elegant Park Avenue hotel is European in the most important way. Why, it even welcomes dogs under 30 pounds as guests. The rooms are fully stocked and room service will bring a special bowl for your pup on request. There is no deposit required for your dog, but you must sign a damage waiver on check-in. Rates are $259–479. 440 Park Avenue, New York, NY 10022; 212/421-0900 or 800/63-SWISS (800/637-9477); website: www.swissotel.com.

Dumont Plaza Suites: This suite-style hotel offers efficiency apartments with full amenities. Dogs are allowed on a case-by case basis, meaning the management has the right to approve your dog before allowing you to stay. A $300 refundable deposit is required. Rates are $150–300 per night. 150 East 34th Street, New York, NY 10016; 212/481-7600; website: www.mesuite.com.

Envoy Club: For haughty hounds looking to stay in the lap of luxury for a month or more, look no further than this upscale East Side apartment hotel.

Dogs of all sizes are welcome to stay with their owners. If price is no object, you'll have all the conveniences of a hotel with the comfort of your own apartment. Studios, one- and two-bedrooms are available ranging from $4,800–10,000 a month. No fee for your pet, but an additional refundable security deposit is required. 377 East 33rd Street, New York, NY 10016; 212/481-4600; website: www.envoyclub.com.

Four Seasons: Well, what can we say about a hotel that provides a room service menu for pets, special pet beds, and even bottled water for your pup? Our dogs know what to say: "When do we check in?" The rates are a bit steep but if you're looking for a place that makes you feel like a pampered pup, this is it. Rates are $615–1,350 per night. 57 East 57th Street, New York, NY 10022; 212/758-5700 or 800/332-3442; website: www.fshr.com.

Metropolitan Hotel: This luxury hotel really rolls out the red carpet for you and your pet. Starting with a special check-in package that includes information about local dog walkers, hotel pet services, and nearby parks and restaurants, your dog will even receive a special place mat, water bowl, toys, and treats. A pet room-service menu is available and a "Did You Forget?" closet provides amenities such as dog beds, leashes, toys, and pooper-scoopers.

Forget waiting for a vacation—you might want to check in now. Rates are $199–600 per night. 569 Lexington Avenue, New York, NY 10022; 212/752-7000 or 800/23-LOEWS (800/235-6397); website: www.loewshotels.com.

Morgans: This trendy hotel, owned by hipster hotelier Ian Schrager, allows pets under 20 pounds. We hear tales that the size requirement is on a sliding scale. Rates are $250–375 and there is a rather stiff, non-refundable $100 cleaning fee due upon checkout. 237 Madison Avenue, New York, NY 10016; 212/686-0300; website: www.ianschrager.com.

The Plaza: Once again, small dogs rule. That's because this New York landmark only allows dogs under 20 pounds. The rooms are exceptional, however, and the staff will provide for a local dog walker on request. George and Inu are getting very tired of the large-dog ban at so many luxury hotels. What can we say? It's a "ruff" world out there. Rates are $350–3500 per night. 768 5th Avenue, New York, NY 10021; 212/759-3000 or 800/545-4000; website: www.fairmont.com.

Regency Hotel: After a recent $35 million face-lift, this grand hotel is ready and waiting to sweep you and your pup off your feet. Featuring such amenities as a pet room-service menu, a "Did you forget. . . ?" closet that is fully stocked with everything from leashes, pet beds, pooper-scoopers, and pet toys, you might never want to check out. The friendly concierges will also arrange for a dog walker, transportation, or even guide you to the closest park and dog-friendly restaurant. Rates are $199–800 for super-elegant suites. 540 Park Avenue, New York, NY 10021; 212/759-4100; website: www.loewshotels.com.

MIDTOWN WEST

Home to the Broadway Theater District, Times Square, Madison Square Garden, and both MTV and ABC studios, Midtown West enjoys the fast-paced whirl of lights, action and the latest commercial trends. Although there is barely a blade of grass to be found for our four-footed friends, there are countless hotels and distractions to keep any city visitor and their party pup busy for days.

Parks, Beaches, and Recreation Areas

32 Bryant Park 🐾 🐾 🐢

This busy Midtown park is always a hub of activity in any season. For this reason, it isn't the best place for dogs. Yes, you can walk along the paved walkways and attend the many concerts and events that are held here, but it is always congested and there are relatively few places to let your dog well, be a dog. We always feel as if we're dodging feet or stares when our dogs do their daily business, and let's face it, the tens of thousands of people walking through here definitely makes a crowd.

But if this is your only option on a daily basis, better come early or late if you want to avoid the crush of humanity. The park is open until 1 A.M. so you'll have plenty of opportunity. Dogs must be leashed. The park is bordered by 40th and 42nd Streets and the Avenue of the Americas. Open 6–1 A.M. 212/408-0234.

Restaurants

Bryant Park Café: On Mondays in the summer, we like to take in dinner and a movie and our dogs think this is the best place in town. Dine at this little café right in Bryant Park and then catch a free flick on the lawn a few steps away. The café serves light American fare as well as desserts and appetizers. 25 West 40th Street; 212/840-6500.

My Most Favorite Dessert Co.: You'd better deliver in the goody department when you make such an audacious claim in the name of your store. Fortunately (or is it *un*fortunately?), this place delivers. With out-of-this-world brownies, pastries, tarts, and cheesecakes, you and your dog will need

EARMARK YOUR CALENDAR–SPRING

Fido Finders: Each year celebrities gather, courtesy of FIDONYC and their founders Bernadette Peters and Mary Tyler Moore, for a fund-raiser dedicated to eradicating pet overpopulation in New York City. Past events have included Broadway Barks, Manhattan Meows, and Loews Hotel's Bark Breakfast. Held each spring, a different event is planned annually. Call for this year's event: 212/227-FIDO (212/227-3436); website: www.fidonyc.org.

EARMARK YOUR CALENDAR–SUMMER

The Reel Thing: HBO hosts the **Bryant Park Summer Film Festival,** an outdoor summer movie series every Monday in July and August in Bryant Park. The lineup includes classic and retro movies sure to be crowd pleasers. The series is very popular so get there early and grab a spot on the lawn. Our dogs think the depiction of animals in Hollywood movies are very unrealistic—I mean, like Air Bud could ever happen? But once we get past their protestations, we have a great time. All movies begin at sundown. 212/512-5700; website: www.hbo-bryantparkfilm.com.

to take a really long walk to work off the damage a visit here inflicts. That's okay with our pups. George thinks a good long walk in Central Park followed by a trip to get our most favorite dessert (cream cheese brownies for JoAnna, lemon tart for George) should be an everyday experience. 120 West 45th Street; 212/997-5130.

Puttanesca: Dine alfresco at this Italian restaurant. With a few sidewalk tables where you can dine on scrumptious fettucine alfredo, eggplant parmesan, and other Italian specialties, New York doggies get the royal treatment here. Make sure you save room for the tiramisu. 859 9th Avenue; 212/581-4177.

Sea Grill: If you're looking for fresh fish grilled to perfection (and who isn't?) you'll be a happy hound at this Rockefeller Plaza outdoor café. With a menu that features different fish each day, you won't get tired of the food or the great people watching at this busy eatery. Dogs allowed at the outside tables only. 19 West 49th Street; 212/332-7610.

Places to Stay

Best Western President Hotel: Adorable teacup-sized mutts (that is, those under 15 pounds) are allowed to stay at this 351-room hotel. But George, at 35 pounds, weighs in more like a large beer mug and he's never had a problem making the cut. Our advice? Make sure your pup is on his best behavior and hope for a sympathetic staffer to let you in. Rates are $120–200. 234 West 48th Street, New York, NY 10022; 212/246-8800 or 800/528-1234; website: www.bestwestern.com.

Crowne Plaza Manhattan: This is a Holiday Inn that went bright-lights, big-city. And although small pets are allowed here, we've discovered "small" is on a sliding scale. So make nice and you shouldn't have a problem. Rates are $225–345 per night, so it isn't a cheap ticket, but you will be in a prime location in the Big Apple. There is a refundable $50 deposit required for your

If I Can Make It There… Calling all dogs who dream of becoming a star. This show's for you! The **New York Pet Show,** held at Madison Square Garden the last weekend in October, is a show for dogs who care more about doing Stupid Pet Tricks than they do flashing their pedigree papers. This annual event is for dogs, kids, adults, and just about anyone who loves their dog. There is a pet talent show, seminars, and demonstrations for dog lovers, a judge who will rate your pup's chance of making it in the movies, a petting zoo, and various contests and entertainment acts for dogs and people. If you're bringing your pet with you, pre-registration is $25; admission for single tickets is $12 per person. For information and dates, call 212/246-0057. 212/662-2133; or Saint Luke's in the Fields at 487 Hudson Street in Greenwich Village, 212/924-0562.

pet. 1605 Broadway, New York, NY 10022; 212/977-4000 or 800/HOLIDAY (800/465-4329); website: www.holiday-inn.com.

Courtyard by Marriott: This comfortable hotel, part of the Marriott chain, is located in the heart of the Fashion District, just blocks away from 42nd Street, Times Square, and the Theater District. Dogs are welcome here on approval. Be sure to announce your pup when making your reservation. There is no size limit. Rates are $199–450. 114 West 40th Street New York, NY 10018; 212/391-0088; website: www.marriott.com.

Hilton New York And Towers: This extremely large (over 2,000 spacious rooms) and extremely extravagant hotel welcomes you and your canine pal. All sizes allowed, which makes our bigger-than-a-bread-box dogs very happy. The service is excellent. Rates are $215–405. 1335 Avenue of the Americas, New York NY 10019; 212/586-7000; website: www.hilton.com.

Le Parker Meridien: Pets are welcome at this upscale, full-service hotel. With 700 rooms to choose from, you'll find all the creature comforts for you and your traveling pup. Many rooms even have kitchens for those who can possibly resist all the great restaurants in the city that never sleeps. Rates are $250–350 per night; there is a non-refundable $50 fee for your dog. 118 West 57th St., New York, NY 10019; 212/245-5000; website: www.parkermeridien.com.

Mainsfield: This charming Victorian hotel will make you feel as if you've stepped back in time. Built in 1904 as a private club for gentlemen, you'll still find the service and elegant rooms suitable for royalty. Located just steps away from the action on 5th Avenue, you and your pup will feel like you've been transported to another world (until you walk outside, that is). Dogs of all sizes are welcome with prior approval. You are required to sign a waiver on check-in. Rates are $200–400. 12 West 44th Street, New York, NY 10019; 212/944-6050; website: www.boutiquehg.com.

Mayflower Hotel: Located steps away from Central Park, your dog will be impressed by this hotel's really big front yard. With 366 dog-friendly rooms to choose from, you and your dog will find location is everything. Rates are $159–420 per night. A refundable $100 deposit and damage waiver are required. 15 Central Park West, New York, NY 10023; 212/265-0060; website: www.mayflowerhotel.com.

Marriott Marquis: Small pets (under 25 pounds) are allowed at this large 2,000-room hotel in the heart of Times Square. Although the location is great for night owls and theater lovers, there aren't a lot of amenities for dogs in this neighborhood, so be sure your dog doesn't mind either crowds or noise. Rates are $250–400 per night. 1535 Broadway Street, New York, NY 10036; 212/398-1900 or 800/228-9290; website: www.marriott.com.

Millennium Broadway: This 630-room hotel is near Times Square and allows dogs under 20 pounds. The rooms are comfortable, with a European flair. Rates start at $225 and go to $400 per night. 145 West 44th Street, New York, NY 10036; 212/768-4400; website: www.stay-with-us.com.

The Muse Hotel: With a muse like this new Midtown hotel, you'll be inspired on every visit. That's because the dog-friendly staff here offer a special Pooch Package with your pup in mind. Your room will be stocked with doggy treats, snacks, and a room-service menu. There's even a twice-daily complimentary dog-walking service. Rates are $195–265 per night. 130 West 46th Street, New York, NY 10038; 212/485-2400; website: www.themusehotel.com.

Novotel: This modern hotel is pet-friendly—welcomes dogs of all sizes with a refundable $100 deposit. The rooms are clean and comfortable and located near busy Times Square. Rates are $189–280 per night. 226 West 52nd Street, New York, NY 10019; 212/315-0100; website: www.novotel.com.

Red Roof Inn: One of the only budget hotels in Manhattan, this comfortable no-frills establishment welcomes dogs up to 80 pounds. All they ask is that dogs are leashed when in the public areas. Rates are $89–159 per night. 6 West 32nd Street, New York, NY 10001; 212/643-7100; website: www.redroofinn.com.

Renaissance New York Hotel: This Times Square hotel is located in the heart of the Broadway Theater District. Smaller than its ostentatious cousin up the street, the Marriott Marquis, this 306-room hotel is quieter and more understated. All the rooms are comfortable and spacious, and dogs of any size are welcome. Rates are $299–450. There is a $65 non-refundable fee for your pet. 714 7th Avenue, New York, NY 10036; 212/765-7676; website: www.marriott.com.

Sheraton Manhattan Hotel: This full service hotel offers just what you might expect from a Sheraton. All rooms are equipped with coffeemakers, mini bars, and clean, comfortable accommodations. Located near Central Park and the Broadway Theater District, you'll be in the heart of Midtown when you stay here. Dogs are welcome with prior approval. Rates are $195–425 per night. 790 7th Avenue, New York, NY 10019; 212/581-3300; website: www.sheraton.com.

Sheraton New York Hotel and Towers: Located just a few blocks from its sister hotel, the Sheraton Manhattan Hotel, your dog will corner the market in this dog-friendly hotel. The rooms are comfortable, if unspectacular, and you'll only be a few blocks away from a walk in Central Park. Rates are $169–389. 811 7th Avenue, New York, NY 10019; 212/581-1000; website: www.sheraton.com.

MORNINGSIDE HEIGHTS

This district runs along Riverside Drive and Broadway from 106th and 123rd Streets on the Upper West Side. Home to Columbia University and Barnard College, Grant's Tomb (located in Upper Riverside Park), and the famous Riverside Church, this neighborhood has always been as eclectic as it is intellectual.

Parks, Beaches, and Recreation Areas
33 Morningside Park 🐾 🐾 🐾

This narrow park located near Columbia University looks a little like some of those Columbia students the morning after a big party. In other words: a little hung over. If you live here, you probably take your dog for a walk along this grassy, if trashy, boulevard, but we think nearby Riverside Park offers much

EARMARK YOUR CALENDAR–OCTOBER

Blessing of the Animals: On the first Sunday in October, on the Feast of St. Francis of Assisi, Catholic and Episcopalian churches throughout the city conduct an annual Blessing of the Animals. It's your chance to bring your pet to church and have him or her anointed for the coming year. Manhattanites bring in a diverse group of animals, including dogs, cats, hamsters, mice, ferrets, snakes, iguanas, and even alligators—just about any animal on Noah's ark. Dogs must be leashed and well-behaved. Head to the Cathedral of Saint John the Divine at 112th Street and Amsterdam Avenue in Morningside, 212/316-7400 or 212/662-2133; or Saint Luke's in the Fields at 487 Hudson Street in Greenwich Village, 212/924-0562.

more for only a few additional blocks of effort. Dogs are allowed to go leashless before 9 A.M. and after 9 P.M.

The park is bordered by 123rd Street, Cathedral Parkway (110th Street), Morningside Avenue and Morningside Drive. Open 6 A.M.–10 P.M. 212/408-0234.

Riverside Park

This lovely park runs from 72nd to 129th Street. See the Riverside Park listing in the Upper West Side section for complete information.

Restaurants

Hudson Beach Café: This no-frills café overlooking the Hudson River is notable only for its close proximity to the 105th Street Dog Run in Riverside Park. You can grab a beer or soft drink, hamburger, sandwich, salad, or dessert and sit out at one of the many outdoor tables located on a large sidewalk area by the river. We can't tell you you'll be getting great food here, but the social benefits are tremendous. Saturday mornings look like doggy rush hour. Riverside Drive and 105th Street; 917/567-2743.

Metisse: Sophisticated uptown canines make this cozy French bistro their restaurant of choice. With a few small tables outside in the summer, poodles can canoodle in style while dining with their owners on delicious breads, French stew, duck with lingonberry sauce, and the best chocolate desserts this side of the Atlantic. 239 West 105th Street; 212/666-8825.

RANDALLS ISLAND/WARDS ISLAND

These two islands located in the middle of the East River between Manhattan and Queens were originally three salt marshes; landfill from construction debris created the current two-island land mass. Used by the city at various times as a potter's field, an insane asylum, and a home for destitute immigrants, this area has never taken hold as a residential area. Today you'll find the Manhattan Psychiatric Center framed by each "island" but only Ward's Island offers public parkland for you and your pup.

Parks, Beaches, and Recreation Areas

34 Wards Island Park 🐾 🐾

Considering this is one of the larger parks in Manhattan, encompassing some 122 acres, you'd expect a lot more for your efforts to get here. Unfortunately it isn't really worth the trek across the East River. Sure, there are large expanses for throwing the ball and shaded picnic areas right along the river, but the park is rather weedy, and it is usually overrun on weekend with ball games and noisy picnickers. We'll take Manhattan and leave the other island to the weekenders.

Dogs must be leashed. The pedestrian footbridge over the East River is located at 103rd Street and the FDR Drive, but we've discovered it isn't always open.

From the FDR Drive, take the Triborough Bridge to the Randall's Island Exit. Follow signs to the Manhattan Psychiatric Center and park at their parking area. Open dawn–9 P.M. 212/360-8111.

SOHO

Soho (which is short for "South of Houston Street) is exactly where it says it is. Located below Houston and above Canal Streets, this neighborhood is known for its upscale restaurants, designer boutiques, and art galleries. The area is a bit tight on park space, however, and for such a trend-setting area, our dogs are mystified why Soho pups are so behind the pack on opening a neighborhood dog run.

Restaurants

Burrito Bar: This funky little Mexican restaurant advertises themselves as "Mexican food for a couple of beans," and we can vouch for that. The prices are very reasonable and the atmosphere fun and casual. The food is pretty darn good, too. So shell out a few beans and then take the whole enchilada to the outdoor tables where you can enjoy the street scene with your Chihuahua. Serving lunch, dinner, and Sunday brunch. 305 Church Street; 212/219-9200.

Once Upon a Tart: When George and JoAnna tire of not being able to afford a thing at the many galleries and boutiques in Soho, they look for a place a little easier on the pocketbook. This cute café provides the perfect haven for shoppers with a sweet tooth. Small tables lining Sullivan Street provide just the spot where you and your dog can relax from your hectic window-shopping spree. Prices for pastries, sandwiches, salads and, yes,

Psychic Salukis: Every Halloween, the **Pet Bar,** a pet store extraordinaire, holds psychic readings for your pup. So if your Irish wolfhound has been baying at the moon, or your King Charles Cavalier thinks he had another life in the English court, find out the answer. Our dogs just want to know if they will get to take a walk soon (as if we ever forget to take them), but your pup may have more probing questions to ask. For more information, call 212/274-0510.

tarts, are reasonable. 135 Sullivan Street; 212/387-8869.

SoHo Grand Bar at the Grand Hotel: You don't have to be a guest at this dog-friendly hotel to enjoy this dog-friendly restaurant. Dogs get treated as royally as their two-legged companions, and we think that's just about as grand as it gets. 310 West Broadway; 212/965-3000.

I Tre Merli: This restaurant has remained trendy and in demand for over a decade, which is no small feat in the fast-paced world of Manhattan restaurants. So put on the dog and come on down to where the beautiful people hang out. The fare is northern Italian, but the attitude is decidedly uptown. Dogs are welcome to dine with you at the sidewalk tables. 463 West Broadway; 212/254-8699.

Places to Stay

SoHo Grand Hotel: This sumptuous hotel treats all its guests in grand style. Even grander, there are two floors just for occupants with pets, a special pet room-service menu, pet beds, and dogs are even allowed in the Grand Bar downstairs. Whether you live in town or out, when you need a break, you can do no grander than checking in here. Grand rates are $290–350. 310 West Broadway Street, New York, NY 10013; 212/965-3000; website: www.sohogrand.com.

TRIBECA

This district picks up where Soho leaves off, taking its name from the abbreviated form of "*Tri*angle *Be*low *Ca*nal." In the 19th century this area was made up of textile and dry goods factories; from 1970–1980, however, residents started moving into the abandoned industrial buildings. Today it is best known for its galleries, trendy clubs, and active neighborhood camaraderie. Washington Market Park, the center of many Tribeca community events does not, unfortunately, allow dogs.

Parks, Beaches, and Recreation Areas

35 Tribeca Dog Run 🐾 🐾 🐾

Located on the grounds of PS 234, this tiny dog run is a privately-run asphalt square on Warren Street between Greenwich and West Streets. The amenities are few: a hose, a small wading pool in the summer, a few benches, and an awning for shade, but this is still the best you can find in park-starved Tribeca. You must become a member (dues are $50 per year) to use this run. For more information, contact the Dog Owners of Tribeca, 310 1/2 Greenwich Street, New York, NY 10013. Open 24 hours; 212/732-9657.

Restaurants

Alfama: This terrific Portuguese restaurant not only offers knockout food, but also a great sidewalk street scene to go with it. Dogs like to watch the world go by from their ringside seats at streetside, while you will enjoy the great food and fine wine list. 551 Hudson Street; 212/645-2500.

Bistro Les Amis: Dogs say bone appétit! at this hearty country French restaurant. And they really sit up and take notice when you tell them they can dine with you French style at the outdoor tables. Make sure you get a table for two at this romantic bistro—and order plenty of legroom for your dogs. 180 Spring Street; 212/226-8645.

Church Lounge at the TriBeCa Grand: Dogs are welcome at this fashionable hotel bar where the couches are comfy and the staff is friendly. Of course we don't know how friendly they'll be if your pup hops on those cozy couches, but well-behaved canines are welcome to sit at your feet. Stop by for some dessert or an appetizer and mingle with the hip crowd. 2 Avenue of the Americas; 212/519-6600.

The Odeon: This cafeteria-style brasserie has been a hip and happening gathering place for over 20 years. With French-American cuisine and a neighborhood flavor, you and your dog will be among friends at the outdoor tables here. Serving good food all day and well into the night, you can satisfy the hungry beast at any hour. Basic diner fare, but the Art Deco décor adds to the experience. 145 West Broadway; 212/233-0507.

Places to Stay

TriBeCa Grand: This lovely hotel, sister to the SoHo Grand, really rolls out the red carpet for you and your pet. With a special pet menu, pet beds, and rooms reserved just for those traveling with four-footed friends, you won't be relegated to the cheap seats here. The staff will coordinate a dog walker for you and basically attend to your dog's every need. Rates are $250–400. 2 Avenue of the Americas, New York, NY 10013; 212/519-6600; website: www.tribecagrand.com.

UPPER EAST SIDE

This district, running along the eastern side of Central Park from 59th to 96th Streets features the Museum Mile (including the Guggenheim, Metropolitan Museum of Art, and Frick Museums, among others), six historic districts and the mayor's residence, Gracie Mansion. Whether your dog's taste runs from shopping along Madison Avenue, taking in the view along the East River or romping with his pals in Central Park, this is the place to satisfy them all.

Parks, Beaches, and Recreation Areas

36 East 60 Pavilion 🐾 🐾 🐕

Located next to the 60th Street Metroport on an elevated platform overlooking the East River, we think this run has dramatic flair. The park was originally a small sheltered area at the beginning of the East River Walk. At some point, the "pavilion" was informally divided between a pedestrian observation point and an open space that became the current dog run. It's a very odd configuration, be we can't complain about the traffic it gets. Although it is really nothing more than a concrete space, locals congregate happily here to enjoy the view and socialize their dogs.

We can't claim this small space offers much for dogs except leash-free freedom and an uncrowded environment, but both points seem to be the main attractions for the dog owners who frequent this place. And, of course, the view is awesome, but bring a warm coat in the winter. The wind off the river can be fierce. Located at East 60th Street and the East River, directly over the FDR Drive. Open 24 hours. 212/755-3288.

37 John Jay Park 🐾

There isn't much to offer dogs here. Composed mostly of playgrounds, dogs are only allowed on the concrete walkways that surround the recreation areas. But if you can't make it a few more blocks to the Carl Schurz Dog Run, this place will have to do. Located between 76th and 78th Streets and York Avenue. Open 6 A.M.–9 P.M. 212/408-0234.

DIVERSION

Fashion Fidos: Canine Styles, the original canine accessory store, opened in 1959 and is still going strong. This store on the Upper East Side led the way in what is now a wave of specialty stores for dogs. They have everything from $250 dog bowls to $1,000 dog bags. Canine Styles also helps cater the Regency Hotel's annual Bark Breakfast. 830 Lexington Avenue; 212/751-4549.

38 Carl Schurz Park & Dog Run 🐾 🐾 🐾 🐕

This park scores points for having two dog runs—one for large dogs, located at 86th Street; and one for smaller dogs, which is near the same location, but closer to the river. We can't say either of these runs are exceptionally impressive, but they are popular and provide much needed leash-free space in the park-starved Upper East Side.

The main run is covered with pea gravel and has a few benches, a hose, and limited space. But the dogs enjoy ruff-housing and meeting to sniff and socialize. Their human counterparts do much of the same. The small-dog run is located on a wooden-planked platform overlooking the East River. The view is great, but there are few amenities in this run. We have to admit, it is very entertaining watching dogs no bigger than toys running around with each other. Sometimes we leave the "big dogs" park just to watch these balls of energy race after each other. You'll have to get your mutt mitts and water, however, from the larger run. Unleashed dogs are allowed in the runs but must be leashed in the park.

Both runs are maintained by the Carl Schurz Park Association, and they also rely on donations from frequent users. To contribute, contact the Carl Schurz Park Association at 217 East 85th Street or P.O. Box 116. New York, NY 10028. Located on East End Avenue between 84th and 90th Streets. Open dawn–1 A.M. 212/288-3304 (dog run), 212/408-0234 (parks department).

Nature Hikes and Urban Walks

East River Walk: For a lovely stroll along the river framed by two dog runs, we highly recommend this scenic river walk along the East River. Starting at the 59th Street Bridge, we suggest you stop at the East 60 Pavilion Dog Run for a little playtime, then continue uptown 30 blocks to Carl Schurz Park. When you arrive, your dog will probably be ready for some more "ruff" and tumble and you'll have two runs to choose from, based on the size of your pooch. Along the way you'll traverse a tile promenade that provides views of Roosevelt Island, Queens and the fast moving river. This is a great alternative to the same old routine on a warm summer's day. 212/408-0234.

Restaurants

Barking Dog Luncheonette: This charming diner doesn't really like barking dogs, but they will allow you and your non-barking pooch to sit at their outdoor tables. Best of all, there is a blue, ceramic dog "bar" (translation: fountain) outside on the corner as you enter the restaurant. You can choose from salads, burgers, and daily blue plate specials. For dessert, a barking dog banana split. Need we say more? Woof! The original location is at 1678 3rd Avenue at 94th Street; 212/831-1800. A second location can be found at 1453 York Avenue at 77th Street; 212/861-3600.

EARMARK YOUR CALENDAR–SEPTEMBER

Canine Buffet: Every year, on the third Wednesday of September from 5 to 7 P.M., the Upper East Side's Corner Book Store really goes to the dogs. For well over a decade the store, under the guidance of dog lover Marian Bell, has sponsored a party just for you and your canine. Marian sends out invitations (in 2001 the list grew to 500) and offers freeze-dried liver snaps for your pup, wine, soda, and popcorn for you. The party has gotten so big it is now held out on the corner of 93rd and Park Avenue. All are invited. For more details or to be included on the mailing list, call 212/831-3554.

Café Nosidam: This trendy Italian restaurant is a bit pricey, but it's a great place to put on the dog. The well-dressed beautiful people who frequent this place are here to see and be seen. If that's your thing, join the crowd and find a place at one of the outdoor tables along the avenue. 768 Madison Avenue; 212/717-5633.

Leaping Frog Café: George and Inu prefer leaping squirrels to leaping frogs but they both agree that this charming outdoor café offers great summer snacks for the hungry canine. Stop by for a quick bite and then go chase some leaping squirrels in nearby Central Park. 830 5th Avenue; 212/717-8918.

Mr. Fresh Bread: This local take-out café offers great bakery items, sandwiches, prepared entrées, and of course, fantastic fresh bread. You can take your food with you, have it delivered, or enjoy your meal at the several tables outside. And for late night hounds, it's open 24 hours a day. 336 East 86th Street; 212/396-3639.

Zocalo: When you're hungering for some food south of the Border, head for the closest thing to it—this Mexican eatery. Offering tasty fajitas, tacos, enchiladas, and the best selection of tequila in the far north. Well-behaved pups get treated to a water bowl and dog biscuits. 174 East 82nd Street; 212/717-7772.

Places to Stay

The Carlyle Hotel: This elegant old world hotel offers charm and comfort for dogs with discriminating tastes. The rooms are bedecked with Oriental rugs, antique furniture, down comforters, and those comfy bathrobes you could live in all day. The staff also will arrange for a dog walker for you if you just have to sneak into the famed Bemelman's Bar for an aperitif. Rates are $350–3,200 per night. 35 East 76th Street, New York, NY 10021; 212/744-1600; website: www.thecarlyle.com.

Hotel Plaza Athénée: This beautiful European hotel rolls out the red carpet for all its guests—which includes dogs of any size. Of course, they also expect good manners, so you'll have to get advance permission to bring your pup. But once you're here, you'll enjoy elegant rooms, great service, and a room service menu to die for (or at least you may die once you see the prices!). Rates are $450–1,900 per night. No additional fee for Fido. 37 East 64th Street, New York, NY 10021; 212/734-9100; website: www.plaza-athenee.com.

The Lowell: This lovely 1926 Art Deco hotel is a little jewel box waiting to be discovered. With only 47 rooms, all are equipped with unique antique furnishings, beds fit for Marie Antoinette, and full-service amenities. There are even fireplaces in select rooms. You and your pampered pup will be wrapped in European luxury on a stay here. With Central Park only steps outside your door, the price tag here is steep. If money is no object, we think this is one of the most beautiful hotels in New York City. Dogs are allowed with prior approval. Rates range $399–1,800 per night. 28 East 63rd Street, New York, NY 10021; 212/838-1400 or 800/221-4444; website: www.lhw.com.

The Mark: This beautiful English-style hotel is an elegant combination of British colonial charm and decidedly modern decor. With an Asian ambience mixed with Edwardian furnishings, your dog will likely not care whether he is wrapped in eastern or western elegance; all he'll care about is getting out to nearby Central Park, which is only a block away. Unfortunately, only shih tzu– or English cocker spaniel–sized pups are allowed. Rates range from a steep $475–2,500 per night. 25 East 77th Street, New York, NY 10021; 212/879-1864; website: www.mandarinoriental.com/themark.

Marmara-Manhattan: This suite-style hotel requires monthly stays. With luxury studio, one- and two-bedroom apartments, you and your dog may not want to leave after a visit here. Dogs are allowed for no additional fee. A refundable security deposit is requested. Rates are $4,500–9,000 per month. 301 East 94th Street, New York, NY 10128; 212/427-3100; website: www.marmara-manhattan.com.

The Pierre Hotel: For little-bitty dogs who demand luxury, look no further than this spectacular New York institution. Each wood-paneled room is decorated with antiques, Victorian furnishings, and linens that may entice you to stay in bed all day. Dogs are provided with a doggy bag on arrival, but if you're over 15 pounds, you're outta luck. Rates are $545–950 per night. 2 East 61st Street, New York, NY 10021; 212/940-8101 or 800/332-3442; website: www.fourseasons.com.

Wales Hotel: This Carnegie Hill landmark has presided over the neighborhood since 1901, and she has held up well, for an old lady. Care has been taken to preserve the beautiful children's illustrations covering the lobby walls and each room has a fireplace, fresh flowers, and oak detailing. Complimentary breakfast is included in your room rate, which ranges from $180–295 per night. Dogs are welcome with advance reservations. 1295 Madison Avenue, New York, NY 10128; 212/876-6000.

UPPER WEST SIDE

This area of Manhattan was originally a series of small ethnic villages known as Bloomingdale. In fact, the street the world now knows as Broadway was once called Bloomingdale Road. Think of it! Bloomingdale's would be the place we go for theater and Broadway would be that department store on Lexington and 59th Street. But history being what it is, all those beginnings have been forgotten, and although the Upper West Side isn't as economically diverse as it once was, it still retains its liberal and bohemian reputation. Best of all, dogs really have it made on the Upper West Side. Sandwiched between Central Park on the east, Riverside Park on the west, and with an additional four dog runs to choose from, this is the best neighborhood in the city to live in if your name is Sparky, Buster, or Rover.

Parks, Beaches, and Recreation Areas

39 Riverside Park 🐾 🐾 🐾 🐾 ⚞

This lovely park, which runs from 72nd to 129th Street, has gone through many incarnations in its long history. In 1873, the Department of Public Parks commissioned Frederick Law Olmsted to create an elegant European promenade out of a long hilly ridge overlooking the Hudson. In the 1880s walking paths were added to broaden the park, but because the New York Central Railroad ran right along the river, the riverfront remained inaccessible until the 1930s.

Today you can stroll along this still lovely promenade on any of the three tiers. The waterfront tier is located across busy Henry Hudson Parkway and is composed mainly of a bike trail that runs from River Bank State Park (where dogs can't go) all the way down to Battery Park in lower Manhattan. The two upper tiers, accessible from Riverside Drive, are composed of sloping walkways and elegantly shaded paths. Dogs must be leashed in the park but there are three dog runs—at 72nd Street, 87th Street, and 105th Street—where your dog can run leash-free.

The park's original dog run is located at 72nd Street, just off Riverside Drive. It is managed and maintained by FLORAL (Friends and Lovers of Riverside Area Life). This is a busy and well-loved dog run with a very active group of dog owners who each pay dues of $25 a year to use the run. There are several benches, some large shade trees, soft hay underfoot, and enough room for your dog to get some good exercise.

Plans were in the works for a new dog run at the 73rd Street Track Infield, but after years of efforts, the plans were scuttled, and it was decided to renovate this run instead. The latest plan is to expand the current square footage, add new benches, fences, and a water fountain. For more information regarding the fundraising efforts, check out FLORAL's website: www.rspfloral.org.

The 87th Street Dog Run is located on the second tier off Riverside Drive; it can be reached by descending the stairway at 86th Street. The largest of the three runs, it is well shaded, has several benches, and a bulletin board heralding events and news for dogs and their owners. FLORAL also maintains this run; the annual dues are $25.

The recently renovated 105th Street Dog Run is a welcome addition. With a state of the art crushed granite undercovering—which is soft on paws and absorbs odors well—old-style benches, a wrought-iron fence, and tons of community support, this run has been a success since it opened in 2000. The park is maintained jointly by the parks department, local civic leaders, and community donations.

Oval-shaped and offering plenty of room to socialize, the run allows the

EARMARK YOUR CALENDAR–MAY

Canines Against Cancer: Join this annual event sponsored by the American Cancer Society as they raise funds for both human and animal cancer research and treatment. Held annually the first Sunday in May, you and your dog can join the thousands of other dog and owners in a walk for the cure. Dog treats are handed out all along the route in Riverside Park, and there are awards given for Best Trick, Best Singer, Best Costume, even Best Smooching Pooch, among others. Proceeds go to the Animal Medical Center and the America Cancer Society. Top fundraisers get great giveaways like free dog food and trips. The walk begins at 11 A.M. at the Soldiers Monument at 89th Street. For details, call 212/237-3872; website: www.dogswalk.com.

many dogs who visit here each day enough room to chase their tail or run after a ball. There are trees to shade the area in the summer, a hose and water bowl, and a bulletin board with local updates. It is well-lit in the evening hours.

Halloween parties, birthday celebrations, and other events are planned on an ongoing basis at all the dog runs. Information is posted at each respective run.

To make a contribution to both the 72nd and 87th Street Runs, contact FLORAL at P.O. Box 330, Planetarium Station, New York, NY 10024; 212/580-6932.

To make your annual contribution of $15 to the 105th Street Run, contact Riverside Park Dog Owners Group, c/o Riverside Park Fund, 475 Riverside Drive, Suite 249, New York, NY 10115; 212/870-3070; website: www.riversidedog.org. Located between 72nd and 129th Streets and Riverside Drive and the Hudson River. The park is open dawn–dusk; the dog runs are open 24 hours. 212/408-0234.

40 Theodore Roosevelt Park & Museum Park Dog Run

After several years living in a tiny makeshift dog run on the corner of Columbus Avenue and 77th Street, the Museum Park Dog Run opened to rave reviews in 2000—so the wait was worth it. The new run is located on the grounds of the American Museum of Natural History in Theodore Roosevelt Park. There are water faucets for dogs (with a step for smaller dogs), several benches, plenty of shade, an undercoat of pea gravel, and ample room for dogs who need to get some exercise. There are plans for a "playground" for dogs in the future.

The local dog owners who come here on a daily basis are a loyal and friendly group, which makes this run especially appealing. With Central Park

Balloons Down Broadway: There's no telling what you will see or how big it will be when you watch the granddaddy of all parades, the **Macy's Thanksgiving Day Parade.** This annual event, started in 1926, is one of our favorite dog walks of the year. We enjoy it all from the confines of Central Park, watching the balloons float down Central Park West from 9 A.M. till noon. Even George and Inu admit they're a bit humbled when Felix the Cat towers above them. That's one cat they have no desire to chase. The parade makes its way from 77th Street and Central Park West down to 59th Street and Broadway, then all the way to Herald Square at 34th Street.

If Thanksgiving morning proves too hectic to escape from the kitchen for a few hours, you and your own Felix can watch the balloons being blown up the day before along West 77th and 81st Streets by the American Museum of Natural History, from 3 P.M. to 10 P.M. 212/494-4495; website: www.macys.com.

---

just steps away, you can come here for happy hour and then take a longer walk in the park before or after.

Dogs are allowed leash-free in the run but must be leashed in Theodore Roosevelt Park. Contributions are relied upon to maintain the run. For information contact the Friends of Museum Park Dog Run, P.O. Box 412, Planetarium Station, New York, NY 10024. Located at the intersection of 81st and Columbus Avenue. Open 8 A.M.–10 P.M. 212/580-2065 (dog run), 212/408-0234 (parks department).

Places to Stay

Hotel Lucerne: Dogs of all sizes are welcome at this boutique hotel. Comfortable, modern rooms with full amenities welcome you and your pup. A walk in scenic Central Park is only a few blocks away. Rates are $189–250 per night. 201 West 79th Street, New York, NY 10024; 212/875-1000 or 212/724-2100.

Restaurants

There are so many outdoor cafés along Broadway, Amsterdam, and Columbus Avenues that we couldn't begin to list all the ones that allow dogs. The bottom line—most of them will allow well-behaved pooches at the outdoor tables. We've listed only a few of our favorites.

Artie's New York: For real deli food—the kind that makes real New Yorkers sit up and take notice—our dogs will trade a bag full of bones for a trip to Artie's. George's favorite is a tongue sandwich; Inu is partial to the matzo ball soup. Make sure you try Artie's own special iced tea. 2290 Broadway; 212/579-5959.

Avenue: Stroll up the avenue to Avenue and have yourself a bite of light summer fare or an excellent brunch at this popular café. Our dogs like the French onion soup, while we prefer the exceptional hot chocolate. 520 Columbus Avenue; 212/579-3194.

Café Mozart: Late night hounds will enjoy stopping by for an after-theater salad, a cup of tea, or a European pastry at this tiny café. Often you'll be treated to live classical music, compliments of Juilliard students and other music lovers. George is partial to Beethoven, but Inu thinks the house specialty—music by Mozart—is the only thing worth interrupting his evening nap for. 154 West 70th Street and Broadway; 212/595-9797.

Columbus Bakery: For decadent desserts and sinful sweets, we make a beeline for this bakery after a long walk in Central Park. We always justify a bite of cheesecake or a scone by waiting until *after* our walk to indulge. Take your treat with you or eat it at one of the benches at the nearby Museum Dog Run only a few blocks away. 474 Columbus Avenue; 212/724-6880.

Isabella's: This reliable West Side restaurant offers superb brunches, lunches, and dinners. Your dog is welcome at the outside patio overlooking the American Museum of Natural History. Choose from Nova Scotia smoked salmon, sandwiches made with Irish soda bread, or an excellent eggs Benedict at this popular American café. 359 Columbus Avenue; 212/724-2100.

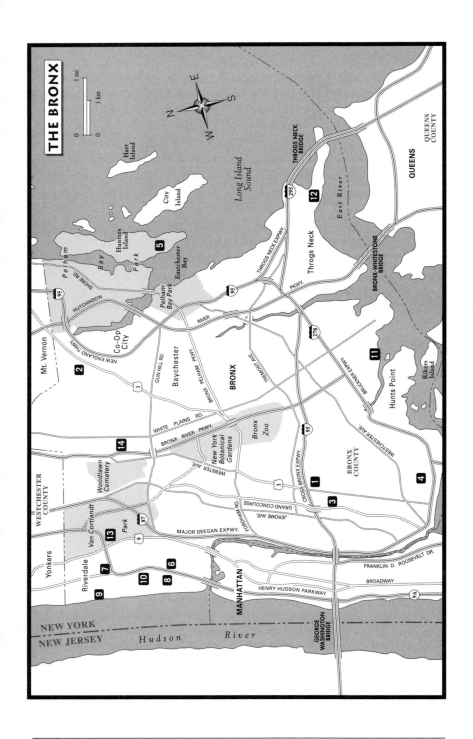

THE BRONX

*Heaven goes by favor; if it went by merit, you would stay out and your
dog would go in.*

—Mark Twain

Before we go any further, let's get rid of any preconceived ideas you might
have about the Bronx, that borough just north of Manhattan, home of the
Bronx Zoo, the Bronx Cheer, and of course the beloved (or hated) Bronx
Bombers. Open minds everyone. Okay? All clear? Good.

The Bronx is named after Johannes Bronck, one of the first settlers in the
only borough connected to the mainland. Slowly annexed by the city in the
19th century, the 42 square miles now known as the Bronx was once intended
to be a vast parkland. Just think of it. Nothing but open fields, streams and a
landscape for happy dogs and people to explore. My, how that well-laid plan
went awry. As we all know, the area has changed significantly since the Dutch
settled this area in 1639. Some things for the worse—like the Cross-Bronx
Expressway, which is number one on everyone's list of Roads Not to Have
Car Trouble On—or the Yankees (if you are a Mets fan or some small market
team in the Midwest). But many things have changed for the better.

The Bronx has an amazingly diverse population and is filled with a lively spirit hard to find anywhere else. Let's not forget all the green space stretching from Riverdale on the Hudson River to Pelham Bay Park on Long Island Sound. In fact, two of the three biggest parks in New York City are here, the aforementioned Pelham Bay Park and Van Cortlandt Park, the latter being home to one of the best dog runs in the city, Canine Court. So, if you already live here, we don't need to tell you about all the hidden treasures in this neck of the woods. And if you don't live here, it's time to reconsider this borough to the north. The Bronx doesn't end at Yankee Stadium, after all.

CROTONA PARK

Parks, Beaches, and Recreation Areas
1 Crotona Park 🐾 🐾 🦀

On Saturday and Sunday in the summer you had better get here early if you want to find a piece of park to call your own. With 127 acres, it's an ample-sized green space in the middle of the Bronx, covering about four city blocks, but picnic tables, playgrounds, ball fields, and a sea of humanity surrounding the duck pond, Indian Lake, take up most of that space.

Despite all the activity, the park holds up remarkably well under the strain of urban use and features a varied terrain of rocky outcroppings, open grassy fields and numerous shade trees; plenty of walking areas make for an enjoyable visit in any season.

Dogs are allowed to go leash-free before 9 A.M. and after 9 P.M. Located between Claremont Parkway, Fulton Avenue and Crotona Park North. Open dawn–dusk. 718/731-0984.

EDENWALD

Parks, Beaches, and Recreation Areas
2 Seton Falls Park 🐾 🦀

This park, bisected by Rattlesnake Creek and covered with a thick 35-acre forest, is falling on hard times. The trails through the woods are well-marked but have far too much broken glass for a comfortable walk with your dog. In fact, this is one time woods are not a welcome addition to a park. Even the creek and the short waterfall are filled with trash.

Dogs are allowed to go leash-free before 9 A.M. and after 9 P.M. Located on Baychester Avenue between 233rd Street and Crawford Avenue, with the main access from 233rd Street. Open dawn–dusk. 718/430-1800.

MORRIS HEIGHTS

Parks, Beaches, and Recreation Areas

3 Claremont Park 😺 😺 🐕

This is another one of the many well-used and lively neighborhood parks that can be found in the Bronx. The park is only about three city blocks in size and, despite the large number of people and dogs that can be found here on any given day, it holds up remarkably well. A quick glance will tell you that baseball, basketball, picnicking, music, and dance appear to be the main activities here, but dogs will still enjoy this park for the wooded areas, grassy lawns and a few hills to explore.

Dogs are allowed to leashless before 9 A.M. and after 9 P.M. Located between 170th Street and Clay Avenue, Teller, and Webster Avenues. Open dawn–10 P.M. 718/430-1800.

MOTT HAVEN

Parks, Beaches, and Recreation Areas

4 Saint Mary's Park 😺 😺 🐕

Saint Mary's Park is located in the heart of the Bronx and, like other inner-city parks in the borough, it gets a lot of visitors. That's not a bad thing. The park is safe, active, and receives the attention and upkeep from the community needed to maintain it. Despite being only two city blocks in size, it has some roomy grassy areas for ball throwing, shady trees, and walkways.

Dogs are allowed to go leash-free before 9 A.M. and after 9 P.M. The park is located between 149th, Saint Ann's, and Saint Mary's Streets and Jackson Avenue. Open dawn–dusk. 718/430-1800.

PELHAM BAY

Parks, Beaches, and Recreation Areas

5 Pelham Bay Park & Dog Run 😺 😺 😺 😺 🐕

Pelham Bay Park is New York City's largest park. At 2,700 acres, there is more room here than anywhere else in the city. And, unlike the large parks in other boroughs, this one was not landscaped to resemble an entirely different place.

Come here today and you can imagine what it must have been like when the Siwanoy lived here or, later, the early Dutch. The Dutch West India Company purchased the land from Native Americans in 1639, but it wasn't until 1654 that Englishman Thomas Pell signed a peace treaty with Siwanoy leader, Chief Wampage, and settled the land that is now Pelham Bay Park.

This is a vast urban wilderness and you and your dog will enjoy exploring a different part of it on each visit. One of our favorite spots is the Bartow-Pell Mansion Museum, built in 1842 by Robert Bartow, a descendant of Thomas Pell. Besides the existing mansion (where your dog can't go), there are beautiful grounds and forest trails that lead down to Pelham Lagoon where your dog can swim. Follow the trail directly adjacent to the gardens and you'll come upon an old family graveyard in the woods. One word of caution, however: in the summer months the grasses on these trails can get quite high and that means ticks. Check your dog faithfully for three days after you take a hike here. Ticks are slow-moving and it often takes up to 72 hours before they try to attach to your pet.

Another great area is Hunter Island, just beyond the man-made Orchard Beach. In the summer you'll have to pay $5 to park here, and you aren't allowed on the swimming beach, but the nature trails here—most of which run along the water—are well worth the price.

In the lower section of the park, separated from the main park by the Hutchinson River, is a small dog run. This run mainly serves the urban neighbors surrounding the park and, given the size of the rest of the park, isn't all that exciting. But dogs are allowed off-leash romping, so if you live here, this is a great daily option. The run is located on Middletown Road at Stadium Avenue, just north of the parking area. If you would like to make a donation towards its upkeep, contact the Friends of Pelham Bay Park, 1 Bronx River Parkway, Bronx, NY 10462.

Dogs are allowed to go leash-free before 9 A.M. and after 9 P.M. and at all times in the dog run. The park is located at Exit 8B off the Bruckner Expressway (I-95) or off the Hutchinson Parkway at Pelham Bridge Road. Open dawn–dusk. 718/430-1890(dog run), 718/731-0984 (parks department).

Restaurants

Tito Puente's: Belly up to the bar at this festive Latin and seafood restaurant. You and your pup are welcome to drink your margarita or eat your mesquite-grilled swordfish at the outdoor tables along City Island Avenue. Or, take it to go and have a picnic in nearby Pelham Bay Park. 64 City Island Avenue; 718/885-3200.

Places to Stay

Le Refuge Bed and Breakfast: This lovely little B&B located on City Island just outside Pelham Bay Park offers 10 small rooms in a quaint and convenient setting. Inside you'll find homey lodging and just outside your window is the boardwalk along the bay. Dogs are allowed in select rooms and rates are $65–140. 620 City Island Avenue, City Island, NY 10464; 718/885-2478; website: www.cityisland.com/LeRefuge.

RIVERDALE

Parks, Beaches, and Recreation Areas

6 Ewen Park & Dog Run 🐾 🐾 🐕

This hillside park is relatively large and roomy for a small neighborhood park. Better still, it has a dog run in the center. The park itself has pockets of grassy lawns and a variety of trees throughout. A few short paths and park benches make it a popular destination for strolling and sitting.

John's Run is a small dog run surrounded by a makeshift fence. There isn't much in the way of amenities—just a dirt floor and some poop bags hung on the gate, but the local dogs don't seem to mind. Give them a little leash-free space and they are happy. Nearby trees provide the run with just enough shade to keep it cool.

Unleashed dogs are allowed at all times in the dog run and in the park before 9 A.M. and after 9 P.M. The park is located along Riverdale Avenue just south of West 232nd Street. Open dawn–10 P.M. 718/430-1800 (dog run), 718/731-0984 (parks department).

7 Frank S. Hackett Park & Dog Run 🐾 🐾 🐕

This little wooded oasis is neatly tucked in between the Henry Hudson Parkway and Riverdale Avenue. It's only one acre in size with a paved path and a bench or two but there are plenty of trees and grass, and the hilly terrain hides the street traffic. The dog run is small with a dirt surface and the fence is at risk of falling over when the big dogs come to play. But hey, it's a leash-free area and a good, clean spot for local dogs.

Dogs are allowed to be off-leash at all times in the dog run and before 9 A.M. and after 9 P.M. in the park. The park is located between Riverdale Avenue, 254th Street and the Henry Hudson Parkway. Open dawn–10 P.M. 718/430-1800 (dog run), 718/731-0984 (parks department).

8 Henry Hudson Memorial Park 🐾 🐾 🏊

This small, hilltop park is well maintained with plenty of grass and trees and a good fence around the perimeter. It is great for dogs in the neighborhood, but we can't encourage you to travel here from a distance. Much of the park is covered by playground and sports facilities, so local dogs have to content themselves with a trot along the stone pathways.

Leashless dogs are allowed before 9 A.M. and after 9 P.M. Located between Independence and Palisade Avenues and Kappock Street. Open dawn–dusk. 718/430-1800.

9 Riverdale Park 🐾 🐾 🐾 🏊

Riverdale Park is a large swath of land along the Hudson River with a rich forest and a few hiking trails. The trick is figuring out how to take advantage of it. Parking spaces are rare. There aren't any official entrances and six rows of railroad tracks limit access to the Hudson River.

The middle section of the park, at the intersection of Palisades Avenue and 248th Street, is the most accessible. There is a small parking area and one main trail running north to 254th Street. Here you'll enjoy a pleasant walk on a flat, wide trail in a very wooded section along the backyards of some very impressive estates.

The southern section is hilly, well wooded, and offers most of the trails, but there is no parking at this end of the park. We park in Seton Park across Palisades Avenue to get here. The trails don't really go anywhere, but the crisscrossing paths make for good exploration.

The northern end of the park at the Riverdale train station at 254th Street is pretty much the only safe way to get to the river. Here you'll find a pedestrian (and therefore, pet-accessible) walkway over the tracks. The shore here is a little rocky and you need to watch out for an occasional broken bottle or fishing hook. Being next to the train tracks is not the most scenic setting but our dogs don't seem to notice. They are too excited about swimming in the

Hudson. There is also parking at the station but you will probably only be able to find a spot on weekends when it is not filled with commuters.

Off-leash dogs are allowed before 9 A.M. and after 9 P.M. Located between 232nd and 254th Streets and Palisade Avenue. Open dawn–dusk. 718/430-1800.

10 Seton Park & Dog Run 🐾 🐾 🐕

Playgrounds and ball fields occupy most of this neighborhood park, but dogs can still find a little room of their own at the park's dog run and a stretch of woods called Wallenberg Forest.

The small run is well protected, but offers little shade and the dogs can really kick up the dust of the dirt in the summer months. This is a busy and popular run with the locals, so if you live in this neighborhood, you probably make this your daily stop. The run is located along 235th Street.

If the dog run is too tame for your Great Dane, try a walk through Wallenberg Forest on the eastern end of the park. The forest is well wooded but the two trails are short and overgrown. What we like to do is grab a parking spot at Seton Park and cut through Wallenberg Forest into the southern end of Riverdale Park just across Palisade Avenue.

Off-leash romping is allowed at all times in the dog run and before 9 A.M. and after 9 P.M. in the park.

The park is located between 235th Street, River Road, Independence and Palisade Avenues. Open dawn–10 P.M. 718/430-1800 (dog run), 718/731-0984 (parks department).

SOUNDVIEW

Parks, Beaches, and Recreation Areas

🔟 Sound View Park 🐾 🐾 🐾 🦀

When visiting this park in the past, located at the apex of the Bronx and East Rivers, we scratched our heads. The only view, through a sea of cattails, was of a sewage disposal plant on the other side of the adjacent Bronx River. The view improved significantly, however, in 2000 when the Parks and Recreation Department completed the Sound View Park Waterfront Esplanade. This one-mile walkway in the southeastern end of the park, runs directly along the East River and what an improvement! There are impressive views up and down the river and across to Queens. The Parks Department, following the Greenway Master Plan, is hoping to expand the Esplanade west through the rest of the park along the Bronx River and east out to Ferry Point Park, but there are no completion dates scheduled as of yet.

The rest of the park's 157 acres is open fields. Although spacious for a city park, up close the parkland is worn and tired from countless visitors. Barbecues, soccer and baseball games dominate the park's weekend activity list. Dogs can enjoy the grassy fields and the short trails through the cattails but watch out for broken glass, especially on the western side.

Dogs are allowed to go leashless before 9 A.M. and after 9 P.M. From the Bruckner Expressway (I-278), take Exit 1 to Morrison Avenue south one block into the park. Open dawn–dusk. 718/430-1800.

THROGS NECK

Parks, Beaches, and Recreation Areas

🔢 Ferry Point Park 🐾 🐾 🦀

Named for the ferries between Queens and the Bronx in the early part of the 20th century, the best thing about this park is its proximity to the water. Located on prime waterfront just under the Bronx-Whitestone Bridge, there are currently plans to renovate this park and create the Sound View Greenway, an eight-mile long recreational corridor from Ferry Point Park to Sound View Park along the Bronx River and East River shorelines. We hope those plans come to fruition. Right now, it's a rather weedy, forgotten piece of waterfront surrounded by landfill from the sanitation department. Along the water, you'll find some shallow beaches where your water dog can take a dip. The view from the tip overlooking the East River across to Queens is truly gorgeous. But the rest of the park, with its open ball fields and shaded pathways, is nothing remarkable. Dogs may be off-leash before 9 A.M. From the Hutchinson River Parkway, take the Ferris Street exit just before the Bronx-Whitestone Bridge. Open dawn–6 P.M. 212/408-0100.

VAN CORTLANDT

Parks, Beaches, and Recreation Areas

🔢 Van Cortlandt Park & Dog Run 🐾 🐾 🐾 🐾 🐕

Van Cortlandt is one of the flagship parks of New York City and with good reason. At 1,146 acres, it's the third-largest park in the city, has two dog runs, miles of hiking trails, and offers open fields, thick forests, Tibbetts Brook, and Van Cortlandt Lake, which is the largest lake in the Bronx.

The two dog runs are actually adjacent to each other at the northern end of the Parade Ground near the intersection of Broadway and West 252nd Street, just south of the Henry Hudson Parkway. Both runs are roomy and have a thick lawn of grass. You might think it strange to place both runs in the same location but that's because one of them, Canine Court, is actually a canine-agility playground complete with a teeter-totter, tunnels, hurdles, and a ladder. In fact, it's so inviting it gets taken over by children at times.

The other run is a traditional fenced-in open space and a popular spot for ball throwing and simply romping about. There isn't much shade for either run, but the lush lawn helps to keep things cool in the summer. And the two runs work out great for our group. Inu likes the enthusiasm and showmanship of the Court and George, ever the ball hound, likes the roominess of the open run. Throughout the year, there are a number of dog events held at Canine Court.

If you are looking for a little exercise for both you and your dog, try the hiking trails. The Putnam Trail (also called Old Putnam Trail and Putnam Rail Trail) was once part of the New York Central Railroad's Putnam Line. The route opened in 1880 and was New York City's first rail link to Boston. Trains ran through here for over 100 years. The tracks are gone now and what remains is a 1.5-mile graded trail through the center of the park. It runs north and south from the Westchester County line through woods and along Van

---

🐕 EARMARK YOUR CALENDAR–APRIL

Who Let the Dogs Out?: You will be asking the same when you see the turnout for the annual Pawswalk in Van Cortlandt Park. This April event is held in the Parade Ground and is one of five walks sponsored in each of the boroughs. The walk also includes a Pooch Picnic, demonstrations, and contests, including owner/pet look-a-likes, Frisbee catching, and newspaper fetching. All proceeds will benefit Van Cortlandt Park and Canine Court, the first public dog agility course/playground in the country. For more information, call 718/430-1890 or 718/601-1460; website: www.pawsacrossamerica.com.

Cortlandt Lake. The southern terminus is at the golf house near the intersection of Van Cortlandt Park south, Putnam Avenue and the Major Deegan Expressway.

The last mile of the Old Croton Aqueduct Trail is also within the park. The trail starts in northern Westchester County and follows an abandoned pipeline. The aqueduct brought water to New York City from 1842 until 1897. (See the Old Croton Aqueduct Trail in the introduction to the Westchester chapter).

The John Muir Trail crosses the park west to east. It runs from the stables in the Northwest Forest along Broadway and then through Croton Woods to the Indian Field Recreation Area in the Northeast Forest along Jerome Avenue. This trail is a 1.5-mile walk and connects with the Putnam and Old Croton Aqueduct Trails.

The Cass Gallagher Nature Trail, unlike the other routes, is a loop path about a mile in length. It starts and ends near the stables in the Northwest Forest off Broadway.

If you just want to keep it simple, the Parade Ground on the western edge of the park along Broadway is a welcoming spot. The huge open lawn has a paved running path and over the years has supported every imaginable activity, including a grazing site for a bison conservation program.

Dogs are allowed off-leash in the dog runs and before 9 A.M. and after 9 P.M. in the park. Trail maps are posted throughout the park or available by calling 718/548-0912.

The park is located between Broadway, Gun Hill Road and Jerome Avenue. It is also bisected by the Henry Hudson Parkway (use Exit 23) and the Major Deegan Expressway (use Exits 11 through 14). Open dawn–10 P.M. 718/430-1890 (dog run), 718/731-0984 (parks department).

WILLIAMSBRIDGE

Parks, Beaches, and Recreation Areas

14 Bronx River Parkway/Greenway 🐾 🐾 🏊

You have to take the good with the bad here. The good is that this corridor of green space follows the Bronx River from the Botanical Gardens into Westchester County. The bad is that the highway of the same name also follows the river and divides much of the park into sections. The size and your enjoyment of each section depend on the bend in the river and the curve of the highway at any point. Many times there are no green spaces and at other times it's hard to tell there is even a highway nearby at all.

The longest, widest, and best section of the greenway is known as Shoelace Park. It is located on the eastern side of the river between East 233rd Street and Gun Hill Road. There are bike paths, benches, river access, open lawns and shade trees; best of all, the highway is as far away as it can get—on the other side of the river.

The Parks Department, along with the State Department of Transportation, plan to expand the park along the southern half or West Farms Segment of the Bronx River from the Botanical Gardens to Sound View Park on the East River. Construction of bicycle paths and bridges is expected to begin in 2003. When completed, the greenway will be over 11 miles long. Dogs are not permitted in the Botanical Gardens.

Dogs may be off-leash before 9 A.M., but because of the highway nearby, use the privilege wisely.

Numerous pockets of the park, on one side of the highway or the other, are reachable from side streets along the Bronx River Parkway. From the Bronx River Parkway (the highway), take the East 233rd Street or Gun Hill Road exits into the park. Open 24 hours a day. 718/430-1800.

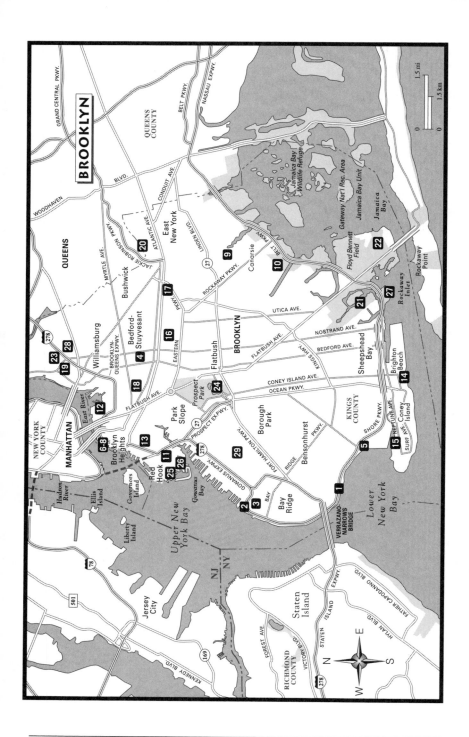

3 BROOKLYN

Learn to distinguish between natural friends and natural enemies. I always warm to gardeners (because we have a mutual interest in digging), clumsy eaters, those who understand the principles of bribery to ensure good behavior, and denture wearers, who find biscuits difficult. To be treated with caution, anyone dressed in white, people who make patronizing inquiries about your pedigree, grumpy old men with sticks, and vegetarians (except at meal time when there is meat on the table that they wish to dispose of discreetly). To be avoided: women who carry photographs of their cats. They are beyond hope.

— From *A Dog's Life*, by Peter Mayle

It would be too easy for us to poke fun at that proverbial tree growing in Brooklyn, but spend any time in this city within a city and you will find green space is no joke. Brooklyn is over 70 square miles in size but, unfortunately, it is also the most under-served in terms of recreation and open space. Currently only nine percent of its area is in city parks and that means you and your dog have to be creative when looking for a spot of green.

PICK OF THE LITTER–BROOKLYN HIGHLIGHTS

BEST CITY PARKS
Fort Greene Park, Fort Greene

Prospect Park, Park Slope

BEST DOG PARKS
Dyker Beach Park & Dog Run, Bath Beach

Hillside Park, Brooklyn Heights

BEST BEACH
Gravesend Bay Beach, Coney Island

BEST RESTURANTS
Brooklyn Ice Cream Factory, Brooklyn Heights

The Gate, Park Slope

Oznot's Dish, Greenpoint

Sparky's, Cobble Hill

Despite this, our social dogs are enthralled with Brooklyn. One visit and you will know that this borough is not about space, but about people—roughly two and a half million—making it the most populous borough in New York City. Brooklynites have a strong sense of home and neighborhood and many have no use for any borough but their own.

Brooklyn's isolationist attitude goes back to 1636 when it was first settled by the Dutch and called *Breukelen* (broken land). Since then, many residents have seen the East River that separates Brooklyn from Manhattan as an ocean too vast to cross. Yes, the completion of the Brooklyn Bridge in 1883—the first link to Manhattan—along with the Williamsburg and Manhattan Bridges, the Brooklyn-Battery Tunnel, and subway lines, all helped to offer Brooklynites a glimpse of the world beyond. But it wasn't until 1957 that Brooklyn saw it couldn't keep the world at bay forever. If the Dodgers could leave, well, then anyone could.

So, whether you're coming or going, George and Inu have found a few good places for you and your dog to walk in the woods, take a swim, or socialize with other four-footed friends. If baseball, in the form of the Coney Island Cyclones, can once again return to this borough, then there's hope you and your pup will find a few good trees still growing here as well.

THINK GLOBALLY, BARK LOCALLY

Brooklyn has two wonderful dog-focused groups: Fort Greene **Park Users and Pets Society (PUPS)** and **Fellowship for the Interests of Dogs and their Owners (FIDO)**, both of which work tirelessly to create more off-leash space for dogs in Brooklyn. Both groups work closely with the Parks Department to improve the lives of dogs (and their owners) in Fort Greene and Prospect Parks. Events are ongoing throughout the year. You can check out these groups and what they're up to at these websites: www.fortgreenepups.org or www.fidobrooklyn.com.

Gateway National Recreation Area: Created in 1972, this vast 26,000-acre shoreline wilderness is located within three New York City boroughs—Queens, Brooklyn, and Staten Island—and in Monmouth County in northern New Jersey. In Brooklyn, it encompasses much of the beachfront along Jamaica Bay and the inner bays facing the Rockaways along the Atlantic Ocean. Jamaica Bay Wildlife Refuge is off limits to dogs. But other sections of the recreation area are dog-friendly and we've detailed them for you in their respective neighborhoods. Maps are available at the Visitor Center located within the Jamaica Bay Wildlife Refuge off Cross Bay Boulevard near the North Channel Bridge. 718/318-4340.

Shore Promenade and Greenway: Running for 13 miles along the water's edge through the entire borough of Brooklyn, this marvelous park/promenade runs on either side of the Belt (or Shore) Parkway. Both sides offer scenic splendor for you and your dog. On the eastern side is the Greenway—a long narrow park that rivals Riverside Park in Manhattan for beauty. It runs for five miles between Shore Drive and Shore Parkway, from Owl's Head Park in Bay Ridge to Dyker Beach Park and Bensonhurst Park in Bensonhurst. Along the way you'll find countless places to enjoy with your canine pal. In the park, dogs are allowed off-leash before 9 A.M. and after 9 P.M.

On the western side of the Parkway is a bike path and pedestrian promenade. Used by joggers, cyclists, in-line skaters, and walkers, this is one of the best esplanades in New York City. Running in sections from Owl's Head Park to the Gateway National Recreation Area and, eventually, all the way out to John F. Kennedy International Airport, you'll have views of Manhattan, New York Harbor, the Verrazano-Narrows Bridge, Staten Island, and everything in between. Along the way are benches, picnic areas and parking turnouts. The view is breathtaking in any season. Both the Promenade and Greenway are open dawn–dusk. 718/965-6980.

BATH BEACH

Parks, Beaches, and Recreation Areas

❶ Dyker Beach Park & Dog Run 🐾 🐾 🐾 🐾 🐕

This park has one of the best dog runs in Brooklyn—this is no end-of-the-block postage stamp–sized dog run or forgotten patch of dirt tucked behind a playground or under an expressway. On the contrary, this run occupies space that is a blissful leap from the many concrete corners or unwanted dust bowls that pass for dog runs in the city.

If you can believe it, this grassy area was once just an unused triangle that served no other purpose than to herald the entrance to the Dyker Beach Golf Course. Although unused, the area was kept manicured and attractive. Local dog owners fought to have it turned into a dog run and the results are wonderful.

There is a block-sized open area for ball throwing, a wrought iron fence to keep dogs from running into the road, plenty of trees and benches, mutt mitts, and trash cans, all adding up to a great doggy social at most hours of the day. You'll find plenty of room to chase your tail or kick up your heels—all leash-free. The dog run is located in a grassy triangle between 86th Street, 7th Avenue, and the Dyker Beach Golf Course entrance road.

Dyker Beach Park itself is located on the other side of the Dyker Beach Golf Course on Cropsey Avenue. It is mainly composed of playground and recreation areas that don't welcome dogs. You can walk on the pathways around the ball fields, but why bother? Head for the dog run.

Dogs allowed off-leash in the run; they must be leashed in all other areas of the park. Located at 86th Street and 7th Avenue. Open 6 A.M.–10 P.M. 718/965-6980.

BAY RIDGE

Parks, Beaches, and Recreation Areas

❷ Owl's Head Park & Dog Run 🐾 🐾 🐾 🐕

This beautiful 27-acre park lies high on a hill overlooking the New York Harbor. Located on the site of a glacial moraine, it is now covered with trees and grass with wide, open hillsides—perfect for whiling away an afternoon or watching your dog chase a stick. No one seems to know the origin of the name, but one theory is that it was once shaped like an owl's head. Another theory is that Eliphalet Bliss, the wealthy manufacturer who donated this land to the city in 1903, had a pair of stone owls at the gate of his estate that once occupied this spot. Whatever the origins, this park is no longer the exclusive enclave of the wealthy but rather a place for you and your dog to enjoy a morning walk, afternoon siesta, or evening view of the harbor.

In fall 2000, a dog run was added on the western side of the park on the corner of Shore Road and 68th Street. Operated by the Parks Department and a group called Friends and Neighbors of Owl's Head Park, it is a small run with dirt flooring, a single bench, and only a little shade. Although a leash-free space is always welcome, the rest of the park is so large and welcoming that this small dog run almost feels like a consolation prize. Located at 68th Street and Shore Road. Open 6 A.M.–10 P.M. 718/965-6980 or 718/745-4218.

3 Leif Ericson Park 🐾 🦫

Named for the famed Viking explorer, we wonder what he would think of this monument to his name. George is fairly certain Leif would be as unimpressed as he is. This promenade park traverses four city blocks, but we can't say it offers much for our canine friends. You can walk along the paths that weave through the many recreation areas, but that's about it. There are a few blades of grass for a doggy to sniff. If you're not desperate, we suggest walking a few more blocks to Owl's Head Park. Located between 66th and 67th Streets between 2nd and 7th Avenues. Open dawn–dusk. 718/965-6980.

BEDFORD-STUYVESANT

Parks, Beaches, and Recreation Areas

4 Herbert Von King Park 🐾

Formerly known as Tompkins Park, this little slice of urban neglect has little to offer either dogs or their human counterparts. Composed mostly of playgrounds and a ball field, you can walk your dog only around the recreation areas. And although we do like the wire sculptures on the ball field fence, it's doubtful that's enough to get your dog very excited on a visit here. Dogs must be leashed. Located between Greene, Lafayette, Marcy, and Tompkins Avenues. Open 6 A.M.–9 P.M. 718/965-6980.

BENSONHURST

Parks, Beaches, and Recreation Areas

5 Bensonhurst Park 🔥

This neglected little park needs a makeover. A really big makeover. Currently it's just a sorry tangle of weeds surrounding some playgrounds. The park gets a lot of use; if you live here, it's probably one of only a few options for your daily stroll but really, for you and your pup, it's only good for a squat on a cold day. Located at Exit 5 off the Shore Parkway. Open 6 A.M.–9 P.M. 718/965-6980.

BOERUM HILL

Conveniently located near Downtown Brooklyn, the Fulton Street Mall and the Brooklyn Academy of Music, this neighborhood has the wonderful attraction of quiet, brownstone-lined streets within walking distance to Brooklyn's Restaurant Row on Smith Street and a wide array of Middle Eastern markets. Still working on getting a dog run, though. (See below.)

Parks, Beaches, and Recreation Areas

As we go to press, Boerum Hill dog owners are clamoring for a dog run of their own. These local activists have petitioned the city, marched for awareness, and continue to collect signatures imploring the city to give them a space to call home. So far, it hasn't happened, but dog owners are making progress. Right now the odds are on a location on State Street. For more information, call 718/237-1261.

Restaurants

The many outdoor restaurants on Smith Street, Brooklyn's prestigious "restaurant row," straddle the neighborhoods of Boerum Hill and Carroll Gardens (see below). Most will allow you to sit with your well-behaved dog as long as you don't have to enter the restaurant in order to reach the outdoor space. We couldn't possibly list them all here, so we picked some of our current favorites. But don't let our suggestions limit your adventurous tastes. Just walk down the street during the warm weather months and discover your own favorites.

Bar Tabac: One of the latest additions on trendy Smith Street, this local bar and French brasserie offers a real Paris café environment right here in Brooklyn. Sit with your poodle at one of the outdoor tables facing the street. The basic café fare is nothing to write home about, but the environment is great. 128 Smith Street; 718/923-0918.

Boerum Hill Food Company: This gourmet take-out café also offers a few benches outside where you and your pup can sit. But the real attraction is their great take-out and delivery menu including daily specials of fish, lamb, beef, and vegetarian entrées. Order a crêpe or dessert to go, and dine in splendor at the park of your choice. 134 Smith Street; 718/222-0140.

Café Luluc: This new restaurant serves one of the best breakfasts around. With fabulous pancakes, exotic egg dishes, and great muffins for Muffin, you'll be hangin' with the pick of the litter here. Lunch and dinner fare is a little bit French and a little bit Cuban (at least that's what we think it is), but our dogs like the morning meal best. Dogs are welcome at the tables outside. 214 Smith Street; 718/625-3815.

The Victory: This comfy neighborhood hangout is popular with local dog owners. In the summer you'll enjoy schmoozing with the neighbors from your

Howling Halloween: Join the fun at the annual **Hillside Dog Park Halloween Party.** Held on the Saturday before Halloween, activities include a canine costume contest, photos taken with the Wicked Witch of Hillside Park (who doesn't fool the dogs for a second), and goody bags for all. The $3 entry fee goes to local animal shelters. For exact dates and times, contact the Friends of Hillside Park at 718/965-6974.

The same weekend, Fort Greene PUPS sponsors their annual **Great PUPkin Costume Contest.** With a raffle, fun prizes, and treats from local pet stores, you and your Halloween hound will have a howling good time. There is a $3 entry fee that assists the ASPCA. The event is held at Fort Greene Park, noon–1 P.M. For current information and photos from last year's event check out the PUPS (Park Users and Pets Society) website: www.fortgreenepups.org.

place at one of the outdoor tables on this tree-lined street. Coffee, bakery items, sandwiches, and a list of daily specials are yours to choose from. 71 Hoyt Street; 718/596-9035.

BRIGHTON BEACH

Once an upscale seaside resort, this neighborhood is now referred to as "Little Odessa" for its large Russian population. So although finding plenty of authentic Russian food, newspapers, and shops here won't be a problem, sniffing out a spot for Spot is an entirely different adventure.

Nature Hikes and Urban Walks

Brighton Beach Boardwalk: In 1878 the area around this neighborhood was named Brighton Beach for that "other" Brighton Beach, the well-known resort on the English Channel. Upscale hotels, not to mention the Brighton Beach Racetrack and the Brighton Beach Baths, offered middle-class visitors a resort destination just east of the more boisterous West Brighton and Coney Island amusement areas. Times change, however, and although the glory days are over for this one-time resort, you can still enjoy the seaside breezes on a stroll along the boardwalk. Connecting Coney Island to Brighton Beach, this historic boardwalk will transport you back to another place and time. Although you aren't allowed to set paw on the sand, the boardwalk allows you to get as close as possible. 718/965-6980.

BROOKLYN HEIGHTS

Once home to residents as illustrious as Charles Dickens, Henry Ward Beecher, and Walt Whitman, this neighborhood boasts of some of the oldest dwellings in New York City. Designated a historic district in the 1960s, a walk here will uncover many examples of the original Federal, Greek and Gothic Revival, and Italianate homes that were so prevalent in the 19th century. With a view overlooking lower Manhattan, residents here have the luxury of being so close and yet so far away from the hectic pace of that borough across the East River.

Parks, Beaches, and Recreation Areas

6 Cadman Plaza Park 🐾 🐾 🐾

Located in the shadow of the Brooklyn Bridge, this large grassy promenade is nothing too exciting, but it does offer some grass and open space, something in short supply in downtown Brooklyn. On the northern end, near the Charles Keck Brooklyn World War II Memorial, is an area ample enough to throw a ball and get in some exercise. You can also reach the entrance to the Brooklyn Bridge Pedestrian Walk (see below) along the far western end.

Dogs are allowed off-leash until 9 A.M. Located between Cadman Plaza and Adams Street. Open 6 A.M. until 9 P.M. 718/965-6980.

7 Hillside Park 🐾 🐾 🐾 🐾 🐕

Hillside Park, once known as Squibb Hill, is one of the most popular doggy gathering spots around. Local pups and their owners have been coming to this patch of green for years, but in 1999 the city designated the whole space an official dog run and now the entire park has gone completely to the dogs. With grass, a hard dirt base, and the use of two acres, there is enough room to throw a ball, sit and relax under one of the multiple shade trees, or just chat up the neighbors. Local dog owners from downtown Brooklyn, Cobble Hill, and Boerum Hill gather with neighbors from the Heights so this is one busy dog run.

One drawback: there are no benches, but an informal BYOC (Bring Your Own Chair) policy is in effect. Several "permanent" portable chairs have also taken up residence here. Located at Columbia Heights and Middagh Street. Open dawn–10 P.M. 718/965-6974.

8 Palmetto Playground 🐾 🐾 🐕

This tiny dog run is as popular as it is small. Which is to say, the neighborhood has a lot of dogs and not many other options for outdoor space. Located on a small patch of dirt smack up against the Brooklyn-Queens Expressway, there are four benches, some shade and a long enough stretch to throw a ball as long as you aren't aiming to get it across an infield. The run is well maintained and who are we to turn our noses up at a little leash-free space? But we prefer

Hillside Park if you're willing to walk a little bit further. Located at Columbia Place and State Street. Open 6 A.M.–9 P.M. 718/855-8996.

Nature Hikes and Urban Walks

Brooklyn Bridge Pedestrian Walk: For an exhilarating and unusual walk over one of the great New York landmarks, take a stroll across the Brooklyn Bridge. On opening day, May 24, 1883, over 150,000 people crossed the bridge. Today you and your pup can add your paws to the millions of people who have walked across this beautiful bridge since its opening.

Built between 1870 and 1883, the bridge spans 1,596 feet across and was, at the time it was completed, 50 feet longer than any other bridge built in the world. This great feat of engineering was beset by many disasters during its push to completion, including the death of the original architect, John A. Roebling, and the debilitating illness of Roebling's son, Washington, who took over the construction after his father's death. Widow and mother Emily Roebling actually supervised the project's completion. Fortunately the bridge, like New York City itself, was bigger than any disaster thrown in its path and today stands as one of New York City's life arteries.

The wood-planked pedestrian/bike path runs directly down the middle of the bridge and although dogs must be leashed, you won't feel you are walking in the middle of New York traffic. (Even though you are!) The views are spectacular and you are well shielded from the cars rushing by on either side.

To reach the bridge walkway, walk up the stairs at the western end of Cadman Plaza and end your 30 minute walk at City Hall Park in Manhattan (see the Civic Center section of the Manhattan chapter). Watch out for joggers and cyclists and stay to the outside of the walkway in the pedestrian lane. 212/360-3000.

Brooklyn Heights Esplanade: This wonderful stretch of waterfront located between Remson and Orange Streets has one of the most spectacular views of the Manhattan skyline anywhere. With unobstructed views of Staten Island, the Statue of Liberty, Wall Street, the Brooklyn Bridge, and other historical landmarks, Abraham Lincoln said in 1864, "There may be finer views than this in the world, but I don't believe it."

Built on what were once the back gardens of 19th century mansions, there had been talk of creating a promenade for wealthy Brooklynites to strut their stuff as far back as 1827. But it wasn't until Brooklyn Heights was designated a historical district in the 1940s and city leaders rallied together to save it from becoming part of the Brooklyn-Queens Expressway that the promenade became a reality.

Originally the city planned to build the expressway right through this historic district. But local residents were properly horrified and had the financial resources to fight Parks Commissioner Robert Moses and his merry highway men. Fortunately a creative alternative was found and the promenade was built directly over the highway, acting both as a roof and a wall to muffle the sounds of the trucks passing underneath. It was dedicated on October 7, 1950 as a public walkway and has been one of New York City's most valuable landmarks ever since.

As you walk, look for the stone marking the spot where the Four Chimneys House formerly stood. This house was used as a headquarters by George Washington during the Battle of Long Island, and, one week later on August 29, 1776, it was the location where the Council of War decided "to withdraw the American Army from Long Island" and escape across the East River to Manhattan. Just north of Pierrepont Street in Garden 5 is a thunderbird constructed from discarded granite paving stones, paying tribute to the Canarsee Indians who lived in this area before the Dutch settlers arrived. 718/965-6980.

Restaurants

Annie's Blue Moon Café: This funky little pub and restaurant offers a traditional menu of burgers, salads, and continental entrées in a scenic environment. Sit out at the outdoor tables with your pup and take in one of the best streets in Brooklyn. 150 Montague Street; 718/596-0061.

Brooklyn Heights Deli: With outdoor tables and a killer deli menu, you can't go wrong at this local hangout. Take your sandwich and saunter on the Brooklyn Promenade or eat it outdoors on Henry Street. Either way, this place serves some of the best NY deli cuisine around. 292 Henry Street; 718/631-1361.

Brooklyn Ice Cream Factory: This newly opened ice cream store, located in a historic fireboat house directly under the Brooklyn Bridge, is proving to be a great addition to the neighborhood. Owner Mark Thompson makes all his ice creams (limiting the selection to only eight classic flavors) and won't rest until he gets every one right. Sit out on the large deck overlooking the bridge and Manhattan's newly diminished skyline, licking a classic cone of chocolate, vanilla, butter pecan, or coffee, and you'll feel you've time-traveled back to a simpler time. Our dogs practically drag us there after a romp at Hillside Park. One visit and you'll be addicted, too. Old Fulton Street at Water Street; 718/246-3963.

Teresa's: Gourmet Polish is the oddly satisfying cuisine at this pleasant outdoor restaurant. Located on trendy Montague Street, this is a great place to people or dog watch while eating your pierogi, mashed potatoes, and other high-calorie comfort food at what has been described as "Warsaw Pact" prices. Dogs are welcome on the outdoor patio. 80 Montague Street; 718/797-3996.

Places to Stay

Garden Green Bed and Breakfast: This cozy little brownstone, nestled in historic Brooklyn Heights, caters to a European clientele in more ways than one. That's because they have set aside their ground floor rooms for visitors and their dogs. With only eight rooms available at this B&B, you have to make reservations early. Well-behaved dogs are welcome on approval. Rates are $90–175. 641 Carlton Avenue, Brooklyn, NY 11238; 718/783-5717.

CANARSIE

Parks, Beaches, and Recreation Areas

9 Bruekelin Park 🐾 🏞️

Although this park is named for the Dutch word for Brooklyn, George and Inu are glad it isn't representative of all the parks in the borough. Composed mainly of ball fields where your dog can't go, the only thing here for retrievers, Dutch or otherwise, is a green promenade with benches, shade trees, and pathways along Williams Avenue. It won't make your dog pant for more, but it will get you out of the house on a nice day.

Dogs must be leashed after 9 A.M. Located between Louisiana Street and Williams Avenue and Glenwood Road and Stanley Avenue. Open dawn–dusk. 718/965-6980.

10 Canarsie Park 🐾 🏞️

Canarsie Park and the surrounding neighborhood are named for the Canarsee Indians, who were the early inhabitants of this area long before the Dutch arrived in the 1630s. Today this 132-acre park bears little resemblance to any place the Dutch, Canarsie, or even Frederick Law Olmsted would recognize, and you might even wonder if it has seen a lawn mower in the last few hundred years.

It does offer some green space in the middle of urban development, but there isn't much to interest your dog other than a large field on its western end. Although you can get in some ball-throwing here, the surrounding area is as scruffy as the park is. Watch for trash and broken glass.

Dogs must be leashed after 9 A.M. Located on Seaview Avenue between Paedergast and Remsen Avenues. Open 6 A.M.–10 P.M. 718/965-6980.

Nature Hikes and Urban Walks

Canarsie Pier: Part of the Gateway National Recreation Area, this historic pier offers fabulous views of Jamaica Bay. Leashed dogs are permitted to wander along the stone tile promenade, sit on one of the many benches that line the walkway, or just take in the view. There are also a few quiet beach trails accessible here on the western end off the bike trail. Take your dog on a short nature walk or, best of all, down to the water for a quick dip. Take Exit 13 off the Belt Parkway and follow Rockaway Parkway south to the end. 718/763-2202.

Restaurants

Sunset Landing on the Pier: This seafood restaurant occupies some pretty choice real estate. Sitting pretty on the Canarsie Pier, you and your dog can order a burger, fish and chips, or ice cream from the snack bar and sit at one of the benches overlooking Jamaica Bay. The indoor restaurant is off-limits but our dogs agree—the service is quicker outside anyway. 2200 Rockaway Parkway; 718/444-5200.

CARROLL GARDENS

Originally a predominantly Italian neighborhood, Carroll Gardens has seen an influx of professionals, artists, and food connoisseurs in recent years. Sharing the title of Restaurant Row with neighboring Boerum Hill, the Carroll Gardens section of Smith Street has some of the best eating establishments anywhere in New York City.

Parks, Beaches, and Recreation Areas

11 Dimattina Park & Dog Run 🐾 🐾 🐕

The dog run at this park scores points for its recent renovation. Originally located on the far side of the Dimattina Playground, the asphalt run was as neglected as the abandoned basketball court it abuts (which is currently also receiving a face-lift). But in early 2001, the renovations began and this run is a great example of what the city can do when motivated by local dog owners.

There is a new ornate fence, a double gate, two great water fountains with built-in dog bowls at their bases, crushed granite flooring, benches, and newly planted trees which are currently protected from doggy leg lifts by a mesh fence. We can't say this is a great location or an overly large one, but it is well planned and has been a welcome addition to the neighborhood since it opened. Let's hope the positive results will lead the way for future dog runs to come. Located at the corner of Hicks and Rapelye Street. Open 6 A.M. until 10 P.M. 718/965-6980.

Restaurants

Banania Café: This French-style restaurant with a Euro-Asian twist offers appetizers like asparagus with gorgonzola sauce, excellent entrées like vegetable Wellington and a crème brûlée to die for. Your dog might not care about the food, but she will like the outdoor tables lining Smith and Douglass Streets. 241 Smith Street; 718/237-9100.

Tuk, Tuk: Although this new Thai restaurant derives its name from the Thai word "taxi," you won't be taken for a ride at this new friendly café. Serving excellent satay, steamed dumplings, vegetarian dishes, and crispy noodles, the prices are reasonable, and the food, good. There are a few small tables outside where you and your dog can dig the cuisine. 204 Smith Street; 718/222-5598.

CLINTON HILL

Parks, Beaches, and Recreation Areas

12 Commodore John Barry Park 🐾

There are little but recreational facilities at this local park—which means it offers few opportunities for you and your pup except a rather poorly maintained open area behind the swimming pool where you can walk your dog. That's about it, folks. The park is bordered by Navy Street, Flushing Avenue, and Elliot Place. Open dawn–1 A.M. 718/965-6980.

COBBLE HILL

Cobble Hill, named for a steep hill that occupied the corner of what is now Atlantic Avenue and Court Street, was once rural farmland covered with orchards and fields. Although that bit of the past is long gone (along with the hill itself), this neighborhood is populated with lovely brownstones, upscale shops, and markets. Dogs looking for leash-free spaces have to go to nearby Brooklyn Heights, but they console themselves with the great selection of places to eat!

Parks, Beaches, and Recreation Areas

13 Cobble Hill Park 🐾 🐾 🐾

The quaint neighborhood of Cobble Hill is home to many shops and restaurants, but not many parks. The one exception is this park, a small half-block haven surrounded by brownstones. Located on Verandah Place, this lovely corner successfully became a park in 1965 after the community fought off plans for more shops and houses—the result is the only open space in Cobble Hill.

Cobble Hill Park was reconstructed in 1989 and won awards for its use of 19th century–era materials. Beyond the distinctive granite columns at its entrance, you'll also find graceful wrought-iron fences surrounding elegant benches, street lamps, and herringbone walkways. We can't say there is much to offer your dog beyond a shady spot to watch the world go by, but if you want a change of pace, you won't find a prettier park or neighborhood than this one. Located on Verandah Place between Clinton and Henry Streets. Open 6 A.M.–11 P.M. 718/965-6980.

DIVERSIONS

Wet, Wild, and Woofing!: Ever get tired of washing your pup in the bathtub at home? And then your wet friend dries herself all over the rugs and sofa? We don't know about you, but having a do-it-yourself dog wash close by is even better than Saturday morning cartoons—and a lot more entertaining. **Woofs and Whiskers** offers an easy-to-use dog wash complete with shampoo, towels, dryers, and gear for keeping you dry while your pup undergoes his ordeal of beauty. We can't say our dogs love this experience, but the socializing on Saturday morning and convenience makes it one of our favorite places to go. The dog wash is open every day except Wednesday from 10 A.M. to 5 P.M. 59 Summit Street; 718/237-0298.

On the other hand, if you only wash your dog once a year (whether he needs it or not) the second Saturday in August is probably the day to choose. Fort Greene PUPS (Park Users and Pets Society) sponsors its annual **dog wash in the park,** 7:30–9 A.M. Donations accepted and all proceeds go to improving the lives of the dogs of Fort Greene Park. 718/965-8998; website: www.fortgreenepups.org

Restaurants

Café Cioforo: This elegant restaurant offers a lovely outdoor setting on the corner of Court and Bergen Streets. Offering a menu of northern Italian cuisine, you'll enjoy pasta with light sauces, veal dishes, and the best *caprese* we've had in a long time. Well-behaved dogs are welcome. 223 Court Street; 718/854-4432.

California Taqueria: This L.A.-style Mexican restaurant offers excellent food at budget prices. With taco, enchilada and burrito platters under $5 and great vegetarian and chicken dishes made to order, you and your dog will probably be regular visitors here. There are tables outside where you and Rover can eat your refried beans, or you can take your meal to-go. 187 Court Street; 718/624-7498.

Sparky's: You might expect that a bar that sounds as if George named it would also be one of the most dog-friendly establishments in town. And you'd be right. Dogs of all sizes are welcome to join their mateys at this local watering hole. That's right, you can drink a pint with your dog by your side. Dogs are served water on request but probably have to show ID for anything stronger. 481 Court Street; 718/624-5516.

Sweet Melissa's Patisserie: Man (or dog) does not live by health food alone. And when you can't live without that luscious brownie or to-die-for pastry, this is the place to make a pit stop. There is a lovely outside garden in the back where you can sit with your dog when things are quiet. On busy days, you'll have to make do with the benches outside on Court Street. 276 Court Street; 718/855-3410.

CONEY ISLAND

As far back as 1824, wealthy New Yorkers were visiting this famous seaside resort, and by the early 20th century Coney Island amusement parks were drawing thousands of visitors every day. By 1920, when the subway lines were built, attendance often reached as high as a million. Today, the parks are a little less exciting, but those longing for the smell of popcorn and gum stuck to the bottom of their shoes will still love a visit here.

Parks, Beaches, and Recreation Areas
14 Asser Levy Park 🐾

This park, formerly known as Seaside Park, bears the name of one of the first Jewish activists in the New York area. It first became a park in 1908 when a bathhouse was built here. The bathhouse is now a historical landmark and lies across the street from the entrance of the Coney Island Boardwalk and Aquarium. Beyond its interesting history, however, there isn't much here for dogs—only a small series of busy walkways surrounding grass that you can't set paw on. But this is Coney Island, so the sights and smells should satisfy curious hounds. The park is bordered by the Boardwalk, Surf, and Sea Breeze Avenues, and Ocean Parkway. Open 6 A.M.–A.M. 718/965-6980.

15 Kaiser Park and Gravesend Bay Beach 🐾 🐾 🐾 🐾 🏊

Okay, we know you're asking yourself why we'd rate a somewhat run-down little park with four paws. Well, this 26-acre park scores points not for its parkland, but for Gravesend Bay Beach, which borders its eastern side. When Inu and George are looking for a little relief from the summer heat, they like to head to this little-known strip along Coney Island Basin where they find a sandy beach and outstanding views of the Verrazano Narrows Bridge, the Manhattan skyline, and the harbor. A great place to watch migrating birds, take a swim (dogs are allowed in the water, but people are not), or a quiet walk on a strip of beach and dunes, this hidden beach is one of our favorite spots. Although it gets a bit trashy and hectic on weekends in the summer (this is also a favorite place for personal watercraft), if you can visit here during the week, you'll find it a welcome oasis from the heat of summer.

Dogs are allowed off-leash before 9 A.M. in the park but should be leashed on the beach so they don't disturb nesting shorebirds. Located on Neptune Boulevard and Bayview Avenue. To reach the beach, drive along Bayview to the end of the park. Open dawn–dusk. 718/965-6980.

EARMARK YOUR CALENDAR–SUMMER

Do You Believe in Mermaids?: You just might after you attend the annual **Mermaid Parade** on the Coney Island Boardwalk. Since 1983 the boardwalk has hosted this annual parade heralding the start of the summer beach season with a wild procession of sea-people. Join in the mer-fun or just take in the jaw-dropping costumes at this annual exhibitionist's rite of summer. Held on the first Saturday in June. Leashed dogs are allowed along the boardwalk—in costume or not. 718/372-5159.

Concerts by the Sea: Join the fun at Asser Levy Park for the Seaside Concert Series every Thursday night in July and August. With a different type of music every week, you and your dog won't get bored of howling at the moon with all the other hound dogs and music lovers. The concerts begin at 7:30 P.M. 718/965-6980S.

Every Friday Is the 4th of July: Every Friday night from July through August, you can watch fireworks fill the sky over Coney Island. If your dog isn't afraid of loud noises, bring her down for a festive Friday. Best viewing is from the boardwalk. 718/222-6464.

Nature Hikes and Urban Walks

Riegelmann Boardwalk: Take in the sights and smells along this boardwalk, which dates back to the mid–19th century. Trivia buffs (and people with far too much time on their hands) might be interested to know that from West 37th Street to Corbin Place, a distance of three miles, there are 1.3 million boards and 15.6 million screws and nails (about 12 to a board). Dogs will only care that they can't run on Coney Island Beach beckoning beyond. 718/965-6980.

Restaurants

Nathan's Famous: Featuring the original Coney Island hot dog, this famous landmark restaurant offers mediocre hot dogs, but plenty of atmosphere for you and your own hot dog. We wish we could rave about the food, but this is one place that's more famous for being famous than it is for being good. Still, you can't beat the name or the location. 1310 Surf Avenue; 718/946-2202.

Totonno's: If you've had enough of the heart-attack-on-a-paper-plate offerings at Nathan's, head over one block to this pizza joint, established in 1924. Well-known for its thin crust and sweet tomato sauce, this pizza is as good as it looks. There are no outdoor tables, so we recommend taking it to the boardwalk for a great lunch or dinner. 1524 Neptune Avenue; 718/372-8606.

CROWN HEIGHTS

Parks, Beaches, and Recreation Areas

16 Brower Park 🐾 🎣

This park is the site of the Brooklyn Children's Museum and while that may be great news for the kids, it isn't so great for your dog. Basically she can't go anywhere except around the perimeter of the museum and the playgrounds. If you live here, it will have to do, but don't make a special trip.

The park is bordered by Park Place and Brooklyn, Kingston, and Saint Mark's Avenues. Open 6–1 A.M. 718/965-6980.

17 Lincoln Terrace Park 🐾 🐾 🎣

The unfortunate reality is that this lovely seven-acre park is located in a not-so-safe neighborhood. Renovated on its centennial in 1996, it has been an urban haven since 1896 and offers an escape from the rush of the city in the daylight hours. But after dark, tread here at your own risk. In a different location, this park would definitely get higher marks, but we have to tell it like it is. You'll find graceful winding pathways through a well-groomed landscape, but we never feel entirely safe here, so use it at your own discretion. Located between the Eastern Parkway and East New York and Rochester Avenues. Open 6 A.M.–10 P.M. 718/965-6980.

EARMARK YOUR CALENDAR–DECEMBER

Make a Joyful Noise: You and your pups are invited to celebrate the holiday season in Prospect Park. Every December, the Prospect Park Dog Owners Association host **Bark! The Herald Angels Sing,** a Christmas caroling and Chanukah singalong in Long Meadow near the Tennis House. The noise, uh singing, starts at 8 A.M. and keeps on howling until 10 A.M. Song sheets, bagels, and hot beverages are provided. For exact dates and information visit its website: www.fidobrooklyn.com.

Ring in the New Year with the family (and dog) friendly **First Night** celebration at Grand Army Plaza. Featuring music, dancing, performers, food, ice sculptures, and fireworks at midnight, this annual event is a must for those who don't want to leave their best friend home alone on New Year's Eve. For more information and a calendar of performances, call 718/965-6975.

EARMARK YOUR CALENDAR–MAY

Strut Your Stuff: Join the pack at the **Paws Across America Annual Dog Walk.** The national fund-raiser, held locally every May in Prospect Park, raises funds for animal shelters across the country. Each doggy participant is sponsored for the three-mile walk. Additional events include a Pooch Picnic, a Dog Walkathon, demonstrations, and contests including owner/pet look-a-likes, Frisbee catching, and newspaper fetching. For more information and dates, call 718/430-1890 or 718/601-1460 or visit the website: www.pawsacrossamerica.com.

FLATBUSH

Flatbush was the neighborhood that once housed Brooklyn's beloved Dodgers. Unfortunately, it's been all downhill since the team moved to Los Angeles; all that's left of the Ebbets Field ballpark is a poorly marked plaque hidden behind a hedge on the wall of a housing project. The "Bums" and the neighborhood deserved better!

Parks, Beaches, and Recreation Areas

Prospect Park

This 526-acre park offers some of the best dog-friendly space in New York City. See the Prospect Park listing in the Park Slope section later in this chapter for complete information.

FORT GREENE

In the past few years, Fort Greene has undergone a culinary and shopping renaissance. With trendy boutiques and cafés moving into the neighborhood as fast as you can say "gentrification," this previously forgotten community is experiencing some of the growing pains that popularity brings. Rents are skyrocketing and Asian-fusion restaurants are co-existing with bodegas. For the most part, the new excitement has produced positive results—especially for dogs with a taste for excellent food.

Parks, Beaches, and Recreation Areas

18 Fort Greene Park 🐾 🐾 🐾 🐾

Fort Greene Park, once called Washington Park in honor of our first president (that guy who has the same name as George), was the very first park in Brooklyn. With an illustrious history during the American Revolution, the hill where the park now stands was the site where the British army forced Washington's troops to retreat to Manhattan during the Battle of Long Island.

The monument on top of the hill commemorates the "prison ship martyrs"—civilians who died as captives on British ships during the war.

Today this 30-acre park is popular with dog owners in the nearby neighborhoods of Boerum Hill, Fort Greene, and Clinton Hill. One of the largest parks in Brooklyn, it is currently undergoing a renovation that is scheduled to be completed by 2008. Located on a gentle hill in the middle of urban sprawl, it offers much-needed green space for dogs and their owners who gather between 7:30 and 8:30 A.M. each morning for a little leash-free socializing. Plans for a new dog fountain near the park information center along DeKalb Avenue are in the works. Through the efforts of PUPS (Fort Greene Park Users and Pets Society) a new dog fountain is slated to be installed near the park information center along De Kalb Avenue in spring 2002.

Currently PUPS (Fort Greene Park Users and Pets Society)sponsors fundraisers such as the annual Holiday Coffee, a Halloween Party and the annual Pup Pin-up Calendar to raise money for more dog fountains and mutt-mitt containers; they are also actively lobbying the city for longer off-leash hours.

Dogs are allowed off-leash before 9 A.M. and after 9 P.M. The park is bordered by Cumberland, De Kalb and Myrtle Avenues. Open 6–1 A.M. 718/965-6980.

Restaurants

We've listed a few of our favorite outdoor restaurants here, but new establishments are opening every day—don't expect this to be a complete list.

Chez Oskar: For exotic French food with a decidedly Jamaican twist, George recommends this quaint restaurant. Located on the corner of Adelphi and De Kalb, you'll have a catbird's seat along the busy avenue while you eat your pheasant or jerked chicken. 211 De Kalb Avenue; 718/852-6250.

Loulou: French seems to be the theme, or maybe just our favorite cuisine, along De Kalb Avenue. This pioneer restaurant, one of the first to ring the dinner bell in Fort Greene, offers fabulous food in a distinctly French bistro atmosphere. There are a few small tables outside and, in true French style, Fifi and Fido are welcome to dine with you. 222 De Kalb Avenue; 718/246-0633.

Madiba Restaurant and Shebeen: For a completely unique experience, stop by this terrific South African restaurant and wine bar. With comfy overstuffed chairs and a welcoming outdoor patio, you and your dog can sit and sip your authentic African wine or rum punch all afternoon. Indulge in Durban bunny chow (George likes to think he caught it himself—although we're happy to report it's actually a vegetarian dish with nary a bunny to be found) or Cape Malay mussels—good enough to lick the shells. The food is excellent and the community vibe is even better. A very popular neighborhood hangout, this may quickly become your

The Reel Thing: Although your dog might prefer *Lassie, Come Home* or *Homeward Bound,* he's sure to enjoy the fun no matter what free family film is showing at Fort Greene Park on Tuesday evenings in July and August. Sponsored by nearby Brooklyn Academy of Music and the Fort Greene Conservancy, this new program offers great classic movies under the stars. The projector rolls at 8:30 P.M. 718/636-4139.

favorite place to greet, meet, and eat with other dog owners. 195 De Kalb Avenue; 718/855-9190.

Á Table: This charming French bistro has been leading the neighborhood renaissance going on in Fort Greene. Sidewalk tables with checkered tablecloths say it all—you'll find provincial French food in a casual environment. Dogs are welcomed to dine here in true French fashion. George favors the escargot, while Inu thinks the goat cheese tart should be eaten in one gulp. Make sure you save room for the chocolate soufflé. Open for breakfast, too. 171 Lafayette Avenue; 718/935-9121.

GREENPOINT

Parks, Beaches, and Recreation Areas

🔟 McCarren Park & Dog Run 🐾 🐾 🐕

There really isn't much space for dogs at this trio of parks. Separated by busy streets, there are more playgrounds here than places to walk your dog, but luckily there is a small dog run on the southwest corner of Driggs and 12th Street. With dirt flooring and a few benches and trees, this small run isn't exciting, but it's the only game in town for both Greenpoint and Williamsburg canines. We can't rave about this park—it is a bit unkempt and seedy—but if you live here, you'd better take what you can get. The park is bordered by Bayard, Berry, Driggs, 12th and Lorimer Streets. Open 6–1 A.M. 718/965-6980.

Restaurants

Oznot's Dish: This coffeehouse café is just down the street from McCarren Park and a great gathering place for local dogs and their owners. Famous for its original "Billyburger," the place can really pack 'em in on the weekends. Brunch is great here too, but getting a table outside to dish with the bohemian crowd always proves challenging. 79 Berry Street; 718/599-6596.

HIGHLAND PARK

Parks, Beaches, and Recreation Areas

20 Highland Park 🐾 🐾 🐾

This well-landscaped park is a mixed bag. Located on the edge of both Queens and Brooklyn, it occupies 141 scenic acres surrounding what used to be the Ridgewood Reservoir. Perched on a hillside that overlooks several area cemeteries, this park offers many options for dogs and owners. There are woodlands, wide-open grassy areas, a new forest that is growing on the former reservoir, and lovely hilly slopes for relaxing on a lazy summer day. Sounds great, right? And it is...mostly. For although the park is well maintained, it just isn't located in an area that is entirely safe.

The main entrance to the park is located along busy Jamaica Boulevard but since this section is composed mainly of recreation areas and playgrounds, this isn't the area you will most want to explore with your dog. The most dog-compatible part of the park is located up the hill in the woods.

To reach this section, we suggest you park at the lot along Highland Boulevard. The only catch is that it is often deserted or there are cars loitering with single occupants waiting for what we aren't sure. Even with a dog by your side, those woods look a little desolate to be exploring on your own. In the final analysis, although we like this park, it falls into the dubious category of "good park, bad location." What more can we say?

Dogs must be leashed after 9 A.M. Located between Jamaica Boulevard and the Interborough Parkway and bisected by Highland Boulevard and Vermont Place. Open 6 A.M.–10 P.M. 718/965-6980.

MARINE PARK

Parks, Beaches, and Recreation Areas

21 Floyd Bennett Field 🐾 🐾 🐾 🐾

This converted 1930s airfield holds the distinction of being New York City's first municipal airport. Famous aviators Howard Hughes, Jacqueline Cochran, and "Wrong Way" Corrigan all used this field for their historic flights. The airport was converted to a naval air station in 1941 and became part of the Gateway National Recreation Area in the 1970s. Many of the historic hangars, airstrips and flight towers still exist, making this one the more unusual parks you and your dog will visit in New York City.

We advise consulting the trail map at the entrance; at 1,000 acres, Floyd Bennett Field is so large that you won't be able to find your way without it. Head over to the picnic areas where you'll find plenty of woodland trails to explore— many of them take you down to Jamaica Bay where your pup can swim.

Dogs are to be leashed throughout the park and are not allowed on the nature trails in the northern section. From the Belt Parkway, take Exit 11S to Flatbush Avenue south for 0.25 miles. The entrance is on your left, just north of the Marine Parkway Bridge. Open 6 A.M.–9 P.M. 718/338-3799.

22 Marine Park 🐾 🐾 🐾 🐾 🐕

This wonderful 800-acre open space along Jamaica Bay offers something for everyone. There are three distinct sections here: the city park along Avenue U, the Nature Center across the street, and the salt marshes running along Gerritsen Creek to Jamaica Bay.

In the park, you'll find a well-maintained city park with open manicured grassy areas under shade trees and walkways. There is plenty of space here to throw a ball, but you must negotiate your way among all the crowds and picnickers. Dogs may be off-leash before 9 A.M., but leashed for the rest of the day.

Across the street at the Nature Center, you'll find a one-mile loop trail and boardwalk that runs over the marshes and along the north side of Gerritsen Creek. Established in 1984, this wonderful nature trail offers many checkpoints and lookout points that offer great views of the surrounding area. Dogs must be leashed at all times in this section. Maps are available at the Salt Marsh Nature Center.

Across the creek is a less-tame section that is actually our favorite—at least in every season but summer. There are trails running over two miles down to the bay, and you will find many swimming areas all along the route. Although the area varies between pristine and downright trashy in the summer months, your dog is allowed off-leash here as long as he is under voice command; you must be respectful of the wildlife. The park is bordered by 32nd and Stuart Streets and Avenue U. Open 6 A.M.–10 P.M. 718/965-6980.

NORTHSIDE

Parks, Beaches, and Recreation Areas

23 Monsignor McGolrick Park 🐾 🐾 🦫

This park, originally called Winthrop Park, was re-named in 1941 for Rev. Edward J. McGolrick, a community leader and pastor of nearby Saint Cecilia's church. Its most distinctive feature is the Pavilion, a Greek Revival structure in the center of the park that is currently slated for renovation. The rest of the park features wide promenades across a two-block shaded greenway. You won't get much exercise here, but if you live in the neighborhood, it is a green alternative to the local sidewalks. The park is bordered by Monitor and Russell Streets and Driggs and Nassau Avenues. Open 6–1 A.M. 718/965-6980.

PARK SLOPE

Located next to beautiful Prospect Park, the 24-block Park Slope historic district offers a great life for dogs and people alike. With busy 7th Avenue acting as the hub of community activity, this neighborhood is home to the Brooklyn Tabernacle Choir, the Brooklyn Museum of Art, an ethnically diverse population and more pups than any neighborhood has a right to enjoy.

Parks, Beaches, and Recreation Areas

24 Prospect Park 🐾 🐾 🐾 🐾 🐕

If you look at the world from a canine viewpoint (and why wouldn't you?), these 526 acres have got to be considered some of the best in New York City. Because of the tireless efforts of local dog owners, this park offers the best off-leash hours anywhere. Dogs can run leash-free, not in dog runs, not on converted asphalt covered playgrounds, not even in unofficial dog areas where rangers look the other way as you skulk around while your dog romps without his leash. No, this park does it right by allowing certain sections of the park to be completely off-leash during set hours.

Prospect Park was created during Brooklyn's Golden Decade, the 1860s. At a cost of $4 million for the land and an additional $5 million for the park's construction, Brooklyn's civic leaders wanted a park that would rival the newly completed Central Park in Manhattan. The years since have proven their investment to be a wise one. Used by millions of visitors each year, the park is home to the Brooklyn Zoo, an ice skating rink, a carousel, a 60-acre lake, a 90-acre meadow, and Brooklyn's last remaining forest land. Designed by the indefatigable Frederick Law Olmsted and his partner Calvin Vaux, this elegant park offers you and your dog endless delights on every visit.

Besides great woodsy trails, open meadows and even a lake to take a dip in, the social life is even better. Between 7 A.M. and 9 A.M. on the first Saturday of every month a "Coffee Bark" is held in the Long Meadow, behind the Picnic House. There is food for you (coffee and muffins) and food for Fifi (dog

---

DIVERSIONS

Saturdays in Park Slope: Every Saturday from 10 A.M.–3 P.M. come down to Grand Army Plaza for the freshest produce, bakery items, and crafts in town. Leashed dogs are welcome and soon you'll know all the local merchants by name. 212/477-3220.

If you want to work up an appetite, rent a pedal boat at the Wollman Center and Rink from mid-May through September. Rentals are $10 per hour plus a $10 refundable deposit. Well-behaved dogs are welcome. 718/282-7789.

---

biscuits) provided by the Fellowship for the Interests of Dogs and their Owners (more conveniently called FIDO). This wonderful group is dedicated to encouraging off-leash time, and we have them to thank for the privileges we can all enjoy here.

The Nethermead, which is located between the Long Meadow and the Ravine, is the hot spot for dogs. This is the place to head for before 9 A.M. and after 5 P.M. Not only does it feature a huge open meadow for games of off-leash tag, but there is also a stream running alongside where your dog can splash and cool off on a hot day.

Beyond the Nethermead to the south is a lake that is fairly clean by urban standards and where dogs are allowed off-leash as well. The Ravine is currently off limits except during the weekends while it undergoes restoration (see the Nature Hikes and Urban Walks section).

The rules for where and when you can walk with your dog off-leash are clearly posted at most park entrances and there is also a handy map for reference. We encourage you to take a look at them both. The only way to make sure dogs keep their coveted privileges is to respect the rules as posted. Here they are:

In the park at large, in winter (November 1–March 31), dogs must be leashed between 9 A.M.–5 P.M.

In summer (April 1–October 31), dogs must be leashed between 9 A.M.–9 P.M.

At all other times dogs may be off-leash only in the Long Meadow, the Nethermead, and the Peninsula Meadow. On weekdays, dogs may be off-leash in the Nethermead after 5 P.M.

Dogs are not allowed in playgrounds, on the bridle paths, or on the ball fields when games are in progress.

Okay, now that you got all that, get out there and enjoy! Located between Prospect Park West and Flatbush, Ocean, and Parkside Avenues. Open 6– 1 A.M. 718/965-6980.

Nature Hikes and Urban Walks

The Ravine: Located in Prospect Park, this newly restored section of Brooklyn's last remaining forest is currently closed to the public but will be open on Saturday and Sunday afternoons by fall 2002 for a walk along waterfalls, a miniature gorge, reflecting pools, and lovely trails. There will be guided tours every Saturday and Sunday at 3 P.M. Self-guided strolls will be every weekend 1–5 P.M. 718/965-6988.

Restaurants

Chip Shop: Okay so this place doesn't have outdoor seating. In fact it doesn't have seating at all—just some of the best English-style fish and chips in the city. This takeout place offers a choice of cod and chips, salmon and chips, sausage and chips, onion pie and chips, and. . .well, you get the idea. So chip in for some chips and take them to Prospect Park for a unique picnic with your dog and a few friends. 383 5th Avenue; 718/832-7701.

Cucina: This upscale transplant from Manhattan started the stampede of trendy restaurants opening along this "other" 5th Avenue. Although you and your dog can't eat at the restaurant, you are welcome at the separate takeout section, which offers all the same scrumptious food as the restaurant. Our favorites include the pumpkin ravioli, mushroom risotto and the veal *saltimbocca*. 256 5th Avenue; 718/230-0711.

Connecticut Muffin: This friendly muffin and sandwich shop has a wonderful outdoor area where you and your dog will enjoy the company of other local dog owners. With cute benches and a shaded circular seating area, you can enjoy your muffin, baked goods, coffee, sandwich or salad with a view of busy 7th Avenue. 171 7th Avenue; 718/768-2022.

Dizzy's Kitchen: This bakery and salad café has benches outside where you and your dog can greet the world as it wanders by. With exotic sandwiches with spreads like apricot mustard or spiced cranberry chutney, whitefish salad, and great desserts, don't be surprised if you attract an audience composed of salivating dogs as they walk by. 52 7th Avenue; 718/230-8900.

The Gate: This dog-friendly bar welcomes dogs both inside the bar and on their outdoor patio. On some nights the dogs outnumber the many patrons. We just have to watch George around the beer. What can we say? One drink and he's under the table. 321 5th Avenue; 718/768-4329.

Sotto Voce: This European-style café offers continental cuisine at its tables outside. Serving lunch, dinner, and weekend brunch, your dog is welcome to join you as you dine on crabcakes, pasta, gourmet salads, or a full selection of meat and fish entrées. 225 7th Avenue; 718/369-9322.

Tutta Pasta: If you and your Italian Greyhound just can't get enough caprese, spinach ravioli, or veal scallopini, better head on over to this Italian restaurant in the heart of Park Slope. You'll get your fill here, as well as some great focaccia served up fresh right at your outdoor table. With you pup at your feet, what could be better? *Mangia!* 160 7th Avenue; 718/788-9500.

RED HOOK

Parks, Beaches, and Recreation Areas

25 Coffey Park 🛉 🛶

This neglected little park is smothered in trash, city debris, and looks like it hasn't been weeded since the 1980s. The benches are worn and unpainted and the criss-crossing sidewalks are cracked and showing their age. In short, this is a stop only after a hard day's night. Dogs must be leashed after 9 A.M. The park is bordered by Dwight, Richards, and Verona Streets. Open 6 A.M.–9 P.M. 718/965-6980.

26 Red Hook Park 🐾 🦀

Only slightly better than its sister, Coffey Park, this larger space is composed mainly of ball fields. But you can walk on the pathways surrounding the recreation areas and playing fields. Not great, but there are few alternatives in this neighborhood. Leashed dogs only, please. Bordered by Clinton, Columbia and Bay Streets. Open 6 A.M.–9 P.M. 718/965-6980.

SHEEPSHEAD BAY

Parks, Beaches, and Recreation Areas

27 Plumb Beach 🐾 🐾

It's hard not to be enthusiastic about a beach that allows dogs, but this little strip of beach bordering the Rockaway Inlet leaves a lot to be desired. Namely, a clean bit of sand, for starters. One of our dog-loving friends calls this place "Rat Beach," and we'll leave it to your imagination why it earned that colorful description. In short, there is approximately a mile in either direction where you and your dog can walk along the surf, and although our dogs don't seem to mind the trash and murky water, if you are looking for a scenic pristine

---

EARMARK YOUR CALENDAR–SUMMER

Summer brings music for the enjoyment of human and canine alike to many Brooklyn parks. Bring a blanket and some dog biscuits and enjoy—it beats any concert hall.

Brooklyn Concerts in the Parks at Fort Greene Park: The City Parks Foundation presents a variety of free outdoor music performances at 7 P.M. Tuesday evenings in July and August. For more information and a schedule of performers, call 212/360-8290 or visit the website: www.cityparksfoundation.org.

Celebrate Brooklyn Festival: An outdoor concert is held at the Prospect Park Bandshell every Thursday, Friday, and Saturday evening throughout the summer. From the Brooklyn Philharmonic to ethnic dance bands to classic film scores, there is an eclectic lineup of music to tantalize every taste. Well-behaved dogs are allowed on the grassy knoll beyond the seating area. For a calendar of events, call 718/855-7882, ext. 33.

Sunset Concerts in Sunset Park: You and your musical hound are welcome to enjoy free music and fun every Wednesday in August. Things get started at 7:30 P.M. or so. 718/636-4139.

---

walk, you'll be disappointed. During the summer, your need to find a spot for Spot to swim may overrule any squeamishness and, in the winter when the trash problem is improved, we suggest you bundle up because the wind can be fierce. Dogs must be leashed.

From the eastbound Shore Parkway, take the small turnout just past Exit 9 (Knapp Road). It is only accessible from the eastbound side. Open dawn–dusk. 718/338-3799.

Nature Hikes and Urban Walks

Sheepshead Bay Esplanade: This horseshoe-shaped urban walkway, which runs along the Sheepshead Bay Piers, offers a half-mile seaside stroll for you and your pup. There are plenty of benches along the promenade and great views of the bay and ocean beyond. To reach either side, you can take the 19th Street footbridge across the bay. 718/965-6980.

Restaurants

For Goodness Steak: This steak and seafood restaurant offers great Sunday brunches and dinners at their outside tables overlooking Sheepshead Bay. The menu isn't adventurous but that doesn't seem to stop folks from stuffing themselves silly on the weekend evenings. You and your dog are welcome at the outdoor tables on approval. 2505 Emmons Avenue; 718/934-3600.

SOUTHSIDE

Parks, Beaches, and Recreation Areas

28 Cooper Park 🔥

This weedy little park offers a few short walkways along the not-so-grassy sections. We'd love to tell you to come here because, for local residents, this is it, but frankly our dogs weren't impressed. The park is bordered by Sharon Street and Maspeth and Morgan Avenues. Open dawn–10 P.M. 718/965-6980.

SUNSET PARK

Parks, Beaches, and Recreation Areas

29 Sunset Park 🐾 🐾 🐾

This 24-acre park looks a little worn, but chances are, if you live here, you take your dog here daily. Located on a large hill overlooking the neighborhood, it is a busy and well-used park that offers enough space to give your dog a good workout. There's a great view of New York Harbor from the top of the hill. But there aren't many outlets for dogs. Covered by recreation spaces, you and your dog will have to make do on the pathways that surround these "no-dog" zones.

Dogs allowed off-leash before 9 A.M. The park is bordered by 41st and 44th Streets and 5th and 7th Avenues. Open 6 A.M.–9 P.M. 718/965-6980.

WILLIAMSBURG

This little neighborhood is the East Village before the East Village became the Upper West Side and its days are numbered. The neighborhood has become so popular it is already well on its way to losing its counter-culture hipness, so catch it while you can.

Nature Hikes and Urban Walks

Bedford Avenue: Take a walk through the heart of Williamsburg along Bedford Avenue between 2nd and 8th Streets. This funky area is filled with clothing warehouses, clubs, flea markets, bookstores, and boutiques. Some of the highlights on your walk include the new designer clothing store, W Warehouse, the old Girdle Factory (which is now basically a mall), Clovis Used Books, and several impromptu alleyway flea markets where everything sells for $5–10. Explore the community bulletin board next to Bliss Bakery where you can find apartment shares, community news and good stuff to buy or sell. 718/875-1000.

Restaurants

Grey Parrot Café: Arguably the most popular restaurant in the neighborhood, this busy café serves one of the best breakfasts around. With the largest area of tables along the avenue and a garden area out back that also allows dogs, you and your pup have a lot of tables-with-a-view to choose from. The food is basic American fare but the portions are large, the food hot and prepared to tasty greasy-spoon perfection. 212 Bedford Avenue; 718/486-9372.

Miss Williamsburg Diner: This diner is one of the most doggone dog-friendly restaurants in town. Take out your burger or bring your pup outside on the patio for a standard diner dinner. George likes the meatloaf; Inu goes for the macaroni and cheese. Dogs are welcomed with their own dog bowl and water on request. 206 Kent Avenue; 718/963-0802.

Squeeze: For great juice concoctions, smoothies, bagels, coffee, and sandwiches, stop by this health bar. There are several tables outdoors where you and your dog can enjoy your wheatgrass shots or marinated tofu sandwich with other local canines. 198 Bedford Avenue; 718/782-9181.

Vera Cruz: For pretty good Mexican food with a great view of the street scene, stop by this neighborhood watering hole. With homemade tortillas and authentic Mexican fare such as *tortas* (a Mexican sandwich) and *olitas*

(Mexican fondue), your dog will want to help you lap up every bite. There aren't any outdoor tables here, but the open air restaurant faces out to the street and your dog may sit directly outside as you sit right next to her inside. 195 Bedford Avenue; 718/599-7914.

EARMARK YOUR CALENDAR

Brooklyn loves a parade. If your pooch does too, there are a number of events throughout the year to choose from.

Brooklyn Irish-American Parade: This annual parade is held on the weekend that coincides with Saint Patrick's Day, March 17. The parade begins in Park Slope at 15th Street and Prospect Park West. Come join the fun with your leashed dog. 718/242-4464.

Brooklyn Bridge Day Parade: This annual parade celebrates the completion of this grand landmark by welcoming revelers and marching bands as they parade across the famous bridge against a backdrop of stunning views. Held on the second Sunday in May, you and your dog may join in the fun. 718/237-4442.

Strike up the Band: Don't be the one person to miss the **West Indian American Day Carnival Parade,** advertised as the largest parade in North America. Over two million spectators, thousands of marchers, and hundreds of bands show up every Labor Day to join the fun as the parade makes its way down the Eastern Parkway. As long as your dog doesn't mind the crowds, you'll find music, food, and booths all along the parade route. Held from 10 A.M.–9 P.M. 718/773-4052.

March for the Run: Each year the dog owners of Boerum Hill hold their annual **Community Dog Run Antic Parade** to raise awareness for their need for a community dog run. Held the last Sunday in September, local dog owners walk through the streets of Boerum Hill in costume or otherwise. For more information, call 718/237-1261.

Three Barks for BARC: If your hound has a hankering to be a star, join the fun at the annual **Brooklyn Animal Resource Coalition (BARC) Parade and Dog Show.** Held every October in McCarren Park, the event includes prizes for such unique talents as: Best Kisser, Best Dressed, Best Trick, and Best Butt. Owners get in on the act with the Dog-Person Look-Alike Contest. The first 200 dogs in attendance receive goody bags from local pet stores. For exact dates and times call 718/486-7489 or visit the website: www.barcshelter.org.

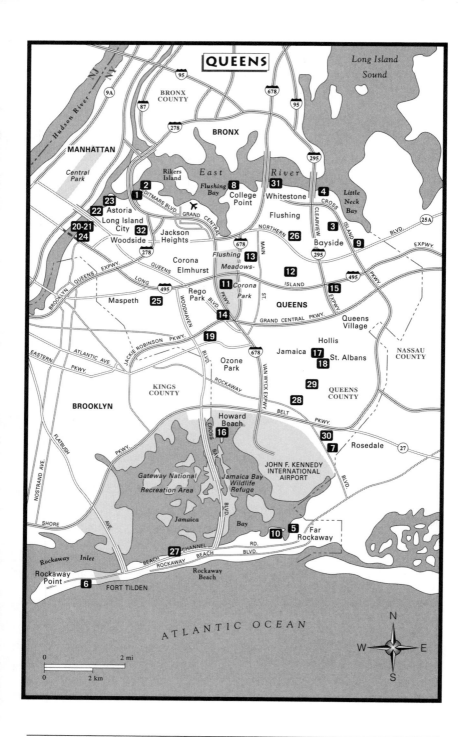

QUEENS

4
QUEENS

If a dog's prayers were answered, bones would rain from the sky.

— Old Proverb

Queens, named for Catherine of Braganza, is the largest borough in New York City. More a series of culturally diverse neighborhoods than a place that fits neatly into a simple description, this mostly residential borough was one of the last boroughs to become urbanized. In fact, between 1910 and 1920, the population of Queens more than doubled, forcing city leaders to begin thinking about park space. And are we lucky they did! Unlike its sister borough, Brooklyn, which was developed and *then* started thinking about open space, today all of us benefit from the parks and green space set aside for recreation.

Most of the large parks existing today in Queens were built during the early and middle years of the 20th century. The 1939–1940 and 1964–1965 World's Fairs led to the further development of Flushing Meadows Corona Park, home of the Mets, the National Tennis Center, and a 1,200-acre park. Although most of the borough is now developed, you can still find plenty of park space and some wonderful beaches where you and your dog can get away from it all.

PICK OF THE LITTER–QUEENS HIGHLIGHTS

BEST CITY PARKS
Alley Pond Park and Environmental Center, Douglaston

Forest Park, Kew Gardens

BEST DOG PARKS
Astoria Park & Dog Run, Astoria

Playground Dog Park, Forest Hills

BEST BEACH
Fort Tilden Park, Breezy Point

Because Queens is not zoned for outdoor restaurants, however, your eating choices are few and far between. We searched high and low and finally decided your best food option is to order take-out at your favorite eatery or bring your kibbles with you.

Queens Greenbelt: Many of Queens' parks are loosely connected by a greenbelt that runs under the major expressways. Beginning at Flushing Meadows Corona Park and running through Queens Botanical Garden, Kissena Corridor Park, Kissena Park, Cunningham Park, and finally to Alley Pond Park, the greenbelt covers more than 10 miles. The route is unmarked, however, so it may take you a few tries to run the whole course.

For a complete map and information, call the Parks Department at 718/520-5936.

Gateway National Recreation Area: Created in 1972, this vast 26,000-acre shoreline wilderness is located within three New York City boroughs—Queens, Brooklyn, and Staten Island—and in Monmouth County in northern New Jersey. In Queens, it encompasses much of the beachfront along Jamaica Bay and in the Rockaways along the Atlantic Ocean. Jamaica Bay Wildlife Refuge, Jacob Riis Park, and the Rockaway beaches are off-limits to dogs. Other sections of the recreation area are dog-friendly, and we've detailed them for you in their respective neighborhoods. Maps are available at the Visitor Center, which is located within the Jamaica Bay Wildlife Refuge off Cross Bay Boulevard near the North Channel Bridge. Call 718/318-4340 for more information.

ASTORIA

This lovely neighborhood overlooks upper Manhattan from across the East River and is becoming a popular alternative to the high-rent neighborhoods of Manhattan. Composed of Greek, Indian, Korean, and European residents, this district is both family-oriented and a magnet for young singles. Musical hounds will be happy to know the very first Steinway factory was built here in the 19th century.

Parks, Beaches, and Recreation Areas

1 Astoria Park & Dog Run 🐾 🐾 🐾 🐾 ✖

Tucked under the shadow of the Triborough Bridge, Astoria Park is a great neighborhood park. With excellent skyline views of Manhattan from the expansive lawn, you and your dog will find a moment of quiet here as you wander the many tree-lined trails that criss-cross through the park. There are plenty of drinking fountains spread throughout the park for you and your thirsty pup, and your dog won't tire of chasing the ball across the wide, open lawn. Although the park hovers along the waterfront, there is no water access for your pup. Dogs are allowed to run sans leash before 9 A.M.

As nice as the park is, the dog run is even better. Located just beyond the park's western boundaries along Shore Boulevard and Astoria Park South, this spacious run is well-supplied with water, chairs (provided by other dog owners), poop bags, and a great view across the East River to Manhattan. Nearby trees and breezes off the water keep it fairly cool in the summer.

Don't be put off by the No Dogs Allowed sign at the parking area. This sign refers to the swimming pool, amphitheater, and ball fields. Dogs are welcome in the rest of the park. The park is bordered by 19th Street and Ditmars and Shore Boulevards. The park is open dawn–10 P.M.; the dog run is open 24 hours a day. 718/520-5936.

2 Ralph DeMarco Park 🐾 🐾 ✖

This tiny five-acre park is really just a strip of green along the waterfront, but if you want excellent views of Manhattan and fresh water breezes, you could do worse. Named for the city councilman who made cleaning up the waterfront area his priority, the park honors his memory.

Dogs must be leashed except before 9 A.M. Located on Shore Boulevard between 20th Avenue and Ditmars Boulevard. Open dawn–10 P.M. 718/520-5936.

BAYSIDE

Parks, Beaches, and Recreation Areas

❸ Crocheron Park/John Golden Park 🐾 🐾 🐾 🐾 🐾

These twin parks are jewels in Queens' crown. With well-maintained trails that roam in and out of the woods and around the ball fields, the park is designed to allow the recreationalists to co-exist with the walkers. Although you will have to watch out for Little Leaguers and softball players (mostly in John Golden Park) in the summer months, there is still plenty of space for you and your dog to romp.

For a break from the ball fields, our favorite section is located in the woodlands off 35th Avenue. Here the smoky smell of leaves and pine needles mix with plenty of grassy spots your pooch will want to sniff. There is also a small lake on the south side of 35th Avenue, although on hot days it is decidedly ducky so use your judgment (and your nose) to decide whether or not you want your pal to take a dip.

Dogs must be leashed except before 9 A.M.

Located between 214th Place, Crocheron Avenue, and Cross Island Parkway. Parking is available at the lot off of 215th Place between 33rd and 34th Avenues, or along 35th Avenue. Open dawn–9 P.M. 718/520-5936.

❹ Little Bay Park 🐾 🐾 🐾 🐾

This wonderful little promenade defines the saying that good things come in small packages. Part bike trail, part park, and located along Little Neck Bay in Long Island Sound, this is one of George's favorite stops.

Start at the beginning of the Joe Michaels Mile, a bike trail that could also be called the Four-Mile Trail because it runs from the Throgs Neck Bridge north four miles along Little Neck Bay. Along the way you can romp on the lawn of Little Bay Park while enjoying views of the Bronx, swim in the Sound at the beach area next to Fort Totten, and walk on the shaded trail next to the bike path as you continue north.

EARMARK YOUR CALENDAR–MAY

Who Let the Dogs Out?: You will be asking the same when you see the turnout for the annual **Pawswalk** in Flushing Meadows Corona Park. This May event is one of five walks sponsored in each of the boroughs. The walk also includes a Pooch Picnic, demonstrations, and contests including owner-pet look-a-likes, Frisbee catching, and newspaper fetching. All proceeds will benefit local animal shelters. For more information, call 718/430-1890 or 718/601-1460 or visit its website: www.pawsacrossamerica.com.

George never tires of walking the rocky jetty here or swimming at low tide from the shore next to the fort. A word of caution, however: as with most of the shoreline along the sound, there can be broken glass and other city hazards in the water, so you should be careful when letting your dog bound through the waves. Also we advise watching out for the in-line skaters and bikers on the bike path. There is plenty of room to dodge the speeders within Little Bay Park, but if you continue north on the trail you'll have to watch your step.

Dogs must be leashed after 9 A.M..

From the Cross Island Expressway, take Exit 32 and turn left onto Totten Avenue. The parking lot and park are on your left. The park closes at 9 P.M. 718/520-5936.

BAYSWATER

Parks, Beaches, and Recreation Areas

5 Bayswater Park 🐾 🏊

This tired little park consists mainly of ball fields and one open weedy field where you can throw the ball for your dog. If you live here, this is your only daily option, but if you don't, this is one park you can live without.

Dogs must be leashed after 9 A.M. Located at the intersection of Far Rockaway Boulevard and Bay 32nd Street. Open dawn–9 P.M. 718/520-5936.

BREEZY POINT

The 2000 census named this area at the end of the Far Rockaways the whitest neighborhood in all of New York City. And a drive down Breezy Point Boulevard might give you the impression that folks here like it just the way it is. We'd love to tell you we found some great parks here, but the truth is there are residential gates on every single street. That means nobody gets in but the local hounds! Fortunately, Fort Tilden lies just outside the castle gates, and with that great beach nearby, who needs anything more?

Parks, Beaches, and Recreation Areas

6 Fort Tilden Park 🐾 🐾 🐾 🐾 🏊

Our friends Scott and dog Clementine gave us the heads up on this fabulous beach park, and George and Inu agree that this is one of the best spots in New York City. But before we tell you about it, we have to ask you to keep the news about this special place to yourself. Once word gets out that not only is this one of the best beaches in town, but that you can also come here with your dog, we're afraid the crowds will descend and ruin this pristine wilderness. So here's the top-secret scoop:

This area has long been used as a military outpost, protecting New York Harbor as far back as the War of 1812. Fort Tilden, also known as "Camp Rockaway," was built in 1917, and the remains of the concrete bunkers that were used in both world wars are still evident today. Fort Tilden operated as part of the U.S. Coast Guard until 1974, when it was acquired by the state of New York and became part of the Gateway National Recreation Area. Today it is being allowed to return to its natural state—a rare occurrence in the New York metro area.

Your dog may not really care about the fabulous history of this place, but she will definitely thank you for bringing her here. On any given day, you'll have this corner of the Far Rockaways mostly to yourself while Jacob Riis Park, only a beach away, is congested, crowded and overrun by radios, hot dogs, and beach towels.

This park is a wonderful mix of beach, dunes, woodlands, and open grassy areas. The ball fields near the entrance can be used for chasing a ball, although our dogs usually head straight for the beach and woodland trails. The long, untamed beach offers a great chance for swimming in the summer and is a place to take in healthy ocean breezes without debris and trash littering the shores.

Beyond the beach are a myriad of woodland trails that lead in chaotic style through overgrown grasses, dunes, trees, and around the deserted bunkers. Many trails are a hodgepodge of eroding concrete—remnants of its Coast Guard days. Other trails are natural animal paths, and a few traverse boardwalk trails that lead over the dunes to lookout points where you can view the Atlantic Ocean and New Jersey shore.

There is an abundance of wildlife here so you need to be respectful of the nesting birds, plant habitats, and fragile dunes. Dogs must be leashed here.

A $25 yearly parking permit is required, although daily passes are issued on exception. Permits and maps are available at the office headquarters, which is open daily from 9 A.M.–4 P.M.

From the Belt Parkway, take Exit 11S onto Flatbush Avenue south across the Marine Parkway Bridge. Turn right onto Breezy Point Boulevard and take an immediate left onto 169th Street. The park entrance will be on your right. Open dawn–dusk. 718/318-4300.

BROOKVILLE

Parks, Beaches, and Recreation Areas

7 Brookville Park 🐾 🐾 🦑

You'll find much to enjoy on a daily basis at this medium-sized park. There are large wooded areas for walking your dog in any season, open grassy lawns, and a path that circles Conseiyeas Pond. The park is well maintained, and there is enough room to get in a good walk with your pooch. During the day, it is frequented by local residents, but we caution you to use discretion after dark and when there aren't plenty of people around.

Parking is available along 147th Avenue and along Brookville Boulevard. Dogs are allowed off-leash before 9 A.M. Located at the intersection of 147th Avenue and Brookville Boulevard. Open dawn–9 P.M. 718/520-5936.

COLLEGE POINT

Parks, Beaches, and Recreation Areas

8 Hermon A. MacNeil Park 🐾 🐾 🐾 🐾

Located on a windy point overlooking the harbor and La Guardia Airport, this quiet waterfront park is a welcome respite from the noisy city surrounding it. Although the out-of-the-way drive means you probably don't come here if you don't live in College Park, the seclusion provides much of its charm.

With 180-degree views of La Guardia, Manhattan, and the Whitestone Bridge, there are grassy fields, large shade trees, and a promenade along the water. This isn't a large park, but you and your dog will find ample room for exercising. There is a wrought-iron fence to keep you from taking a dip (and the currents are fast so we wouldn't recommend it anyway), but the harbor breezes are wonderful on a hot summer day. Of course this means they are also rather brisk in the winter.

A Mister Softee ice-cream truck makes frequent stops to the playground in the summer, and although you may wish to pony up for an ice cream, your dog is not allowed in the play area.

Dogs are allowed off-leash before 9 A.M. Located on Poppenhusen Avenue and the end of College Place and 119th Street. Plenty of parking is available along Poppenhusen Avenue. Open dawn–9 P.M. 718/520-5936.

DOUGLASTON

Parks, Beaches, and Recreation Areas

9 Alley Pond Park and Environmental Center 🐾 🐾 🐾 🐾 🐾

This large 654-acre park sprawled under the Long Island and Cross Island Expressways provides a welcome green space from the chokehold of surrounding concrete. Although ball fields encompass much of the southern end, you can escape the ball games by heading through the woods from the parking area at Springfield Boulevard and 76th Avenue. Here you will find trails that meander through the trees and meadows, and you'll also find plenty of shade to beat the summer heat. In the winter you and the other dog walkers will often enjoy a quiet stroll by yourself.

To reach the best trails in the center of the park, follow the signs to the

Environmental Center parking area via a service road off Douglaston Parkway. The nature preserve is one of the last remaining undeveloped spots in New York City. Although it is mainly an education center, there is wonderful trail system that runs over the saltwater marshes, along the ponds and trees, and through the woodlands and meadows. You and your leashed dog are allowed on the boardwalk trail as long as you respect the wildlife in the area.

Nature trail maps are available at the Environmental Center headquarters. You can also request a map of adjoining Alley Pond Park.

For shorter walks on the western side of the park, you'll find the Gertrude Waldeyer Promenade, which circles Oakland Lake along Springfield Avenue. This "lake" is really a marshy duck pond, but the walk is quiet and scenic.

Dogs must be leashed after 9 A.M.

The Center is located on Northern Boulevard just past the Cross Island Parkway (Exit 31). The park has multiple entrances' it's accessible from the Cross Island Parkway at Exits 29, 30, and 31, and from Douglaston Parkway and Springfield Boulevard. The Environmental Center is open 8 A.M.–6 P.M. daily. The park is open dawn–9 P.M. 718/520-5936 or 718/229-4000.

EAST ELMHURST

Restaurants

Jackson Hole Airline Diner: This old-fashioned diner has plenty of tables outside where you and your frequent flyer can dine; place your order through the take-out window. Although it is right along the busy Grand Central Parkway, and you'll have to contend with the planes of La Guardia overhead, the grub is sloppy, cheap, and good. Just the way we like it. 35-01 Bell Boulevard (35th Avenue); 718/281-0330.

Places to Stay

La Guardia Marriott: This large airport hotel offers roomy rooms and comfy quarters for travelers and their pets (as long as the pet is under 25 pounds). So if you meet the size restriction or can get your retriever to shrink down to the size of a cat, this place is for you. A refundable $100 deposit is required for your pet. Rates are $149–450 per night. 102-05 Ditmars Boulevard, East Elmhurst, NY 11369; 718/565-8900 or 800/228-9290; website: www.marriott.com.

EDGEMERE

Parks, Beaches, and Recreation Areas

10 Edgemere Park—Rockaway Community Park 🐾 🐢

This park is less "park" and more undeveloped open space. The trick is accessing the "space"—a few trails through tall marsh grasses. First you have to go through Rockaway Community Park, a small, not particularly attractive park in an equally scruffy neighborhood. Walk to the western end of Rockaway Community Park behind the ball field, and you'll reach a narrow dirt path that leads through high grasses along Sommerville Basin. The trail is not well-groomed, so walk in this area at your own discretion. George thinks it's not really worth all that effort, but you be the judge.

Dogs are allowed off-leash before 9 A.M. and must be leashed all other hours. Parking is available along 54th Avenue.

From Beach Channel Drive, take Alameda Drive north and turn left on 54th Avenue. The park is on your right. Open dawn–9 P.M. 718/520-5936.

FLUSHING

Parks, Beaches, and Recreation Areas

11 Flushing Meadow Corona Park 🐾 🐾 🐾 🐾 🐾

Many know these 1,275 acres as the site of the 1939–1940 and 1964–1965 New York World's Fairs, but before that it was a landfill—and before that it was a swamp. Fortunately for present and future generations, the rush of pride that propelled businesses to ante up for the World's Fair also created this lush present-day recreation site that includes Shea Stadium, the National Tennis Center, the Queens Zoo, and, yes, plenty of open space for you and your pooch.

If you want to avoid the hustle and bustle around Shea Stadium (where dogs can't go), we recommend that you enter on the northern side. You can reach several parking lots either from the Van Wyck Expressway or off College Point Boulevard. From here you can choose from acres of open walkways through picnic areas, shade trees, and meadows perfect for ball throwing. Or, head straight to Meadow Lake, New York City's largest artificial lake. This 84-acre lake isn't really fit for a swim unless you and your dog don't mind the muck of a city lake, but there is a trail that leads along its edge that makes for an enjoyable jaunt. This is Queens' largest park, so your tireless pup might actually burn all that extra apartment energy here.

On the lower eastern section is Willow Pond, a marshy duck pond. There is no access to the water here, so don't expect to take a dip. You can saunter along the pond in peace, however, because this is the least-congested area of the park.

Dogs must be leashed 9 A.M.–9 P.M.

Located between Grand Central Parkway and Van Wyck Expressway from 111th to 134th Streets. The park is open from dawn until 1 A.M. 718/760-6565.

12 Kissena Park 🐾 🐾 🐾 🐾

This 127-acre park is a favorite with local dog owners. There are plenty of woods, hills, and open spaces to vary the terrain, so local residents won't get

Boating on the Bayou: Take your dog out on Meadow Lake in Flushing Meadows Corona Park. Paddle boats and rowboats are available at the boathouse located along the lake at the parking area on the northern side of the park. Boats are $10 per hour. Dogs ride free, but since there's no such thing as a free ride, you may want to decide up front who has to row. Boats are rented on a first-come, first-served basis. 718/760-6565.

tired of the locale. For exercise enthusiasts, there is a bike and fitness trail in the center of the park circling the "nature center," an untamed marshy area where wildlife and birds are abundant. George and Inu don't care much for doing sit-ups, but they are happy to wait while JoAnna takes a shot at the slant board.

There is a pond long 164th Street and Oak Avenue that your dogs may think is just ducky. Of course, this may not be a good thing if you have to bring your soggy pooches home with you after their energetic pursuit of their feathered friends. We suggest avoiding the pond and just heading for the woods beyond the water. Dogs are not allowed in the playground or on the tennis courts and ball fields. Dogs must be leashed after 9 A.M. The park is bordered by 164th Street; Memorial, Rose, and Oak Avenues; and Kissena Boulevard. Open dawn–9 P.M. 718/520-5936.

13 Queens Botanical Gardens 🐾 🐾

As we go to press this park is currently under construction, so it is short on gardens and long on torn-up dirt. But the interior still has large grassy areas where you can throw the ball for your dog or kick up your heels. The walkways are wide and stretch over the expansive lawns. It should really look great when construction is finished in 2003.

This park connects to the Kissena Corridor, which eventually connects to Kissena Park. At present you can't walk the entire distance between each park. Dogs must be leashed at all times. Located between Main Street and College Point Boulevard Park. Open dawn–9 P.M. 718/520-5936.

FOREST HILLS

Parks, Beaches, and Recreation Areas

14 Playground Dog Park 🐾 🐾 🐾 🐾 🐕

This is one of the better dog parks in the area—certainly the best one in Queens. Located directly under the footbridge that leads over Grand Central

Parkway into Flushing Meadow Corona Park, it is spacious, covered with wood chips, shade trees, benches, and plenty of trash cans. Unlike so many dog runs in New York City, this one actually seems to have been designed with a dog's needs in mind. It's one block long and one block wide, so there's enough room to throw the ball; its undersurface absorbs the wear and tear of many dogs treading at once; and if you want a longer walk the park beckons over the bridge. Located at 64th Avenue and 64th Street, next to the Grand Central Parkway. Open 7 A.M.–9 P.M. 718/760-6565.

FRESH MEADOWS

Parks, Beaches, and Recreation Areas

🟦 Cunningham Park & Dog Run 🐾 🐾 🐾 🐕

This large 350-acre park encompasses plenty of acres, but not all of them provide the things that most interest dogs. Most of the western side, which runs along Francis Lewis Boulevard, is covered with ball fields, where dogs are not welcome in the summer, although in the winter months you can enjoy the open space with your pooch. On the eastern side, along Hollis Hills Boulevard, there are woodlands to wander through, but you have to enter the forest paths via the street, which makes the area a little too secluded for our taste.

Our favorite area is the smaller southern section, which has looping paths that circle the playing fields and a small dog run. This dog park isn't large—really just a tiny dirt enclosure—but it gets a lot of action. If your dog is a social butterfly like Inu, this is a good spot to make connections. The dog run is on 193rd Street just south of Union Turnpike.

Dogs may run off-leash in the dog run and before 9 A.M. in the park.

Parking is available along Francis Lewis Boulevard or at the parking area off Union Turnpike between the boulevard and 193rd Street. The park and dog run are open dawn–9 P.M. 718/760-5700 (dog run), 718/520-5936 (parks department).

GLENDALE

Parks, Beaches, and Recreation Areas

Highland Park

This park covers 141 acres at the edge of both Queens and Brooklyn. See the Highland Park listing in the Brooklyn chapter for complete information.

HOWARD BEACH

Parks, Beaches, and Recreation Areas

16 Frank M. Charles Memorial Park 🐾 🐾 🐾 🦀

Part of the Gateway National Recreation Area, this small seaside park has three things going for it: location, location, location. When you're a hot dog sweltering in the summer sun, location is everything. Perched along Jamaica Bay, this is one of the few parks that offers easy access to the water *and* welcomes your canine pal. Although the park itself is really a series of tennis courts and ball fields, if you venture past the courts, you'll find a grassy beach with a large swimming area. Dogs are allowed to be off-leash before 9 A.M., but leashed the rest of the day, so if you're looking for a little sun and want to share it with your pooch, you will enjoy this place. A word of caution: watch out for glass along the water. Located on 165th Avenue between 95th and 103rd Streets. Open 6 A.M.–10 P.M. 718/520-5936.

JAMAICA

Parks, Beaches, and Recreation Areas

17 Detective Keith L. Williams Park 🐾 🦀

Formerly called Liberty Park, this tiny neighborhood park doesn't offer much for dogs, but if you live here, this is your only option. Although the park is composed mostly of ball fields and other recreation areas where dogs can't go, you and your pal are allowed on the path that circles the several block–long area park. Dogs must be leashed after 9 A.M.

From Jamaica Avenue, turn left on Merrick Boulevard, and right on 105th Avenue. Parking along 105th Avenue. Open dawn–10 P.M. 718/520-5936.

18 Saint Albans Park 🐾 🐾 🦀

This small park was completed in the summer of 2001 and has proved to be a welcome addition to the neighborhood. Located on 15 acres of open, well-groomed space, you and your dog can look forward to spending some good walk time here if you live in this neighborhood. Throw a ball for your pooch, sit on one of many well-placed benches, or meander along the pathway that weaves across and around this newest addition to the New York City park system.

Dogs must be leashed after 9 A.M. Located on Sayres Avenue and Merrick Boulevard. Open dawn–9 P.M. 718/520-5936.

Harmonizing Hounds: Join the fun at the free Sunday afternoon concerts held at the George Seuffert Bandshell in Forest Park. The music begins at 2 P.M. in July and August and ranges from blues to big band to musical theatre tunes. Leashed dogs are not allowed in the formal seating area but are welcome to hang out in back or along the outer areas. For dates and performers, call 718/235-0815.

KEW GARDENS

Parks, Beaches, and Recreation Areas

19 Forest Park 🐾 🐾 🐾 🐾 🌊

This 530-acre park is the third-largest park in Queens and serves many surrounding neighborhoods of dogs and their owners. Conceived in 1895 as part of a planned greenbelt system that would lead from Manhattan to the Atlantic Ocean, Forest Park was originally called Brooklyn Forest Park until the present-day boundaries between the boroughs required a shortening of the name. Well-named for its vast forest woodland, this large park offers an impressive choice of terrain for active two- and four-legged folk.

The western side of the park is mainly composed of ball fields, tennis courts, and other recreation activities your dog will want to avoid. On the eastern side are seven miles of hiking and bridle trails perfect for curious hounds. An extensive trail system runs through hilly forests and open meadows; the latter are perfect for sunning, ball throwing, or just chasing your tail. Forest Park Way, a paved road that runs through the park, is closed to traffic and serves as another recreation trail for you and your pup.

Dogs are allowed off-leash before 9 A.M. but must be leashed throughout the day. Maps are available at the park entrance on Woodhaven Boulevard and Forest Park Drive. Parking is available along Myrtle Street or at the band shell parking area at the entrance to Forest Park Way. There is additional parking at the golf course on the western end. Located between Union Turnpike and Myrtle Avenue off Exit 6 of the Jackie Robinson Parkway. Open dawn–10 P.M. 718/235-0815.

LONG ISLAND CITY

This part-residential, part-industrial neighborhood has long been the focus of gentrification talk. When Citibank moved its headquarters here in the 1980s, everyone was sure this would be the next hot spot. Now that the United Nations is building residential towers along the waterfront, the rumors are heating up again. With great views and easy access across the river to midtown Manhattan, this area certainly can't be beat for location. But despite the several dog parks here, the industrial dominance of this neighborhood means that for Spot, this neighborhood isn't all that hot.

Parks, Beaches, and Recreation Areas

20 Granary Plaza State Park 🐾 🐾

To call this a park may be stretching things a bit, but a beautiful promenade overlooking Manhattan is certainly an appropriate description. The only state park that allows dogs in the New York City area, this lovely plaza is one of the best uses of waterfront property in Queens. Gravel paths coexist with graceful walkways and piers that jut out into the East River. For the desperate water dog, there is a small area with water access, but you'll need a very long leash to reach the water from the path above.

An energetic dog won't get much exercise here, but if you're looking for an unobstructed view of the skyline, this is an ideal spot. If you need to stretch your legs, the Vernon Boulevard Dog Run is just up the street. At Queens Landing between 48th and 49th Avenues. Open until 10 P.M. 718/858-4708.

21 Murray Playground & Dog Run 🐾 🐾 🐕

There's a small local dog run located in this playground that is frequented by local residents. It's only a small dirt fenced-in area that really won't give your dog much of a run, but it's a good place to meet the local canines. Most of the dog owners continue to "unofficially" use the playground area to throw the Frisbee and give their dog some exercise, though be advised that there is a leash law in the playground. Located on 21st Street and 44th Avenue. Open dawn–10 P.M. 718/520-5936.

22 Queensbridge Park 🐾 🐾 🐢

This neighborhood park isn't anything to cross the Queensborough Bridge for, but if you live here, it's one of the few green spaces along the waterfront where you can walk with your dog. Naturally, it gets a lot of use. Although located right on the waterfront under the Queensborough Bridge, you can't actually access the water here. The promenade started sinking into the East River in 1999 and has been under construction ever since. George tried sneaking under the fence, but another wrought iron gate stopped his progress and there are danger signs posted. Better to wait for the reconstruction, which could be several more years. Still, there are large shade trees, a well-lit path circles the playing fields, and the sod has recently been replaced.

Dogs are allowed off-leash before 9 A.M. Located on Vernon Boulevard at 41st Avenue just north of the Queensborough Bridge. Parking is on Vernon Boulevard. Open dawn–10 P.M. 718/520-5936.

23 Rainey Park 🐾 🐾 🐢

This neighborhood park is a well-groomed patch of green located along the East River. Not much more than a couple of city blocks, you won't go out of your way to visit here, but if you live here, this is an adequate spot to exercise your pup. The No Dogs Allowed sign you'll see refers to the playground area.

The morning leash-free law is in effect here until 9 A.M. Leashes are required the rest of the time. Located on Vernon Boulevard between 35th and 33rd Avenues. Parking available along Vernon Boulevard. Open 6 A.M. until 10 P.M. 718/520-5936.

24 Vernon Boulevard Dog Run 🐾 🐾 🐕

This recently completed dog run isn't much to get excited about. The only thing worth mentioning is that it's leash-free. With grass under paw, poop bags, and just enough room for five dogs and their owners to do little but stand around, we can only recommend it as a place to meet and greet your neighbors. And hey, that's not such a bad thing, is it? To get any real doggy exercise, unfortunately, you'll have to leave the neighborhood. Located on Vernon Boulevard between 48th and 49th Avenues. Open 24 hours. 718/520-5936.

MIDDLE VILLAGE

Parks, Beaches, and Recreation Areas

25 Juniper Valley Park 🐾 🐾 🐢

This 55-acre local park is in a lively area of town, so you can be sure you'll meet up with the locals on a visit here. Split into two sections by 80th Street, the eastern side is mostly playing fields where your dog can't go, but the western section offers some shade trees and grass for doggy socializing.

Dogs must be leashed after 9 A.M. Located on Juniper Boulevard North and South between 71st and 81st Streets. Open dawn–9 P.M. 718/760-5700.

MURRAY HILL

Parks, Beaches, and Recreation Areas

26 Bowne Park 🐾 🐾 🐢

This pleasant neighborhood park offers a small duck pond in the center of a well-manicured park. Popular with local dogs and owners, you'll find many other tail waggers to hang with here. Although this park is nice enough, we can't recommend it as a must-see if you aren't already in the neighborhood. If you live here, you'll enjoy making this a daily stop with Spot. Located between 155th and 159th Streets and 29th and 32nd Avenues. Open until 9 P.M. 718/520-5936.

ROCKAWAY PARK

Parks, Beaches, and Recreation Areas

27 Marine Park 🐾 🦴

This is more a promenade than a park and not a particularly great one at that. Located on the Jamaica Bay side of the Rockaways, a narrow concrete pathway runs along the bay. You and your dog are welcome to enjoy the view but you'll have to contend with the many anglers who populate this park each day.

Dogs must be leashed because it is so close to the road and parking area. Located off Beach Channel Drive at 116th Street. Open dawn–9 P.M. 718/520-5936.

SPRINGFIELD GARDENS

Parks, Beaches, and Recreation Areas

28 Baisley Pond Park 🐾 🐾 🦴

This long park offers a little green space surrounding a duck pond, but we can tell it wants to be much more. Located in a rather ratty neighborhood (sorry, folks, but it's true), this park also shows its wear and tear. Yet the landscaping is really quite lovely. Graceful trees line the park boundaries as wrought-iron bridges slope over the mucky pond. There are plenty of benches lining the worn grassy areas and room to let a dog stretch his legs. But until the area residents decide to take more pride in their park, there is only so much this place can improve. Let's hope for the best.

Dogs may go leash-free before 9 A.M. Leashes required all other times. Located at the intersection of Baisley, Rockaway, and Sutphin Boulevards. Open dawn–9 P.M. 718/520-5936.

29 Roy Wilkins Southern Queens Park 🐾 🦴

Although this park has a large expansive lawn that stretches into ball fields and recreation areas, it doesn't really offer much for dogs except a few scruffy patches of grass straddling the residential area. Our dogs' tails start hanging when we try to convince them this is a good place to walk. If you live here and it's your only option, go right ahead.

Dogs may go leash-free before 9 A.M. Leashes required all other times. Located at the intersection of Baisley and Merrick Boulevards. Open dawn–10 P.M. 718/520-5936.

30 Springfield Park 🐾 🦴

This small city park offers a little green space in a tough neighborhood. Local dogs have few options, but if you don't live here, you probably can choose other places to walk on a daily basis. Dogs may go leash-free before 9 A.M. Leashes required all other times. The park is bordered by 184th Street,

145th and 147th Avenues, and Springfield Boulevard. Open dawn–9 P.M. 718/520-5936.

WHITESTONE

Parks, Beaches, and Recreation Areas

31 Francis Lewis Park 🐾 🐾 🖾

This waterside park is located in the shadow of the Whitestone Bridge. Although there is an excellent view across the river to upper Manhattan and the Bronx, this tiny park isn't a must-see. But if you're feeling the need for an ocean breeze, you could do worse. There are a few walkways and grassy areas for your dog to sniff and smell. If you're a local pup, this is certainly an adequate solution for a daily walk.

Dogs may go leash-free before 9 A.M. Leashes required all other times. Located at the intersection of 3rd Avenue and 147th Street at the Whitestone Bridge. Open dawn–10 P.M. 718/520-5936.

WOODSIDE

Parks, Beaches, and Recreation Areas

32 Windmuller Park & Dog Run 🐾 🐾 🐕

We wish we could get a little more excited about the dog run in this park. I mean, it *is* a leash-free space, after all. But our dogs barely gave it a glance, and when we went inside they just looked at us as if to say, "And now what?" It has a pebbly-dirt floor and is set on the hillside next to the playground; it offers little room in which to run or even to play once a few large dogs enter the enclosed area.

So who are we to bash the city for at least opening up another leash-free space? Still, if it could just be a little larger. . . . The park is bordered by 54th and 56th Streets and Woodside Avenue. Open dawn–dusk; 718/520-5936.

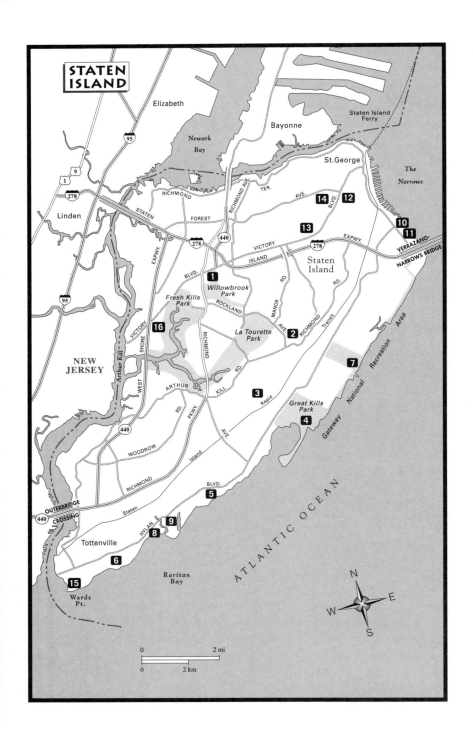

STATEN
ISLAND

Elizabeth

Bayonne

Staten Island
Ferry

Newark
Bay

St.George

The
Narrows

RICHMOND

FOREST

RICHMOND AVE.

TER.

AVE.

BLVD.

14 **12**

13

Victory

ISLAND

EXPWY

10

11

VERRAZANO-
NARROWS BRIDGE

Linden

STATEN

EXPWY.

BLVD.

278

440

278

Staten
Island

1

Willowbrook
Park

MANOR

RD.

RICHMOND

Transit

RD.

ROCKLAND

VICTORY

Fresh Kills
Park

16

RICHMOND

AVE.

La Tourette
Park

2

SHORE

NEW
JERSEY

Arthur Kill

WEST

ARTHUR

KILL

Rapid

3

7

Gateway

National

Recreation

Area

440

PKWY.

RD.

Great Kills
Park

4

WOODROW

Island

AVE.

RICHMOND

BLVD.

Staten

5

ATLANTIC OCEAN

OUTERBRIDGE

CROSSING

440

HYLAN

9

8

Tottenville

6

15

Wards
Pt.

Raritan
Bay

N

W   E

S

0   2 mi

0   2 km

5 STATEN ISLAND

Dogs are our link to paradise. They don't know evil or jealousy or discontent. To sit with a dog on a hillside on a glorious afternoon is to be back in Eden, where doing nothing was not boring—it was peace.

— Milan Kundera

The smallest and most suburban of all the boroughs, Staten Island was originally called *Monacnong,* from the Raritan word for enchanted woods. By all descriptions it was a wonderland of dense forests, rolling hills, lakes, and plenty of wildlife. In 1776, a British officer wrote, "Surely this country is the Paradise of the world." But all good things come to an end, and today Staten Island is known more for its ferry and its landfill than for its beauty. Who can blame residents here if they feel a little "dumped" on by the rest of New York City?

When Fresh Kills Landfill opened in 1948, it had the dubious distinction of being the world's largest garbage dump. Located on 3,000 acres of a once-beautiful marshland, the landfill was supposed to close in 1960. The trash, however, kept piling up and Staten Island kept enduring another 40 years of

PICK OF THE LITTER–
STATEN ISLAND HIGHLIGHTS

Clove Lakes Park, Sunnyside

Great Kills Park, Great Kills

High Rock Park Conservation Area, Egbertville

Miller Field, New Dorp Beach

Wolfe's Pond Park, Prince's Bay

trash jokes. Finally, in November 2001, the landfill finally bit the dust, and we are happy to report that plans are already underway to turn this site into parkland. Since we don't doubt that the world's biggest compost heap will also provide great fodder for a new park, do we hear any support for starting a new distinction—that of, "world's largest dog run," anyone?

Although Staten Island has long been either dissed or ignored and rumors of its secession from the city surface every few years, we were pleasantly surprised to discover some excellent park space—and without a doubt the best beaches anywhere in the New York City area. Staten Island offers several large city parks, clean stretches of beach in the Gateway National Recreation Area, an 18th century colonial village, a beautiful conservation center, and more green space per person than anywhere else in New York City—we think you and your dog may wish to reconsider this suburban island and ante up for the $7 fare across the Verrazano-Narrows Bridge. And that's no rubbish!

Staten Island Greenbelt: In 1984, approximately 2,500 acres were designated as the Greenbelt by the Parks Department. This greenway connects many of the parks in the interior of the island, including Willowbrook Park, La Tourette Golf Course, High Rock Park, and Clove Lakes Park. Considered an oasis within the city, you'll find some sections of these trails better than others; and while we don't have a high opinion of the almost non-existent trail markers, there is enough land here that you can explore a different section on each visit. Leash laws must be followed while in the respective parks, but your dog may roam leash-free on the connecting trails. Maps are available (and needed, if you want to make sense of where you are) through the Staten Island Greenbelt, 200 Nevada Avenue, Staten Island, NY 10306; 718/667-2165.

Gateway National Recreation Area: Created in 1972, this vast 26,000-acre shoreline wilderness is located within three New York City boroughs—Queens, Brooklyn, and Staten Island—and in Monmouth County in northern New Jersey. In Staten Island, it encompasses much of the beachfront along the western side of the island including Miller Field and Great Kills Park. Maps are available at the Visitor Center at Great Kills Park or the Jamaica Bay Wildlife Refuge Visitor Center in Queens. The Center is located off Cross Bay Boulevard near the North Channel Bridge. Call 718/318-4340 for more information.

BULLS HEAD

Parks, Beaches, and Recreation Areas

1 Willowbrook Park 🐾 🐾 🐾

This large park lies in the center of the island and connects with the Staten Island Greenbelt. There are a myriad of woodland trails that lead up and through the hilly terrain. You'll also find a mucky duck pond at the parking entrance. You and your dog will probably enjoy the trail that leads around it, but keep your dog from swimming in it—it's truly only a pond a duck could love. Dogs are permitted off leash before 9 A.M. Located on Morani Street between Victory Boulevard and Richmond Avenue. Open dawn–dusk. 718/390-8020.

Places to Stay

Hilton Garden Inn: This comfortable hotel allows dogs 18 pounds and under, which in our opinion is hardly a dog at all. But if you make the cut, this place is for you. All rooms are clean and spacious and cost $189–249 per night. Dogs are an additional $35 per day. 1100 South Avenue, Staten Island, NY 10314; 718/477-2400; website: www.hiltongardeninn.com.

DONEGAN HILLS

Restaurants

Royal Crown Pane Antico: This Italian restaurant offers a huge menu of subs, hero sandwiches, pizza, Italian entrées, pastries, and gelati to hungry dogs and their companions. With a large outdoor seating area and a friendly wait staff, you and your pup will get the "royal" treatment. 1350 Hylan Boulevard; 718/668-0285.

EGBERTVILLE

Parks, Beaches, and Recreation Areas

2 High Rock Park Conservation Area 🐾 🐾 🐾 🐾

This wonderful conservation area is a treat you'll want to indulge in again and again. Located up a hill (or high rock) in the middle of a residential area, the park offers a glimpse of what Staten Island must have looked like before it became a true "bedroom community." Once you enter the stone gates at the entrance, you'll be immediately transported into a secluded and serene world.

The beautiful, well-tended trails wind through trees and woodlands. Along the way you'll pass over a boardwalk and a pond that is off-limits for swimming but a great spot for bird-watching. It's hard to rave too much about this special place. The delights offered you and your dog are evident on each visit. Our dogs always know when we drive up the steep, winding road leading to the entrance that we are in for a great afternoon.

Dogs must be leashed. Take Rockland Avenue to Nevada Street. Parking area is at the end of the road. The park is open dawn–dusk, but the parking area gates close at 6 P.M. 718/667-2165.

GREAT KILLS

Parks, Beaches, and Recreation Areas

3 Evergreen Park 🐾 🐾

It's hard to get very enthusiastic about this parcel of woods and trails. Set in a residential tract, the only reason to come here is if you live here. The overgrown trails are not well maintained, but they certainly provide local canines and their owners with a walk in the woods.

Dogs are permitted off-leash before 9 A.M. Located between Greaves and Corbin Avenues with entrances on Greaves, Corbin, and Evergreen Avenues. Open dawn–dusk. 718/390-8020.

4 Great Kills Park 🐾 🐾 🐾 🐾

This is simply one of the best parks in this book. Only a $7 toll away from Manhattan, your money will be well spent on a visit here. If you live on Staten

Island, you're even more fortunate because you can come here any time.

In 1860, a man name Crooke purchased the peninsula that now bears his name, Crooke's Point. In 1913, the Army set up a short-lived military post here, and 10 years later New York City purchased both parcels of land to develop into a city park. In 1974, the city offered the land, along with Miller Field in New Dorp Beach (see section below) to the National Park Service as part of the Gateway National Recreation Area.

Today you can fish, swim, and hike through marshlands, dunes, beaches, and oak forest. The color coded nature trails out on Crooke's Point are our favorite. You'll find them easy to traverse and varied in terrain. Best of all, there are miles of beach here, and your dog is free to splash in the surf and run on the sand on all of them—with the exception of the designated swimming beach in the center of the park. There are also woods trails near the park entrance. Maps are available at the ranger station in the center of the park.

Dogs must be leashed. From the Staten Island Expressway, take Hylan Boulevard south for three miles. The park is on the left. Open dawn–dusk. 718/351-6970.

HUGUENOT PARK

Parks, Beaches, and Recreation Areas

5 Blue Heron Pond Park 🐾 🐾 🐢

At press time this park is under construction so it's hard to know what its final incarnation will be. As of the summer 2001, the park consists of woodlands intercut with overgrown trails. If you live nearby, you probably walk your dog here. If not, there is no reason to make a special trip. We'll keep you posted.

Dogs are permitted off-leash before 9 A.M. From the Staten Island Expressway, take Hylan Boulevard south for three miles and turn right onto either Barclay or Poillon Avenues. The park will be on your left or right, respectively. Open dawn–dusk. 718/390-8020.

MIDLAND BEACH

Nature Hikes and Urban Walks

FDR Boardwalk: This boardwalk runs the length of Father Capodanno Boulevard from South Beach to Miller Field. Although your dog can't set paw on the beaches here, and we don't recommend the area around South Beach because of the amusement park–atmosphere, you *can* enjoy a good four-mile seaside walk overlooking the Atlantic Ocean. Your leashed dog will enjoy the many sights and salty smells to be found here. 718/390-8020.

MOUNT LORETTO

Parks, Beaches, and Recreation Areas

6 Mount Loretto Conservation Area 🐾 🐾 🐾 🐾 🐕

This unusual property is owned by the archdiocese at Mount Loretto and managed by the New York State Department of Environmental Conservation. This is a long way of saying that, for the time being, it is open space that you and your dog can enjoy. Located on the site of Saint Elizabeth's Orphanage, which burned down in the late 1980s, this land is now open to the public for hiking, swimming, or chasing sticks through tree-lined paths. There are several miles of hiking trails at this little-known treasure and, best of all, an open beach that you and your dog will have to yourselves. This is a great spot to escape to in any season and, until the state or the church decides otherwise, we recommend you hightail it over here because this park has a flexible leash law: if your dog is under voice control, she may skip the leash.

There is no parking allowed on the property, so you'll have to park either on Hylan Boulevard or Richard Avenue. The entrance is located fight on Hylan Boulevard, between Richard Avenue and Cunningham Road. Open dawn–dusk. 718/482-4900.

NEW DORP BEACH

Parks, Beaches, and Recreation Areas

7 Miller Field 🐾 🐾 🐾 🐾

Also part of the Gateway National Recreation Area, this is another fine property managed by the National Park Service. Built right after World War I as a military airfield, these 187 acres were converted to park space in 1974. As you enter the area, you will see wide, open ball fields—off-limits during the summer months, but great for ball chasing in the "off-season." The best part of this park, however, is the beach access, which you can reach by going past the ball fields and parking at the end of New Dorp Lane. From here you can walk along Cedar Grove Beach all the way to Great Kills Park. Our dogs love visiting here and don't especially care that the beach area isn't white and sandy. If the sand here is a bit dusky, that just means fewer sunbathers and more room for trying to catch the surf.

Dogs must be leashed. From the Staten Island Expressway, take Hylan Boulevard south for 2.75 miles. Turn left onto New Dorp Lane. Parking and the park are on the left. Open dawn–dusk. 718/351-6970.

Restaurants

Trattoria Romano: Italian fare is the cuisine of choice on this island off Manhattan and this friendly family restaurant is one of our favorites. Serving traditional Italian food ranging from eggplant parmesan and lasagna to brick-oven pizza, the owners go out of their way to make you and your pup welcome. Expect kisses for the ladies, exuberant greetings for the gents, and pats and a water bowl for your dog. The atmosphere on busy Hylan Boulevard is less than intimate, but since this is one of the few outdoor restaurants on the entire island, we won't complain. 1476 Hylan Boulevard; 718/980-3113.

PRINCE'S BAY

Parks, Beaches, and Recreation Areas
🐾Lemon Creek Park 🐾 🐾 🐾 🐾

This recently renovated park is a delightful combination between park and open space. In the park section, there are crushed granite paths that weave through the tall grasses of the surrounding marsh area, around the green manicured lawn and to Lemon Creek, which empties into the Atlantic here.

If you want to go to the beach, the paths make their way down to the sand as well. Our dogs like to swim in the saltwater or the freshwater of the creek—both spots offer relief from the hot summer sun. In the winter, the winds can get quite chilly off the ocean, but you'll have the place to yourself. It's a tradeoff, but one worth making. Dogs may be off-leash until 9 A.M.

From the Staten Island Expressway, take Hylan Boulevard south for 3.25 miles. Turn left onto Seguine Avenue to the end of the end of the road and turn right onto Trenton Court. The park is at the end of the road. Open dawn–dusk. 718/390-8020.

🐾Wolfe's Pond Park & Dog Run 🐾 🐾 🐾 🐾 🐕

After a face-lift in 1998, this 341-acre park has something for every canine taste. There's beach access, a lovely freshwater lake, woodland trails, open grassy lawns, and Staten Island's newest (and only) dog run.

In 1992, when winter storms threatened the barrier separating Wolfe's Pond from the ocean, the city constructed a new pond embankment to protect both the beach and the pond. More recently, a new picnic area, landscaping, paths, drainage and lighting systems, and more were installed. The result is a wonderful mix of recreation and natural environment.

The dog run was approved by the city in July 2001 after local dog owners collected 1,200 signatures pleading for an off-leash space. As we go to press, the proposed run is scheduled to open in the summer of 2002 in a previously overgrown corner on the southern side of the park off Cornelia Avenue.

Dogs are allowed throughout the park and you'll find plenty of other canine companions on any weekend afternoon. Dogs are allowed off-leash before 9 A.M. but must be leashed the rest of the day. Leashes are not required in the dog run.

From the Staten Island Expressway, take Hylan Boulevard south for 3.25 miles. Turn left, taking Cornelia Avenue to the end, where you'll find the parking area. Open dawn–dusk. 718/390-8020.

RICHMOND

Nature Hikes and Urban Walks

Historic Richmond Town: Take a walk through this historic town, preserved in its 17th–19th century glory by the Staten Island Historical Society. First established as a village in the 1690s, the 100 acres here include 28 historic buildings, most of which are still located on their original sites. During July and August, visitors can witness daily exhibitions of 18th and 19th century living history. Leashed dogs are allowed on all the walks but cannot enter the buildings. Maps for self-guided tours are available at the Visitor Center at 441 Clarke Avenue. Open Wednesday–Saturday 10 A.M.–5 P.M.; Saturday–Sunday from 1–5 P.M. 718/351-1611.

ROSEBANK

Parks, Beaches, and Recreation Areas

10 Austen House Park 🐾 🐾 🐾 🐾

This historical landmark was once the home of photographer Alice Austen, who lived here until 1945. It is also a wonderful 14-acre park perched on a gentle hill overlooking the New York Harbor. Here you can wander the grounds along the water, take a walk on nearby Buono Beach, or sit on a bench and look at the gorgeous view of Manhattan and the nearby Verrazano-Narrows Bridge. You have your choice of a small waterfront promenade or trails along the restored 1890 farmhouse. Dogs must be leashed at all times here, but we think this site makes for an unusual departure from much of the parkland in New York City. From the State Island Expressway, take Hylan Boulevard east a half mile to the end and Edgewater Street. Open dawn–dusk. 718/390-8020.

SAINT GEORGE

Nature Hikes and Urban Walks

North Shore Esplanade: Walk along the waterfront on this promenade that runs from Jersey Street to Clove Road. You'll have great views of Manhattan, the Statue of Liberty, Ellis Island, and the Staten Island Ferry as it goes back and forth to Battery Park. There are plenty of benches to stop and enjoy the view. 718/390-8020.

High Rock Music: Join the fun at the **summer concert series** held at High Rock Park Conservation Area every Sunday afternoon in July and August. Enjoy a different style of music each week surrounded by the beauty of this natural setting. Concerts start at 2 P.M. Dogs must be leashed. 718/667-2165.

SHORE ACRE

Parks, Beaches, and Recreation Areas

11 Von Briesen Park 🐾 🐾 🐾 🗘

This 12-acre park was once the estate of lawyer Arthur Von Briesen, who provided legal aid to the poor of New York in the early part of this century. In a tongue-in cheek reference to his prominent location across from Manhattan, he referred to his estate as First House on the Left, America.

The city acquired the land in 1949, and today you can walk on three winding paths that lead through shade trees and lovely park benches to views of Manhattan, the Statue of Liberty, and the Verrazano-Narrows Bridge. There is plenty of room for you and your pooch to take a quiet stroll. A recent facelift, including new paths, benches, overlook, and parking area, was completed in July 2001.

Dogs must be leashed after 9 A.M. Located at Bay Street and Wadsworth Avenue. Open dawn–dusk. 718/390-8020.

SOUTH BEACH

Places to Stay

The Harbor House: This 1890 home has lovely views of New York Harbor and the Verrazano-Narrows Bridge. The 10 rooms are comfortable with full amenities included. Pets are allowed on approval and if your dog is large, be prepared to sit up and beg. Rates are $49–110 per night including a continental breakfast. 1 Hylan Boulevard, Staten Island, NY 10305; 718/876-0056 or 800/626-8096; website: www.bestinns.net/usa/ny/harborhouse.html.

STAPLETON

Parks, Beaches, and Recreation Areas

12 Hero Park 🐾 🐾 🗘

This park is a lovely three-acre memorial to the 144 Staten Island soldiers who died in World War I. Perched on a hill overlooking the Silver Lake Reservoir, this graceful park has a single winding trail and 144 trees, one planted in memory of each soldier. If you're looking for a peaceful quiet place to sit or contemplate, you might try this park. If you're looking for a little exercise, we recommend going across the street to Silver Lake Park. Located at the intersection of Victory Boulevard and Louis Street. Open dawn–dusk. 718/390-8020.

SUNNYSIDE

Parks, Beaches, and Recreation Areas

13 Clove Lakes Park 🐾 🐾 🐾 🐾 🐾

This 195-acre park is one of the most beautiful parks on Staten Island. There are miles of trails that criss-cross along three ponds and woodlands. Simply put, you can wander the trails through the woods, or follow the 2.5-mile trail around Clove Lake and never get bored. Our dogs enjoy trying to sneak into the rather murky lake for a dip, running in the meadow, or chasing a squirrel up a tree. Trivia pups will be happy to know that this park is also home to Staten Island's largest living thing, a tulip tree. Rumored to be 107 feet tall and at least 300 years old, it survived the extensive logging of the 19th century. You and your dog will enjoy coming here in all seasons. Located between Clover and Royal Oak Roads and Victory Boulevard. The main entrance is off Clover Road. Open dawn–dusk. 718/390-8020.

14 Silver Lake Park 🐾 🐾 🐾 🐾

This graceful park surrounds the Silver Lake Reservoir, which, unfortunately, is off-limits to you and your dog. But if you can keep your pooch from looking longingly at the clear cool water, you can enjoy walking along the water's edge on well-kept pathways and open lawns. There are plenty of trees to shade your walk and benches along the way. There's even a fountain on the top of the hill along Victory Boulevard that has been known to serve as a stand-in for the reservoir below.

From the Staten Island Expressway, take Clove Road north, turn right onto Victory Boulevard. The park is on the left. Parking available along Victory Boulevard. Open dawn–dusk. 718/390-8020.

TOTTENVILLE

Parks, Beaches, and Recreation Areas

15 Conference House Park 🐾 🐾

This most interesting thing about this park is the meeting that took place here between British Lord Admiral Richard Howe and Benjamin Franklin,

John Adams, and Edward Rutledge on another historic September 11—this one in 1776. Held at the home of British sympathizer Captain Billopp, Lord Howe tried to convince the colonists to end the war peacefully. But Franklin and the others refused and the rest is history. In 1929 the Conference House Association took over operations and has maintained the house since then, in cooperation with the Parks Department and the Historic House Trust of New York City.

The rest of this 226-acre park, which lies at the southern tip of Staten Island across from New Jersey, is a rather scruffy mess of tangled woods and unmarked trails. There is a lot of land here, but little of it is accessible. We suggest you stick to the main section by the Conference House. You can also take a swim from the small beach at the foot of the lawn.

Dogs are to be leashed at all times around the museum. The house itself is off-limits to four-footed visitors. Take Hylan Boulevard to the end and turn right on Satterlee Street. The Conference House is 100 feet on the left. Open dawn–dusk. 718/390-8020.

Restaurants

Ciao Bella: This little Italian café serves up great pasta and northern Italian fare. Best of all, it's located in the heart of Main Street. You and your dog will enjoy dining on linguine and eggplant at the outdoor tables in the summer months. 192 Main Street; 718/966-4434.

TRAVIS

Parks, Beaches, and Recreation Areas
🔟 Schmul Park 🐾 🦮

This scruffy little playground and park have seen better days. With all the great parks in nearby neighborhoods, you'll only visit here out of desperation. We can't believe you'll ever be that desperate.

Dogs must be leashed after 9 A.M. Located at the intersection of Wild and Melvin Avenues. Open dawn–dusk. 718/390-8020.

WOODROW

Places to Stay

Staten Island Hotel: When it comes to hotels, you won't have many choices, so it's lucky that this one is also dog-friendly. There are 189 rooms here, and you and your pup will be comfortable in all of them. Rates are $159–175 per night. 1415 Richmond Avenue, Staten Island, NY 10304; 718/698-5000 or 800/532-3532; website: www.statenislandhotel.com.

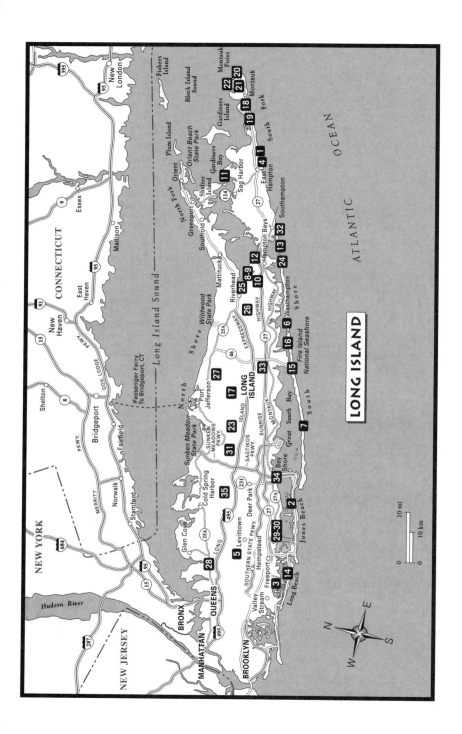

LONG ISLAND

6 LONG ISLAND

Men have had hundreds of years to learn the secret of the sun, which is so simple every dog knows it. A dog knows enough to go lie down in the sun when he feels lazy. . .You will note, too, that a dog never makes the mistake of lying in the hot sun right after a heavy meal. A dog lies in the sun early in the day, after a light breakfast, when the muscles need massaging by the gentle heat and the spirit craves the companionship of warmth, when the bugs crawl on the warm, painted surfaces, and the day settles into the blackberry bushes. That is the whole secret of the sun—to receive it willingly. What more is there to unlock?

—From *Fred on Space,* by E. B. White

Mention Long Island and what comes to mind? Perhaps you think of the daily traffic nightmare on the Long Island Expressway or, better yet, the siren song of the Hamptons? Maybe you weigh the lure of the rocky necks and woodlands of the North Shore against the white sandy beaches of the South Shore? Connoisseurs may relish the upscale wineries while cynics rail against Levittown's cookie-cutter suburban neighborhoods. Or maybe what you're

---

PICK OF THE LITTER–
LONG ISLAND HIGHLIGHTS

BEST BEACHES
Cupsogue Beach County Park, East Moriches

Fire Island National Seashore, Fire Island

Montauk Point State Park, Montauk

Shinnecock West County Park (Ponquogue Beach), Hampton Bays

BEST DOG PARK
West Hills County Park & Dog Run, West Hills

BEST FOREST
Hither Woods, Montauk

BEST RESTAURANTS
Amagansett Farmer's Market, Amagansett

BEST PLACES TO STAY
Capri, Southampton

Inn at Quogue, Quogue

Stearns Point House, Shelter Island

BEST EVENT
Dogs Walk against Cancer, Old Westbury

really thinking is about what time you'll need to leave Manhattan on a Friday afternoon and still make it to Montauk by midnight?

The one thing you probably *don't* think is, "Great place for dogs." But we are here to tell you that there are a surprising number of places to go, things to see, and fun to treasure if your name is Fido, Rover, or Muttley. And speaking of treasure, rumor has it that Gardiner's Island, a private island off the northeastern coast, holds the hidden treasure of Captain Kidd. If only they'd let dogs out there, we're pretty sure they'd dig up that chest in no time!

Although none of the state park or conservation lands on Long Island allow dogs, in Suffolk County *all* of the county parks and many of the town beaches are open to your furry friend—many of them year-round. Even better, East

Hampton has a flexible leash law, which means your dog may be off-leash if under your direct control. In neighboring Nassau County, however, we suspect business is booming for those folks who make the No Dogs Allowed signs; there is an almost complete ban on dogs in most of the city and county parks. In the villages of Great Neck and Manhasset, a dog can't set paw in any park. In the rest of Nassau County all the best trails, beaches, state parks, and county preserves are also off-limits to canines. So to save your pup a little angst and you a little gas money, we list only the few parks in Nassau County that have dog runs. Otherwise, our advice is head for the border. The border of Suffolk County, that is. You'll find all the hot spots for you and your dog there.

One word about how to find your favorite park in this chapter. In both Nassau and Suffolk Counties, smaller villages are clustered under the jurisdiction of larger towns. For example, the *villages* of Amagansett, Montauk, East Hampton, and Wainscott all fall under the township of East Hampton. In order not to confuse you, we've organized the material by village with the township included in parentheses, so that no matter what you decide to call your own corner of the world, you'll still be able to find it. Confused? Think of the words of the Cheshire Cat who said, "No matter where you go, there you are." Just bring a good map.

Green Key Cards: If you are a Suffolk County resident, you should purchase a Green Key Card. It will identify you as a county resident and insure reduced fees for all park activities. Non-residents do not need a Green Key Card to hike in the parks, but if you plan to camp, you must purchase one. Cards can be purchased for $20 at pro shops, major parks, or the administration office; they expire three years from the date of purchase. Non-residents have the option of purchasing a Tourist Reservation Key for $35 at the Parks Administration Office. This card allows access to the golf and camping reservation system on a limited basis and expires on December 31 of the year purchased. For more information, contact the Parks Department at P.O. Box 144, West Sayville, NY 11796; 631/854-4961; website: www.co.suffolk.ny.us.

Fire Island National Seashore: This wonderful beach wilderness provides not only a wild and intoxicating walk along the Atlantic but is also one of the very few beaches where you can take your dog year round. Running 32 miles in four sections from the William Floyd Parkway in Shirley to Robert Moses State Park in West Islip (broken occasionally by developed areas), this untamed area offers you and your dog a chance to swim, walk for uninterrupted miles, view wildlife, and truly get away from it all. Although the Seashore is only an hour away from New York City, it is about as far from the rush of midtown Manhattan as a dog can get. One of the reasons this wilderness area hasn't succumbed to the frantic building of the Hamptons and other vacation spots on Long Island is its location. Simply put, it's hard to get to.

By car, there are two parkways that anchor Fire Island. The Robert Moses Causeway takes you to Robert Moses State Park on the western end, and William Floyd Parkway delivers you to Smith Point Park on the eastern end. In between, you must take a ferry from Patchogue, Bay Shore, or Sayville. And although dogs are allowed in Smith Point Park, they aren't allowed in Robert Moses State Park. Parking is allowed, however, at Field 5 where you may leave your car and then hike a mile on the road to the Fire Island Lighthouse and enter the seashore from there.

Needless to say, this limited access has kept miles of seashore preserved, protected, and in its natural environment—which is great news for you and your pup. Okay so it's a bit of a hassle, but once you get there, you'll be glad you made the effort. With soft sandy beaches, gentle dunes, marsh grasses, a natural forest, and even a seven-mile wilderness area on the eastern end, a walk here is unlike any other place you've visited.

Dogs must be leashed here at all times. The park hours are 6 A.M.–10 P.M. Maps are available at the Visitor Center at the Otis G. Pike Wilderness Area at the end of William Floyd Parkway or by calling the Visitor Center at 631/597-6183 or the Ranger Station at 631/597-6210.

Pine Barrens Preserve: Long Island is home to the second largest pine barrens preserve in the United States. Located east of Hampton Bays and running between Smithtown and Islip, these 52,000 acres scattered throughout Suffolk County are home to the last remaining pitch pines in New York state. Currently, you must have a permit to hike in the three remaining areas, which are managed by the New York State Department of Environmental Conservation: David A. Sarnoff Preserve, Rocky Point Preserve, and the Navy Co-op Preserve. Sears-Bellow, Flanders, and Hampton County Parks are also protected areas, but are open to the public without permit.

The Pine Barrens Preserve Trail runs 50 miles through the heart of the three protected preserves. Eventually there are plans to extend the trail all the way out to Montauk, but at present the trail is interrupted in large sections. The landscape surrounding the pine barrens is dry and sandy; scrub oaks and low-lying pitch pines will be your only shade. We think the best time for a walk here is in the cooler months. If you do hike here in the summer, make sure you bring water for your pup as there are few natural water spots along the way.

You can pick up trail maps, permits and information at the Trails Information Center on County Road 111, Manorville, NY; 631/369-9768.

AMAGANSETT
(EAST HAMPTON TOWNSHIP)

Parks, Beaches, and Recreation Areas

1 Atlantic Avenue Beach 🐾 🐾 🐾 🐾

Good news for surf hounds! In the summer months between Memorial Day and Labor Day, dogs are permitted on this Atlantic Ocean beach before 10 A.M. and after 6 P.M. The rest of the year you may visit at any time. Although you must avoid the roped-off swimming area, leashed pups are allowed within

---

DIVERSIONS

Ferries for Fido: For many residents, ferries to and from the local islands are everyday transportation, but they can also be a fun activity for your and your favorite canine.

Fire Island ferries: All ferries to the island are seasonal, running between April and October. Leashed dogs are allowed on the Fire Island–Patchogue ferry. For schedules and information, call 631/665-3600; website: www.fireislandferries.com.

To ride to Sunken Forest, check out the Sayville Ferry Service at 631/589-0810; website: www.sayvilleferry.com.

If you want to avoid all the hassle usually reserved for those who want to get away for the weekend, Tommy's Taxis will transport you and your pup from New York City to the Fire Island Ferries in style for a mere $10 per dog. Spaces get filled fast, so reservations are required. Rates are $17 to $20 per person. 631/665-4800.

Port Jefferson Ferry: This shuttle makes a scenic crossing of Long Island Sound to Bridgeport, Connecticut. Leashed dogs are allowed in the outdoor area of the ferry. For schedules, rates, and information, call 631/473-0286.

Orient Point Ferry: Another ferry operates between Orient Point and New London, Connecticut. Leashed dogs are allowed in a crate or on deck. For schedules and information, call 800/443-5281; website: www.longislandferry.com.

Shelter Island Ferry: Take a ride from Sag Harbor to Shelter Island on this small 10-car ferry. The ride is only 8 minutes door-to-door, but the view from either side is wonderful, and your dog will love getting out in the salty air. Reservations not needed. Fare is $7 round-trip. Island ferries are operated by North Ferry Company, 631/749-0139; and South Ferry Inc., 631/749-1200.

---

300 feet on either side of the restricted section. This will give you plenty of running room and our dogs agree: this is a great place to run.

Dogs must be leashed. From the Montauk Highway (Rte. 27), take Atlantic Avenue south three blocks to the end. Parking permits are available at the East Hampton Town Hall. Open dawn–dusk. 631/324-4143.

Restaurants

Amagansett Farmer's Market: This is the best place in town to kick back and absorb a little local color. And we don't mean working on your tan. There are tables and chairs spread all around the several-acre family farm; you and your dog will feel right at home at this family-owned mainstay. Breakfast is the busiest meal of the day at this part grocer, part deli, part coffeehouse. Pick up muffins, eggs cooked to order, or coffee cake and eat them under the shade trees. Or take a sandwich or salad to go from the gourmet deli to your favorite local beach or park. Whatever you're hungry for, you'll be sure to find it here. Main Street (Rte. 27); 631/267-3894.

O'Malley's Saloon: This traditional Irish pub and restaurant, located right in the heart of town, has a lovely outdoor patio that is open during warm weather. You and your pup can dine on fish and chips, fresh seafood and shepherd pie under a canopy of umbrellas and shade trees. 209 Montauk Highway (Rte. 27); 631/324-9010.

Places to Stay

Gansett Green Manor: Situated on two acres of land with gardens and a pond, these lovely cottages all have full kitchens and private entrances. Well-behaved pets are welcome here on approval. Rentals are $150–450 per night. 273 Main Street, Amagansett, NY 11930; 631/267-3133; website: www.gansettgreenmanor.com.

Red Door Guest House: Located right in the heart of town, this historic 1690 house still has its original beam ceilings and country charm. You'll know it by its signature red door. There are six rooms available but not all allow dogs, so make your reservations early. Rates are $100–250 per night. 293 Main Street, Amagansett, NY 11930; 631/267-6694.

AQUEBOGUE (RIVERHEAD TOWNSHIP)

Places to Stay

J & S Reeve Summer Cottages: This small three-cottage complex is located right on quiet Reeve's Creek. Each cottage is equipped with a kitchenette, full amenities, a water view, and shaded porch for whiling away a summer day.

Dogs are welcome. Rates are $189–250 per night. 28 White's Road, Aquebogue, NY 11931; 631/722-4096; website: www.liny-cottages.com.

BABYLON (BABYLON TOWNSHIP)

Parks, Beaches, and Recreation Areas

2 Gilgo State Park 🐾 🐾 🐾 🐾

This undeveloped state park has no official paths or roads—not even any signs to help you find it. Sandwiched between two no-dog zones—Jones Beach and Robert Moses State Park—dogs are only allowed to access the beach via the parking area off Ocean Parkway on the eastbound side. You'll see a sign that says "Restricted Area—permits only." And if you want to park here, you'd better have a four-wheel drive, because the sand is thick and deep. Permits are available through the New York Environmental Protection Agency at 290 Broadway, New York, NY 10007-1866; 212/637-3000; website: www.epa.gov/region02.

If you make it through that gauntlet, you and your dog will enjoy several miles of open, uninterrupted beach. Dogs must be leashed so they won't disturb nesting shore birds along the dunes. From the Robert Moses Causeway, take the Ocean Parkway west about 0.5 miles to the unmarked parking area on your left. Open dawn–dusk. 212/637-3000.

BAY PARK (HEMPSTEAD TOWNSHIP)

Parks, Beaches, and Recreation Areas

3 Bay Park & Dog Run 🐾 🐾 🐕

This beach park has a very uninviting "No Dogs Allowed" sign at the entrance, but this is one sign you can ignore. While it's true that dogs are not allowed on the public swimming beach, there is a small dog run off 1st Avenue—on the far eastern side of the park. The run doesn't offer much more than some room to throw a short ball, but considering there are few other places that will let you set paw on dry land in the area, this run at least offers your pooch a little off-leash action. From Main Street, take Rhame Avenue south six blocks. Turn left onto North Boulevard and proceed one block. The park is on the right. Open dawn–dusk. 516/571-7250.

Restaurants

Dock's Dog House: How can your resist a place with a name like this? This roadside eatery has a shaded patio where you and your dog can eat your sandwich, burger, or fries by the bay. Oh, and yes, they serve hot dogs, too. Located just up the road from Bay Park, we recommend stopping here after a visit to the dog run. 14 Front Street; 516/887-4249.

East Point Inn Café: You and your pup will enjoy eating on the outdoor patio at this café overlooking the bay. Whether you enjoy a salmon Caesar salad or soft-shell crabs, your dog and you will agree that enjoying good food and a view on a warm summer's day is one great way to go. After lunch take a walk over to the dog run at Bay Park. 1 Main Street; 516/599-0044.

DIVERSIONS

Cabernet Canines: Dogs with discriminating tastes will be happy to know that daily tours are available at many of the wineries on Long Island, and well-behaved, leashed dogs are welcome. New York wineries may not have the history of their California cousins, but you won't be disappointed with these Long Island offerings. Your pet will need to be 21 (in people years) to lap a glass of wine, but if you have a dog that old, she deserves a glass. All the wineries have lovely grounds for walks and picnic areas for lunching.

Aquebogue:
Palmer Vineyards, 108 Sound Avenue; 631/722-WINE (631/772-9163); website: www.palmervineyards.com; open daily, 11 A.M.–6 P.M.
Paumanok Vineyards, 1074 Main Road; 631/722-8800; website: www.paumanok.com; open daily, 11 A.M.–5 P.M.

Cutchogue:
Bedell Cellars, County Road 25, Main Road; 631/734-7537; website: www.bedellcellars.com; open daily, 11 A.M.–5 P.M.
Castello di Borghese/Hargrave Vineyard, Rte. 48 and Alvah's Lane; 631/734-5111; website: www.castellowdiborghese.com; open daily, 11 A.M.–6 P.M.
Galluccio Estate/Gristina Vineyards, 24385 Main Road; 631/734-7089; website: www.gristinawines.com; open daily, 11 A.M.–5 P.M.
Peconic Bay Winery, 31320 Main Road; 631/734-7361; website: www.peconicbaywinery.com; open daily, 11 A.M.–5 P.M.

Peconic:
Lenz Vineyard and Winery, Main Road; 631/734-6010, 800/974-9899; website: www.lenzwine.com; open daily, 10 A.M.–6 P.M.
Osprey's Dominion Vineyards, 44075 Main Road; 631/765-6188, 888/295-6188; website: www.ospreysdominion.com; open daily, 11 A.M.–5 P.M.

Greenport Village:
Ternhaven Cellars, 331 Front Street; 631/477-8737; website: www.ternhaven.com; open Tuesday through Sunday, 11 A.M.–6 P.M.

BETHPAGE (OYSTER BAY TOWNSHIP)

Places to Stay

Battle Row Campground: This 44-acre campground offers 31 RV sites and 21 tent sites, all equipped with picnic tables and surrounded by a dense woods. Well-behaved dogs are welcome, and there are plenty of trails to walk along. Reservations are made on a first-come, first-served basis. The campground is open both to residents and non-residents of Nassau County. Nightly rates range from $15 for residents to $20 for non-residents. 321 Claremont Road, Old Bethpage, NY 11804; 516/572-8690.

BRIDGEHAMPTON (SOUTHAMPTON TOWNSHIP)

Restaurants

World Pie: This local gourmet pizza restaurant is as popular for its outdoor patio as it is for its great pizza selections. Pizza offerings include taco (spicy beef, cheese guacamole, and sour cream), Mr. Tang (duck, scallions, goat cheese, and cilantro), and our favorite, the Stevie Cheese which features the house specialty—skamozz (an Italian cheese) and spedini sauce (an anchovy sauce). It's an original. Your taste buds will be as happy as your eyes as you take in the view from your table. Well-behaved dogs welcome. 2402 Montauk Highway (Rte. 27); 631/537-7999.

COPIAGUE (BABYLON TOWNSHIP)

Parks, Beaches, and Recreation Areas

Indian Island County Park

This lovely 275-acre county park offers several hiking trails through the woods and along the water. See the Indian Island County Park in the Riverhead section below for complete information.

EAST HAMPTON (EAST HAMPTON TOWNSHIP)

East Hampton has a flexible leash law—which means your dog may go sans leash as long as she is under your control at all times. And even better, dogs are allowed on all town beaches year round. The rules are listed below.

Before 10 A.M. and after 6 P.M. dogs are allowed to set paw on the town beaches as long as they stay clear of the marked swimming areas. After September and before May, there are no hourly restrictions.

During the summer season, most town beaches require you to display a parking permit, which may be obtained at the town hall on Montauk Highway. Resident passes are $25 per season; non-residents must pay $130 per season. Many local hotels will provide weekend visitors with temporary passes.

Three beaches don't require parking permits on the weekdays: Main Beach, Atlantic Avenue Beach, and Kirk Park. You must display a parking permit on weekends.

Parks, Beaches, and Recreation Areas

4 Main Beach 😺 😺 😺 😺 🐕

This Atlantic Ocean beach is one of the few that doesn't require parking permits during the hectic summer months. Of course that also means it gets very busy. Finding a clear patch of sand becomes a challenge even New Yorkers find daunting. The good news, however, is that the crowds don't start arriving until mid-morning and your pup is allowed here before 10 A.M. and after 6 P.M. We think those are the best times to visit (even if we had a choice).

You must steer clear of the roped-off swimming area, and your dog must be leashed. But we think that's a fair tradeoff. After September, you'll have the place to yourself. From Montauk Highway (Rte. 27) take Indian Well Plain Highway south two blocks to the parking area. Open dawn–dusk. 631/324-4142.

Restaurants

Babette's: Although you might gasp at the price tag for a turkey sandwich ($14.95) or a smoothie ($6), the view from the outdoor eating area on Newtown Lane goes a long way to make you forget the sticker shock. And hey, you're on vacation. Who thinks about money at a time like this? Entrées include seafood, vegetarian, and free-range chicken dishes. 66 Newtown Lane; 631/329-5377.

Barefoot Contessa: Have a craving? You want gourmet entrées, great muffins, or sandwiches? Desserts to die for? Well, luckily, you can find all of the above here. Pick up nearly anything your tummy desires at this well-known specialty food shop and take it to one of the many benches out on Newtown Lane or to the nearest beach, park, or preserve. 46 Newtown Lane; 631/329-6972.

The Spot on Newtown: Just about everything hits the spot here. Especially those outdoor tables where you and your own Spot can stop. Continental cuisine is on the menu, but we think the food is there just so we can sit and enjoy the street scene. 64 Newtown Lane; 631/907-8800.

Turtle Crossing: This gourmet take-out place specializes in Southwestern cooking. Try the BBQ ribs, garlic mashed potatoes, or

George's favorite—the rotisserie chicken. Complete meals, from soup to sorbet, are available to take on a hike or back to your house or hotel. 221 Pantigo Road (Rte. 27); 631/324-7166.

Places to Stay

Accommodations Plus: This rental realty has a few listings that allow dogs. Rentals are available throughout the Hamptons, but they specialize in properties in Easthampton. All rentals include maid service, grocery services and beach passes. Call for more details on their many properties. Rates range from the expensive to the very expensive. 172 Newtown Lane, East Hampton, NY 11937; 631/324-1858.

Bassett House Inn: With a name like this, we knew we were in the right place. This comfortable 1830 country inn is close to the village and town beaches. There are 12 antique-filled rooms and a full breakfast served each morning. Dogs are allowed in the designated smoking rooms for an additional $5 fee. Rates are $155–225. 128 Montauk Highway, East Hampton, NY 11937; 631/324-6127; www.bassetthouseinn.com.

Bend in the Road Guest House: This farmhouse set on 20 acres offers a jogging path, a dog-friendly swimming pool, and two rooms with private baths, refrigerators, and king-sized beds. Located close to town and the beaches, the rates are $100–175 per night. 58 Spring Close Highway, East Hampton, NY 11937; 631/324-4592; website: www.bendintheroadguesthouse.com.

The Dutch Motel and Cottages: This comfortable motel, located just outside of town, is clean and convenient and best of all, it allows pets. For an additional charge of $10 per night, dogs up to 25 pounds may stay here with their owners. One pet allowed per room. Rates are $65–250 per night. 488 Montauk Highway, East Hampton, NY11937; 631/324-4550; website: www.thedutchmotel.com.

East Hampton Point Resort: This luxury hotel allows pets in its one- and two-bedroom cottages. All the cottages have full kitchens, living areas, porches, and French doors that look out onto the marina. Weekly rentals are given reservation preference in the summer season. Rates are $100–475 per night. 295 Three Mile Harbor Road, East Hampton, NY 11937; 631/324-9191; website: www.easthamptonpoint.com.

The Pink House: This 19th century pink colonial house is also a gracious bed and breakfast that welcomes "friendly" dogs. (Translation: Dogs on approval only.) Each of the five rooms is unique and tastefully decorated. A full breakfast is made to order each morning. With service like this, you and your pup will definitely be in the pink! Rates are $175–450. 26 James Lane, East Hampton, NY 11937; 631/324-3400; website: www.travelguides.com/inns.

Rose Inn: Several private rooms are available in this quaint guesthouse. You'll find the owners very dog friendly and will make you and your pet feel welcome. They'll also furnish beach passes and chairs for the resident-only beaches in the summer. Rates are $85–125. 6 Clinton Street, East Hampton, NY 11937; 631/324-4181.

EAST MARION (RIVERHEAD TOWNSHIP)

Places to Stay

Blue Dolphin Motel: This standard 29-room motel isn't fancy, but the rooms are clean and offer refrigerators and small kitchenettes in each room. You can walk to the beach and, best of all, dogs of all sizes are welcome on prior approval. Rates are $85–125 per night. Open seasonally May–October. 7850 Main Road, East Marion, NY 11939; 631/477-0907.

EAST MEADOW (HEMPSTEAD TOWNSHIP)

Parks, Beaches, and Recreation Areas

5 Eisenhower Park 🐾 🐾

Although this is the largest town park in the county, you must be a Nassau County resident to use it. So if you live here, you may bring your leashed dog here for a walk. If you don't, you're out of luck. The park offers picnic areas, ball fields, and outdoor concerts, but only a few places for your dog to wander. From the Meadowbrook State Parkway, take Merrick Avenue north for 0.25 miles to the Stewart Avenue intersection. The park entrance is at the end of Stewart Avenue, on the right. Open dawn–dusk. 516/572-0348.

EAST MORICHES (BROOKHAVEN TOWNSHIP)

Parks, Beaches, and Recreation Areas

6 Cupsogue Beach County Park 🐾 🐾 🐾 🐾

This beach park seems like a small miracle. Located on prime real estate at the tip of Westhampton's barrier dunes you'll think it must be divine intervention when you discover dogs are actually allowed here all year. Okay, so it's true they must be leashed, but hey, just to be allowed on the sand seems like somebody up there must like dogs.

Covering 296 acres, this beautiful beach offers plenty of walking opportunities, and in summer the water dogs will thank you for the chance to swim. All dogs must stay clear of the supervised swimming area, however.

Make your way to the path on the western side of the parking area and from there, you're home free!

There is limited beach camping available for trailers and campers (no tents) May–September. Reservations are recommended, and you must have a Green Key Card. Sites are $15–24 per day. For reservations, call 631/244-7275.

Dogs must be leashed at all times in the park and camping areas. From Montauk Highway (Rte. 27A), take Jessup Lane south over the bridge. Turn right onto Dune Road to the end and the park. There is an $8 parking charge May–September. Open dawn–dusk. 631/852-8111

Places to Stay

Cupsogue Beach County Park Campground: See Cupsogue Beach County Park above.

FARMINGVILLE (BROOKHAVEN TOWNSHIP)

Nature Hikes and Urban Walks

Suffolk County Vietnam Veterans Memorial Park: Your dog won't get much exercise here, but if you are looking for a spectacular view of Long Island, this memorial site is probably worth a visit. Perched on top of Bald Hill, one of the highest points on Long Island, you'll find an unobstructed view of the surrounding area for miles and miles in all directions. Your dog may not give two sniffs for the view, but she'll probably enjoy the ocean breezes. From the Long Island Expressway, take Exit 63 to North Ocean Avenue (Rte. 83) north. Follow signs to the parking area. 631/854-4949.

FIRE ISLAND

This elusively exclusive enclave is the choice of New Yorkers who want a different kind of experience than the Hamptons offer. With funky little bungalows for lodging and weather-beaten storefronts and restaurants, a visit here offers rustic charm and natural beauty.

Most of Fire Island is national seashore with the exception of a few commercial areas. To reach the retail district of Ocean Beach, you must take a seasonal ferry from Bay Shore. Everything is within walking distance of the ferry, and you'll find most of your eating establishments along Bay Walk, which runs parallel to the dunes and Atlantic Ocean. Don't worry about directions. Once you get there, everything is easy to find. The ferries run seasonally April–October.

Kids on Parade: Join the fun along Bay Walk for the annual **Labor Day Kid's Parade.** Families and children dress in crazy costumes as Ocean Beach residents celebrate the end of summer. Food, fun, and festivities abound. Dogs welcome to parade in costume or au naturel. Leashes required. 212/929-6415.

Parks, Beaches, and Recreation Areas

7 Fire Island National Seashore—Watch Hill 😊 😊 😊 😊

In Patchogue, you can take a ferry to Watch Hill where you'll find a boardwalk nature trail that loops across salt marsh, maritime forest, and over dunes rising to 40 feet or more. This section was designated a national wilderness in 1980 and the wildlife has prospered because of it. On a recent visit here George and JoAnna observed a doe and her fawn wander through low-lying shrubs not 50 feet away. For this reason, your dog must be leashed, no matter the temptation to release her.

There are 150 tent sites located along the dunes in Watch Hill. Rates are $20 per day, but where else can you get beachfront property for that price? For reservations call 800/365-2267.

Take the Patchogue ferry from Beach Avenue and once on Fire Island, walk east three blocks to Watch Hill. Open 6 A.M.–10 P.M. 631/289-4810.

See the Mastic Beach section below for information on Otis G. Pike Wilderness section of the Fire Island National Seashore, the only designated wilderness area in the New York City vicinity.

Nature Hikes and Urban Walks

Fire Island National Seashore—Sunken Forest: This 1.5-mile boardwalk runs through a 300-year-old holly forest. Because the "forest" is nestled among the dunes, at points it actually appears lower than the towering sand, hence the name: sunken forest.

There are many informative signposts along the way. Dogs must be leashed, and all walkers (two- and four-legged) are to stay on the wooden boardwalk at all times. The boardwalk is located on the western end of Bay Walk. Signs will lead you there. 631/289-4810.

Restaurants

The restaurants in the Ocean Beach section of Fire Island come and go with the seasons, so what's here one year may be gone the next. All of the restaurants listed below are mainstays, but don't hold us to anything. Also, there are many outdoor establishments that will allow you to sit and sup, and most of them are dog-friendly. Just use our suggestions as a first-time guide while you discover your own favorite hangouts. Most of the Fire Island establishments are open seasonally April–October.

The Mermaid Market: When you and your dog are looking to enjoy a gourmet picnic on the beach, you can do no better than making a stop first at The Mermaid Market. This nifty deli/bakery/coffee house located right in the center of Ocean Beach serves up delicacies for the most finicky of appetites. Choices include smoothies, vegetarian sandwiches and entrees, prepared chicken, seafood, and pasta dishes, pastries, and great coffee. Take your Neptune-worthy feast to the beach or enjoy it at any of the benches along Bay Walk. If you prefer to dine without the walk, the Island Mermaid Restaurant next door allows pups to dine al fresco on their deck during off-peak hours. Both establishments are located at 780 Bay Walk; 631/583-0303.

Rachel's Bakery and Restaurant: Grab a cup of coffee and a pastry-to-die-for at this Ocean Beach mainstay. You and your dog can sit at the outdoor tables or take it to go. Join the locals and other regulars at this anything-but-regular bakery. 325 Bay Walk; 631/583-5953.

Maguire's Bay Front Restaurant: For great seafood, salads, and chowder, with an even better view of the beach and dunes from the outdoor deck, stop by this popular beachfront restaurant. You and your dog will be sitting pretty by the bay. 1 Bay Walk; 631/583-8800.

Places to Stay

Clegg's Hotel: This quaint seaside hotel right in the heart of Fire Island allows dogs in its studio apartments. Believe us when we tell you that the rooms disappear as quickly as ice cream in summer. So make your reservations well in advance and enjoy your summer home away from home. Rates are $125–450 per night. 478 Bayberry Walk, Ocean Beach, NY 11770; 631/583-5399.

Dune Point Fire Island Rentals: Studio and full-sized apartments are available at this condominium complex. All units have kitchenettes, private terraces, and access to a private waterfront beach. Short-term and long-term stays are available. Dogs are welcome. Rates are $450–2,400 per week. Lewis Walk, Cherry Grove, NY 11770; 631/597-6261.

The Season's Bed and Breakfast: This lovely bed and breakfast welcomes well-behaved pups in the small efficiency apartments on the property that are just steps away from the beach and all the action. Vacancies are rare, so make sure you call well in advance. Rates are $130–400 per night. 468 Denhoff Walk, Ocean Beach, NY 11770; 631/583-8295.

Watch Hill Campground: See the Fire Island National Seashore—Watch Hill section above.

FLANDERS (SOUTHAMPTON TOWNSHIP)

Parks, Beaches, and Recreation Areas

🔢 Flanders County Parkland 🐾 🐾 🐾

This small county park is located on the western side of Flanders Bay. The most rustic of the parks clustered along the bay (including Hubbard, Sears-Bellow, and Indian Island County Parks), this Pine Barrens Preserve has a series of access roads that lead down to Flanders Bay from Rte. 24. We can't rave about this park because there is no parking area and no real trails. It offers quiet and water access—and you'll have it to yourself most days.

Park along the turnouts on Rte. 24 and walk down the sand-covered service road. When you come to the deserted green service buildings, continue past them to the bay for a marshy dip in the water. This is also a great place to bird-watch, so be sure to bring your binoculars.

From Sunrise Highway (Rte. 27), take Exit 64 to Pleasure Drive north for about 1.5 miles to the end. Right onto Flanders Road for a mile. The service road and entrance is on the left between Birch Avenue and Birch Creek Road. Open 8 A.M.–dusk. 631/854-4949.

🔢 Hubbard County Park 🐾 🐾 🐾

This out of the way park, hugging the southern shores of Flanders Bay, is a wetlands surrounded by one of the last remaining pine barrens forests on the East Coast. Privately owned and used as a hunting area since the 1890s by wealthy New Yorkers such as E. F. Hutton, the area became a county park in 1974 and was designated as part of the Pine Barrens Preserve in 1995.

Today you can walk along sandy trails that lead through a desolately beautiful pine forest and through marshy wetlands out to Flanders Bay. Black Duck Lodge, Hutton's hunting lodge, is located at the parking area, and you'll see the remains of concrete duck blinds and other reminders of the park's hunting era as you wander the trails. You'll also find several marshy ponds that were created by duck hunters who altered the water flow in Hubbard Creek.

There isn't much room for swimming here unless you don't mind a muddy, mucky dog for the drive home, and you should definitely bring the bug spray in the summer months. But if you're looking for an unusual park with a bit of history, this is a great place to visit. Maps are available at the Sears-Bellow County Park headquarters (see below). Dogs must be leashed.

From Sunrise Highway (Rte. 27), take Exit 65 to Rte. 24 west for one mile. Turn right onto Red Creek Road and take an immediate left into the park entrance access road. This entrance is only open 8 A.M.–4 P.M.; if you visit the park later, you can park along Red Creek or Upper Red Creek Roads. Open 8 A.M.–dusk. 631/854-4949.

DIVERSIONS

Row, Row, Row Your Boat: Enjoy a leisurely row on the pond with your pup. Rowboat rentals are available at several Long Island parks, typically on a first-come, first-served basis.

Stump Pond in Blydenburgh County Park off Veterans Memorial Highway from May to September. Rates range from $10 for an hour to $18 per day. 631/854-3713.

Alewife Pond in Cedar Point Park, Alewife Brook Road, Flanders. Rates range from $20 per hour to $65 for a full day. 631/852-7620

Bellows Pond in Sears-Bellows County Park. Bellows Pond Road, Flanders. Rates range from $10 for an hour to $18 per day. 631/854-1422

Southaven County Park in Southampton along the Carmens River. Rates are $20–65 for an hour or a day. 631/854-1414.

⑩ Sears-Bellows County Park 🐾 🐾 🐾

This Pine Barrens Preserve has a series of trails that weave throughout its 979 acres. There are several small ponds scattered throughout—the largest are Bellows Pond at the park entrance and Sears Pond in the western section. Both have excellent swimming and a protected beach. If you take the trail that leads from one to the other, you will also pass Division, Little House, and Bog House Ponds. Maps are available at the entrance to help guide you.

Sears-Bellows County Park is also home to the Big Duck, which is reputed to be Long Island's most famous landmark. In 1931, a Riverhead duck farmer named Martin Maurer built this 20-foot-tall concrete duck and sold eggs from its belly. Its eyes, which glow red at night, were taken from a Model T Ford. We can't say it's art, but it is unusual, so check it out. Frankly, the only interest our dogs showed was to sniff it suspiciously and start to lift their legs, but we trust that others may respond with a bit more enthusiasm.

There is a network of bridle trails throughout the park, but these are for horses only.

Camping is available here during the summer. There are 70 tent and trailer sites, all with water and electric hookups. Rates are $16–23 per night. Reservations are recommended, and dogs must be leashed in the campground and park. For reservations, call 631/852-8290. From Sunrise Highway (Rte. 27), take Exit 65 to Rte. 24 west for about 0.5 miles. Turn left onto Bellows Pond Road. The park entrance will be on your right. 631/854-1422.

Places to Stay

Sears-Bellows County Park Campground: See Sears-Bellows County Park listing above.

GARDEN CITY (HEMPSTEAD TOWNSHIP)

Places to Stay

Garden City Hotel: This full-service hotel offers all the amenities for you and a friendly welcome for your dog. Each room has a refrigerator, some are equipped with Jacuzzis, and room service is available. A health club and restaurant are also on site. Dogs under 30 pounds get a free pass, but large dogs are only allowed on approval and there's a $50 fee per day. Rooms are $175–500 per night. 45 7th Street, Garden City, NY 11530; 516/747-3000 or 800/547-0400; website: www.gchotel.com.

GRACE ESTATE (EAST HAMPTON TOWNSHIP)

Parks, Beaches, and Recreation Areas

11 Cedar Point Park 🐾 🐾 🐾

When the days are hot, the Hamptons are crowded, and you and your dog can't set paw on any of the town beaches except after hours, seek a little relief at Cedar Point. Not only will you find seclusion, woodland trails, and a great beach, but you'll also enjoy fabulous views of Sag Harbor, Shelter Island, and Long Island Sound. This underused little park is located on a peninsula that was once the entrance to Sag Harbor. The Cedar Point Lighthouse, built in 1860, once stood on an island 200 yards from shore, but the Great Hurricane of 1938 rearranged the shoreline so you can now walk out to the lighthouse on a narrow strip of sand.

Water dogs can take a swim in Alewife Pond, a saltwater estuary near the entrance of the park that leads to the sound. Or you can enjoy a walk through the pine trees as you head for the beaches on the northern side of the park. Dogs are not allowed at the protected swimming beach but can romp beyond the barriers on either side. A hike all the way out to Cedar Point is definitely recommended for the glorious view.

Camping is available here. Rates are $16–23 per night. For camping reservations call 631/244-7275.

Dogs must be leashed in the park and campground. From Montauk Highway (Rte. 27) in East Hampton, take Stephen Hands Path north for a mile. Left onto Old Northwest Road for two miles. Left onto Alewife Brook

Holy Hounds: Take your dog to church with you. At least on the second Sunday in February you can. For that's the day that All Saints Church salutes mixed breed and rescued dogs at the **Bark-Minster Dog Show and Service.** (George and Inu, are you listening?) Well-behaved dogs of all breeds, mixed or otherwise, will receive special blessings, win prizes and awards, compete in contests, and generally experience a little heaven on earth. The service starts at 10:30 A.M. at All Saints Church, 855 Middle Neck Road. For more information, call 516/482-5392.

Road. The park entrance is nearly 100 yards down the road. Open dawn–dusk, except in the campground. 631/852-7620.

Places to Stay

Cedar Point Park Campground: See the Cedar Point Park listing above.

GREAT NECK (NORTH HEMPSTEAD TOWNSHIP)

Places to Stay

Inn at Great Neck: Okay we know this is weird. There are *no* parks that allow dogs to set paw within any of this city's parks, yet here is a lovely inn that allows pets. But beggars can't be choosers, so who are we to complain? Stay at this stately inn and drive across the county line to walk your dog at West Hills County Park (see the West Hills section). The 85 rooms are pure luxury with an Art Deco theme. Pets can stay by offering a refundable $200 deposit. Rates are $185–350. 30 Cutter Road, Great Neck, NY 11021; 516/773-2000; website: www.innatgreatneck.com.

GREENPORT (SOUTHOLD TOWNSHIP)

Restaurants

Claudio's Crabby Jerry's: Sit on the wharf and watch the world go by with some of the best take-out seafood around. Claudio's self-serve restaurant offers fish and chips, clams, and a raw bar in a casual atmosphere. Your dog will enjoy picking up the leftovers as he sits next to you at the café tables outdoors. Main Street Wharf; 631/477-8252.

HAMPTON BAYS (SOUTHAMPTON TOWNSHIP)

Parks, Beaches, and Recreation Areas

12 Meschutt Beach County Park 🐾 🐾

This beach park allows leashed dogs as long as you stay clear of the designated swimming area. Located on Great Peconic Bay, this is a very small slice of beach so you won't get a great walk in—but if you're looking for some water action, your dog will be a happy camper here.

And while we're on the subject, camping is available (no tents). Rates are $16–23, and you must obtain a Green Key Card. Reservations can be made by calling 631/852-8205.

EARMARK YOUR CALENDAR–SUMMER

The Sound of Music: They don't call it a sound for nothing. Several outdoor summer concert series are available on Long Island. Non-singing dogs are welcome (the entertainers hate the competition!). Bring a blanket or chair, pack some snacks for both humans and canines, and enjoy a musical night under the stars.

Friday Night Blues: Be nothin' but a hound dog every Friday night at 7 P.M. From June to August you and your dog can sing the blues on the grounds of the East End Arts Council at 133 East Main Street, Riverhead. For dates and information, call 631/727-1215.

Sunday Singers: Join the fun at the free Sunday concerts on the Stonybrook Village Green in Brookhaven township each Sunday evening in July and August. Entertainment ranges from Dixieland to disco and Broadway to big band. For dates and schedules, call 631/751-2244.

Concerto Charlie: Discriminating dogs will enjoy the elegant setting and musical fare offered at Lake Agawam Park in the center of Southampton Village. Every Tuesday evening in July and August, you and your dog can join the crowds on the lawn here for a summer concert sponsored by the Cultural and Civic Center of Southampton. The music varies from Big Band to orchestral. Festivities begin at 8 P.M. 631/283-0402.

Song of the Sirens: Come on down to the Village Green in the center of Westhampton for the Concerts By The Sea. The musical concerts are sponsored by the Westhampton Cultural Consortium. Concerts begin at 7:30 every Thursday night in July and August. 631/288-3337.

Dogs must be leashed throughout the park.

From Sunrise Highway (Rte. 27), take Exit 66 to Canal Road north for a quarter mile to the park entrance. Open 8 A.M.–dusk. 631/728-4099.

13 Shinnecock West County Park—Ponquogue Beach 🐾 🐾 🐾 🐾

Shinnecock West County Park is made up of two beaches in two separate towns: Ponquogue Beach in Hampton Bays and Tiana Beach in Quogue. Here in Hampton Bays, this beautiful stretch of beach is the highlight of any visit. Although dogs are banned during the summer months, the town of Southampton passed an ordinance in September 2001 that allows dogs on the beach October 1–March 15. So bring your shades, sunblock, pail, and shovel and head for the sand. Think of it this way—you may be out there with icicles on your tail, but you'll have it to yourself!

From Montauk Highway, take East Tiana Road south about a mile. Turn right on Lynn Avenue and cross the Ponquogue Bridge to the park. Open dawn–dusk. 631/283-6011.

Places to Stay

Bowen's by the Bays: Dogs are allowed with advance approval in the seven quaint cottages at this lovely country inn. Located on 3.5 country acres, the inn is close to the beaches and town and all the cottages have fully-equipped kitchens. Rates are $99–250 per night. There is a pet fee of $7 per night or $35 per week. 177 West Montauk Highway (Rte. 27), Hampton Bays, NY 11946; 631/728-1158 or 800/533-3139.

Meschutt Beach County Park: See listing above.

HAUPPAUGE (ISLIP TOWNSHIP)

Places to Stay

Wyndham Windwatch Hotel and Hamlet Golf Club: Located near several beaches, this 360-room, full-service hotel allows pets under 40 pounds. Rates are $129–230 per night with an additional $50 fee per pet, per week. 1717 Motor Parkway, Hauppauge, NY 11788; 631/232-9800 or 800/WYNDHAM (800/996-3426); website: www.wyndham.com/newyork.

HUNTINGTON STATION (HUNTINGTON TOWNSHIP)

Places to Stay

Huntington Country Inn: This resort-style hotel offers a wide variety of rooms and amenities. There are suites, rooms with Jacuzzis, and large "executive-style" rooms. All rooms have coffeemakers, CD players, and other luxuries. Dogs of all sizes are welcome with advance notice. Rates are $140–160 per night. No extra fee for Fido. 270 West Jericho Turnpike, Huntington Station, NY 11746; 631/421-3900 or 800/739-5777; website: www.huntingtoncountryinn.com.

LIDO BEACH (HEMPSTEAD TOWNSHIP)

Parks, Beaches, and Recreation Areas

14 Nassau Beach Park & Dog Run 🐾 🐾 🐾 🐕

This small beach park on the Atlantic Ocean is the only beach in Nassau County that allows dogs. That's because there is a pleasant little dog run on the western side of the parking area. Located on the sandy dunes, your dog can kick up some sand while socializing with her friends—even in the summer months. We can't say this is entirely satisfactory, considering your pup still can't set paw on the sand and the surf of the main beach, but in this dog park–starved county, this is as good as it gets.

In the summer months, there is a stiff parking fee of $6 for residents and $17 for non-residents. Fortunately most of the attendants will wave you through if you tell them you're going to the dog area. Parking is free September 15–Memorial Day.

Camping is also available—for residents of Nassau County and their guests only. Leashed dogs are welcome if under control at all times. Reservations must be made in person, and are available on a first-come, first-served basis. Tent and RV sites available. Rates are $10–20 per person. From Sunrise Highway (Rte. 27), take Long Beach Road south, and turn left onto Lido Boulevard. In about two miles, the park will be on your right. Open dawn–dusk. 516/571-7700.

Places to Stay

Nassau Beach Campground: See Nassau Beach Park listing above.

MANORVILLE (BROOKHAVEN TOWNSHIP)

Nature Hikes and Urban Walks

Pine Barrens Preserve Trail Information Center: This comprehensive visitors center will provide you with a history of this area and a glimpse of what much of Long Island looked like before rampant development destroyed most of the pitch pines in the second half of the 20th century. Located near several trailheads in the Pine Barrens Preserve, you can pick up a permit, trail maps, directions, and brochures here. The short, interpretive

Blueberry Loop trail will give you a sample of your experience out on these trails. Dogs are allowed on all the trails here, and on the grounds of the Center, but not inside the Center. The center is open Friday–Monday, May–October. County Road 111; 631/369-9768.

MASTIC BEACH (BROOKHAVEN TOWNSHIP)

Parks, Beaches, and Recreation Areas

15 Fire Island National Seashore—Otis G. Pike Wilderness 🐾 🐾 🐾 🐾

This fantastic seven-mile stretch of beach is the only designated wilderness area in the New York City vicinity. Just think of it. In a city of millions, you are only a little more than an hour away from the wilderness. We're pretty sure that our dogs think about it every day.

With 1,300 acres to explore along dunes, marshes, and grasslands, you'll feel like you've been cast up on some deserted island. Only you and your pup, alone in all the world. Although it's a hike to get here (you must drive all the way to the eastern end of Fire Island National Seashore), if you have a day or a weekend to visit, we can guarantee you won't be disappointed.

The wilderness area runs from Smith Point County Park (where you'll need to park your car) all the way to Watch Hill. Along the way you'll be certain to see plenty of wildlife—deer, fox, and shorebirds are some of the common animals you'll be likely to spot. So, out of respect for this pristine area, make sure you keep your own Spot on-leash. From the Long Island Expressway (I-495), take Exit 68 to the William Floyd Parkway south all the way to the end at Fire Island. Open 6 A.M.–10 P.M. 631/289-4810.

16 Smith Point County Park 🐾 🐾 🐾 🐾

Smith Point is Suffolk County's largest beachfront park, and your dog will thank you for bringing him here. Covering five miles along the Atlantic Ocean on the eastern end of Fire Island, this is one of our favorite places to make an escape from the hustle and bustle of city life. Best of all, you can visit in any season.

You can swim, sniff, and really kick up some sand. The long beach offers a great place to stretch your legs, although you must avoid the main swimming beach from June through September. There are dune trails as well, but you must keep your dog leashed and away from the protected nesting areas.

In the winter, the winds can be fierce, but we find we usually have the place to ourselves. If you're looking for a long solitary walk with your dog, you can find no more beautiful spot than here.

Maps are available at the entrance on request. Dogs must be leashed on the beach and in the campground.

May–September, there are 75 campsites available for trailers and campers (no tents). Sites are $15–24 and you must apply for a Green Key Card. For reservations, call 631/244-7275. From the Long Island Expressway (I-495), take Exit 68 to the William Floyd Parkway south all the way to the end at Fire Island. Open dawn–dusk, except at the camping area. 631/852-1313.

Places to Stay

Smith Point County Park Camping: See the Smith Point County Park listing above.

MIDDLE ISLAND (BROOKHAVEN TOWNSHIP)

Parks, Beaches, and Recreation Areas

🐾17 Cathedral Pines County Park 🐾 🐾 🐾 ⤚

This 320-acre park runs along the Carmans River, offering plenty of places to wander through the pitch pines or take a dip with your pup. Although most of this park is developed with camping sites and picnic areas, there is also a dog run where you can let your dog go leashless. Just a small enclosed area, the run is mostly for camping guests and their pups, but locals occasionally use it, too.

We like this park for the water access and the hiking in nearby Prosser Pines Nature Preserve, which features a stand of white pines planted in 1812. From here you can add on to your hike for another eight miles into the Pine Barrens Preserve.

There are 100 camping sites, all with water and electric hookups. Nightly fees are $15 for Green Key Card holders, $24 for non-residents.

On weekends there is a day-use fee of $2 for Green Key Card holders and $4 for everyone else. Dogs must be leashed at all times. From the Long Island Expressway (I-495) take Exit 66 to Sills Road north, turn left onto Yaphank Road. The park is on your left. Open dawn–dusk, except in the camping area. 631/852-5500.

Places to Stay

Cathedral Pines County Park: See listing above.

MONTAUK (EAST HAMPTON TOWNSHIP)

Parks, Beaches, and Recreation Areas

🔢18 Ditch Plains Beach 🐾 🐾 🐾 🐕

During the summer, your dog is allowed on this Atlantic Ocean Beach before 10 A.M. and after 6 P.M. Dogs may be off-leash if under voice command. They must stay 300 feet on either side of the protected swimming area. Resident parking permits are required and are available at the town hall. From Montauk Highway (Rte. 27), take Seaside Avenue south two blocks to the end, where you'll find the parking area. Open dawn–dusk. 631/324-4142.

🔢19 Hither Woods Preserve 🐾 🐾 🐾 🐾

Although dogs are not allowed at Hither Hills State Park, this slice of woodland is jointly managed by the town of East Hampton, Suffolk County, and the state of New York. This is a long-winded way of saying that the usual state park rules don't apply and that dogs are allowed on the trails here. And what great news that is! This is one of the most pleasurable and scenic walks you'll find at the tip of Long Island.

Park at the Hither Hills Overlook at Petticoat Hill and take the Serpent's Back Trail into the preserve. The trails are well marked, and there is a map board (and, occasionally, free maps) to help guide you. From this trail you can head all the way down to Block Island Sound by way of the Stephen Talkhouse Trail, which runs parallel to the shore for several miles. Along the way, a low-lying scrub forest, some scenic overlooks, and plenty of seclusion will surround you.

If you really want to make a day of it, you can also enter Theodore Roosevelt County Park (listed below) from here. Take the Serpent's Back Trail to Flaggy Hole Road and into the preserve. The only fresh water available for swimming is Fresh Pond (located along the Stephen Talkhouse Trail), so be sure to bring drinking water with you on a hot day. There isn't much shade on this walk, and the heat can be brutal for both you and your dog in the summer.

Dogs must be leashed. From Montauk Highway (Rte. 27) just east of the turnout for Old Montauk Highway, go about 0.5 miles, and turn left into the parking area. Open dawn–dusk. 631/668-2461.

🔢20 Montauk Point State Park 🐾 🐾 🐾

Dogs are not allowed in any state parks on Long Island, but an exception is made here in the undeveloped sections on the western end that abut Theodore Roosevelt County Park (see listing below). From the parking area at the end of Montauk Point, go to the left of the gift shop and restaurant. There are signs to point you to the fire roads that will take you down to the water's edge; from here you can wander for several miles along Block Island Sound, take a swim, or just take in the view.

Our dogs think they are definitely getting away with something when we visit here—we enjoy it so much, it seems like it must be illegal. Fortunately, you are welcome here—but in order to continue this privilege, make sure you are respectful of this natural area and always clean up after your dog!

Dogs must be leashed. There is a parking fee of $5, 8 A.M.–4 P.M. From Montauk Highway (Rte. 27), take Old Montauk Highway all the way to the end. The parking area is on your left. Open 8 A.M.–dusk. 631/668-2461.

21 Outer Beach Park 🐾 🐾 🐾 ⋙

Dogs are allowed at this small barrier beach before 10 A.M. and after 6 P.M. as long as they stay 300 feet away from the protected swimming area on both sides. The beach isn't large, but our dogs get their exercise in a straight line as they follow the path of a tennis ball directly out into Block Island Sound. Due to the flexible leash law, dogs under voice command may go leash-free. From Montauk Highway (Rte. 27), take East Lake Drive north to the end. Parking is for residents only in the summer months. Permits are available at the town hall. Open sunrise–sunset. 631/324-4142.

22 Theodore Roosevelt County Park (formerly Montauk County Park) 🐾 🐾 🐾 🐾 44 ⋙

Nestled between the Hither Hills and Montauk Point State Parks, this county-managed preserve offers relief from those No Dogs Allowed signs. And what a relief it is! This wonderful county park offers over 800 acres of woodsy nature trails, ponds, rolling hills, open meadows, and outer beach access. And there's more than enough room to make you feel you have the place to yourself—even during the busy summer months.

This park is as historic as it is beautiful. In 1898, Teddy Roosevelt and the Rough Riders, along with 28,000 other soldiers, were quarantined here after their victory in the Spanish-American War. You can see where they stayed at the Third House, located in the middle of the park.

There are two ways to access the park. The main entrance is located off Montauk Highway. This is the most developed area of the park: horse stables and riding trails, picnic areas, and campgrounds all cluster close to the entrance and you must keep an eye on your dog around the horses.

The other entrance off East Lake Drive has more immediate access to the three nature trails: the Blue Trail, the Green Trail, and the Brown Trail. The Brown Trail is the longest loop at 1.3 miles. Follow this path to Oyster Pond and the edge of Montauk Point State Park. The mile-long Blue Trail leads to Big Reed Pond, where your dog can take a dip or two. Continue on from a side trail at the pond to the beach about 0.5 miles farther. The Green Trail is a loop connecting to both the Blue and the Brown Trail.

There is a map board at the trailhead to help you find your way or you can pick up trail maps at the park entrance.

Camping huts are available and provide a rustic, beautiful setting for you and your leashed dog. Reservations are required. Rates are $25–35 per day. 631/852-7879.

The park entrance is off of Montauk Highway (Rte. 27) east of the village of Montauk. To reach the nature trails, take East Lake Drive north a mile and there is a small dirt parking area on your right. Open sunrise–sunset. 631/852-7878.

Restaurants

The Clam Bar: This roadside fish joint is a popular local favorite. There are plenty of outdoor tables, but they can get very crowded during summer weekends, so be sure to get here early during the lunch or dinner hours. Choose from a standard menu of fish and chips, clams, fresh fish, and fish salads. Table service is available or you can take your dinner to-go. 2025 Montauk Highway (Rte. 27); 516/267-6348.

Places to Stay

Ann Breyer's Cottages: This little cluster of four charming cottages welcomes well-behaved dogs of all sizes. Each cottage has a full kitchen, bedroom, and sitting room. All are close to the beaches and town. Beach passes are provided. The cottages are available April–June and September–December only. Rates are $105 per night with an additional $20 fee for Fido. 560 Westlake Drive, P.O. Box 167, Montauk, NY 11954; 631/668-2710.

Born Free Motel: This well-situated motel sits overlooking the dunes between Montauk and Ditch Plains Beach. With beachfront efficiencies in each room, you and your dog will feel right at home here (if home includes the

EARMARK YOUR CALENDAR

On Long Island, there are plenty of opportunities to walk your dog in the name of a good cause.

Sea Dog Walk: The Animal Rescue Fund of the Hamptons (ARF), sponsors this annual dog walk to raise funds for its no-kill shelter in Wainscott. The one-mile walk takes place at Mulford Farm on the first Saturday in May. Local merchants donate prizes, doggy bags, and there are contests and competitions for you and your dog. For exact dates and information, call 631/537-0400.

Dog Walk against Cancer: Leashed pets, with their owners in tow, gather for this one-mile walk held on the first Sunday in May at SUNY Old Westbury to benefit cancer research. Included at the event are demonstrations, refreshments, raffles, and doggy bag giveaways. For more information, contact the American Cancer Society at 516/229-4100, ext. 3018.

Hamptons Summer Race Fest: The festival features 5K- and 10K-runs to benefit the Guide Dog Foundation, a provider of guide dogs free of charge to the visually impaired. The course begins and ends at Turtle Bay in Quogue and runs through the streets of Southampton. Guide dog training events as well as refreshments and food are waiting at the finish line. The event is held on the last Sunday in August; the race begins at 9:30 A.M. For more information, call 631/283-6011 or visit its website: www.tracs.net.

Love on a Leash: This annual fundraiser is sponsored by Bide-A-Wee, a Westhampton animal shelter. Proceeds go to Bide-A-Wee's Golden Years Retirement Home, a home for abandoned dogs eight years and older. A parade of animals begins at 6 P.M., followed by a swing band concert and dancing at 8 P.M. For details and dates, call Bide-A-Wee at 212/532-6395 or 212/532-4455.

---

sound of waves lulling you asleep each night). Rates are $90–150 per night. 115 South Emerson Avenue, Montauk, NY 11954; 631/668-2896.

Hither House: This elegant eight-room hotel offers efficiencies in most rooms and is only a short walk to the local beaches. All rooms have sun decks, and dogs are welcome with prior approval. Rates are $70–275 per night. 10 Lincoln Road, Montauk, NY 11954; 631/668-2714.

Oceanside Beach Resort: This 30-room resort hotel overlooks the dunes of the Atlantic Ocean. All units have kitchenettes and terraces equipped with barbecues. Dogs are welcome on approval. Rates are $55–245 per night. 626

Montauk Highway, Montauk, NY 11954; 631/668-9825; website: www.montaukmotel.com.

Sepp's Surf-Sound Cottages: Pets are welcome at any of the nine cozy cottages here. Each cottage is equipped with a kitchen and patio and is within walking distance to Ditch Plains Beach. Rates are $90–135 daily; weekly rentals required in July and August. Weekly rates are $800–950 per week. Ditch Plains Road, Montauk, NY 11954; 631/668-2215.

Theodore Roosevelt County Park: See listing under Parks, Beaches, and Recreation Areas.

NESCONSET (SMITHTOWN TOWNSHIP)

Parks, Beaches, and Recreation Areas

23 Lake Ronkonkoma County Park 🐾 🐾

This small county park is mostly composed of recreational areas. Trails are non-existent with the exception of a mile-long paved walkway that leads down to the shores of Lake Ronkonkoma. Although dogs are not welcome at the main swimming beach, you can walk along the shore a short way to find some water access. This isn't a must-see park, but on those days you feel shut out of all the beach action, this provides a good alternative. From the Long Island Expressway (I-495), take Exit 59 to Ocean Avenue north. Turn left onto Rosevale Avenue. Turn right onto Lake Shore Road. The park entrance will be on your left. Open 8 A.M.–dusk. 631/854-9699.

OLD WESTBURY (NORTH HEMPSTEAD TOWNSHIP)

Nature Hikes and Urban Walks

Old Westbury Gardens: This elegant 1906 mansion is located on over 150 acres of gardens, lakes, and woodland trails. Owned by the Phipps family, it has also been featured in movies such as *Love Story, Age of Innocence,* and *North by Northwest.* Your dog will probably only want to know if he can swim in the manmade lake (he can't), but you will enjoy the exquisite setting. Dogs must be leashed and are not allowed inside the mansion. Open April–December. Old Westbury Road; 516/333-0048; website: www.oldwestburygardens.org

PLAINVIEW (OYSTER BAY TOWNSHIP)

Places to Stay

Residence Inn by Marriott: Studios and one- and two-bedroom suites are available for extended-stay guests. Each suite has a fully equipped kitchen, and a complimentary breakfast is served each morning. You probably won't stay here on a short visit because there is a one-time non-refundable $100 cleaning fee for your pet. In addition, there is a $20 daily fee for your pup. Room rates are $159–275 per day. 9 Gerhard Road, Plainview, NY 11779; 516/433-6200 or 800/331-3131; website: www.marriott.com.

PORT JEFFERSON
(BROOKHAVEN TOWNSHIP)

Places to Stay

Danfords on the Sound: Located in the heart of historic Port Jefferson, this elegant inn has 85 guestrooms, views of Long Island Sound, and refrigerators in each room—not necessarily in that order. Well-behaved pets are welcome on approval and with advance reservations. Rates are $150–250. 25 East Broadway, Port Jefferson, NY 11777; 631/928-5200 or 800/332-6367; website: www.danfords.com.

Ransome Inn Bed and Breakfast: This quaint two-room country bed and breakfast is located near the waterfront in historic Port Jefferson. A full breakfast is served each morning. Dogs are welcome with advance reservations. Rates are $85–145 per night. 409 East Broadway, Jefferson, NY 11777; 631/474-5019; website: www.bbdirectory.com.

QUOGUE
(SOUTHAMPTON TOWNSHIP)

Parks, Beaches, and Recreation Areas

24 Shinnecock West County Park—Tiana Beach 🐾 🐾 🐾

This lovely white sand beach is part of Shinnecock West County Park. Running west from Southampton's Ponquogue Beach (which is also included in the park), these thousand feet of beachfront is all your dog will need to make her happy. Even more happily, as of October 2001 dogs are allowed on the beach between October 1 and March 15. Previously dogs were banned all year. We can live with that, can't we?

Dogs must be leashed. From Montauk Highway (Rte. 27A), take East Tiana Road south about a mile. Turn right onto Lynn Avenue across Ponquogue Bridge, and then take another right onto Dune Road to the beach. Open dawn–dusk. 631/283-6011.

Places to Stay

Caffrey House: As we go to press this wonderful Victorian resort inn is up for sale. We can't promise the new ownership will still allow dogs, but here's the scoop as it exists at press time. With 16 luxurious rooms and its own private beach, you and your dog will be treated like royalty here. Continental breakfast is served each morning overlooking the beaches of Shinnecock West County Park. Dogs are welcome in designated rooms. Rates are $80–150 per night. 2 Squires Road, East Quogue, NY 11942; 631/728-9835; website: www.caffreyhouse.com.

Inn at Quogue: Stay in the lap of luxury—and not just lap dogs need apply! This historic inn offers wicker-attired cottages and a great location that will make you feel right at home. One of the only inns that allows dogs in this quiet Hampton village, the amenities speak loudly. Bicycles, continental breakfast, and a private beach are just a few of the perks you'll receive when you stay here. Dogs are welcome in specific rooms for an additional $50 per stay. Rates are $125–400. 47-52 Quogue Street, P.O. Box 521, Quogue, NY 11959; 631/653-6560.

RIVERHEAD (RIVERHEAD TOWNSHIP)

Parks, Beaches, and Recreation Areas

25 Indian Island County Park 🐾 🐾 🐾

Located on a peninsula on Flanders Bay, this lovely 275-acre county park has several hiking trails that lead through the woods and along the water. An especially appealing walk is to Indian Island, a small point that was once an actual island but is now joined to the rest of the park by a white sandbar. The peninsula makes for a great swimming and picnicking spot on the white, sandy beach.

You can also wander along the Peconic River, which empties into the bay. The trails are a little more overgrown along the river, but there are a few water access points.

Trail maps are available at the entrance.

There are also trailer and tent sites here, but they are *very* popular in the summer months, so reservations are required. For reservations, call 631/854-4949.

There is a day use fee of $2 for Green Key Card holders and $4 for non-residents. From the Long Island Expressway take Exit 71 to Rte. 24 east two miles, through the Riverhead Traffic Circle. Turn left onto Cross-River Drive (Rte. 105). The entrance is on the right. Open 8 A.M.–dusk. 631/852-3232.

Places to Stay

Best Western East End: Formerly a Ramada Inn, this full-service hotel throws open its doors for all dogs. With 100 comfortable and spacious rooms, you and your dog will stay in style at this newly remodeled hotel. Rates are $169–229 per night with a refundable $50 deposit for your dog. 1830 Rte. 25, Riverhead, NY 11901; 631/369-2200; website: www.bestwesterneastend.com.

DIVERSIONS

Most activities on Long Island involve getting out on the water. As long as your dog has her sea legs, we suggest paddling along the shores of Alewife Pond or heading out to Long Island Sound for a day of kayaking.

East Coast Adventure Tour Company, 216A Main Street, Amagansett, 631/267-2303, offers kayak rentals from April through October. Guided tours, hourly or daily rentals, and free delivery to any location throughout the Hamptons are also available.

Main Beach Surf and Sport, Montauk Highway, East Hampton, 800/564-4386, rents canoes or kayaks for use at any of the ponds or beaches in the East Hampton area. Free delivery and pickup is included in your rental price. Rates $45–75 for a half- or full-day rental. Tours are also available starting at $65 per person.

Maryanne's Kayaks, Oak Walk, Fire Island, 631/583-5282, offers kayak rentals near the Great South Bay, a perfect place to get out on the water. Rentals are by the hour, the half day or full day. Rates $20–45.

Peconic Paddler, Riverhead, 631/369-9500, supplies canoes for a day or an hour for paddling down the Peconic River, including stops in the Pine Barrens Preserve. Sea kayaking on Peconic Bay is also available, from two hours to all day. Rates are $16–69 for kayaks; canoes are $13–45.

Shelter Island Kayak, 23 North Ferry Road; 631/749-1990; website: www.kayaksi.com. The closest you and your dog will get to Mashomack Nature Preserve (where dogs can't go) is just offshore via kayak or canoe. Guided tours are $45 a person (dogs ride free) or $15 an hour to explore on your own.

RIVERSIDE (SOUTHAMPTON TOWNSHIP)

Parks, Beaches, and Recreation Areas

26 David A. Sarnoff Preserve 🐾 🐾 🐾 🐾

With over 2,100 acres to explore, this Pine Barrens Preserve is the most easily accessible of all the permit-only preserves on Long Island. With entrances and trailheads located off Nugent Drive, Riverhead-Quogue Road, and Riverhead-Moriches Road, there is plenty of access and miles of sandy trails through the pitch pines of the Pine Barrens Preserve.

From the entrance at Riverhead-Moriches Road, take the trail to Frog Pond. Although this isn't exactly a swimming hole, the marshes do support an array of flowers and wildlife in the wet season. For a longer hike, you can access the five-mile Red Trail off Nugent Road, or take the Blue Trail almost three miles into the sandy wilderness. The only thing missing from these peaceful trails is water access, so you should definitely bring your own drinking water on a hike here. Permits are required and maps are available from the New York Environmental Protection Agency (see the section on the Pine Barrens Preserve at the beginning of this chapter). There is also a very good map posted at the trailhead turnout on County Road 63, so make sure you take a good look before setting out on your walk.

From the Long Island Expressway, take Exit 71 to Rte. 24 south to the Riverhead traffic circle. Take the first right onto County Road 63 (Riverhead-Moriches Road), and go south 0.25 miles. The parking area is on the right. Open dawn–dusk. 631/444-0273.

ROCKVILLE (HEMPSTEAD TOWNSHIP)

Places to Stay

Holiday Inn of Rockville Centre: You know what to expect at a Holiday Inn, and you get it here. There are 99 comfortable rooms located in a convenient spot. Dogs are welcome on approval. Rates are $120–150 per night. 173 Sunrise Highway, Rockville Centre, NY 11570; 516/678-1300 or 877/241-7544; website: www.holiday-inn.com.

ROCKY POINT (BROOKHAVEN TOWNSHIP)

Parks, Beaches, and Recreation Areas

27 Rocky Point Preserve 🐾 🐾 🐾

This park is the official starting point to the proposed 50-mile Pine Barrens Preserve Trail. This 5,100-acre preserve was once used as a base for transatlantic broadcasting towers, but was purchased by the state of New York in 1978. In June 1994 the Pine Barrens Preserve Trail opened. As you walk you'll see the remains of the towers and electronic equipment that was left behind.

Although most of the trail features the traditional dry terrain of the sandy pine barrens, you'll also pass through a section of hardwood forest and weave around several glacial kettleholes. We prefer visiting here in the off-season, mostly because it can get very hot in the summer months. If you do visit here during hot weather, be sure to bring water. Maps of the entire nine-mile loop trail are available at the Pine Barrens Preserve Trail Information Center in Manorville, where you can also obtain the required hiking permit.

Dogs must be leashed. From Rte. 25A, take Rocky Point Road south into the preserve. Open dawn–dusk. 631/369-9768.

ROSLYN
(NORTH HEMPSTEAD TOWNSHIP)

Parks, Beaches, and Recreation Areas

28 Christopher Morley Park & Dog Run 🐾 🐾 🐕

This lovely park is located on over 30 acres of woodland and, until recently, your dog was banned from all of them. And although he's still not welcome on the trails, there is now a dog run where local pups can meet and mingle. As usual, it's in the cheap seats, but until the Nassau County Parks Department decides to lighten up and let dogs in, we'll have to be happy with having a place at all.

This run is always busy, and the dogs here have enough room to play with each other or chase a favorite ball. The run has a hard-packed dirt floor, and there is one small bench and some shade. Not bad, but oh how those woods beckon. . . .

Dogs may go leashless in the run but cannot set paw anywhere else in the park. From Rte. 25A (Northern Boulevard), take Searingtown Road south for about a mile. The park and its entrance will be on your left. Open dawn–dusk. 516/571-8113.

SAINT JAMES
(SMITHTOWN TOWNSHIP)

Restaurants

Saint James General Store: This general store, operating since 1847, is the only "official" general store on Long Island. Pick up some great sandwiches, picnic supplies, and home-baked desserts and bone up on a little history—all with the knowledge that you are supporting a disappearing way of life. 516 Moriches Road at Harbor Hill Road; 631/862-8333.

SEAFORD (HEMPSTEAD TOWNSHIP)

Parks, Beaches, and Recreation Areas

29 Cedar Creek Park 🐾 🐾 🐾 🐕

As usual, dogs are relegated to the back of the bus in this bayside park. While everyone else is at the beach, your dog gets to go to the treatment plant. Located at the southern end of the park (next to the treatment facility), the good news is that this dog run is fairly large, with a dirt floor and some shade.

The bad news is that you can't set paw anywhere else in the park—even on a leash. So, it may not be scenic, but it is leash-free. And we never turn up our noses at that.

The run is closed the first Tuesday of each month for maintenance. From Wantagh State Parkway, take the Merrick Road exit. Go east on Merrick Road, and make your first right into the park. The dog run is at the end of the loop road. Open 9 A.M.–dusk. 516/571-7473.

30 Wantagh Park 🐾 🐾 🐾 🐕

This residents-only park offers a small dog run for Nassau County dogs. And while we're not big fans of local parks that exclude the rest of us, we have to agree that there are so few places for dogs to walk in this county, maybe they deserve one place all their own. In any event, they have it, so if you live in the county, you are welcome to this tiny run. Just don't get too excited. Yes, it's an off-leash area, and, yes, it's well attended, but large it is not.

The dog run is located in the middle of Wantagh Park, adjacent to the boat launch.

Dogs are not allowed in the rest of the park. The run is closed the first Tuesday of each month for maintenance. From Wantagh State Parkway, take Merrick Road west. Take the first left onto Kings Road into the park. Open 9 A.M.–dusk. 516/571-7460.

SHELTER ISLAND

Places to Stay

Stearns Point House: This restored farmhouse in Shelter Island Heights has spacious rooms, private baths, and, best of all, is dog-friendly. Dogs of all sizes are welcome with advance reservations. Rates are $110–150 per night. 7 Stearns Point Road, Shelter Island Heights, NY 11964; 631/749-4162.

SMITHTOWN (SMITHTOWN TOWNSHIP)

Parks, Beaches, and Recreation Areas

31 Blydenburgh County Park 🐾 🐾 🐾 👣

This lovely and spacious 627-acre park is one of those good news/bad news stories. Although it is true there is a lot of room here, the park can get quite crowded on warm summer days, and much of its space is dedicated to recreation enthusiasts. This is always bad news for dogs. The more development, like camping, bridle trails, picnic areas, and fishing spots in a park, the fewer places a dog can run unencumbered and welcomed. Our advice? Visit in the off-season. You'll enjoy it more.

The good news is, if you do visit in any season, there are plenty of trails through hilly forests and open valleys that lead to the Nissequogue River and Stump Pond. Trails along the river are our favorite water spots, but watch out for anglers and the strong current.

History hounds will enjoy the historic district, which features a gristmill and other remains of a long-ago life on Long Island. There are also guided hikes throughout the park sponsored by the Greenbelt Trail Conference. Leashed dogs are welcome on many of these hikes. For more information, call 631/360-0753.

Camping is allowed here, and dogs are welcome in the camping area. Reservations and a Green Key Card are required. Sites are $10–20 per night. For reservations, call 631/244-7275.

The main entrance to the park is off the Veterans Memorial Highway. The northern entrance is at New Mill Road. Open 8 A.M.–dusk, except in the camping area. 631/-854-3713.

Places to Stay

Blydenburgh County Park: See the Blydenburgh County Park listing above.

SOUTHAMPTON

Southampton, undoubtedly the grand lady of the Hamptons, was first settled by Europeans when Puritans from Lynn, Massachusetts, arrived here in 1640. The original occupants, of course, were the Shinnecocks, Native Americans who lived here for more than 8,000 years before the Europeans arrived. They called this place Agawam.

Regardless of what you call it, this lovely area on the Atlantic has been one of the most popular destinations for New Yorkers since 1870, when the railroad was completed and folks from New York City began to arrive in droves. Drawn by the quaint seaside villages and the beautiful sandy beaches, they are still arriving, as any day sitting in traffic on busy Sunrise Highway will demonstrate.

Please note that the township of Southampton umbrellas several villages — one of them is the village of Southampton, which has its own dog regulations, as detailed in the following sections.

Parks, Beaches, and Recreation Areas
32 Southampton Beaches 🐾 🐾 🐾 🐾

Unlike the county beaches in the town of Southampton (including Tiana and Ponquogue Beaches), which ban dogs entirely between May 15 and October 1, the beaches in the village of Southampton allow dogs to set paw on the sand before 10 A.M. and after 6 P.M. We think this is doggone civilized and you'll meet plenty of other happy canines who agree. The beaches along Dune Road

all welcome you and your leashed pup on some of the most expensive beachfront property in the country. And it isn't hard to see why this is such a desirable area. There are miles of gorgeous white beaches for you to enjoy and, as long as you avoid the roped off bathing areas, you and your dog can enjoy all of it.

The catch, of course (and isn't there *always* one?), are those darn parking permits, which are required at most of the beaches. You may obtain a season permit at no charge with proof of residency. Non-residents may obtain a seasonal pass for $130. And those of you who are here just for the weekend can pay a $20 daily fee or go to Road D Beach or Fowlers Road Beach where there is no parking permit requirement. Dune Beach is for residents only.

Maps, information, and permits are available at the Town Hall at 23 Main Street. All of the beaches are off Dune Road, which becomes Beach Road. Open dawn–dusk. 631/283-0247.

Restaurants

The Driver's Seat: This little pub restaurant has outdoor seating in the summer. The tables are tucked away down a little alley, but they are shaded and private. There is no table service here, but you can take your food to-go and sit outside with your pup. 62 Jobs Lane; 631/283-6606.

Golden Pear Café: This bakery-restaurant offers a few tables outside where you can enjoy a fresh coffee and muffin in the morning, or gourmet salads, specialty sandwiches, and vegetarian pizzas at lunch. There are also plenty of benches along Main Street if you wish to take your food to-go. 99 Main Street; 631/283-8900.

Village Cheese Shop: In sidewalk-challenged Southampton, there aren't many outdoor cafés, so your best bet is to take your food to-go and settle along one of the many benches on Main Street or take your meal to the beach. This specialty food store is a safe bet to find unusual and tasty items for your picnic basket. With choices of domestic and imported cheeses, caviar, salmon, foie gras, chocolate, and made-to-order sandwiches and salads, you and your dog will be eating like, well, like you're in the Hamptons. 11 Main Street; 631/283-6949.

Places to Stay

Atlantic: This lovely resort, located on five acres, provides luxurious lodging with a European flair. Small dogs are welcome, although well-behaved larger dogs will be considered. Rates are $250–500 per night. 1655 County Road 39, Southampton, NY 11968; 631/283-6100; website: www.hrhresorts.com.

Bayberry Inn: This medium-sized inn is more motel than hotel, but the rooms are comfortable, clean, and affordable, so it's a go in our book. Better yet, this place is as pet-friendly as it is centrally located. Rates are $85–150. Continental breakfast served each morning. 281 Country Road, Southampton, NY 11968; 631/283-4220 or 800/659-2020.

Capri: This retro-style inn has the ambience and charm of a 1950s motor lodge, and although the rooms are more extravagant than any motel we've been in, they are still cozy and comfortable. Close to all the action in Southampton Village, you and your dog will be able to stay here without selling the family jewels to afford it. Rates are $180–300 per night. 281 County Road Southampton, NY 11968; 631/283-6100 or 631/287-0908; website: www.hrhresorts.com.

Oak Tree Inn: This three-room bed and breakfast offers lovely rooms furnished with antiques. Dogs are allowed on approval. All rooms have a private bath. A full breakfast is served each morning. Rates are $100–150 per night. 606 Majors Path, Southampton, NY 11968; 631/287-2057; website: www.hamptons.com/oaktree.

Southampton Inn: There are 90 charming rooms at this resort located in the heart of Southampton village. Dogs are welcome in all rooms—at no extra fee. Rates are $119–300 per night. 91 Hill Street, Southampton, New York 11968; 631/283-6500 or 800/832-6500; website: www.southamptoninn.com.

Village Latch Inn Hotel: This historic inn offers country quaintness on the expanse of five acres where guests are welcome to roam. Dogs are allowed in the cottages for an additional $20 per night. Rates are $175–400 per night. 101 Hill Street, Southampton, NY 11968; 631/283-2160 or 800/545-2824; website: www.villagelatch.com.

SOUTH HAVEN (BROOKHAVEN TOWNSHIP)

Parks, Beaches, and Recreation Areas

33 Southaven County Park 🐾 🐾 🐾 🐾

This beautiful county park has miles of hiking trails, a river walk, freshwater lake, and plenty of places where you and your dog can stretch your legs. Located along the Carmans River, you'll find shady, quiet trails in a pine and oak forest. In the summer, we suggest you head into the woods away from the developed areas as the park can get quite crowded. Fortunately with over 1,300 acres of parkland, you shouldn't have any trouble escaping the masses—in the off-season we usually have the place to ourselves.

Maps are available at the main entrance. There is a day-use fee of $2 for Green Key Card holders and $4 for non-residents.

Camping is also available here. Tent and trailer sites have water and electric hookups. Rates range from $15 for residents and $24 for non-residents. For reservations, call 631/244-7275. From Sunrise Highway, take Exit 58 to William Floyd Parkway north. Take an immediate left onto Victory Avenue. Follow signs to main entrance. Open dawn–dusk, except in the camping areas. 631/854-1414.

Places to Stay

Southaven County Park: See the Southaven County Park listing above.

STONY BROOK (BROOKHAVEN TOWNSHIP)

Nature Hikes and Urban Walks

Walking Tour of Stony Brook Village: This area dates back to the American Revolution when Washington's spy ring operated here and British soldiers came to the Stony Brook Gristmill for supplies. The historic village was created in 1941 to demonstrate colonial life. Over 35 shops and restaurants are here for you and your dog to explore, including the famed gristmill, a mechanical eagle that flaps its wings atop the post office each hour, the historic Three Village Inn (built in 1751), and ships along the harbor that date back to the early nineteenth century. Maps are available at the Stony Brook Village Center on Main Street on the harbor. For more information, call 631/751-2244 or visit website: www.stonybrookvillage.com.

Restaurants

Golden Pear Café: Enjoy a scrumptious salad, sandwich, or special dessert at this comfortable café. Take your food to-go and enjoy it on any of the many benches along Main Street, or eat at one of the outdoor tables. 97 Main Street in the Inner Court Complex; 631/751-7695.

UNIONDALE (HEMPSTEAD TOWNSHIP)

Places to Stay

Long Island Marriott: If you are not one of the "Islanders," but only a visitor here, this full-service hotel is of Stanley Cup caliber. It offers all the creature comforts you might expect from a Marriott and, even better, your own hockey hound can enjoy the comforts with you. "Small" dogs are welcome—size is negotiable, so be sure your pup is on her best behavior to avoid a trip to the penalty box. Rates are $125–150 per night. 101 James Doolittle Boulevard, Uniondale, NY 11553; 516/794-5936 or 800/228-9290; website: www.marriott.com.

WAINSCOTT (EAST HAMPTON TOWNSHIP)

Places to Stay

Country Bed and Breakfast: This five-room bed and breakfast on the East Hampton–Southampton town line offers in-room refrigerators and private terraces. Dogs are allowed with approval in selected rooms, so make your reservations early. Rates are $100–150 per night. 344 Wainscott Harbor Road, P.O. Box 1037, Wainscott, NY 11975; 631/537-0907.

WEST BAY SHORE (ISLIP TOWNSHIP)

Parks, Beaches, and Recreation Areas

34 Gardiner County Park 🐾 🐾 🐾 ◀●

One of the only parks available to dogs on Great South Bay, this lovely county park has hiking, nature trails, water access, and countless places to take in the beautiful scenery. Originally part of the Gardiner estate (Long Island's first white landowners and the current owners of private Gardiner Island), these 231 acres are located right on the water and hearken back to a time when Suffolk County was a rural jewel along the sea. This place is definitely worth a visit in any season.

The park entrance is off Montauk Highway (Rte. 27A), about 0.5 miles east of the Robert Moses Causeway. Open 8 A.M.–dusk. 631/854-0935 (Memorial Day–Labor Day) or 631/854-4949.

WESTHAMPTON BEACH (SOUTHAMPTON TOWNSHIP)

Dogs are not allowed on any Westhampton town beach during the summer months. After September 15, they are allowed before 10 A.M. and after 6 P.M. For doggy entertainment, see the listing for Cupsogue Beach County Park in the East Moriches section.

Nature Hikes and Urban Walks

Tree Walking Tour: Nature lovers and dog lovers unite on this unique walk through town. Saunter along Main Street and the surrounding side streets while identifying the plant and tree species indigenous to Long Island. A brief description and history of each tree is given on the handy map available at the library or Lynne's Cards and Gifts on Sunset Avenue. Maybe you'll learn a few things and your dog will appreciate trees in a whole new way; this is one way to discover a tree is more than just something to lift a leg on. For information, call the Chamber of Commerce at 631/288-3337.

Restaurants

Beach Bakery: For the best breakfast yummies around, pick up a muffin, pastry, or breakfast sandwich at this excellent bakery. Convenient benches are located outside where your dog can help you with the crumbs. 112 Main Street; 631/288-6552.

Hampton Coffee Company: You'll find this gourmet coffee shop in a quiet courtyard located just off the beaten path of Main Street. There are plenty of shaded tables outside the shop where you and your dog can enjoy your cup of java. 127-1 Main Street; 631/288-6726.

John Scott's Raw Bar: Even if you can't set paw on the beaches, you can come close to the sand at this local seafood restaurant on Dune Road. With the usual offerings of clams, oysters, and fish and chips, you won't come here for the food, but rather the local beach atmosphere. There are plenty of tables outside on the patio where your dog can join you for a meal. We like it best at lunch. The dinner and late-night crowd can be fairly noisy. 546 Dune Road; 631/288-5810.

Margarita Grille: This Mexican restaurant has the best outdoor patio in town. Sit out under the protected patio and watch the world go by. Enchiladas, tacos, and other standard Mexican fare are on the menu. 83 Main Street; 631/288-5252.

Sydney's: For fully prepared specialty food, stop at this gourmet market and food shop. Entrées, desserts, breakfast items, and lunch specialties are all available to you and your drooling dog (of course, you may actually be the one doing the drooling). 194 Mill Road; 631/288-4722.

Places to Stay

Woodland Bed and Breakfast: This comfortable bed and breakfast offers rooms at the inn for well-behaved dogs. There is even a fenced-in run in the back. Dogs of all sizes are welcome for an additional $5 per night. Rates are $80–135 per night. 12 Woodland Avenue, Westhampton Beach, NY 11978; 631/288-1681.

WEST HILLS
(HUNTINGTON TOWNSHIP)

Parks, Beaches, and Recreation Areas

35 West Hills County Park & Dog Run 🐾 🐾 🐾 🐾 🐕

This wonderful park has countless trails for you and your dog to explore. Located right over the border from Nassau County and all those No Dogs Allowed signs, we expect a lot of park-starved pups are crossing the line to get to this place. Hiking the Walt Whitman Trail to the top of Jayne's Hill (the highest peak on Long Island at 400 feet), wandering through wide-open meadows, traversing over 15 miles of well-groomed trails, and running leash-free with the rest of the pack are just some of the highlights.

The dog park is located on High Hold Drive in the northern section of the park. Park at the youth camp and go to your right as you face the lodge. You will probably hear the many happy yips coming from the meadow beyond. Let those be your guide. On weekend mornings this run is one busy place, which in our humble opinion only attests to the need for more leash-free space in this neck of the woods.

Although dogs are only allowed off-leash in the dog run, there are countless other spots to explore here. Most trails are a terrific combination of woodland paths and open meadows, so you can get in a varied walk with your pal. Pick up a map at the entrances off High Hold Drive or Sweet Hollow Road. Avoid the bridle paths as they can get quite muddy in the wet season. Take the Long Island Expressway (I-495) to Exit 48 and High Hold Drive north. The park entrance is on the right. Open 8 A.M.–dusk. 631/854-4423.

WOODBURY (OYSTER BAY TOWNSHIP)

Places to Stay

Ramada Inn: Dogs are welcome at this 100-room chain hotel. The rooms are clean and comfortable and dogs of all sizes are welcome with prior approval. Rates are $75–90 per night. 8030 Jericho Turnpike, Woodbury, NY 11797; 516/921-8500 or 800/2-RAMADA (800/272-6232); website: www.ramada.com.

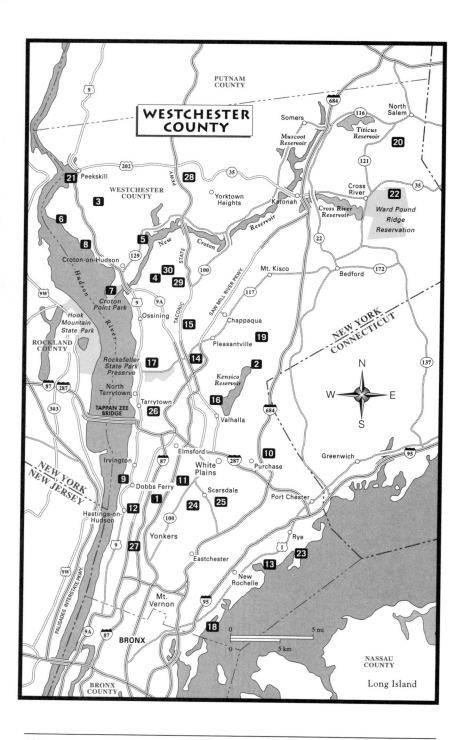

7 WESTCHESTER COUNTY

Dogs never talk about themselves but listen to you while you talk about your-self, and keep up an appearance of being interested in the conversation.

—Jerome K. Jerome, English humorist

Westchester County is only a short car trip away from the heart of Manhattan, but to many it may as well be as far as the moon. Historically it was the site of many decisive battles of the American Revolution, and Washington Irving memorialized it in his stories of Rip van Winkle, the Headless Horseman, and the other eccentric characters of "The Legend of Sleepy Hollow." Today the elite neighborhoods of Scarsdale, New Rochelle, Rye, and Dobbs Ferry work hard to keep their neighbors to the south out of their neck of the woods, but with a little effort you'll discover a place rich in trails, bike paths, and preserves where you and your dog can get away from the hectic pace of the city. In no time you can be kicking up your heels in the hills of Ward Pound Ridge Reservation and Blue Mountain or splashing in the waters at Mountain Lakes Camp or Teatown Lake Reservation. Although it is true that many of the suburbs lining the Long Island Sound have gone a little crazy with the

PICK OF THE LITTER–
WESTCHESTER COUNTY HIGHLIGHTS

Blue Mountain Reservation, Cortlandt

Hardscrabble Wilderness Area, Mount Pleasant

Teatown Lake Reservation, Yorktown

Ward Pound Ridge Reservation, Pound Ridge

"No Dogs Allowed" signs, we promise a trip to Westchester County will offer many options to keep your pooch's tail wagging.

We haven't listed each and every park in the county, just the ones we think are worth a trip out of the city. If you'd like more information about other smaller city parks in the county, we suggest you contact the Westchester Parks Department at 25 Moore Avenue, Mount Kisco, NY 10549; 914/864-7000 or the website: www.westchestergov.com.

Westchester County Parks: Dogs are not allowed in any county-run preserves in Westchester County (the private preserves that we list are the exception to this rule), but are welcome in all the county parks. Although there is a day-use fee required in these parks during the busy summer season, you won't need to pay to use the trails in the off-season. Residents who plan to access these parks often, however, should consider obtaining an Empire Pass. This park pass is available to all residents of Westchester County for a fee of $30; the pass is good for three years. The Empire Pass allows discounted fees in all county parks, golf courses, pools, beaches, and historic sites. Passes may be obtained at most county park locations or by calling 914/864-7000.

Bronx River Reservation Pathway: There are three stretches of pathways along the Bronx River that you and your dog will enjoy exploring. You'll discover woods, streams, two lakes, and plenty of trails off the beaten path here. In its entirety, the trail runs from Mount Vernon to the village of Valhalla in Mount Pleasant, but the path doesn't yet run contiguously. Beginning in the Bronx River Reservation, there is a one-mile loop in Mount Vernon, a 3.5-mile section between Bronxville and Scarsdale, and a five-mile section from Hartsdale to the Kensico Dam Plaza in Valhalla. A section of the Bronx River Parkway from Scarsdale Center to County Center is closed to traffic every Sunday in May and June, and again in September and October, 10 A.M.–2 P.M. Trail parking is available at exits off the Bronx River Parkway, at the Metro–North Harlem Line station and at Kensico Dam. Maps are available from the Westchester County Department of Parks and Recreation. Open dawn–dusk. 914/593-2600.

Briarcliff-Peekskill Pathway: This pathway covers a strip of land that was once a planned parkway. Purchased in the 1920s, the route was slated for development until the 1970s when the acreage was taken over by the Westchester County Parks and Recreation Department and turned into a trail. You'll find most of the trailheads are marked with the green Westchester county logo.

The trail runs 13 miles from Briarcliff to Peekskill, taking you through Teatown Lake Reservation, Blue Mountain Reservation, and Croton Gorge Park. Parking is available at all those locations, and the trail is fairly easy to follow throughout its entire stretch. For a trail map or information, call 914/864-7000.

Old Croton Aqueduct Trail: The Old Croton Aqueduct Trail is a 26-mile walking path that follows the route of the Old Croton Aqueduct. A historic feat of engineering, the aqueduct once carried as much as 100 million gallons of water a day to New York City, from 1842–1955, contributing to New York's phenomenal 19th century growth. Most of the structure is intact underground and has been designated a National Historic Landmark.

The trail begins at New Croton Dam in northern Westchester County and ends in Van Cortlandt Park at the New York City line. Primarily a walking trail, horses are welcome in certain sections, as are bicycles when it is not rainy or muddy. Because the trail follows the gently sloping path of the aqueduct, you'll find this an easy walk. Along the way you'll be treated to views of the Hudson River, historic homes, and two nature preserves, Croton Gorge Park and Teatown Lakes Reservation. The trail also runs through the village of Sleepy Hollow, memorialized in early American author Washington Irving's stories. Unfortunately, the surrounding mansions and Dutch settlements in this town are off-limits to dogs; the closest you'll get to them is on this trail which runs along the property boundaries of several sites. In Ossining, a museum highlighting the construction of the aqueduct is within walking distance of the trail. In all, the trail passes through 11 communities, and although most of the time you'll be on a rural pathway, there are sections that cross busy streets and sidewalks.

Parking is available on local streets. To receive a map of the entire trail, contact the Old Croton Trailway State Park, 15 Walnut St., Dobbs Ferry, NY 10522-2109 or the Friends of the Old Croton Aqueduct at 914/693-5259.

South County and North County Trailways: These two wonderful biking and hiking trails run 36 miles along the Saw Mill Parkway between Hastings-on-the-Hudson to Elmsford in the south and from Tarrytown Lakes to Putnam County in the north. Located on the old Putnam section of the New York Central Railroad, this trailway slices through some of the most scenic parks and woodlands in the entire county. You'll meet many other recreation enthusiasts along the way and there are enough diversions (translation: lakes, streams, and other dogs) to keep your dog very happy during a walk here. Remember, this is also a bike trail, so keep an eye out for speeding cyclists. For more trail information, call the Westchester County Department of Parks and Recreation at 914/864-7000 or download a map from website: www.westchestergov.com/parks.

ARDSLEY

Parks, Beaches, and Recreation Areas

❶ V. Everett Macy Park 🐾 🐾 🐾

This long and narrow park is spliced into a section between the Saw Mill Parkway on one side and the New York State Thruway (I-87) on the other. But don't let the nearby rushing cars scare you away. Other than the sounds of a little distant traffic, this small oasis will make you feel like you are miles away from civilization.

Walk for several miles on the dirt trail that runs along the western side of Woodland Lake and the Saw Mill River or traverse the South County Trailway which runs along the eastern side. Wildflowers are abundant in the spring and summer, and the trees are lush and shady. The lake is clean in the lower section right by the parking area, but we wouldn't recommend swimming elsewhere.

Dogs must bring their leashes. Entrance located off the Saw Mill Parkway northbound between Exits 7 and 7A. Open dawn–dusk. 914/946-8133.

ARMONK

Parks, Beaches, and Recreation Areas

❷ Betsy Sluder Nature Preserve 🐾 🐾 🦮

Formerly known as Whippoorwill Ridge Park, this small nature preserve isn't large, but it does offer four leash-free trails. The longest of these, extending three-quarters of a mile, is the White Trail. It leads to a lookout point with a view of the valley below. Those who wish to stick to the lowlands can take the Blue Trail to marshy Agnew Pond. Although it may be tempting, you will probably want to discourage your dog from swimming in this pond unless she is dressing as the creature from the Black Lagoon for Halloween. The woodsy trails make for a pleasant but short walk, and dogs are allowed off-leash if under voice command. A handy map board is located at the trailhead.

From Rte. 684, take Exit 3 to Rte. 22 west and proceed for about 0.5 miles. Turn right onto Rte. 128, and take an immediate left onto Old Rte. 22 for 0.25 miles. The small turnout is on your right. Open dawn–dusk. 914/946-8133.

Restaurants

Schultz's Cider Mill: Stop at this friendly little roadside cider mill, and you'll be in for a treat. Make that several treats. Whether you're longing for the homemade doughnuts served only on Saturdays and Sundays (which are so popular they limit the orders to one dozen per person), fresh cider and juices, freshly-picked produce, or homemade candy and pies, you can be sure to find something you and your dog can agree upon. There is even a grill where you can order hamburgers and hot dogs. Sample your fare at the shady outdoor tables or take your loot to a park nearby. We dare you to make the doughnuts last until your next stop! 103 Old Route 22; 914/273-8125.

Places to Stay

Ramada Inn: This standard chain hotel offers 141 clean, comfortable rooms with the usual amenities. Most rooms feature small refrigerators, microwaves, and coffeemakers. Dogs are welcome for an additional $6 per night and a $100 refundable deposit per stay. Rates are $100–140 per night. 94 Business Park Drive, Armonk, NY 10504; 914/273-9090; website: www.ramada.com.

CORTLANDT

Parks, Beaches, and Recreation Areas

❸ Blue Mountain Reservation 🐾 🐾 🐾 🐾

This 1,600-acre reservation was once part of Van Cortlandt Manor—a section of the area that Dutch settler Stephen Van Cortlandt purchased from the Delaware Indians in 1677. There are over 15 miles of trails here separated by two mountains, Blue Mountain and Mount Spitzenberg. Climb to the top of either for a fabulous view of the Tappan Zee Bridge, the Hudson River, and the mountains to the north and south. From the entrance, a sign points you toward a five-mile trail that leads to both summits.

The reservation features a myriad of woodland and self-guided nature trails. Loundsbury Pond is great for swimming, and there are several meadows for picnicking or just hanging out on a dog-day afternoon.

For a longer hike, the Briar-Peekskill Pathway runs through the park. You can connect with this green-blazed trail at Montrose Station Road. Energetic dogs may also want to take this path to the top of Mount Spitzenberg or continue north out of the reservation towards Peekskill.

Although the trails are color-blazed, they aren't always well-marked along the way, so maps are recommended. You can pick up a map at the entrance in the summer or contact the Westchester County Parks Department.

Dogs must be leashed. In the summer there is an entrance fee of $3.50 for Empire Pass holders; $7 for all others. From U.S. 9W, take Welcher Avenue east to the park entrance. Open 8 A.M.–dusk. 914/737-2194.

4 Cliffdale Farm 🐾 🐾 🐾

This working farm is open to nature lovers on the two-mile loop that traverses the meadows of the farmland through the surrounding woodland. The trail also connects to the western side of Teatown Lake Reservation (see the Yorktown section, below), so if you wish to take a longer walk you can travel south into Teatown Lake from the loop trail. Maps for both parks are available at the Nature Center at the Teatown Lake Reservation. There are farm animals here, so dogs must be leashed at all times. From Rte. 9A in the village of Crotonville, take Quaker Bridge Road north one mile. Turn right onto Quaker Ridge Road and proceed for one mile. Turn right onto Teatown Road and proceed for one mile. The park is open dawn–dusk; the parking area closes at 5 P.M. 914/762-2912

5 Croton Gorge Park 🐾 🐾 🐾 🔶

This scenic park overlooking the Croton Reservoir offers countless woodland trails, rolling fields, a bubbling brook, a gorge-like overlook, and bike paths that you and your dog will enjoy over and over again. Although your dog must be leashed here, the paths are well maintained, and the natural setting converges harmoniously with the park atmosphere. Our friends Scott and dog Clementine love this 98-acre park for its quiet beauty, and we agree—it's one of the most scenic parks in Westchester County. For a longer hike, you can also access the Old Croton Aqueduct Trail from here.

Dogs must be leashed and maps are available at the ranger office. From Rte. 9A, take Rte. 129 (Croton Dam Road) east for almost two miles. The parking area will be on your right. Open dawn–dusk. 914/271-3293.

6 George's Island Park 🐾 🐾 🐾 🐾

We like to think this beautiful park is named for a certain canine who, on every visit here, races for the beach as soon as he gets the chance. But no dog is an island, and this means all dogs can visit here, even ones named Max, Joe, and Pixie. Perched on a point along the Hudson River, this "island" features four nature trails, a lake called Whoopee, and a swimming beach along the river. Although you and your leashed dog must avoid the roped-off swimming beach, you're welcome everywhere else—there are plenty of other water access points along the trails.

The 1.5-mile Trail One leads out to Sundance Point and is the longest hike. Trail Two leads about 0.5 miles to Whoopee Lake. Trail Three leads to the picnic areas along the river. Finally, climb up Trail Four to Dugan Point for a view along the river.

George wants to know why the trails have such boring names when the destinations seem rather colorful. Nobody seems to know the answer, so just enjoy. A map is available at the main entrance and is recommended.

From Memorial Day to Labor Day, there is a day-use fee of $3.50 for Empire Pass holders and $7 for all others. From Rte. 9A, take Dutch Street west. Follow it to the end into the park. Open 8 A.M.–dusk. 914/737-7530.

Places to Stay

Comfort Inn: This 66-room hotel isn't big on luxury, but, like the name says, it's comfortable. It offers all the usual amenities, including a continental breakfast each morning for you. Rates are $75–100. 2 1/2 Locust Avenue, Cortlandt, NY 10520; 607/753-7721 or 800/228-5150; website: www.comfortinn.com.

Econo Lodge: Okay, it isn't plush, but your dog won't care. Rooms are $50–90. A free continental breakfast is included each morning. 3775 Rte. 11, Cortlandt, NY 10520; 607/753-7594 or 800/55-ECONO (800/553-2666); website: www.econolodge.com.

Holiday Inn: Located close to the heart of town, this hotel offers 150 rooms at reasonable prices. Dogs are allowed for an additional $20 per stay. All the usual amenities are included. Rates are $75–100 per night. 2 River Street, Cortlandt, NY 10520; 607/756-4431 or 800/HOLIDAY (800/465-4329); website: www.holiday-inn.com.

CROTON-ON-HUDSON

Parks, Beaches, and Recreation Areas

🐾 Croton Point Park 🐾 🐾 🐾

This large 505-acre county park has more camping and picnic areas than hiking trails, but you can access the Hudson River here, and in the off-season you and your dog will find many place to sniff and explore without the busy summer crowds. The Croton River runs through the park, so even when the beach areas are off-limits you can still find some water to help you beat the heat.

Camping is also available here and many of the sites are along the Hudson River. Tent and trailer sites are $15–20 per day. Reservations are required and dogs are permitted as long as they are well-behaved.

There is a day-use fee of $3.50 for Empire Pass holders and $7 for all others from Memorial Day to Labor Day. Dogs must be leashed. From Rte. 9A, take Croton Point Avenue west into the park. Open 8 A.M.–dusk. 914/271-3293.

🐾 Oscawana Park and Nature Preserve 🐾 🐾 🐾 🐕

The good news is that this little park, nestled along the Hudson River, occupies some great real estate. But, unfortunately in this case, location isn't everything. Although the park leads to the river where your dog can swim, there is trash everywhere—which certainly ruins a potentially good thing.

To reach the river, take the left fork after you cross Furnace Brook; this trail leads over the MTA Metro-North tracks that run along the Hudson. The view across to New Jersey is panoramic, but you'll have to pick your way through the leftover Coke cans, broken bottles, and chip wrappers to get to it. (Or in Inu's case, *eat* through the leftovers before taking a much-desired swim).

In the eastern section across Cortlandt Street there is another trail that runs along the Furnace River. This area doesn't seem to attract the trash as much, so if you are looking for a less scenic but longer walk, head for the hills. Dogs may be off-leash if under voice command. From Rte. 9A, take Maiden Lane west for about 0.5 miles. Turn left onto Cortlandt Street. The park will be on both your left and right; the parking area is on your immediate right. Open dawn–dusk. 914/737-7530.

Places to Stay

Croton Point Park Campground: See the Croton Point Park listing, above.

DOBBS FERRY

Parks, Beaches, and Recreation Areas

🄉 Old Croton Trailway State Park 🐾 🐾 🐾

This park celebrates the Old Croton Aqueduct and its 26-mile journey from the Croton Dam all the way to reservoirs in Central Park and the present site of the New York Public Library on 5th Avenue in Manhattan. You can view a map of the entire trail here as well as a history of the aqueduct. Arrangements can be made at the ranger station for tours of the tube that carried the flow of water along the aqueduct.

Although dogs may not give two biscuits for all the history, they will enjoy hiking the scenic trail that leads north to Tarrytown or south to Yonkers from here. 15 Walnut Street; 914/245-4434.

Thank God It's Thursday: That's because Thursday is our night for outdoor movies and a picnic on the grounds of Mercy College in Dobbs Ferry. Every Thursday night in August you and your pup can see a family film in the great outdoors. Just bring the popcorn, the city will do the rest. The college is located at 555 Broadway. For times and information, call 914/674-7562.

Restaurants

Louisiana Marketplace: If you've got a hankering for some good old-fashioned comfort food, come on down to this Cajun-style restaurant and take-out market. Slow-cooked ribs, cornbread, and seafood gumbo are the house specialties. There are a few small tables outside the restaurant, or you can order your meal at the market and take it to the park or beach for a rib-sticking meal. George is partial to the Saint Louis–style spicy ribs; Inu likes the sausage gumbo. 25 Cedar Street; 914/674-0706.

New York Bagel Authority: For a quick spot to pick up some breakfast food, bagels, and coffee, this bagel café offers a wide variety to choose from. There are tables outside if you want to nosh on site; otherwise, pick up your cinnamon raisin bagel to-go and head over to the Old Croton Aqueduct Trail for a morning walk and views of the Hudson. 24 Cedar Street; 914/674-4828.

ELMSFORD

Places to Stay

Hampton Inn: This centrally located hotel is only minutes from the Hudson River and the heart of town. Continental breakfast is served each morning, and dogs are allowed for an additional $5 per night. Rates are $65–95 per night. 200 Tarrytown Road, Elmsford, NY 10523; 914/592-5680 or 800/HAMPTON (800/426-7866); website: www.hamptoninn.com.

HARRISON

Parks, Beaches, and Recreation Areas

🔟 Silver Lake Preserve/John Passidomo Park 🐾 🐾 🐾

Although Silver Lake is more lily-pad green than it is silver, you and your water pup will definitely want to put this on your list of places to visit. With trails on both sides of the lake, a large meadow overlooking the water, and a myriad of trails leading in and through the woods, this park scores high on George and Inu's check list.

The main entrance is through John Passidomo Park. This park is really just a small green space with playground facilities and picnic tables nestled along the lake. Continue past the playground, though, and you will reach a lakeside trail leading into Silver Lake Preserve. (There's no sign, so you'll have to take our word for it.) From here you can walk along the eastern side of the lake for about 0.5 miles. You can access the lake all along the trail, and our dogs run from point to point expecting to swim.

You can also enter the park at Merritt Hill, an open meadow that was the site of the Battle of White Plains. On October 28, 1776, the British advanced southward only to be thwarted by the American army here and pushed back to White Plains. Today there is a stone marker commemorating the event and a large open meadow where your dog will enjoy kicking up her heels in the tall grasses overlooking Silver Lake. There are several trails that lead down to the lake from here.

There is an additional entrance off Lake Street where you can access the trail along the western side of the lake.

Dogs must be leashed in the park.

From Rte. 287, take Exit 8E to Underhill Avenue north for a mile, (Underhill Avenues becomes Veterans Memorial Boulevard). Make an immediate right into the John Passidomo Park parking area. Only residents displaying resident stickers on their cars can park here.

Continue another 0.5 miles on Veterans Memorial Boulevard to Merritt Hill. Take a left at the fork of Old Lake Road and the parking area will be on your immediate left. Another small parking turnout is located off Lake Street. Turn right into the turnout at the White Plains town marker. Open 8 A.M.–dusk. 914/737-7530.

HARTSDALE

Parks, Beaches, and Recreation Areas

⓫ Ridge Road Park/Secor Woods Park 🐾 🐾

These adjacent parks are most easily accessed through Ridge Road Park. From the parking area off Ridge Road, you can hike along the western side of Ridge Road Park into Secor Woods. Odds are you won't be able to tell when you're in one and not the other.

There are two simple trails accessible from the parking area: the eastern trail leads through picnic areas where your dog is not welcome. The other leads to the aforementioned Secor Woods. Although we can't get too excited about these pleasant, but unspectacular 70-acre parks, they do provide an easy woods walk. If you live here, you probably make this an occasional stop. If

Come Alive with the Season: The Hartsdale Pet Cemetery, the first pet cemetery in the country, is enjoyable in any season, but it really comes alive (no pun intended) at the annual **Christmas Tree Lighting Ceremony.** That's right, canines have their very own festival of caroling (howling is more like it), trimming the tree and, most importantly, assisting canines less fortunate than they are. Bring a donation of pet foods and treats for the animals in local shelters when you attend this festive event. For information and dates, call 914/949-2583. For a history of this wonderful place, check out its website: www.petcem.com.

you don't, we like visiting across the street at the quieter Harts Brook Preserve (see the Nature Hikes and Urban Walks section below).

There is a day-use fee of 3.50 for Empire Pass holders; $7 for non-residents. From Sprain Brook Parkway north, take the Underhill exit east. Make an immediate left onto Sprain Road, which in about a mile will veer right onto Ridge Road. The park entrance will be about 0.5 miles on your left. Open 8 A.M.–dusk. 914/946-8133.

Nature Hikes and Urban Walks

Harts Brook Preserve: This peaceful conservation area is a refreshing alternative to some of the bigger and busier Westchester County parks. Located on the grounds of the Marian Woods Convent, directly across the street from Ridge Road Park, you and your dog will enjoy many blessings on the one-mile scenic woodland trail that runs the length of the property. The trailhead can be found to the right of the small parking area near the parish house. Filled with wildflowers in warmer weather and a quiet solitude during the winter, this is a great place to visit when you're looking to get away from the crowds. Please be respectful of the convent and its family. Dogs must be leashed. 914/683-7393.

Restaurants

Harry's Steakhouse: This traditional steakhouse has several outdoor tables where you and your discriminating pup can dine. The menu offers a great variety of cuts for red-blooded meat eaters, so if you're salivating for a steak, look no further. 230 East Hartsdale Avenue; 914/472-8777.

HASTINGS-ON-HUDSON

Parks, Beaches, and Recreation Areas

12 Hillside Park 🐾 🐾 🐾

This tucked-away spot of woodland is located in and around a residential neighborhood; if you didn't already know it was here, you certainly wouldn't discover it from the city's maps. There are no signs to direct you and no formal parking areas. But local residents know what a find it is, and now you will, too.

There are several entrances, all on local streets. The most direct entrance is at the end of Judson Road. Here you'll find a small turnout and a trail that leads you into the woods. From here you'll find a series of unmarked trails that criss-cross throughout the wooded area.

You can also access the park off Ferndale Road. At the end of the road there is a turnout for one car. An easy-to-follow trail leads into the woods from here. Our favorite time for a visit is in the fall when the lush woods are ablaze with glorious color. This is a lovely, quiet, and isolated park that you and your dog will enjoy visiting whether you live in the neighborhood or not.

From Saw Mill Parkway, take Ashford Avenue west. Just after it becomes Broadway in the center of town, turn left onto Clinton Avenue past the Masters School. Turn left on Judson and follow it to the end. To reach the other entrance, take Clinton Avenue past Judson Road until it turns into Villard Avenue. Turn left on Ferndale Drive and go to the end. Open sunrise–sunset. 914/478-2380.

Restaurants

La Vera Gastronomia: When all the summer outdoor cafés have closed for the season, and you and your dog are longing for a gourmet supper, stop by this take-out restaurant. Serving great brick oven–pizza and Italian specialties, you and your dog will be enjoying your own gastronomia in the privacy of your own home. 598 Warburton Avenue; 914/478-1212.

Scoops-on-the-Hudson: There's little we like better than a scoop of ice cream after (or before or during) a good long walk. When the scoops are as scrumptious as the ones at Scoops, our taste buds take on that glow of expectation. Inu likes plain vanilla, but George goes for fresh blueberry every time. There aren't any tables outside so you'll have to take yours to-go, but we've never found this to slow us down a bit. 575 Warburton Avenue; 914/478-0784.

KATONAH

Nature Hikes and Urban Walks

John Jay Homestead: The beautiful home of the first chief justice of the U.S. Supreme Court is open for walking tours and your dog is welcome to join. Jay's illustrious career included serving on the Supreme Court and as the second governor of the state of New York State. He lived at this elegant estate until his death in 1829; five generations of Jays maintained the residence until 1926, when the home was given to the state of New York. There is a one-mile self-guided nature trail that leads through the gardens and over the grounds on this country estate. Leashed pets are welcome. The historic site is open 8 A.M.–sunset. Rte. 22; 914/232-5651.

Restaurants

Katonah Restaurant: This pleasant diner is located right in the heart of Katonah. With the usual standard diner fare to choose from, we won't claim there is anything very exciting about the food, but because location is everything you won't get any complaints from your four-footed pals. Especially when they discover the many shaded tables outside on Main Street. So order an all-American burger, fries, chocolate shake, and a mixed green salad with bleu cheese dressing and enjoy a slice of small town Americana. And speaking of slices—make room for the apple pie. 63 Katonah Avenue; 914/232-9241.

LARCHMONT

Dogs are not allowed in any Larchmont parks. Grr!

Restaurants

Tequila Sunrise: Enjoy great Mexican food, cocktails, or brunch outside on the patio at this festive restaurant. Tequila Sunrise serves an excellent choice of Mexican and Southwestern cuisine, so you and your *amigo* will be begging for *mas*. Dogs allowed outside at the outer tables. 145 Larchmont Avenue; 914/834-6378.

Watercolor Café: This intimate little café has two outdoor tables where you and your dog may indulge on such varied items as grilled lamb, paella, or vegetarian dishes. There is an excellent rotating selection of wines by the glass. Serving lunch, dinner, and Sunday brunch. 2094 Boston Post Road; 914/834-2213.

MAMARONECK

Parks, Beaches, and Recreation Areas

13 Harbor Island Park 🐾 🐾 ◀●

This lovely park isn't large and isn't very hospitable towards dogs, but it *is* scenic and located along the Long Island Sound. However, dogs are only allowed here in those seductively swimmable months of December through March. Yes, it's true. After enduring all the No Dogs Allowed signs in most of the towns along the sound, discovering that dogs are allowed here only during the coldest months of the year is hardly cause for celebration. But the policy in many of these towns along the Sound seems to be that beggars (or dogs) can't be choosers, so be happy you can have an ocean view at least a few months a year. This park isn't large enough to give you a workout, but our dogs are happy enough to sniff and wander along the water's edge, blissfully unaware that they are experiencing a rare treat. Dogs must be leashed. From I-95 (New England Thruway) north, take Exit 18A to Fenmore Road east. Turn left onto U.S. 1 (Boston Post Road). The park is immediately on your right. Open 8 A.M.–dusk. 914/864-7000.

MOUNT PLEASANT

Parks, Beaches, and Recreation Areas

14 Graham Hills Park 🐾 🐾 🐾 ✕

This secluded wilderness park covers 70 acres of hilly woodland with several miles of trails criss-crossing through it. Popular with mountain bikers, you'll have to watch your back, but hikers, dog walkers, and cyclists seem to coexist fairly well here on the busy weekends. During the weekdays you'll usually have it to yourself.

There is a small stream that trickles through the forest and the well-marked trails are easy to follow. Be sure to bring your bug spray on hot summer days; it can get quite thick with mosquitoes. The best thing about this county park is that your dog may wander leash-free as long as she is under voice control; our dogs give it a big paws-up for this rare exception.

Take the Taconic Parkway north just past the Saw Mill Parkway. There is a park entrance to the east, immediately after you cross the Saw Mill Parkway. Open dawn–dusk. 914/864-7000.

15 Hardscrabble Wilderness Area 🐾 🐾 🐾 🐾 ✕

You may not be in real wilderness when you visit here, but your dog won't mind because she gets to run off-leash here with plenty of other canine pals. This 235-acre park, an understandably popular meeting place for local dog walkers, is one of the best parks in the county and once you visit, you'll see why.

ARROOOOOOOOOOO

There are miles of lovely woodland trails, a waterfall, gurgling brook, a great swimming lake, and lots of room to stretch your legs. The four loop trails are well marked, thanks to the tireless effort of local residents, and there are enough spots here that Spot will exhaust himself trying to see them all. Trail maps are available at the entrances; we recommend you use them.

Our favorite entry into the park is off Hardscrabble Road, because it puts us in sniffing distance of Hardscrabble Lake. You'll find plenty of local dogs and their owners hanging around the old swimming hole in every season. Trails lead off into the woods from there. Dogs may be off-leash if under voice control.

From Taconic Parkway take Pleasantville Avenue. Turn left at the off-ramp and take an immediate right onto Dogwood Lane. Go to the end and park.

Other parking and entrances are along Washburn Road and on Hardscrabble Road. Open dawn–dusk. 914/742-2310.

16 Kensico Dam Plaza 🐾 🐾 🐾 🐾

On your first visit to the Kensico Dam, you'll be forgiven if you mistake this awesome structure for an Aztec pyramid. Named for the Siwanoy sachem "Cokenseko" and built in 1915, the huge stone dam measures over 300 feet high and 1,830 feet long. And although your dog may not give two sticks for such an imposing piece of architecture, he'll be very happy to discover the surrounding park is equally impressive.

There are several miles of beautiful woodland trails that run in and around the dam. Although the reservoir is off-limits to your pup, there are enough sniffs and smells along the trails to keep an adventurous dog happy.

One note of caution: The trails are also popular with mountain cyclists so keep an eye out. Dogs must be leashed. There is a parking fee of $2.25 for non-residents; $1.75 for residents with an Empire Pass. Located at the northern terminus of the Bronx River Parkway (Exit 27) and the southern end of the Taconic Parkway. Open dawn–dusk. 914/737-7530

17 Rockefeller State Park Preserve 🐾 🐾 🐾 🐾

With an extensive network of trails weaving throughout this 1,000-acre park, you won't get tired of visiting here over and over. Once part of the Rockefeller estate, there are over 20 miles of carriage paths for you and your wandering pup to explore. This is one time your dog's good nose will help you, because the trails are not especially well-marked and seem to make sense only to a horse.

One of our favorite hikes is along the Sleepy Hollow Trail, which leads to the Pocantico River. If you prefer lake swimming, head for Swan Lake. (That's right, if watching for the Headless Horseman on the Sleepy Hollow Trail doesn't give you the willies, then a visit to Swan Lake certainly will.) Here you can circumvent the 24-acre lake or dive right in.

From the lake, take a short walk up to the overlook for great views of the lake and beyond. Pick up a map at the main entrance or take a look at the posted maps at the visitor center and Swan Lake. From U.S. 9, take Rte. 117 east 1.3 miles. The park and the entrance are on your right. Open 8 A.M.–dusk. 914/631-1470.

NEW ROCHELLE

New Rochelle isn't a place we'd call dog-friendly. In fact, it's downright unfriendly when it comes to our four-footed friends. With some of the most beautiful parks located along Long Island Sound, we can understand protecting these lovely spots of green—but between the No Dogs Allowed and the Residents Only signs, we started getting the picture that we really weren't very welcome here. So, with the exception of one residents-only county park, making a special trip to New Rochelle with your dog probably isn't the best way to spend a Saturday afternoon.

Parks, Beaches, and Recreation Areas

18 Glen Island Park 🐾 🐾 🐾

If it weren't for Glen Island Park, dogs would be completely shut out in New Rochelle. Of course, if you don't live in New Rochelle, you, too, will be shut out. This residents-only park is the only park in the city that allows dogs. Located along the water, you'll find well-maintained picnic areas, a sandy beach (where dogs are not allowed in the summer months), and several grassy areas for ball throwing. The price is step; however. A $30 annual resident pass is required (not to be confused with the Empire Pass, which is good in all county parks). Passes are issued at the park office and ID is required. Dogs must be leashed. Got all that?

From the New England Thruway (I-95), take Exit 15 to U.S. 1 (Boston Post Road) north for one block. Turn right on Weyman Avenue. Take the Glen Island Approachment across the bridge into the park. Open 8 A.M.–dusk. 914/632-9500.

Places to Stay

Rose Hill Guest House: This quaint bed and breakfast welcomes dogs of all sizes. With three private rooms and a master suite (only available on request), you and your pup will feel right at home at this French country inn. Continental breakfast is served each morning and there is an enclosed dog run out back for Fido. Rates are $89–135 plus an additional $10 per stay if your dog uses the run. 44 Rose Hill Avenue, New Rochelle, NY 10804; 914/632-6464; website: www.bnbfinders.com.

NORTH CASTLE

Parks, Beaches, and Recreation Areas

19 Wampus Pond Park 🐾 🐾

This park is the story of pond triumphing over park. The park part is really just a 500-yard section of green hugging the edges of a lovely lake. The good news is that if you're looking for a bit of cool clean water to alleviate the dog days of summer, you'll find it here. The bad news? The banks leading to the water's edge slope in a way that doesn't allow a truly easy way to access the water. But water dogs will find a way, so if you need to beat the summer heat, this pond, uh park, is a good place to go. Leashed dogs are welcome.

From I-684, take Exit 3S to Rte. 22 south. Turn right on Rte. 128 (Main Street/Mount Kisco Road) and proceed for two miles. The park is on your left. Open dawn–dusk. 914/273-3230.

NORTH SALEM

Parks, Beaches, and Recreation Areas

🐾20 Mountain Lakes Camp 🐾 🐾 🐾 🐾

Although this camp is more camping than hiking, the lakes are the real attraction for our dogs. There are three beautiful lakes here: Pine, Spruce, and Hemlock Lakes. Although Hemlock has the deadliest name, it happens to be our favorite. That's because all the crowds tend to hang out at the swimming beach at Spruce Lake—you'll find you usually have Hemlock to your Socrates-loving self.

There are over 1,000 acres here, mostly composed of camping sites and cabins. The trails tend to weave in and out of the developed areas, but the woods are plentiful and the lakes clean and clear. Our water dogs really don't care about hiking when they have the option of swimming, so we have to give this place a major paws-up for the wet world it provides.

Camping is available throughout the park and reservations must be made in advance. There are tent sites and cabin camping. For seasonal rates and reservations, call 914/669-5793.

To get to Hemlock Lake, follow the Boating sign past the main beach area on Mountain Lakes Road and turn at your next left. Dogs are to be leashed in all county parks.

From Interstate 684, take Exit 6 to Rte. 35 east about three miles. Turn left onto County Road 121 north about five miles. Right onto Hawley Road. Turn left onto Mountain Lakes Road into the park. Open 8 A.M.–dusk. 914/669-5793.

Places to Stay

Mountain Lakes Camp: See the Mountain Lakes Camp, above.

DIVERSION

Say Grace at Gracelane: Although we don't usually list kennels, this one is rather special. Built in 1911, Gracelane is the oldest canine boarding facility in the country and the accommodations are more like camp than kennel. Private indoor cabins facilities, with an outdoor run that the dogs can utilize all day, offer ample room for your pup to enjoy a home away from home. So if you must, absolutely must, leave your dog for a weekend, you can do no better than this homey spot. 46 Gracelane; 914/762-6188, 888/734-6188; website: www.gracelane.com.

DIVERSIONS

Farmer Fidos: Our dogs like to people watch while we choose from an array of fresh produce, bakery items, and crafts at Westchester's local farmer's markets.

Ossining: Main and Spring Streets; 914/923-4837. Pick a peck of pickled peppers every Saturday, 8:30 A.M.–2 P.M. at this farmer's market, held from May through October. Leashed dogs are welcome.

Peekskill: Bank Street; 845/737-2780. You can bring your leashed dog with you, but you should do the picking at this weekly farmer's market, held every Saturday, May through October, 8:30 A.M.–2 P.M.

Tarrytown: At Patriot's Park on U.S. 9; 914/631-1705. Pick one potato or a whole bag of them at Tarrytown's weekly farmer's market. Your leashed dog is welcome to come help you do the picking every Saturday, May to October, 8:30 A.M.–2 P.M.

Yonkers: Saint John's Church at 1 Hudson Street; 914/963-3033. The musical *Guys and Dolls* may feature references to Yonkers, but you won't find any dancing girls or backroom craps games at the weekly farmer's market here. Only fresh produce and great baked goods. Even better, your leashed dog is welcome to help you make your weekly choices. Held every Saturday morning, May through October, 8:30 A.M.–2 P.M.

PEEKSKILL

Parks, Beaches, and Recreation Areas

21 Riverfront Green 🐾 🐾

This waterfront park is a half-mile strip of green along the mighty Hudson River. Composed mainly of picnic tables, grass, and a great view, its best feature is the much-needed water recreation it provides in the hot summer months. It's a good option if you live here, but we can't get too enthusiastic about it when Blue Mountain Reservation is just up the road.

Dogs must be leashed here. From U.S. 9, take Main Street west one block. Turn left onto Water Street. The park is on your right. Open dawn–dusk. 845/346-4188.

Places to Stay

Peekskill Inn: There are 53 rooms at this suburban motel; most have panoramic views of the Hudson River and plenty of space for you and your four-footed friend. Stay here and you'll be within walking distance to the river and driving distance to the fabulous Blue Mountain Reservation. Pets allowed on approval; small pets preferred. Rates are $75–100. 634 Main Street, Peekskill, NY 10566; 914/739-1500 or 800/526-9466; website: www.peekskillinn.com.

POUND RIDGE

Parks, Beaches, and Recreation Areas

🐾 Ward Pound Ridge Reservation 🐾 🐾 🐾 🐾

This park is the real deal. Dogs, birders, hikers, cross-country skiers—in other words, just about anybody who likes the outdoors—will agree this 4,300-acre park has something for everyone. With over 35 miles of hiking trails, open meadows, hills, woodlands, and rocky overlooks, you and your dog will never grow tired of visiting this wonderful reservation.

The northern section of the park is also the most developed. The park entrance is on Boutonville Road; from here, follow signs to the Trailside Nature Museum. You can pick up trail maps here—a must if you want to explore this park efficiently. Our favorite walk is a five-mile loop (marked with white blazes) that follows the Cross River. The trail, accessible from the picnic area, is a quiet woodland walk. The Cross River varies from a bubbling brook to a muddy flow depending on the season. From the picnic area you can also branch onto the Blue Trail, which will take you to the highest point in the park—an overlook of 860 feet.

In the southern section, accessible from Michigan Road, the Red Trail leads across the meadow to a wetland trail that eventually arrives at some open ledges that look out over Stone Hill River Valley and the Cross River Reservoir. This section is the most varied and secluded in the park, but also the swampiest; in the summertime, bug spray is mandatory and, despite the dampness, there is little drinkable or swimmable water for your dog.

There are some interesting side paths off the Red Trail, however. The most famous is the path that leads to the Leatherman's Cave, named for a leather-clad hermit who lived here from 1858–1889. The Leatherman retraced his steps along the same path through New York and Connecticut every 33 days. He may have been a bit odd, but he knew a good view when he found it. From the Red Trail, take the white-blazed path when you reach a large intersection at the two-mile mark; the left fork will take you directly to the cave and a breathtaking view. (A map will definitely help you here unless your dog can pick up the scent of ancient leather!)

Camping is permitted in the open-face shelters throughout the park; the cost is $7 per night. Water and toilet facilities are nearby and each shelter comes with an outside grill and picnic table. Tent sites are available on a first-come, first-served basis although you must obtain a permit at the park office. For more information, call 914/864-7317.

Dogs should be leashed in the public picnic and camping areas.

On summer weekends there is an entrance fee of $3.50 for Empire Pass holders and $7 for all other visitors. From I-684, take Exit 6 to Rte. 35 west for four miles. Turn right onto Rte. 121 and take an immediate left onto Boutonville Road into the park. Open 8 A.M.–dusk. 914/864-7317.

Places to Stay

Ward Pound Ridge Reservation Campground: See the Ward Pound Ridge Reservation listing, above.

RYE

Parks, Beaches, and Recreation Areas

23 Rye Town Beach and Park 🐾 🐾 🐾

George and Inu give a major paws-up to the town of Rye for not only allowing dogs at this beach park, but for also allowing non-residents. Of course, the welcome mat only gets extended so far because dogs are not allowed on the swimming beach May–October, but in the off-season you and your leashed pup may enjoy this lovely stretch of sand.

The beach area is surrounded by a lovely tree-lined park; you and your dog are welcome to take your daily walk here all year round. The park isn't large, so we wouldn't recommend a special trip here, unless you can also expand your walk to include the beach. But if you live here, we suspect this is your daily stop with Spot. Parking is a challenge during the summer. There is no street parking, so you'll have to cough up the parking fee of $3 for residents and $5 for non-residents. Leashed dogs only, please.

From the New England Thruway (I-95), take Exit 19 to the Playland Parkway east for a mile. Turn right onto Forest Avenue and proceed for two blocks. The park is on your left. Open 7 A.M.–midnight. 914/967-0965.

SCARSDALE

Parks, Beaches, and Recreation Areas

24 Garth Woods 🐾 🐾 🐾

Although most of the Bronx River Reservation is accessible from the Bronx River Reservation Pathway, Garth Woods is an especially lovely section that has several woodland trails branching off from the main path. Here you can wander in a shaded glen and play in the river as it gurgles by. Inu likes this section in the summer when so many of the water spots are crowded or off-limits. George likes it in the fall, when the leaves turn color and he can get especially muddy in the river and shake himself all over JoAnna's occasionally clean car.

This section of the adjacent parkway is also closed to car traffic on Sunday in May and June and in September and October, 10 A.M.–2 P.M. Dogs must be leashed. From the Bronx River Parkway, take Exit 4 to Scarsdale Center. Park on Scarsdale Road or in the small parking area on Carpenter Street. Open dawn–dusk. 914/593-2600.

25 Saxon Woods Park 🐾 🐾

Before the county golf course and the town swim club cut into it, Saxon Woods was quite large. What remains today of the once-rustic woods is a county park with a few short trails.

For the best access to the woods we suggest you enter from the swim club parking lot. From here you can follow a short loop trail through the thick pine forest or take the path along the Mamaroneck Brook and Mamaroneck Avenue to the park's picnic area. This route is a little overgrown, but does give you access to the brook. The picnic area is composed of just a few tables and is also accessible by car.

Dogs need to be leashed and, because of the overgrown foliage, you will find a number of signs warning of the ticks here. From Hutchinson River Parkway, take Exit 23 to Mamaroneck Avenue south for a third of a mile. The park's two entrances are on the right. The swim club entrance is first and the picnic area is next. Open 8 A.M.–dusk. 914/995-4480.

TARRYTOWN

Although we'd love to tell you that dogs are welcome at Washington Irving's home, Sunnyside, we should warn you that dogs can't set paw on any of the many historic estates in the land of the Knickerbockers. The injustice is enough to make the Headless Horseman ride again!

Parks, Beaches, and Recreation Areas

26 Tarrytown Lakes 🐾 🐾 🐾

This series of lovely woodland trails surrounding the Tarrytown Reservoir make for a great afternoon walk. There are pathways that lead along the shores of both small reservoirs, but the best access here is along the North County Trailway, which begins at the parking area off Neperan Road. You'll walk along the shore on a paved path that meanders through a woodland only a heartbeat away from the road. Despite that, you'll feel like you're away from everything. Just watch out for the cyclists who use the trailway, as well. The North County Trailway is described in more detail in the South County and North County Trailways section at the beginning of this chapter.

Dogs must be leashed and are not allowed in the water. From the Saw Mill Parkway, take Neperan Road west about 0.5 miles. Parking area is on your right by the dam. There is another parking area two miles west, also on Neperan Road at the other side of the reservoir. Open dawn–dusk. 914/864-7000.

Nature Hikes and Urban Walks

Old Croton Aqueduct Trail: You can pick up the Tarrytown-to-Scarborough section of this county-long trail at Hamilton Place, which is just off North Broadway, a block past Main Street. A little over a mile up the trail, you'll enter Rockefeller State Park Preserve (described in the Mount Pleasant section, above) and eventually arrive in the village of Scarborough. In all, this section is about five miles long. 914/693-5259.

Restaurants

Horsefeathers: This well-known restaurant offers reliable cuisine at reasonable prices. Whether you're hungry for such diverse fare as garlic bread with basil and parmesan, Alaskan king crab, or shepherd's pie, you can find it here. You will also find a great outdoor patio where your dog is welcome. Located on the main drag, this restaurant is certainly no drag. 94 North Broadway; 914/631-6606.

Lago di Como Ristorante: This excellent Italian restaurant serves the best focaccia bread we've tasted. It smells so good that our dogs always want to sneak a bite from their seat under our outdoor table. But we don't ask them to share their kibbles, do we? Fortunately, the management makes them feel better by offering a bowl of water and a great view of Main Street. 27 Main Street; 914/631-7227.

Main Street Café: We have a suspicion that the merchants of Tarrytown were struggling to come up with names for their establishments, so they just named them all Main Street something or other. In keeping with tradition, Main Street Café offers American café food on Main Street; you shouldn't have any trouble finding it. The food isn't original, but it is very good—and the outdoor tables make it even better. Dine alfresco with your main mutt at Main Street Café. 24 Main Street; 914/524-9770.

Main Street Sweets: When your sweet tooth is killing you, make a killing at this old-fashioned ice cream parlor located on (where else?) Main Street. Serving homemade ice cream and plenty of sugary treats, you can be sure you'll need to take a walk on the Old Croton Aqueduct Trail to work off the calories. 35 Main Street; 914/332-5757.

Places to Stay

Hilton Tarrytown: Dogs are welcome at this faux "country estate," which is really more of a countrified conference center. Located near the woods made famous by Washington Irving's "The Legend of Sleepy Hollow," the staff at this comfortable resort hotel will make you and your dog feel at home. Rates are $109–159 per night. No extra fee for your dog, but you must make reservations in advance. 455 South Broadway, Tarrytown, NY 10591; 914/631-5700 or 800/HILTONS (800/445-8667); website: www.hilton.com.

Marriott Westchester: Pets are welcome at this full-service hotel. Located close to all the parks and historical sites, this large hotel almost always has room at the inn. Pets are welcome, but larger dogs (over 40 pounds) must be approved. Rates are $125–175 per night. A refundable deposit is required for Fifi. 670 White Plains Road, Tarrytown, NY 10591; 914/631-2200 or 800/228-9290; website: www.marriott.com.

WHITE PLAINS

Restaurants

The Little Spot Ltd.: This little roadside hot dog stand makes for a good stop on your way to or from Silver Lake Preserve (see the listing in the Harrison section). The proprietors brag that they offer the "best dogs in town" and although George claims he's had better, we have to admit they're pretty doggone good. There are plenty of shaded tables outside. 854 North Broadway; 914/761-1334.

Sweetwaters: This elegant little café offers continental cuisine in a French-style atmosphere. With a varied menu ranging from roasted chicken, steamed artichokes, and quiche, you can satisfy the most finicky eaters here. A lovely outdoor garden is open to you and your well-behaved dog on request. 577 North Broadway; 914/328-8918.

Places to Stay

Residence Inn by Marriott: Studios and one- and two-bedroom suites are available at this extended-stay hotel. With kitchen facilities and full amenities in all rooms, you and your dog will feel at home here. Rates are $150–295 a day. Dogs are an additional $15 a day plus a non-refundable $75 cleaning fee per stay. 5 Barker Avenue, White Plains, NY 10601; 914/761-7700 or 800/331-3131; website: www.residenceinn.com.

Summerfield Suites by Wyndham: This extended-stay property offers 150 one- and two-bedroom suites, all with kitchens and living rooms. Dogs are allowed with a $10 daily fee and one-time $150 cleaning fee per stay. Rates are $99–189. 101 Corporate Park, White Plains, NY 10604 914/251-9700 or 800/833-4353; website: www.wyndham.com.

YONKERS

Parks, Beaches, and Recreation Areas

27 Sprain Ridge Park 🐾 🐾

Although you will see "No Dogs Allowed" signs as you drive to the entrance of this county park, don't be alarmed. It is true that dogs are not allowed at the pool area that dominates the northern section of the park, but fear not, your dog is welcome on the trails through the surrounding woods.

We can't get too excited by this park, even though it does encompass over 300 acres. It gets very busy during the summer, and it is difficult to find a little corner of the world where your dog can, well, be a dog. But in the off-season when the park isn't so overrun by two-legged folk, you may wish to explore some of its woodsy trails. The Sprain Reservoir, which beckons so tantalizingly in the distance is, unfortunately, off-limits.

Dogs must be leashed. There is a parking fee of $5.75 in the summer. To reach the southern section from I-87 (New York State Thruway), take Exit 6A into the park. To reach the northern section, take Sprain Brook Parkway to Jackson Avenue west. Go about 0.5 miles and turn left into the park entrance. Open 8 A.M.–dusk. 914/231-3450.

YORKTOWN

Parks, Beaches, and Recreation Areas

28 Franklin D. Roosevelt State Park 🐾 🐾

This small state park is composed mainly of camping and boating facilities. There are only a few trails above the campground for dogs to enjoy, but the water access makes up for what is lacking in trails. Crom Pond and the larger Mohansic Lake are perfect places to cool down your hot dog, but you must avoid the boat launch and the gigantic 1.000-person swimming pool located by the main parking area.

On weekends, there is a $5 day-use fee. Dogs must be leashed in all state parks. From the Taconic Parkway, take the state park exit directly into the park, just north of Rte. 132A and south of Rte. 202. Open 8 A.M.–dusk. 914/245-4434.

29 John E. Hand Park at Bald Mountain 🐾 🐾 🐾 🐕

This park is more trail than playground. Which is exactly what our dogs like. Leading to the top of Bald Mountain, the trail follows a gentle incline through a deciduous forest and hounds that like to actually get somewhere on their walk will enjoy this one. The views that span out over the New Croton Reservoir to the north and Teatown Lake to the south are more than worth the short 1.5-mile round trip. If you are hankering for more, detour south into neighboring Teatown Lake Reservation.

In the winter, during skiing season, you won't be able to access the trail all the way to the top of Bald Mountain.

Dogs under voice control may be off-leash. From Taconic Parkway, take Rte. 134 west 0.25 miles to Spring Valley Road. Take a right onto Blinn Road; a small parking turnout will be on your right just past Journey's End Road. Open dawn–dusk. 914/864-7000.

30 Teatown Lake Reservation 🐾 🐾 🐾 🐾

Visit here once, and you'll wonder what took you so long to find this place. Your dog may be asking the same question. Visit here twice, and you'll wonder why you don't come here every weekend. In our estimation, these 636 acres offer some of the best trails around. With over 15 miles of pathways, boardwalks, and trailways running through here, your only problem will be which walk to choose next.

For help with that problem, maps can be picked up at the Nature Center. One of our favorite walks is the two-mile Lakeside Trail that circles Teatown Lake—it even has a 600-foot boardwalk that crosses one section of the water. The lake isn't really swimming material, but there are a few places where your dog can probably wade without getting swamp mud all over her.

EARMARK YOUR CALENDAR–OCTOBER

Teatown Lake Reservation Annual Harvest Festival:
Held the first Saturday in October, this family celebration of nature is a day enjoyed by all. Featuring music by local and international bands, plenty of food, a raffle, games, face painting, and general fun for the whole family, this annual event is held at the Nature Center at Teatown Lake Reservation near Yonkers from 10 A.M. to 5 P.M. Admission is $15 per person and all proceeds go to support this wonderful preserve. Leashed dogs are welcome. 914/762-2912; website: www.teatown.org.

Another path worth exploring is the 2.5-mile Hidden Valley Trail that wanders through a hemlock grove, meadow, and a scenic gorge. It connects to the Overlook Trail for a satisfying view of the valley below.

Both the Old Croton Aqueduct Trail and the Briarcliff-Peekskill Pathway run through the reservation. (These trails are described more fully at the beginning of this chapter.) The Briarcliff-Peekskill Trail can be accessed at the northern tip of the Lakeside Trail; pick up the Old Croton Aqueduct Trail at the western end of the lake near Teatown Road.

From the Taconic Parkway, take Rte. 134 west 0.25 miles to Spring Valley Road. Turn right and follow the road about 1.5 miles to the Nature Center parking area on your right. The trails are open from dawn–dusk. The Nature Center is open Tuesday–Saturday, 9 A.M.–5 P.M.; Sunday, 1–5 P.M. 914/762-2912.

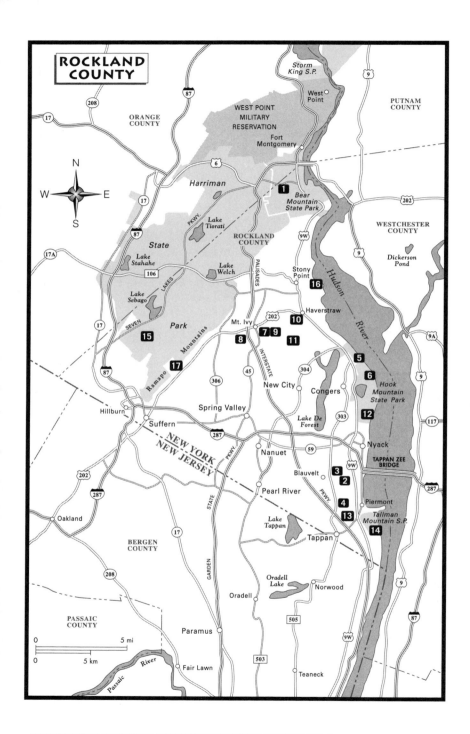

ROCKLAND COUNTY

8 ROCKLAND COUNTY

*It changes every day, you know, the forest, perhaps not to the eye of man,
but certainly to the informed nose. You can smell where hunting dogs have
been, whether or not the rabbits have been out and about, as well as traces
of human passage. And below it all, the dry, sharp smell of pine needles
and wild herbs mixing, on a good day, with the bouquet of a stale ham
sandwich left behind by a passing hiker. Full of surprise, nature.*

— From *A Dog's Life*, by Peter Mayle

This tiny county, only 25 miles from midtown Manhattan, is often an
afterthought for New York City dwellers. Tucked into a triangle next to New
Jersey and the Hudson River, it's easy to forget this rural county is actually
part of New York State. But with 32,000 acres of parkland, your dog won't
ever let you forget. Home to Bear Mountain and Harriman State Parks and
Palisades Interstate Park, the options listed here are simply some of the best
in this book.

Escaping from big city life in New Amsterdam, the Dutch settled this
county along the Hudson River in the 1600s. Today you and your dog will
find your own easy escape from the big city, just minutes over the George

PICK OF THE LITTER–ROCKLAND COUNTY HIGHLIGHTS

BEST DOG PARKS

Kakiat County Park & Dog Run, Suffern

Kennedy-Dells County Park & Dog Run, New City

BEST FORESTS AND NATURAL AREAS

Bear Mountain State Park, Bear Mountain

Harriman State Park, Sloatsburg

BEST BEACH

Nyack Beach State Park, Nyack

Washington Bridge. We haven't listed each and every city park—if you live here, you know where your local park is. If you don't, we only tell you about the ones worth getting in your car and driving out of the city for. And believe us, there are quite a few.

Whether you want to experience a little American Revolution history at Stony Point Battlefield, enjoy the artistic community of Nyack, hike an original section of the Appalachian Trail, roam free in the three splendid state parks, or enjoy the spacious lands of the many county parks, there is a little something for everyone in this county—especially for hounds in need of a quick trip out of the concrete jungle. For more information contact the Rockland County Office of Tourism, 10 Piermont Avenue, Nyack, NY 10960; 845/353-5533; website: www.rockland.org.

Appalachian Trail: The very first section of this famed 2,160-mile trail that runs from Maine to Georgia began right here in New York at Bear Mountain State Park. Running 88 miles from the Hudson River, through Bear Mountain and Harriman State Parks and into Sterling Forest in Putnam County, the Appalachian Trail was the brainchild of naturalist Benton MacKaye. MacKaye, fearful of the loss of open space in the east way back in 1921, championed the idea of a trail that would run along the mountain ridges of the northeastern and southeastern United States.

Thankfully, his dream came true. The Appalachian Trail, of course, went on to become much larger than even MacKaye envisioned. Here in New York you and your dog can still enjoy this scenic section, preserved for us since 1923. Need we say it? Treat it respectfully so future generations will be able to enjoy it as well. For more information, or to contribute to the Appalachian Trail Conference, contact the organization at P.O. Box 807, Harpers Ferry, WV 25425; 304/535-6331; website: www.appalachiantrail.org.

Palisades Interstate Park: By 1900, development and mining threatened the very existence of the Palisades, the spectacular cliffs along the western shore of the Hudson River. Fortunately, conservationists stepped in with a monumental plan to create a giant park encompassing all of the Palisades and much of Orange, Rockland, Sullivan and Ulster Counties in New York and northern Bergen County in New Jersey. Just describing this plan is difficult and actually preserving all of this land has yet to happen. However, much has been done and today, a scattered group of beaches, forests, historic sites and the cliffs themselves form the Palisades Interstate Park. To manage so many parks across state lines, the Palisades Interstate Park Commission was established under the state park systems of both New York and New Jersey. All together, the Palisades Interstate Park is made up of over 20 parks covering some 100,000 acres, and is the inspiration for the movie term "cliffhanger"—a reference to the many movies filmed here in 1920s and 1930s.

Many of the parks listed in this chapter are part of the Palisades Interstate Park and managed by the Palisades Interstate Park Commission.

The park's Visitor Center is on the Palisades Interstate Parkway between Exits 16 and 17. You can purchase trail maps and historical information here. Open 8 A.M.–5 P.M. daily. 845/786-5003.

Additional information and maps are available at the Park Headquarters in Alpine, New Jersey at Exit 2 off the Palisades Interstate Parkway and at website: www.njpalisades.org. The Palisades Interstate Park Commission also has its own website: www.pipc.org.

BEAR MOUNTAIN

Parks, Beaches, and Recreation Areas

1 Bear Mountain State Park 🐾 🐾 🐾 🐾

This wonderful state park, a part of the Palisades Interstate Park, regularly makes everyone's top 10 list. With over 5,067 acres located along and above the Hudson River, George and Inu never get tired of "bearing" a visit here.

The centerpiece of any visit is beautiful Hessian Lake. Originally called Lake Sinnipink by local Native Americans, it was changed to Bloody Pond after unsuccessful British raids on Fort Clinton and Fort Montgomery on September 16, 1777. According to legend, the bodies of the mercenary Hessian soldiers killed in this attack were dumped into the 40-foot deep water. Later, in the 1800s when blocks of ice were cut from the lake and shipped to New York City, it was renamed Highland Lake (maybe the city thought they might have a slight PR problem selling ice from Bloody Lake).

EARMARK YOUR CALENDAR

Bear Mountain offers gatherings to keep you and your dogs busy winter, spring, summer, and fall.

Farmer's Market: Every weekend from 10 A.M. to 6 P.M., you and your dog can sniff your way through delicious fresh produce, honey, baked pies, and other exotic offerings at the farmer's market. Held from May through October at the Bear Mountain Inn parking area, this is one farmer's market worth visiting. Admission is free to the market but there is a $5 parking fee. For more information, call 845/786-2731.

Octoberfest: Bring your pup along for a whole lotta fun at the annual **Bear Mountain Inn Octoberfest.** Held the last two weekends in September and the first two weekends in October at Hessian Lake in Bear Mountain State Park, the event features plenty of German comfort food, beer from around the world, and various Rhineland bands. Admission is free and your leashed dog is welcome at all outdoor events. 845/786-2731.

Bear Mountain Holiday Festival: Join the fun for the **annual tree lighting** at the Bear Mountain Inn at Bear Mountain State Park. See Santa arrive and watch the festival kick off with a firework show. Leashed dogs are allowed at all outdoor events. The festival runs from the first week in December through New Year's Day, but the tree lighting occurs the first Saturday in December. For information, call 845/786-2731.

Finally, when Bear Mountain State Park opened in 1910, the name was change to Hessian Lake.

The good news—this is one of the most beautiful lakes in the metropolitan region. The bad news—your dog is not allowed to swim here. We like to saunter along the promenade that leads around it, but our dogs are completely dumbfounded that we don't let them cut loose and go for a swim. If your dogs are as water-happy as ours are, you might want to distract them at the southern section of the lake by the lodge, and take the White Trail or the Yellow Trail. Or, if you still want to stay close to the water, pick up the Red Trail. This trail leads along the western side of the lake and then north to a wonderful lookout spot where you'll get an excellent view of the Hudson River Valley. If you're feeling really frisky, you can continue on the Red Trail (also called the Major Welch Trail) for a three-mile trek all the way to the top of Bear Mountain.

If you want an easy way up to the top of the mountain, you can drive up Perkins Road to the same spectacular overlook. Our top choice is hiking on the Appalachian Trail, which runs through the park. This part of the 2,150-mile trail is actually the original section completed in 1923 and has the lowest elevation of any segment. You can pick it up off Seven Lakes Road about 0.5 miles past Exit 19 off Rte. 6. You can also park at the lot off Exit 17 of the Palisades Interstate Parkway. Take the Appalachian Trail, marked by white blazes, north three miles to the top of scenic Bear Mountain.

Another favorite trail is up Dunderberg Mountain, where you and your happy dog will gape at magnificent views overlooking the Hudson River. The best access—and the one that offers countless craggy viewpoints along the way—is along either the Rampopo-Dunderberg Trail or the Timp-Torme Trail. Park at the lot off U.S. 9W just south of Jones Point, and follow the trail for 0.25 miles. The Rampopo-Dunderberg Trail leads to your right and the Timp-Torme Trail veers off to the left. Both are rather steep trails and should be tackled only by experienced hikers.

For an easy scenic nature walk, take the trail out to Iona Island. The trail is surrounded by marshes and high reeds, and you can't actually reach the Hudson River, but the walk is beautiful and makes for a great change of pace from the surrounding forests. Look for the marked turnout off U.S. 9W a mile south of the main lodge.

To make sense of all these trails, we strongly recommend that you pick up a map at the ranger station along Seven Lakes Road in Harriman State Park in Sloatsburg or at the Bear Mountain Inn off U.S. 9W. The infinite number of combinations you can weave together within Bear Mountain State Park and adjoining Harriman State Park is unparalleled in the New York City area.

Dogs need to be leashed and are not allowed in the Trailside Museum and Zoo. From the Palisades Interstate Parkway, take Exit 19 to Seven Lakes Drive east for three and a half miles into the park. Open 8 A.M.–dusk. 845/786-2701.

BLAUVELT

Parks, Beaches, and Recreation Areas

🐾 Blauvelt State Park 🐾 🐾 🐾

If peace and quiet is your aim, this 590-acre state park may just fill the bill. Accessible through Tackamack Park, it often gets lost in the shadow of the larger parks that make up the Palisades Interstate Park, so odds are you and your dog will probably enjoy a private walk in these woods. Originally built in 1910 as a National Guard rifle range, it was abandoned soon after opening and later served as an ROTC training area during World War I. It became a state park after World War II.

No evidence of a military presence remains, but you can hike on patriotic red- and white-blazed trails up hilly Clausen Mountain and through the forest. Autumn is an especially glorious time in these woods. Although most of these paths are through forest roads, on any given day you'll be sure to see wild turkeys, deer, and plenty of migratory birds. Dogs need to be leashed in all state parks.

From the New York Thruway (Interstate 87), take Exit 12 to Rte. 303 south for a quarter mile. Left onto Nyack Road. Immediate right onto Greenbush Road for three quarters of a mile. Left onto Clausland Mountain Road for a half mile. The park is on the left. The parking areas close at 6 P.M. but the park is open dawn–dusk. 845/786-2701.

🐾 Buttermilk Falls County Park 🐾 🐾

This 72-acre park is composed mostly of undeveloped woodlands with a single marked trail for you and your pup. Located right next to Blauvelt State Park, it is hard to know where one park ends and the other begins, but your dog won't really care as long as you enjoy these woods on a brilliant fall day. We aren't thrilled with this park in the summer because there isn't any water for swimming and the humidity attracts plenty of bugs, but when the weather is cool and dry, you're both in for a treat.

Dogs must be leashed.

From the New York Thruway (I-87), take Exit 12 to Rte. 303 south for about 0.25 miles. Turn left onto Nyack Road and then take an immediate right onto Greenbush Road and proceed about 0.25 miles. The parking area is on the left. Open 8 A.M.–sunset. 845/354-7900.

🐾 Tackamack Park 🐾 🐾

This 105-acre park adjoins Blauvelt and Clausland Mountain State Parks, providing several woodland trails that you can extend into a longer walk through the state parks if you like. The main trailhead begins off Clausland Mountain Road and continues up the mountain into Blauvelt State Park. You can also walk across the road from the parking area and enter Clausland Mountain State Park via a shady woodland trail through some swampy woods. Beware of bugs and mosquitoes in the wet season.

From the New York Thruway (I-87), take Exit 12 to Rte. 303 and proceed south for about 0.25 miles. Turn left onto Nyack Road and take an immediate right onto Greenbush Road and proceed for a mile. Turn left onto Clausland Mountain Road to enter the park. Open dawn–dusk. 845/359-5100.

CONGERS

Parks, Beaches, and Recreation Areas

🐾 Hook Mountain State Park 🐾 🐾 🐾

This long and narrow 676-acre park runs along the Hudson River within the Palisades Interstate Park. The Long Path, which is the main trail here, runs high along the Palisades Ridge and up Hook Mountain, which rises 728 feet—

the second highest point in the Palisades. There isn't a lot of room for running and romping here (and we definitely don't advise ball throwing unless your dog can fly), but if you're looking for a scenic walk, you won't do much better than here.

The Hook Mountain Bike Path runs along the Hudson River below and can be reached through the Ticor Quarry in Dutchtown. Essentially a long narrow trail along the Hudson River, you and your dog will enjoy great water views here, alternating from water's edge up to 60 feet or so above the water. Along the way you'll come across the remains of abandoned quarries and one intriguing rock that bears the inscription: Andre the Spy Landed Here September 21, 1780. This refers to the British major, John Andre, who was executed by the Americans for colluding with Benedict Arnold in 1783 in what is now Tallman State Park. Usually George the Dog attempts a leg lift on the remains of Andre's memory, but we're impressed by the landmark nonetheless. The bike path runs six miles within Hook Mountain State Park and another six miles through Rockland State Park into Nyack Beach State Park.

To reach the southern section of the park, park at Rockland State Park and follow the Long Trail into Hook Mountain. From U.S. 9W (just north of Rte. 304), take Short Clove Road east one block. Sharp right onto Riverside Avenue past the quarry to the end of a road where there is a small parking area and the trailhead. Open dawn–dusk. 845/268-3020.

6 Rockland Lake State Park 🐾 🐾

Although there are 1,079 acres and a glorious lake in this Palisades Interstate Park, we can't say this is a great place for dogs. Once known for its superior Rockland ice, which was in demand at all the best New York City restaurants in the 19th century, the crystal clear lake is still popular for swimming and recreation in the summer months. But as you drive up to the entrance, you are greeted by No Dogs Allowed signs posted everywhere. They refer to the lake area itself and mean that dogs are forbidden at the formal swimming and picnicking areas.

The rangers tell us leashed dogs are welcome on the outer ring road and the back trails that lead into Hook Mountain State Park and Nyack Beach State Park via the Long Path. George thinks you're better off just going to those other parks and not bothering trying to navigate your way through all those No Dogs Allowed signs.

If you wish to take a slightly more scenic walk on the western side of the lake, park at the back entrance to the part, located on U.S. 9W north of the main entrance. About a mile past the main gate, you'll see a picnic area on your right. Again, your dog won't be allowed to swim in the lake, but at least this road is a little more exciting than the outer ring road. On our last visit we watched a very unhappy beagle walking his owners along the outer road while cars zipped by on their way to the lake. Who needs that?

The park entrance is located off U.S. 9W four miles north of Nyack. Turn right onto Rockland Lake Road and follow signs to the main parking area. There is an $8 parking fee in summer. Open dawn–dusk. 845/268-3020.

MOUNT IVY

Parks, Beaches, and Recreation Areas

🐾 Gurnee Quarry County Park 🐾 🐾

You'll probably need a nose better than a hunting hound to find this small county park but once you do, you'll have it to yourself, not surprisingly. Located just off busy Rte. 45, the park has a single trail that leads through open woods, continuing into South Mountain County Park (see below) for a two-mile walk. The park sits perched up on High Tor Mountain, affording glimpses of the valley below. For a continuous walk of over five miles, begin your stroll here and keep going all the way to High Tor State Park.

Dogs must be leashed. From Rte. 202, take Rte. 45 south and make an immediate left onto Andreana Park Road. A small lot is located here and the single trail leads from this parking area into the park. Open 8 A.M.–sunset. 845/354-7900.

🐾 Mount Ivy County Park 🐾 🐾 🐾

This spacious park offers acres of woodlands for you and your pup to explore. Located at the end of Fireman's Memorial Road, it is also right next to the Hi-Tor Animal Shelter that has a volunteer dog walking program. If your dog likes other pups (and is current on all her shots), stop by the shelter and offer to walk one of the loving dogs waiting to be adopted. On any given Saturday you'll meet up with lots of families taking their favorites out for a short jaunt in the woods. For information on the walking program, call 845/354-7900.

There is ample space to kick up your heels at Mount Ivy County Park, and two small brooks criss-cross their way throughout the park. Our dogs enjoy the wide, open trails and the many trees sprinkled with the scents of all the dogs that pass by. They take the job of marking each with a doggy decal that says, "Inu and George were here." It probably lasts for about 15 minutes, but don't tell them. They like to think their 15 minutes of fame lasts forever.

Dogs must be leashed in all county parks. From Palisades Interstate Parkway, take Exit 12 to Rte. 45 west. Take the first right on Pomona Road and then an immediate right onto Fireman's Memorial Road. Drive to the end of the road and park. Open 8 A.M.–sunset. 845/354-7900.

🖕 South Mountain County Park 🐾 🐾 🐾

Here's another county park that takes a good nose and an even better map to find. Part of the three-park triangle that includes Gurnee Quarry County Park and High Tor State Park, you'll find these 273 woodland acres situated smartly between the other two; odds are, if you visit one of the others, you will also venture into South Mountain County Park.

This park offers a pleasant, if unremarkable, saunter along a single path overlooking the southern part of Rockland County. In the winter, your view is the best; in the summer, the woods can get a bit buggy so be sure to bring bug spray for you and water for your pup. If you venture to the west, you'll wander into Gurnee Quarry County Park. To the east of busy Rte. 33 lies High Tor State Park. Dogs must be leashed.

From Rte. 202, take Rte. 33 south one mile. A small parking area is located on the left at the crest of the hill. Make sure you're watching for it because the turnout is difficult to see at high speeds. Open 8 A.M.–sunset. 845/354-7900.

NEW CITY

Parks, Beaches, and Recreation Areas

🔟 High Tor State Park 🐾 🐾 🐾

These 564 acres mark the highest point in both Rockland County and Palisades Interstate Park. Once used as a signal point by the colonists during the American Revolution, it was in danger of becoming a traprock quarry during the early part of the 20th century until the improbable success of a Broadway play called *High Tor* renewed sentimental interest in the ridge. The Rockland County Conservation Association rallied their forces, and in 1943 their conservation efforts were rewarded when High Tor became part of Palisades Interstate Park.

Although there aren't many trails here and dogs aren't allowed at the swimming area, you can park at the recreation area and hike north up a woods road to an overlook called Little Tor. In total, your hike will be about 3.5 miles through woods and up a gradual rocky ascent.

Enter from South County Mountain Park off Rte. 33 and you can extend your hike another three miles.

Dogs must be on leash. Take U.S. 9W north to South Mountain Road (Rte. 90). Turn left and follow South Mountain Road two miles to the entrance on your right. Go up the hill about 0.5 miles to the parking area on your left. The trail begins up the access road north of the swimming area. Open dawn–dusk. 845/634-8074.

1️⃣1️⃣ Kennedy-Dells County Park & Dog Run 🐾 🐾 🐾 🐾 🐕

We love this wonderful 177-acre county park. Not only does it offer a lovely mix of recreation areas, manicured trails, and open woodlands, but the new dog run is also a big hit with the community. And, for once, this is a dog run that actually has enough room to, uh, run. What a concept!

The dog run is located past the ball fields and through the woods (hmmm. . .sounds like a song) on a rather odd open field that has been partially groomed to make room for a flat, grassy area where your pup can recreate. The enclosure is about the size of a football field and there are several benches, a trash can, and mutt mitts provided. There is little shade except for the trees in the woods beyond, so it can get a bit warm on summer days. But don't tell that to the fleet of happy hounds cavorting on any given day. With tongues hanging, they romp in any weather until their owners drag them home. But even if your dog won't complain, we encourage you to bring your own water and bowl when the weather is hot.

For a longer walk (or if your dog is antisocial) continue across the field into the woods beyond. There, you'll walk on a wide, dirt-packed trail through a quiet woodland, perfect for sniffing and chasing sticks.

There is a map of all trails at the southern end of the parking area. Dogs must be leashed except in the dog run. From Rte. 90 (South Mountain Road) take Rte. 29 (Haverstraw Road) south. At the intersection of Rte. 20 and Main Street North, turn left onto Main Street and take an immediate right into the park. There is another small parking area off Phillips Hill Road. Open 8 A.M.–sunset. 845/354-7900.

NYACK

Only 16 miles from upper Manhattan, this lovely town along the Hudson River represents the heart and soul of Rockland County. One visit confirms the charm and magic of this small town. With countless galleries, shops, and restaurants along Main Street, and river views that have inspired painters as far back as the 18th century, Nyack has been the home of such diverse artists as Edward Hopper, Lotte Lenya, Helen Hayes, and Kurt Weill.

Parks, Beaches, and Recreation Areas

12 Nyack Beach State Park 🐾 🐾 🐾 🐾 🐾

This scenic strip of a state park is located on 564 acres right along the Hudson River and is part of Palisades Interstate Park. One of the best places to actually get up close and personal with the river, you and your dog will meet up with plenty of other happy canines on a walk here.

The park can most easily be accessed through the town of Nyack at the northern end of Broadway. From here you can saunter the scenic Haverstraw Trail, a five-mile river trail that runs along the base of the Palisades cliffs. At the 1.5-mile marker, you'll reach Peninsula Picnic Area, a sandy beach where you can splash in the river. Dogs are not allowed at the swimming beach between the hours of 9 A.M. and 5 P.M. during the summer months, but there are plenty of other places along the trail to get your feet wet.

After another 0.5 miles, you can access the Knickerbocker Fire House Trail, which leads to Rockland Beach State Park. Stay on the Haverstraw Trail if you want to keep close to the water, because dogs aren't allowed to swim at Rockland Lake.

We should warn you that the currents in the Hudson River are strong here, so if your dog is not an experienced swimmer, then you might want to stick to wading instead of your usual swim. Bikes are allowed on the river trail, so keep an eye out and keep your dog leashed.

From U.S. 9W, take Old Mountain Road east for about 0.25 miles. Turn left onto Broadway and proceed about 0.25 miles into the park. Open sunrise–sunset. 845/268-3020.

Nature Hikes and Urban Walks

Downtown Nyack: Take a walk through the artistic downtown of Nyack.

EARMARK YOUR CALENDAR

Food, music, sunshine. . .what more could any dog ask for? Check out these local gatherings in Nyack.

Septemberfest Street Fair: Held the last Saturday in September, 10 A.M.–5 P.M., this annual street fair and block party is so much fun that you'll want to make it a yearly event. Main Street and South Broadway are blocked off to cars so pedestrians (and their dogs) may enjoy street musicians, bands, plenty of food, and art exhibits throughout town. Leashed dogs are welcome at all outdoor events. 845/353-2221.

Farmer's Market: The freshest produce in town is available every Friday, 9 A.M.–2:30 P.M., on Main Street. Leashed dogs are welcome. 845/353-2221.

Jazz Sundays: Every summer Sunday, there's a free outdoor jazz concert at 2 P.M. in the restored garden at the Hopper Museum at 82 Broadway. Well-behaved dogs are welcome. 845/358-0774.

You and your dog are welcome at many of the shops and restaurants—window-shopping at the many galleries along Main Street is a popular activity. Modernist artist Edward Hopper's childhood home is located at 82 Broadway, just a block off Main Street. You aren't allowed in the building, but you are welcome on the grounds. 845/358-0774.

Restaurants

Casa del Sol: This funky little restaurant offers Mexican and South American cuisine in a garden setting. Metal tables and chairs are located along busy Main Street where you and Muttley can dine alfresco. There is also a garden courtyard at the interior entrance where you can sit on cloudy or rainy days. 104 Main Street; 845/353-9846.

Hudson House: Part gallery and part bistro, this restaurant offers great food for adventurous eaters. And since Inu and George rarely discriminate between dirt-encrusted pizza and foot-trampled chicken pieces, we get few complaints from them no matter where we take them. Fortunately at this restaurant you have your choice of more edible fare like chilled artichoke with wasabi dip, Caribbean crab, and polenta pudding with blueberries. There are tables outdoors on Main Street during the warmer weather. 134 Main Street; 845/353-1355.

The Kyack in Nyack: This charming little restaurant offers an assortment of healthy wraps, sandwiches, and "protein platters" served under large umbrella-shaded tables in a garden setting. A scrumptious bakery and coffee bar completes the experience. Take-out available, too. 188 Main Street; 845/358-8002.

Lanterna: Pasta like Mama made is the cuisine at this charming Italian bistro! George likes the lasagna, but Inu is partial to the veal. Try both as you dine alfresco with a bottle of chianti on a warm summer night. 3 South Broadway; 845/353-8361.

ORANGEBURG

Parks, Beaches, and Recreation Areas

🔟3 Clausland Mountain State Park 🐾 🐾

This woodland park is really more woods than park, even though it is part of Palisades Interstate Park. There are a few poorly marked turnouts along Greenbush Road where you can park and enter the woods, but the trails are not clearly marked, so we don't recommend this place for anyone but residents who are already very familiar with this area. The best way to both find a trail and enter the park is through Tackamack Park (see Blauvelt).

On the top of Clausland Mountain is a newly groomed area called Nike Overlook; energetic hikers will be rewarded with a gorgeous view of the Hudson River Valley, picnic areas, and open fields for ball throwing. Dogs must be leashed.

From the Palisades Interstate Parkway, take Exit 5 to Rte. 303 north for about 0.5 miles. Turn right onto Greenbush Road. The park is on the right. It's open from 8 A.M.–sunset. 845/638-5484.

PALISADES

Parks, Beaches, and Recreation Areas

🔟4 Tallman Mountain State Park 🐾 🐾 🐾

This lovely 687-acre park is located at the border of Rockland County and New Jersey in the Palisades Interstate Park. It runs along the Hudson River through the villages of Palisades to Piermont. Charming Dutch houses from an era long past still dot the landscape in a place rich with historical significance.

In 1775 Mollie Sneden carried Martha Washington across the Hudson from here to join George Washington in Cambridge. The old stone house where Mrs. Washington stayed still stands at the base of the cliff along Oak Tree Road. Further along this road the British saluted the American flag for the first time in 1783; it was also the site of the execution of John Andre, head of the British secret service during the Revolution.

There are several trails here, including the Long Path and the Tallman Bike Path. To reach both trails, take the southern entrance road to the parking lot and follow the woodland trail that parallels the river and the bike path. The Long Path diverges to the left on a turquoise-blazed trail and the bike trail continues along the marshes near the river. The Hudson River is not accessible here, because there is about 0.5 miles of marshland between the park and the water. The bird-watching is terrific and the wildflowers in the spring are worth a trip to see. From the Palisades Interstate Parkway at the New Jersey border, take Exit 4 to U.S. 9W north for 1.5 miles. The park is on the right. Open dawn–dusk. 845/359-0544.

PEARL RIVER

Places to Stay

Hilton Pearl River: This elegant full-service hotel is located on a country estate, complete with its own lake. (Sorry, as tempted as your dog will be to dive in, the only animal life allowed in the lake are the ducks and geese!) There are 150 beautiful rooms available, but not all are available to travelers with pets. The management asks that you reserve in advance if your pup is accompanying you. Rates are $99–189 per night. 500 Veterans Memorial Drive, Pearl River, NY 10965; 845/735-9000; website: www.hilton.com.

PIERMONT

This quaint little town along the Hudson River was originally the terminus for the Erie Railroad—an all–New York train system whose original charter stated that it was to be built entirely within the state. The mile-long pier in the center of town was originally built for the sole purpose of transferring passengers from the train to a ferry that would transport them across the river. The railroad's founder, Eleazer Lord, renamed the town in honor of his pier. Today you and your dog can enjoy walking along the wildlife sanctuary at the end of the pier, dining at the many outdoor restaurants in town, or window-shopping in the countless galleries and shops. The Tallman Mountain State Park (a part of the Palisades Interstate Park) is accessible from this town.

Nature Hikes and Urban Walks

Piermont Pier: This unusual nature walk runs along a mile-long pier that juts out into the Hudson River. Originally built as part of a ferry system to neighboring Westchester County, today the paved walkway overlooks the Piermont Marsh. With spectacular views of the river and Tappan Zee Bridge and a variety of bird life to enjoy, this pier is a far cry from the fish-splattered decor associated with most piers. Take a look back to town when you reach the end and you can see Lord's Castle, the home of Piermont founder Eleazar Lord, which still stands on a hill overlooking the pier. 845/359-1258.

Restaurants

Pasta Amore: For a scenic view of Piermont Pier and the harbor, you can do no better than this cute little Italian restaurant. There are outdoor tables along the pier during warmer weather where you and your dog can dine on the pasta or gourmet pizza of your choice. A bottle of red wine and some tiramisu for dessert make for a perfect way to watch the sun go down. 200 Ash Street; 845/365-1911.

Sidewalk Café: Well, the name says it all. It's on a sidewalk, and it's definitely a café. This popular local restaurant offers outdoor patio dining in the summer and you better get your table early, because the joint is jumpin'. The menu offers American continental cuisine with a southwestern flair. We like the vegetarian specials, but we can't keep our dogs' paws out of the blue corn tortillas and guacamole. 482 Piermont Avenue; 845/359-4439.

SLOATSBURG

Parks, Beaches, and Recreation Areas

🐾 Harriman State Park 🐾 🐾 🐾 🐾

It's hard to find enough superlatives to describe this wonderful park. Named for Edward H. Harriman, a railroad magnate whose family originally donated 10,000 acres to the state upon his death in 1910, the land has expanded to nearly 50,000 acres and is one of the best, if not *the* best, parks in this book. Harriman State Park has so many trails that there have been entire books written to cover them all in detail. Since we obviously can't do justice to the many routes you can explore here, we recommend you buy *Harriman Trails: A*

Guide and History by William Myles, published by the New York–New Jersey Trail Conference. At the very least, purchase a trail map for $11.95 at the various ranger stations throughout the park. You'll need it.

We think the best hiking is in the northern section of the park, but really, if you stop anywhere that strikes your fancy, you'll find a lovely trail and, most likely, a great lake. With more than 235 miles of marked trails in the park (and this doesn't include the unmarked trails, of which there are plenty) we don't think you'll have a tough time finding a favorite.

One of our personal favorites is along Silvermine Lake. From the parking area off Seven Lakes Drive, head for the yellow-blazed trail on the far side of the lake from the picnic area. This trail will take you along the southern edge of the lake for about 0.5 miles and then continues along Bockey Swamp Brook for another mile. You'll be surrounded by water the entire time, a detail that always makes it a major favorite with our dogs. If you're looking for a shorter lakeside walk, set off along the unmarked path on northern side of the lake. Parking is available at the ski lift lot off Seven Lakes Road.

This might be a good moment to discuss the swimming policy here at Harriman State Park. No swimming is allowed for humans or dogs at any spot other than the formal swimming areas. Unfortunately, no dogs are allowed at any of the formal swimming beaches—not even in the off-season. There are countless lakes in this park, and when we questioned why dogs weren't allowed to swim in the out-of-the-way spots, we were told that, for insurance reasons, park officials were afraid if a dog drowned, or a person drowned trying to save their dog, then there would be trouble. As a coda, they added that as long as you were warned of the policy, it was up to you how you wanted to handle it. Translation: No one will either save you or ticket you as long as your dog can swim. Hey, we're just reporting the facts here. What you do with them is up to you.

If you'd like to explore several lakes (from shore, of course) along one trail, we suggest heading to the southern end of the park and taking the Long Path, which meanders by Lake Askoti, Lake Skannatati, Lake Kanawauke, and Little Long Pond. The path is marked by blue blazes and passes by several deserted mines along the way. Park at the Lake Askoti parking area off Seven Lakes Drive.

Camping is allowed May–October at Beaver Pond Campground, which is actually located along beautiful Lake Welch. Tents or trailers are allowed for $15 per night. Reservations can be made for an additional $8 fee and are recommended in the busy months of July and August. 800/456-2267.

The park Visitor Center is located off the Palisades Interstate Parkway between Exits 16 and 17. Dogs must be leashed and are not allowed in any of the public swimming areas. From Rte. 17, take Seven Lakes Road east into the park. Open dawn–dusk. 845/786-2701.

Places to Stay

Harriman State Park Campgrounds: See the Harriman State Park listing above.

STONY POINT

Parks, Beaches, and Recreation Areas

16 Stony Point State Historic Site 🐾 🐾 🐾

For dogs that want to bone up on a little history, this unique park in the Palisades Interstate Park offers plenty of opportunity. This battlefield marks the site of the 1779 surprise attack by General "Mad Anthony" Wayne and 900 American soldiers on the British-held fort. The battle was a decisive turning point in the Revolution because after being defeated by the Americans, the British were pushed north and never again established a stronghold in the Hudson Highlands.

In 1899, Theodore Roosevelt made this battlefield a historic site and today you can walk along a lovely country trail that leads about 0.5 miles to Stony Point Lighthouse, the oldest light on the Hudson. Built in 1826 and still working, this historic light also offers scenic views of the Hudson River in all directions. For a walk that is secluded, scenic and unusual, this tops George's list.

Dogs must be leashed and the parking area closes at 5 P.M. From U.S. 9W in the village of Stony Point, take Park Road east two blocks into Battlefield Road into the park. Open 10 A.M.–5 P.M. 845/786-2521.

Restaurants

Annie's: Stop by this little roadside eatery, owned and operated by the original "Annie" since 1952. The restaurant features a variety of seafood, pasta and sandwiches, all of which you can order at the outdoor counter and eat at

---

DIVERSION

Praise the Lord and Pass the Ammunition: German shepherds and Saint Bernards will feel right at home on this guided nature walk that recreates the battle between the American colonists and a British garrison at Stony Point Battlefield. The walk is short and easy, and you will stop at each historical point as you make your way out to the lighthouse on the Hudson River. Held the third weekend of September at Stony Point Reservation. Call for more information at 845/786-2521.

---

colorful picnic tables outdoors. Make sure to save room for any of the homemade pies and baked goods or, George's favorite, butterscotch pudding. Woof! 149 U.S. 9W; 845/942-1011.

SUFFERN

Suffern may have been put on the map by TV's *Sex and the City,* but before it was Sarah Jessica Parker's idea of a forced march to nowhere, it was, and still is, a very pleasant place to take your dog. In fact, Suffern can boast of being the first town in Rockland County to create its own dog park.

Parks, Beaches, and Recreation Areas
17 Kakiat County Park & Dog Run 🐾 🐾 🐾 🐾 🐕

This 353-acre park has the fortune, or misfortune, of being in the shadow of massive Harriman State Park. Often confused for being part of the mammoth park, this smaller county park also offers great hiking not far from New York City. Even better, it has a large dog run located right at the parking area, so your dog may not even *want* to venture into the vast area of Harriman State Park.

The dog run is an enclosed area about the size of a football field. With an underlay of wood chips, several benches, and mutt mitts, it is a popular place to let your dog run leashless. And although we applaud the county for providing an off-leash area, the rest of the park is so terrific, we find we only stay a short time in the dog run before our restless pups want to roam. This is a great place to come to socialize your dog, but don't forget the rest of the park, leash or not.

From the parking area, take the trail past the Old Mill, a deserted gristmill from the 19th century. From here you can take a very scenic half-mile walk on the orange-blazed trail to your left, or the longer Kakiat Trail, which leads to your right and continues on into Harriman State Park. To reach the larger park, follow the white blazes and continue on past the power lines to Grandma and Grandpa Rocks, an odd rock formation at the apex of the white-blazed trail and the yellow-blazed trail.

If you wish to make a two-mile loop of both trails, take the unmarked path to the left of the white-blazed trail right after you pass the power lines. Dogs must be leashed except in the dog run.

From the New York Thruway (I-87), take Exit 15A to the Orange Turnpike (Rte. 59) south for about 0.5 miles. Turn left onto Haverstraw Road (Rte. 202) for two miles. The park is on the left. Open 8 A.M.–dusk. 845/364-2670.

Places to Stay

Wellesley Inn: There is nothing unusual about this chain hotel except that your dog is welcome here, so in our opinion, it's remarkable. There are 97

DIVERSION

You're in the Army Now: Take a full-day cruise up the Hudson River originating from the quaint village of West Haverstraw to the United States Military Academy. From May to October, the M.V. *Commander* will steam up the river and stop for two hours at historic West Point, before cruising past scenic Bannerman's Island and a return trip to West Haverstraw. The outing takes a full day—10 A.M.–4:30 P.M.—and leashed dogs may ride on the outer deck. Adults are $24; dogs are free. 845/534-SAIL (845/534-7245); website: www.commanderboat.com.

clean and comfortable rooms and a free continental breakfast is included each morning. Rates are $80–95 per night. There is no additional fee or size restriction for Fido, but you must sign a damage waiver and dogs are usually placed in the ground floor rooms. 17 North Airmont Road, Suffern, NY 10901; 845/368-1900 or 800/444-8888; website: www.wellesleyinnandsuites.com.

WEST HAVERSTRAW

Restaurants

Hoyers Ice Cream: Stop at this seasonal homemade ice cream stand after a long day on the trails. With an exhaustive menu of ice cream flavors, we usually take forever trying to make up our minds. Then Inu predictably goes for the vanilla, George for the strawberry, and, well, JoAnna and Chris settle the indecision by taking just about everything else. 289 U.S. 9W; no phone.

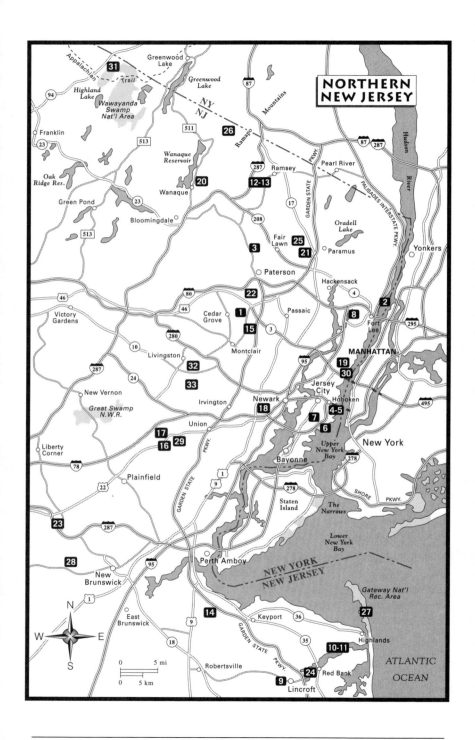

NORTHERN NEW JERSEY

Now, Charley is a mind-reading dog. There have been many trips in his lifetime, and often he has to be left at home. He knows we are going long before the suitcases come out, and he paces and worries and whines and goes into a state of mild hysteria, old as he is.

— From *Travels with Charley*, by John Steinbeck

In 1776, when George Washington crossed the Delaware River from Pennsylvania into New Jersey, it was an event that would live on in American history. To many New Yorkers today, the idea of going into Jersey remains an equally monumental task, starting with the realization there is a world on the other side of the Hudson River.

If you do venture across the George Washington Bridge or through the Lincoln and Holland Tunnels, you will find there really is merit to the nickname, the Garden State. And while it's true that most opinions of New Jersey are formed on its many highways and the "what exit?" joke of the Garden State Parkway, a closer look reveals sandy beaches, farms, forest-

PICK OF THE LITTER– NORTHERN NEW JERSEY HIGHLIGHTS

BEST PARKS

Hartshorne Woods Park, Locust

Palisades Interstate Park, Fort Lee

Ramapo Valley County Reservation, Mahwah

Thompson Park & Dog Run, Lincroft

Watchung Reservation, Mountainside

BEST BEACH

Sandy Hook, Sandy Hook

BEST EVENT

Santa Paws, Eatontown

covered mountains, and plenty of opportunities for you and your dog to kick back in the wide open spaces.

The Ramapo and Watchung Mountains, the cliffs of the Palisades, and the beaches of Sandy Hook are all great destinations for Jerseyites and New Yorkers alike; best of all, these spots are easy-to-reach afternoon getaways for those willing to cross the river and state lines. Just be careful not to stay too long—your dog may get a hankering for suburbia, his own backyard, and a chance to chase the mailman every day.

CEDAR GROVE

Parks, Beaches, and Recreation Areas

🚹 Mills Reservation 🐾 🐾 🐾

When Davella Mills donated these 157 acres to the Essex County Park Commission in 1954, she asked that the land be preserved in its natural state. And lucky for us, apart from a parking lot and about five miles of hiking trails and forest roads, that's the way it remains. George and Inu will be the first to tell you that this is a good thing. The woods are dark, thick, and tall. The terrain is rough, hilly, and adventurous. And it's a fact that the fewer facilities a park has, the more dog-friendly it is. Limited facilities mean fewer visitors to contend with and dogs don't have to watch out for no-dogs-allowed picnic areas and playgrounds. In fact, every time we visit, we either have the park to ourselves or share it with other dog walkers. Mills Reservation is *the* destination for local dog owners.

Access to the park is on the north side and, from the parking lot, the main route is the dirt and gravel forest road. It runs south and forms a figure eight or two connecting loops. Follow it to the far end of the second loop and you'll reach Quarry Point, a rocky outcrop with good views of the Manhattan skyline. Along the way, a number of hiking trails intersect with the road and help to vary your visits.

Dogs need to be leashed in all Essex County parks.

From the intersection of Rte. 3 and 46, take Rte. 46 west for about 0.25 miles. Turn left onto Clover Road and proceed for about 0.5 miles. Turn right onto Normal Avenue and proceed for two blocks. The park entrance and a parking lot are on the left. Open dawn–10 P.M. 973/268-3500.

EAST BRUNSWICK

Places to Stay

Motel 6: All Motel 6 locations allow dogs as long as you don't leave them unattended. The motel is about a mile off Exit 9 of the New Jersey Turnpike and 35 miles outside of New York City. One dog is welcome per room. Rates $55–66. 244 Rte. 18, East Brunswick, NJ 08816; 800/4-MOTEL6 or 732/390-4545; website: www.motel6.com.

EAST HANOVER

Places to Stay

Ramada Hotel: This chain hotel may not be luxurious, but it welcomes canine travelers—which makes it lavish in our book. With 255 clean and comfortable rooms, you and your dog will have all you need here. Dogs under

EARMARK YOUR CALENDAR–SEPTEMBER

Mutts Marathon: You won't have to run 26.2 miles to feel like you accomplished something at the annual Mutts Marathon. The two-mile walk is a great way to help raise funds for the orphan pets of the Mount Pleasant Animal Shelter. Participants are charged a $15 registration fee. The outing also includes demonstrations, games, food, vendors, and entertainment. The walk takes place the last weekend in September on the Kraft Company campus at 100 DeForest Avenue (Rte. 10). For exact date and time or for more information, call the Mount Pleasant Animal Shelter at 973/386-0590.

40 pounds preferred, but Inu shrinks his 65-pound frame into a sweet and winsome ball and makes the cut every time. Rates $65–145 per night. 130 Rte. 10, East Hanover, NJ 07936; 201/386-5622; website: www.ramada.com.

EATONTOWN

Places to Stay

Crystal Motor Lodge: This simple motel isn't big on glamour, but what it lacks in luxury, it makes up for in dog-friendliness and convenience. With

---

EARMARK YOUR CALENDAR–DECEMBER

Holiday Hounds: You and your dog will both get into the holiday spirit at these New Jersey events.

Lights of Remembrance: The holidays are a great time to recognize how much our pets mean to us and to help those animals less fortunate than George and Inu. The Lights of Remembrance tree at the Mount Pleasant Animal Shelter lets you do both. The shelter's annual holiday tree lighting ceremony glows with lights in remembrance of thousands of pets. Holiday visitors are asked to make a donation for a light in memory of their loyal pet. Caroling, festive food and holiday spirits are also included. The Lights of Remembrance takes place the first week in December at the shelter located at 194 DeForest Avenue (Rte. 10), East Hanover. For exact date and time or for more information, call the Mount Pleasant Animal Shelter at 973/386-0590.

Be a Pinup Pup: Is your dog worried that her wish list of chew toys won't make it to the North Pole in time for Christmas? Well, she can give Santa the list in person at the Monmouth County Society for the Prevention of Cruelty to Animals' annual **Santa Paws.** All pets get a photo with Santa and can partake in the holiday festivities. The small fee for the photo benefits the SPCA's animal protection and humane education programs. Call the SPCA for exact dates and time in December. The shelter is located at 260 Wall Street, Eatontown. 732/542-0040.

Caroling Canines: Get the holiday season off with a yuletide glow with the annual **Holiday Tree Lighting Ceremony and Charity Drive** at Watchung Reservation. The festivities take place the first Friday in December from 6:30 to 9:30 P.M. and include the tree lighting, caroling, a visit from Santa, and a mounted drill team demonstration. Everyone is asked to bring an item of dry or canned food or new, unwrapped toy for donation to a local charity. For more information, contact the Union County Parks and Recreation Department at 908/527-4900.

---

refrigerators and microwaves in every room, a stay here is easy and comfortable. Dogs are allowed with a $5 fee. Rates are $75–95 per night. Rte. 35, Eatontown, NJ 07724; 908/542-4900 or 800/562-5290.

ENGLEWOOD

Nature Hikes and Urban Walks

Palisades Avenue: The cliffs of Palisades Interstate Park may be breathtaking, but the heartbeat of the Palisades community comes from trendy Palisades Avenue. The many shops and restaurants make for an enjoyable afternoon or evening stroll. Wander along the avenue with your dog and be sure to notice that these businesses strike an interesting balance by servicing both the upper crust from the mansions of adjacent Englewood Cliffs and the regular needs of the rest of Englewood. The action runs from Grand Avenue to Knickerbocker Avenue. For more information contact the Englewood Chamber of Commerce at 201/567-2381.

Restaurants

Palisades Avenue hosts a number of fine cafés and eateries, including standards like Ben & Jerry's and Starbucks. We list two of our favorites, but don't limit yourselves to our choices. There are plenty more to try.

Blue Moon Mexican Café: Rice and beans are some of the simplest ingredients on any menu, but blend them together with a little salsa and sour cream—and you'll have one of our posse's favorite meals. Mix in some outdoor seating off Palisades Avenue and you'll be dining here more than once in a blue moon. 21 East Palisades Avenue; 201/848-4088.

Sol 'n' Sol Kosher Delicatessen: Great Jewish delis aren't just located in New York City. S 'n' S, in business since the 1940s, is a great example. Whether it's breakfast, lunch, or dinner, the menu teems with classic favorites from knishes and potato pancakes to hot open-face turkey sandwiches, chicken-in-a-pot, and Hungarian goulash. Sidewalk seating makes family dining possible. 34 East Palisades Avenue; 201/541-6880.

Places to Stay

Radisson Hotel: This top-of-the-line hotel has 194 rooms and is located just two miles from the George Washington Bridge and New York City. Some of the amenities are an indoor heated pool, a well-equipped exercise room, and shuttle service to New York. Rates $180–240. The hotel requires guests with pets to sign a release waiver and pay a refundable deposit of $150. 401 South Van Brunt Street, Englewood, NJ 07631; 201/871-2020 or 800/333-3333; website: www.radisson.com.

FORT LEE

Parks, Beaches, and Recreation Areas

🐾 Palisades Interstate Park 🐾 🐾 🐾 🐾

New Jerseyites always enjoy the impressive Manhattan skyline, but that doesn't mean New Yorkers don't have anything to look at. The dramatic, plunging cliffs of New Jersey's Palisades along the Hudson River are impressive in their own right. Designated a National Natural Landmark in 1983, the Palisades make for a quick destination when you need to get out of the confines of city living.

The park, which runs from the George Washington Bridge in Fort Lee to the New York state line, covers 13 miles and 2,500 acres. Part of a grouping of parks along the Hudson River in New York and New Jersey, Palisades Interstate Park is jointly managed by both states. The New York portion of the Palisades Interstate Park includes Bear Mountain, Harriman, Rockland Lake, and Tallman Mountain State Parks, among others. (See the Rockland County chapter for more information.)

The park is covered with rich forest and offers 30 miles of trails. The two primary trails are the Long Path and the Shore Trail. They both run the length of the park and are each about 11 miles long. The Long Path runs along the top of the cliffs and accesses State Line Lookout, the highest point on the Palisades at 532 feet. The Shore Trail follows the Hudson River at the base of the cliffs. You can find plenty of river access along the way, but we caution you that the river runs deep and may not always be safe for swimming. The two trails connect at the Giant Stairs in the northern end of the park, although this steep route over a boulder field is not recommended for out-of-shape dogs (or people!).

Another good place for hiking is along Henry Hudson Drive when it is closed to vehicle traffic from the last Sunday in October to the first Saturday in April. This park road is seven miles long and covers the southern half of the park from George Washington Bridge to the park headquarters. It's a popular route for cyclists coming over the bridge from New York City.

For something a little adventurous, you may want to try a walk on the George Washington Bridge. The bridge has walkways on both sides and has great views of the cliffs, Manhattan, and straight down to the water below! Access is from the southern end of the park.

Information and maps are available at the park's headquarters in Alpine at Exit 2 off the Palisades Interstate Parkway. Pets need to be leashed and are prohibited in all developed areas, including picnic areas. There are numerous parking areas in the park. Most of them require a $4 fee from April through October. Limited free parking is available at the southern end of the park on Main Street at the Edgewater town line.

Stories of people falling off the cliffs are not uncommon. Use care when hiking on them. From I-95 at the George Washington Bridge, take the Palisades Interstate Parkway north for seven miles. Take Exit 2 into the park. Open during daylight hours. 201/768-1360; website: www.njpalisades.org.

Restaurants

Callahan's Roadstand and Hiram's Roadstand: It's not the cola wars or the Hatfields and the McCoys, but to residents of Fort Lee and many people of New Jersey there is no middle group when it comes to these two old-time hot dog restaurants on Palisades Avenue. The rivalry goes back to 1950 when Callahan's opened just a few yards from Hiram's, which started selling hot dogs in 1932. Neither has outdoor seating, but the food is just as tasty to-go, and both are a convenient stop if you are crossing the George Washington Bridge. The menus have plenty of burgers, chicken, fries, and ice cream too.

We try to take the politically correct approach by not publicizing our personal favorites, but we do admit having to make two stops when we are out with our dogs for dogs. Hiram's Roadstand is at 1345 Palisades Avenue; 201/592-9602. Callahan's Roadstand is at 1365 Palisades Avenue; 201/592-9580.

Fort Lee News Bar: Get the latest gossip and a good cup of coffee at this local hangout. The sidewalk café also serves pastries and sandwiches. 140 Main Street; 201/944-9779.

HAWTHORNE

Parks, Beaches, and Recreation Areas

🛂 Goeffle Brook Park 🐾 🐾 🐾 🐕

This 103-acre park is an enjoyable stop in its own right, but what gets our dogs really excited is knowing that it's home to one of New Jersey's first dog runs. The fenced-in run is a good size, covered with wood chips, dirt, and some grass with shady trees, benches, and chairs—and a water pump to quench the thirst of playful pups.

The rest of this Passaic County park runs a mile in length, nestled between Goeffle Brook and Goeffle Road. Although it's bisected by some cross streets, there's pleasant walking on the dirt trails and sidewalks through brookside woods and numerous, well-maintained grassy lawns—good places for picnics, Frisbee, and ballgames.

Dogs need to be leashed outside the run.

From Rte. 208, take Goeffle Road south for about 0.25 miles. The park and a number of parking areas are on the left. The dog run is located at the southern end of the park near the intersection of Goeffle Road and Diamond Bridge Avenue. Open sunrise–sunset. 973/881-4832.

HOBOKEN

Parks, Beaches, and Recreation Areas

◳ Church Square Park & Dog Run 🐾 🐾 🐕

Located right in the middle of town, this park is only two city blocks in size and the basketball courts, gazebo, and dog run take up most of the space. Although the park is not large, the triangle-shaped dog run is spacious and well fenced, with benches, two trees, a doggy water fountain, and good lighting at night. One problem with the run is that the flooring consists of stones or large pebbles. The dogs don't seem to mind, but we find it makes the usual poop scooping a little tricky. Maybe this is why the run has a slight odor. We know—picky, picky. At least it's a leash-free space.

Outside of the run, dogs need to be leashed.

The park is bordered by Fourth, Fifth, Garden, and Willow Streets. Open 6 A.M.–11 P.M. 201/420-2349.

◱ Stevens Park & Dog Run 🐾 🐾 🐕

A run with a view is the best way to describe this park and dog run. And what a view it is! Hoboken sits right across the Hudson River from Greenwich Village and Stevens Park offers impressive views of both Midtown and the Financial District. Sitting pretty on a bluff, you will have a bird's eye view of Manhattan while your dog romps with the local pups. The park and run are both small, but green and shady and just a block off action-packed Washington Street.

Outside of the run, dogs need to be leashed. The park is bordered by River Drive and Fourth, Fifth and Hudson Streets. Open 6 A.M.–11 P.M. 201/420-2349.

Restaurants

Countless Manhattan-bound commuters pass through Hoboken every business day without ever noticing the city's revitalization. The ones who have stopped and smelled the coffee (and the wine and tequila), however, have made Hoboken's Washington Street and the area around the Erie-Lackawanna Train Terminal alive with bars and restaurants. There are many more for you to dine at, but here are a few dog-friendly establishments with outdoor seating.

East LA: Not only can you take in the scene of Hoboken's busy Washington Street from this sidewalk café, you also get to enjoy pretty good Mexican food and a margarita or two. Although Mexican food on the East Coast is never as good as the West Coast version, this place comes close. 508 Washington Street; 201/798-0052.

Hoboken Cottage: They describe their menu as exotic Chinese cuisine. We call it loaded. You name it, if something was eaten just once in China, it's listed on the menu. Seafood, tofu, dim sum, and desserts prepared in every way possible are just some of the delights. 516 Washington Street; 201/798-6788.

Park Pastries: This French café is the perfect stop for coffee, something sweet or sandwiches. Enjoy their outdoor seating or take your coffee to the nearby dog runs. 517 Washington Street; 201/386-1020.

Tutta Pasta: If we didn't list at least one Italian restaurant, we would certainly receive a visit from some of Hoboken-born Frank Sinatra's "friends." This lively restaurant saved us from "swimming with the fishes," so to speak, by offering wonderfully zesty pasta dishes and drinks. Best of all, our dogs can join us at the outdoor patio and for that we are even more grateful. 200 Washington Street; 201/792-9102.

JERSEY CITY

Parks, Beaches, and Recreation Areas

⑥ Liberty State Park 🐾 🐾 🐾

For many immigrants in the 19th and 20th centuries, this land across from the Statue of Liberty and Ellis Island provided a first taste of the America mainland. The centerpiece of the 1,212-acre Liberty State Park is the Central Railroad of New Jersey Terminal. From 1889–1954, eight million immigrants boarded trains from this terminal for destinations all over the United States. Today it is has been converted to a museum commemorating this colorful past.

With or without an illustrious history, this park is spectacular. There are great views and plenty of space. The most popular section of the park for dogs is the Morris Canal Peninsula Park. Separated from the rest of the park by the Morris Canal, it is the quietest and easiest part of the park to get to for many residents of downtown Jersey City. Located right on the Hudson River, you'll find a half-mile stretch of green grass here, enough for a lovely romp.

Another good place for a jaunt is the Liberty Walk. This two-mile promenade runs the length of the park's waterfront with unsurpassed views of the Statue of Liberty and Ellis Island. There are great views of New York City and New York Harbor, as well.

Two other nice areas for a jaunt include Green Park and Liberty Park Natural Area. Green Park has spacious lawns, gardens, bike paths; the Natural Area offers a 36-acre salt marsh with an interpretive nature trail.

Dogs need to be leashed in all state parks.

From the New Jersey Turnpike, take Exit 14B Jersey City to Morris Pesin Drive east for about 0.5 miles into the park. Follow the signs to the park. Open 6 A.M.–6:30 P.M. 201/915-3400.

7 Lincoln Park 🐾 🐾

Finding space in the city is tough, even here at Lincoln Park. At 273 acres, it is the largest park in Hudson County, but on first glance the design proves challenging to all but the most determined canine cadet. A large piece of the park is devoted to a driving range. The ball fields and the running track are off-limits to dogs, and watch out for busy Rte. 440, which runs through the middle of this community green space.

But fear not, what remains are about 123 acres of undeveloped land along the Hackensack River with a cross-country trail, bike paths, and three small ponds. Everything fits so well together that, on second and third glance, the design actually meets the needs of all the visitors, dogs included. In other words, the furniture is arranged so that the room appears bigger than it is.

Dogs need to be leashed in all Hudson County parks.

The park is bordered by County Road 440, and Communipaw and West Side Avenues. Open 6 A.M.–11 P.M. 201/915-1385.

Dog Day Afternoon: Join the Kennel Club of Northern New Jersey in Overpeck Park as they celebrate National Dog Week with **Dog Day in the Park.** The annual September event features a day full of dog demonstrations, education, literature, and fun. Activities include obedience, agility, arson detection, dancing demonstrations, breed literature, and dog product information. There's plenty of room for picnicking, too. Admission and parking is free. Dogs must be leashed. For more information, call the Kennel Club of Northern New Jersey at 201/337-8933.

LEONIA

Parks, Beaches, and Recreation Areas

🐾 Overpeck County Park 🐾 🐾

For a park that was originally intended to rival New York City's Central Park, it has certainly missed its mark. The park has 811 acres scattered along Overpeck Creek, but apparently the need for superhighways took precedence over green space. Both I-80 and I-95 slice through it, creating a series of smaller, multipurpose parks. The biggest and best is the Henry Hoebel Area.

The main attraction of the Henry Hoebel Area is the set of oval walking paths around open fields and athletic fields. The paths are popular places for walking, running, and in-line skating.

The Palisades Park Area offers a number of open fields and better views of the river, but the omission of a walking path keeps the crowds away. Although you may want to frequent this section for a good game of throw and fetch, the use of space leaves much to be desired. The river is wide, lined with waving cattails, and offers scenic views—but up close it is not very appealing for swimming.

There is a lot of landfill here, and you probably don't want to know much more than that, but apparently a sinkhole suddenly appeared during a Leonia High School football game. During an investigation of the field, an old car was found. Apparently, the roof rusted out and caved in, collapsing the field above.

Dogs need to be leashed in all Bergen County parks and are not permitted in the picnic or stable areas. From Rte. 4 in Englewood, take Grand Avenue (Rte. 93) south for about 0.5 miles into Leonia. Turn right onto Fort Lee Road for an eighth of a mile. The Henry Hoebel section is on the right. The Palisades Park section is further down Grand Avenue at the intersection with Roosevelt Place. Open sunrise to a half hour after sunset. 201/336-PARK.

LINCROFT

Parks, Beaches, and Recreation Areas

9 Thompson Park & Dog Run

When people say, "get it right the first time" they must be thinking of the Monmouth County Park System and the dog run it created in Thompson Park. Opened in 1999, it was the first dog park in Monmouth County and simply one of the best ones we know of. If your pet enjoys running with the pack, then this run is a real treat.

The enclosure is a grassy 1.25 acres, giving everyone plenty of room. It also has a sturdy, six-foot chain-link fence around it with a double-entry gate, water spigot, poop bags, and trash cans; top it off with plenty of parking and nearby restrooms, and you end up with a beautiful setting in a peaceful and secluded corner within the park.

The rest of Thompson Park is also very attractive and well maintained. There are plenty of hiking opportunities on 665 acres of open lawns, rolling meadows, and hardwood forests nestled along the Swimming River Reservoir. For a pleasant hike and a nice break from the pack at the dog run, take the grassy path through the soybean and wildflower field. The path is located near the run across from the craft center.

Except for the run, dogs need to be leashed in all Monmouth County parks and are not permitted on the ball fields or in the playgrounds. From the Garden State Parkway, take Exit 109 to Newman Springs Road (County Road 520) west for two miles. The park is on the left. There are multiple sections and entrances to the park. For the dog run, use the second entrance after Brookdale Community College and follow signs to the Craft Center. Open 8 A.M.–dusk. 732/842-4000.

LOCUST

Parks, Beaches, and Recreation Areas

10 Hartshorne Woods Park

Covering 736 acres, Hartshorne Woods Park is the largest park in the Monmouth County Park System and one of the most popular. If you have a trail hound, it will soon be on your list, too. With 11 miles of trails through a rich hardwood forest and some of the hilliest terrain on the Jersey shore, one visit and you'll see why.

This area of the shore is known as the Jersey Highlands and is well named. At times, the hilltops rise to 245 feet above the adjacent Navesink River. In addition, you will find a number of scenic overlooks above the river and the nearby Atlantic Ocean and a few bunkers from World War II that are fun to explore. In the woods you'll discover a variety of hiking routes to choose from. The longest and most difficult is the Grand Tour Trail, appropriately marked with black diamonds. It's about 3.5 miles long over somewhat rough terrain.

If mountain climbing isn't in the cards for you and your pet, the Rocky Point Section of the eastern portion of the park is a bit more level and has three miles of paved paths closed to auto traffic. This section is great for in-line skating, biking, or walking. Accessible from Portland Road, you'll also find it easy to reach the Navesink River for a quick dip.

Dogs need to be leashed. Mountain bikes and horses are plentiful here, so avoid collisions by sharing the trails and being alert. From Rte. 36 in Atlantic Highlands, take Navesink Avenue south for half a mile into Locust. The park and a parking lot are on the left. Open 8 A.M.–dusk. 732/842-4000.

11 Huber Woods Park 🐾 🐾 🐾

If the Monmouth County Park System could acquire a little bit more land or get a special right-of-way easement, Huber Woods Park and Hartshorne Woods Park could be come one giant park. They are very similar, on rugged terrain near the Navesink River, and are only separated by about 0.5 miles or so.

Huber Woods is the more moderate of the two parks, smaller in size with 258 acres of forests and meadows and less of the hilly Jersey Highlands terrain. That means that most of the seven miles of trails are fairly flat and accessible to just about everyone.

The most challenging route is the Many Log Trail in the western half of the park, which is more bumpy than hilly. The easier trails are on the eastern side of the park near Brown's Dock Road.

Dogs need to be leashed. Dogs are not permitted at the stables or at the environmental center. In addition, mountain bikes and horses are plentiful, so avoid collisions by keeping any eye out and sharing the trails. There is limited water access at the park. From Rte. 35 in Middletown, take Navesink River Road east for 3.5 miles. Turn left onto Brown's Dock Road into the park. Open 8 A.M.–dusk. 732/842-4000.

MAHWAH

Parks, Beaches, and Recreation Areas

12 Campgaw Mountain County Reservation 🐾 🐾 🐾

One of a number of state and county parks in the wooded Ramapo Mountains, this park has seven hiking trails totaling over six miles. The Old Cedar Trail is the longest at just over two miles, but because all the trails cross each other, you can pretty much make your own route.

Be sure to explore the pond in the center of the park. A trail leads around and beside the water, making for a pleasant walk, although you may have to do some explaining to make your dog understand she's not allowed in the refreshing water. (Our dogs still don't get it, no matter how many times we tell them swimming is not allowed.) If you are looking for even more exercise, the trails connect to bridle paths in the southern end of the park. Half of the paved park road is closed to auto traffic on Saturday and Sunday and after 4 P.M. Monday through Friday.

Dogs must be leashed in all Bergen County parks. In season, skiing is available here and dogs are not permitted on the slopes. The park permits camping from April 1–November 30. Camping is allowed by permit only and campers are limited to a total of two weeks per year. Campsite fees are $5 per night. For more information and reservations, contact Darlington County Park, 600 Darlington Avenue, Mahwah, NJ 07430; 201/327-3500.

From I-287, take Exit 66 to U.S. 17 and proceed south for about 0.5 miles. Take Ramapo Valley Road (Rte. 202) south for a mile. Turn left on Darlington Avenue, and proceed for an eighth of a mile. Turn right onto Campgaw Road for about 0.5 miles. The park entrance is on the right. Open sunrise to a half hour after sunset. Information and trail maps are available through Darlington County Park on nearby Darlington Avenue (no dogs allowed there) at 201/327-3500.

13 Ramapo Valley County Reservation 🐾 🐾 🐾 🐾

So, your dog wants some exercise? Well this park in the Ramapo Mountains is definitely the place. In fact, some of the trails here provide such a workout that members of the New York Giants football team train on them in the off-season. Luckily, you don't have to run up Rocky Mountain or Drag Hill (both over 1,000 feet) or slap each other on the butt to have a great outing here. With 15 miles of trails of all degrees of difficulty, destinations like Bear Swamp Pond, the Ramapo River, and Scarlet Oak Pond make this Bergen County park one of the favorite parks for Jersey dogs.

Most of the hiking trails and wider tote roads head up into forest-covered mountains where you can explore hidden ponds, swamps, brooks, and old ruins. From the higher elevations, there are also impressive views of the distant Manhattan skyline. But, even with all of this splendor, the most widely used route is the path around Scarlet Oak Pond just beyond the parking lot and the footbridge over the Ramapo River.

Dogs need to be leashed in all Bergen County parks, and swimming is not permitted in Scarlet Oak Pond. The park permits camping from April 1–November 30. Camping is allowed by permit only and campers are limited to a total of two weeks per year. Campsite fees are $5 per night. For more information and reservations, contact Darlington County Park, 600 Darlington Avenue, Mahwah, NJ 07430; 201/327-3500. Snake sightings are not uncommon.

From I-287, take Exit 66 to U.S. 17 south for about 0.5 miles. Take Ramapo Valley Road (Rte. 202) south for a mile. The park entrance is on the right. Open sunrise to a half hour after sunset. Information and trail maps are available through Darlington County Park on nearby Darlington Avenue (no dogs allowed there) at 201/327-3500.

Places to Stay

Campgaw Mountain County Reservation: See Campgaw Mountain County Reservation listing, above.

Ramapo Valley County Reservation: See the Ramapo Valley County Reservation listing, above.

Sheraton Crossroads Hotel: Since childhood, Chris has never thought of this building as a hotel but as a spaceship preparing to lift off from Cape Canaveral. You might have a different opinion of the futuristic, 22-story structure, but we all agree the rooms are great and the views of the surrounding Ramapo Mountains are impressive. There are 228 rooms, a fitness facility, tennis courts, and pools. Room rates are $125–185. Guests with pets are asked to sign a waiver. 1 International Boulevard, Route 17 North, Mahwah, NJ 07495; 201/529-1660 or 888/625-5144; website: www.sheraton.com.

MATAWAN/OLD BRIDGE

Parks, Beaches, and Recreation Areas

14 Cheesequake State Park 🐾 🐾 🐾

Some argue that the Garden State Parkway should not run through the middle of this beautiful park; others say, "It sure is convenient to get here." Whatever your opinion and however you get here, you and your dog are sure to enjoy a trip to this state park.

The park covers 1,274 beautiful acres along the fresh- and saltwater marshes, creeks, ponds, and swamps of Raritan Bay with nine miles of hiking trails. Throw in plenty of open fields, woods, some pine barrens, and opportunities for wildlife viewing and you've got yourself one wonderful afternoon.

The best trails are in the eastern half of the park, and most are accessible from the first parking area past the ranger station. They explore the park's untamed area, which includes White Cedar Swamp and Hooks Creek. Trail maps are available at the park entrance and the ranger station.

Dogs need to be leashed in all state parks and are not permitted in the picnic or camping areas. From Memorial Day weekend through Labor Day, there is a $5 weekday and $7 weekend and holiday entrance fee. A State Park Pass is available for $35 and is good for a year at all state parks. From the Garden State Parkway, take Exit 120 to Matawan Road south for an eighth of a mile. Turn right onto Cliffwood Avenue and proceed for about 0.25 miles. Turn right onto Gordon Road and drive for about 0.5 miles into the park. Open during daylight hours for day-use. 908/566-2161.

MONTCLAIR

Parks, Beaches, and Recreation Areas

15 Brookdale Park 🐾 🐾

As Inu gets older (12 as we go to press), he doesn't need or want to be bounding down trails on a daily basis, but the old boy never tires of getting out to socialize. Good thing that Brookdale is a good place for an easy walk to meet the neighbors. This Essex County park is popular enough to bring in people to meet even Inu's insatiable social demands, but is secluded and spacious enough to give everyone plenty of room to breathe.

The park encompasses 121 acres, including a one-acre duck pond. A good portion of the park is devoted to an outdoor stage, tennis courts, and ball fields for summer soccer camps. These features can really draw crowds to the park, but our dogs enjoy a visit here because of the park's other features. They like meandering on the 1.5-mile bike path, rolling in the lush grass of the open lawns, or picnicking under one of the many shade trees. There is even a quarter-mile track and a formal rose garden too. In fact, we'd give this park a higher rating, but because it is so manicured, that also means a very strict (we'd call it extreme) leash law. It makes it hard to relax and enjoy when you have a ranger breathing down your neck.

Dogs need to be leashed in all Essex County parks. From the Garden State Parkway, take Exit 151 to Watchung Avenue west for about 0.5 miles. The park is on the right. Open dawn–10 P.M. 973/268-3500.

Strike Up the Band: The **Essex County Summer Concert Series** really knows how to put on the dog. The free outdoor concerts in Branch Brook and Brookdale Parks feature performances by major attractions such as the Metropolitan Opera, Tommy Dorsey, and the Latin jazz artist Tito Puentes. Performances are generally on weeknights from the end of June through August. For more information, dates and a list of performers, contact the Essex County Department of Parks, Recreation, and Cultural Affairs at 973/268-3500.

Restaurants

Arturo's Brick Oven Pizza Company: Take in all the action of this college town from one of its main thoroughfares, Bellevue Avenue, while indulging in pizza with your favorite toppings or assortment of heroes and pasta. Sidewalk tables are available so your dog doesn't get left behind. 223 Bellevue Avenue; 973/744-2300.

Beyond the Bagel: Located right in the quaint downtown section of Montclair, this sidewalk café is perfect for a morning pick-me-up or a lunchtime bagel sandwich. Small café tables outdoors mean your pup can snack on the crumbs as they fall from your plate. 215 Bellevue Avenue; 973/744-9238.

MOUNTAINSIDE

Parks, Beaches, and Recreation Areas

16 Echo Lake Park 🐾 🐾

This park along with Lenape and Nomahegan Parks in nearby Cranford and Springfield (see description under Springfield section) make up a trio of connecting parks in the Rahway River Basin. Offering easy strolls on meandering bike paths, this Union County park provides ample opportunities to meet plenty of passersby. The park and the tree-lined paths running through it follow two babbling brooks and a series of small duck ponds—the largest being Echo Lake. There are also a few grassy meadows for picnicking or ball playing. The paths and brook continue into adjacent Lenape Park, if you wish to expand your outing.

Dogs need to be leashed in all Union County parks. From I-78, take Exit 49 to Springfield Avenue south and proceed for 1.25 miles into Mountainside. Turn right into Mill Lane into the park. Open 6 A.M.–9 P.M. 908/527-4900.

EARMARK YOUR CALENDAR–SUMMER

Howling to the Hits: Howl and sway to the hits under the stars at Echo Lake Park in Mountainside with the **Union County Summer Arts Festival.** The outdoor concerts are held on the lawn of the park's natural amphitheater and feature a wide range of performances including oldies, reggae, jazz, country, and the New Jersey Symphony Orchestra. The free concerts run from the end of June through August on Wednesday evenings at 7:30 P.M. Remember to bring a chair or blanket. For more information, contact the Union County Parks and Recreation Department at 908/527-4900.

17 Watchung Reservation 🐾 🐾 🐾 🐾

In days long ago, the Lenape Indians called the mountain range between the Passaic and Rahway Rivers "Wachunk" or "high hills." Today, it's known as the Watchung Mountains and is home to a number of great parks in both Essex and Union Counties. One of them is Watchung Reservation, a 2,000-acre county park with over 40 miles of hiking trails and 26 miles of bridle trails through mountainside and hidden valley forests. Meadows, deserted villages, copper mines, and farms, along with plenty of water areas, complete the idyllic scene.

The best way to see all of this is to walk the Sierra Trail. The 10-mile route is the longest path in Watchung Reservation and loops through the entire park, which allows you and your faithful companion to explore all of the highlights. The trail can be picked up at almost any point in the park. Look for it near the southwestern entrance at Seeley's Pond, at the Trailside Nature & Science Center in the center of the park or at Lake Surprise in the northern end of the park. Of course, it's no surprise that we like to head for Lake Surprise. The water is great, and there are paths all along the shoreline.

Other hiking routes are the shorter Green, Orange, Red, and Yellow Trails that start from the Trailside Nature & Science Center. They range from 0.25 to 1.5 miles.

Dogs need to be leashed in all Union County parks. You can pick up a trail map at the park's Trailside Nature & Science Center in the northern end of the park at the intersection of Coles Avenue and New Providence Road. The Watchung Stables is located in the park, so watch for horses if you are using the bridle trails. From I-78, take Exit 43 to Diamond Hill Road east for an eighth of a mile. Turn left onto Valley Road into the park. The main park road, Sky Top Drive, branches off Valley Road to the right at the entrance. Open 6 A.M.–9 P.M. 908/527-4900.

Pumpkin Pups: Linus never saw the Great Pumpkin, but you can see hundreds of them, floating on water no less, at the **Great Pumpkin Sail** in Echo Lake Park in Mountainside. Launch your own jack-o'-lantern on Echo Lake with a pumpkin patch of others. The sail happens the day after Halloween, November 1, 6–9:30 P.M. A $5 fee per family covers entertainment, hot chocolate, and marshmallows. For more information, contact the Union County Parks and Recreation Department at 908/527-4900.

NEWARK

Parks, Beaches, and Recreation Areas

18 Branch Brook Park 🐾 🐾

In 1895 a city reservoir, formerly a Civil War training ground, and a murky marsh were given to the newly formed Essex County Park Commission, creating the first county park open to the public in the United States. In the first half of the 20th century, the Commission worked to dramatically improve the park. Through land acquisition, it expanded to 360 acres—about four miles in length and a quarter-mile wide—to become one of the largest city parks in Essex County and even the country. The marsh, Old Blue Jay Swamp, was transformed into a sparkling lake surrounded by lush lawns and pathways. Gardens were also created and thousands of cherry trees were planted. In fact, it is estimated that the park has more cherry trees than Washington, D.C.

These impressive credentials attracted many city dwellers between 1930 and 1950, but now, after a hundred years, the grand park is showing some wear and tear. Although still impressive and worth a visit, the surrounding community seems to be pushing in on all sides.

For dogs, the park highlights are Branch Brook, which flows through the park from north to south, and the spacious fields, especially the meadows at the northern and southern ends. Bike paths and tree-lined walking trails follow the brook. While you are strolling, look for a number of notable architectural works in and near the park. Among these sights are pedestrian and former railroad bridges, the park's administration building, which was built in 1915 and is listed on the national historical register, and the arched entrance to the Sacred Heart Cathedral overlooking the park. Also, be sure to plan a visit in April when Branch Brook is in the pink during the Cherry Blossom Festival. Park officials estimate they have 5,000 visitors a day to view the cherry blossoms.

Dogs need to be leashed in all Essex County parks. From I-280, take Clifton Street north. The park and access to the park's loop road are on the left. Open dawn–10 P.M. 973/268-3500.

Places to Stay

Sheraton Hotel: Okay, so it's at the airport. Not exactly the most glamorous of locales. But if you need a room at the inn, you could do far worse than this comfortable full-service hotel. There are 500 rooms here, and they all welcome dogs. Rates are $120–200 per night. 128 Frontage Road, Newark, NJ 07102; 201/690-5500 or 800/325-3535; website: www.sheraton.com.

NORTH BERGEN

Parks, Beaches, and Recreation Areas

19 North Hudson Park and James J. Braddock Run 🐾 🐾 🐾 🐕

For communities along the shores of the Hudson, finding extra space is a rare and wonderful thing. Open land is one of the reasons why North Hudson Park is so popular. At 167 acres, it's the county's second-largest park. It's also home to Woodcliff Lake, the largest lake in the county. Unfortunately for our water dogs, swimming is not permitted in the Woodcliff Lake (but fishing is). There are two island bird sanctuaries in the middle of it. (To which Inu and George offer a collective snore.) Fortunately, if you can keep your dog from the water, the paved paths around the lake make for a pleasant stroll. Throughout North Hudson Park there are plenty of places for walking or romping with your dog. Tree-lined bike and walking paths cross through the park, and there are numerous fenced-in, grassy sections for ball throwing.

The park's off-leash area is the James J. Braddock Run, located near 85th Street and Bergenline Avenue. It has a water fountain for dogs, benches, and a dirt base with some trees and grass. The run has a good fence, too, so you won't have to worry about your dog's well being.

The park, and all of North Bergen, is located on the southern end of the Palisades, so you can catch a glimpse or two of the Manhattan skyline through the trees and apartment towers that surround the park. Outside of the run, dogs need to be leashed. The park is bordered by 91st Street, JFK Boulevard, and Bergenline and Woodcliff Avenues. Open 6 A.M.–11 P.M. 201/319-3747.

OAKLAND

Parks, Beaches, and Recreation Areas

20 Ramapo Mountain State Forest 🐾 🐾 🐾 🐾

Go anywhere in the Ramapo Mountains and you are bound to find a great wilderness paradise. But we have to admit that even amidst a number of excellent parks, Ramapo Mountain State Forest is the pinnacle of parks out here. This park covers 4,161 acres of hardwood forests, miles of trails, breathtaking vistas, a lake, and unusual places to explore just a short drive from the confines of Manhattan.

At the center of the park is Ramapo Lake, a beautiful mountain lake. If you can believe it, the lake is also known as Rotten Lake, a poor translation of the Dutch name originally given to the pond—*Rotten Poel,* meaning Muskrat Pond. From the southern parking lot on Skyline Drive, the Blue Trail gives visitors their main access into the park. The trail climbs up into the heart of the forest and Ramapo Lake. You can walk all the way around the lake and even cross the dam that extends the original acreage of the lake.

From Ramapo Lake, you pick up the Red Trail, which has a number of lookout points with amazing views of the surrounding mountains and even New York City. You can also access the White Trail from here. This trail explores the northern section of the park and leads to Van Slyke Castle, the ruins of a mansion built by a former landowner in 1909. The White Trail can also be reached from the northern parking lot on Skyline Drive.

The longest trail in the park is the Cannonball Trail. It runs north-south for the length of the park on an old forest road that dates back to the American Revolution and the days when the iron industry dominated these hills. Part of the trail is a footbridge over I-287, which makes for a surreal crossing as traffic races under foot. This trail also runs beyond the park's northern boundary into the adjacent park, Ramapo Valley County Reservation.

Dogs must be leashed. Hunting is permitted here in season, generally October–February. You will be sharing the trails with horses, mountain bikers, bears, and snakes. Trail maps for Ramapo Mountain and many other surrounding locations can be purchased at Campmor, located at 810 Route 17N, Paramus, NJ. 201/445-5000. From I-287, take Exit 57 to Skyline Drive north for either a 0.25 miles or 0.5 miles to two main parking areas on the left. Open 8 A.M.–8 P.M. Information is available through Ringwood State Park at 973/962-7031.

Restaurants

Mike's Dog House: You won't be in the doghouse with a stop here. Located near the numerous parks, this hot dog stand is a handy stop on the way to or from an outing in the Ramapo Mountains of Mahwah and Oakland. There is no outdoor seating, so get your hot dogs and drinks to-go. 21 West Oakland Avenue; 201/677-0999.

PARAMUS

Parks, Beaches, and Recreation Areas

Saddle River County Park

This large park that has sections in Glen Rock, Saddle River, and Rochelle Park. See the Saddle River County Park listing in the Ridgewood section below for complete information.

21 Van Saun County Park 🐾 🐾

This Bergen County park is loaded with amenities, including a zoo, carousel, pony rides, train, playground, ball fields, and picnic areas, among others. For our four-footed friends, however, this list doesn't generate too much enthusiasm. And that's where the 1.5-mile bike path comes in. Perfect for dogs who don't need to be hoofing it down a mountain trail every day, the level blacktop path runs the entire length of the 140-acre park and circles the duck pond at the southern end.

The park, which is surprisingly green despite all the facilities, is a direct five miles from the George Washington Bridge, so you'll find it's a popular destination for New Yorkers on summer weekends.

Dogs need to be leashed in all Bergen County parks and are not permitted in the zoo or playgrounds. From Rte. 4, take Forest Avenue north for about 0.5 miles. The park entrance is on the right. Parking available. Open sunrise to a half hour after sunset. 201/262-2627.

Places to Stay

Radisson Inn: Free associate the word Paramus and what usually comes to mind is another word: malls. The Radisson puts you in the heart of this crazed shopping district. It is also conveniently located near New York City, the Meadowlands Sports Complex, and Newark Airport. With 120 upscale rooms, rates are $79–110. Guests with pets are asked to sign the hotel's pet policy. 601 From Road, Paramus, NJ 07652; 201/262-6900 or 800/333-3333; website: www.radisson.com.

PARK RIDGE

Places to Stay

Park Ridge Marriott: This four-story, 289-room hotel is newly renovated and offers a health spa and indoor and outdoor swimming pools, although pets are not allowed in the pools. They are permitted without any additional charges in the first floor rooms. Rates are $145–235. 300 Brae Boulevard, Park Ridge, NJ 07656; 201/307-0800 or 800/228-9290; website: www.marriott.com.

PARSIPPANY

Places to Stay

Parsippany Hilton: This recently renovated 510-room hotel offers a new fitness center, business center, and a convenient location near I-287. New York City is only 27 miles away. There is a refundable $50 pet deposit required per stay; room rates are $85–140. 1 Hilton Court, Parsippany, NJ 07054; 201/267-7373 or 800/744-1500; website: www.hilton.com.

Red Roof Inn: Conveniently located near I-80, this chain motel allows one small pet per room. Rates are $65–85. 855 U.S. 46, Parsippany, NJ 07054; 973/334-3737 or 800/RED-ROOF (800/733-7663); website: www.redroof.com.

Residence Inn: This extended-stay hotel has 156 suites all with separate living and sleeping areas and a fully equipped kitchen. Rates range $130–165 per night, including breakfast and dinner. With a $200 non-refundable pet fee per stay you probably won't stop here for a one-nighter, but if you need to call this area home for a week or more, the fee seems more reasonable. 3 Gatehall Drive, Parsippany, NJ 07054; 973/984-3313 or 800/331-3131; website: www.residenceinn.com.

PATERSON

Parks, Beaches, and Recreation Areas

22 Garret Mountain Reservation 🐾 🐾 🐾 🐾

Folks in these parts say that this is a rough area. That's not because this park is in Paterson, but because the steep slopes and sheer drops of the cliffs give even the most energetic dogs a good workout. The park's 569 acres cover all of Garret Mountain and, in turn, offer miles of hiking trails, bridle paths, and a park loop road with a pedestrian/bike lane. Just about every one of these routes has some kind of incline so even the healthiest of dogs better be prepared for some aerobic exercise. Luckily, the heavily wooded mountain also features some open lawns that give you a place to catch your breath.

At the base of the mountain is the entrance to Highland Lake. No swimming is permitted in the reservoir, but it is a picturesque area and probably the flattest spot in the park. Throughout the rest of the park you will also find numerous jaw-dropping views and plenty of options for adventure and relaxation.

This Passaic County park is located right off I-80. We actually drove right by it for years before stumbling upon it one day. Now it's a favorite stop any time we are headed west of the city. Dogs need to be leashed and should step carefully along the cliffs. From I-80, take Exit 56 to Squirrelwood Road south for about 0.25 miles. Turn right onto New Street and proceed for an eighth of a mile. Turn left onto Mountain Avenue and proceed for about 0.25 miles. The park entrance is on the right. Open sunrise–sunset. 973/881-4832.

PISCATAWAY

Parks, Beaches, and Recreation Areas

23 Johnson Park 🐾 🐾 🐾

Whether your dog is the scholarly type or more inclined to enjoy mud wrestling, Johnson Park has something for every taste. The Middlesex County park stretches out between the Raritan River and the campus of Rutgers University for a distance of over three miles. The park offers plenty of access to the river, but the shallow water along the shoreline can be quite muddy in places—a minor inconvenience that, if pointed out, will most likely elicit the response "so what's your point?" from your dog. If she does get a little muddy or wet, however, the park also has plenty of places to dry off, so don't sweat the little things.

There are 473 acres of open fields and woods with a few hiking trails and a 2.5-mile bike path that runs the length of the park. If you need more, you can always take a walk through the Rutgers campus next door.

Dogs need to be leashed in all Middlesex County parks and are not permitted on the ball fields. From I-287, take Exit 9 to River Road east for two miles. The park and its four entrances are on your right. Open sunrise–sunset. 732/745-3930.

Places to Stay

Motel 6: All Motel 6 locations allow dogs. This motel is near the intersection of the New Jersey Turnpike (Exit 10), the Garden State Parkway, and I-287 (Exit 5). It is about 38 miles outside of New York City. One dog is welcome per room. Rates are $55–76. 1012 Stelton Road, Piscataway, NJ 08854; 732/981-9200 or 800/4-MOTEL6 (800/466-8356); website: www.motel6.com.

EARMARK YOUR CALENDAR–OCTOBER

Stepping Out with the Big Dogs: Dogs of all shapes and sizes come out for the **Pet Walk and Fair.** The annual event is held at Red Bank's Marine Park in mid-October to raise money for the Monmouth County Society for the Prevention of Cruelty to Animals. The walk features a two-mile stroll through downtown Red Bank. There are also various street performers, vendors and dog contests like Best Kisser, Celebrity Look Alike, and Best Fetcher of the *Asbury Park Press*. Walk participants are asked to raise donations through sponsorship—there are great prizes for top fundraisers. To obtain a sponsor sheet or for more information, call the Monmouth County SPCA at 732/542-0040.

RED BANK

Parks, Beaches, and Recreation Areas

24 Marine Park 🐾

This small riverside park doesn't offer much in the way of exercise, but it does have scenic views overlooking the Navesink River and the town marina. With less than one acre of grass in a two-acre park, some of it devoted to picnic tables, your pet might rather walk along the nearby marina walkway instead.

Dogs need to be leashed. From Rte. 35, take County Road 10 (Main Street) east for about 0.5 miles. Turn left on Wharf Avenue and proceed into the park. Open dawn–dusk. 732/530-2762.

RIDGEWOOD

Parks, Beaches, and Recreation Areas

25 Saddle River County Park 🐾 🐾 🐾

Even though this is a relatively simple county park, finding all of the nooks and crannies here is almost impossible. It covers 596 acres, loosely following the Saddle River and stretching over five miles in five different towns. The park sections are the Wild Duck Pond Area in Ridgewood, the Dunkerhook Area at the intersection of Dunkerhook and Paramus Roads in Paramus, the Glen Rock Area in Glen Rock, the Otto Pehle Area in Saddle River, and the Rochelle Park Area in Rochelle Park. A paved bicycle path and pedestrian bridges connect all sections.

For dogs, the bike path is the main focus of any visit. It's well used and is a popular place for exercising and socializing. The main route is about two miles in length, but it has numerous loops and dead ends that branch off from it. If you're not back in two hours, we'll send out a search party!

Dogs need to be leashed in all Bergen County parks. From U.S. 17 in Paramus, take Ridgewood Avenue west for about 0.5 miles into Ridgewood. The park is on the right. The Dunkerhook area is off Paramus Road in Paramus. Open sunrise to a half hour after sunset. 201/796-0324.

Nature Hikes and Urban Walks

Downtown Ridgewood: Yes, there is something to be said for the high adventure of the dusty trail or a good muddy pond, but when you really want to put on the dog, step out with the upper crust in downtown Ridgewood. The shops and cafés along Ridgewood Avenue and Broad and Chestnut Streets beckon with a welcoming charm and equally affluent clientele. (Well, until *we* show up, that is!) Whether you are resigned to window-shopping or leave carrying armfuls of shopping bags, an afternoon or evening outing along these flower-strewn, lamp-lit streets is a must. For more information, contact the Ridgewood Chamber of Commerce at 201/612-2425 or check out its website: www.webridgewood.com.

Restaurants

If we listed all of the dog-friendly restaurants in Ridgewood's downtown section, we would be competing with Zagat restaurant guides. And since it is staying away from dog guides, we'll return the favor and only list a few of the cafés and restaurants that really make us howl.

A & B Ridgewood Bakery and Caffe: Whether you just need a mocha to keep you going on your downtown stroll or want to relax at the outdoor tables with something sweet, this is the spot to stop with Spot. If you're looking to watch the world go by, A & B is as easy as 1-2-3. 18 East Ridgewood Avenue; 201/612-6888.

Latour: The outdoor seating at this French-American restaurant is close enough to the downtown action to see and be seen, yet enough out of the way to relax and enjoy a delightful meal of lobster bisque, escargot, salmon, or duck. In true French fashion, our dogs are partial to any tidbit that drops from our forks to their places under our table. 6 East Ridgewood Avenue; 201/445-5056.

Tastefully British: If you enjoy bangers, kidney pork pie, scotch eggs, and fish and chips, or if you are simply one of the few who actually know what these dishes are, you will have a jolly old time at Tastefully British. Your dog will, too, because the sidewalk tables allow you both to dine together. 2 East Ridgewood Avenue; 201/612-0009.

Zarolé: If you are tired of the same old, same old, Zarolé's French-American menu, with a dash of Asian influence, will help shake things up. Try the pan-seared halibut with Israeli couscous or the grilled lobster salad. The outdoor dining at the corner of East Ridgewood Avenue and South Broad

Street puts you and your dog in the heart of downtown. 20 East Ridgewood Avenue; 201/670-5701; website: www.zarole.com.

RINGWOOD

Parks, Beaches, and Recreation Areas

26 Ringwood State Park 🐾 🐾 🐾 🔶

The land that this 5,237-acre state park now occupies first became attractive during the 1700s, when much of the colonial iron production came from here. The iron industry, in turn, helped finance some of the exclusive estates and gardens found within the park today. Dogs are not permitted at the park's Botanical Gardens, Skylands Manor, or Ringwood Manor, but they are welcome to use the miles of endless trails that run through the roomy Skylands Forest. You and your pack have an assortment of paths to choose from, including hiking trails and wide bridle and carriage paths covering dense forests, rocky vistas, and the popular Shepherd Lake. Also popular here is mountain biking, so remember you and your dog are sharing these trails.

Dogs need to be leashed in all state parks and are not permitted at the designated beach area of Shepherd Lake. Trail maps are available at the ranger station at the entrance. From Memorial Day Weekend through Labor Day, there is a $5 weekday and $7 weekend and holiday entrance fee. The State Park Pass is available for $35 and is good for all state parks for a year.

From I-287, take Exit 57 to Skyline Drive north for five miles. Turn right onto Greenwood Lake Turnpike and proceed for five miles (past the Botanical Gardens). Turn right onto Sloatsburg Road and proceed for two miles into the park. Follow signs for specific sections of the park and trailheads. Open during daylight hours. 973/962-7031.

SANDY HOOK

Parks, Beaches, and Recreation Areas

27 Sandy Hook 🐾 🐾 🐾 🐾 🔶

Sandy Hook, a 1,665-acre barrier beach, is the northern end of the Jersey shore and part of the majestic gateway into New York Harbor. The six-mile long peninsula is home to endless beaches along the Atlantic Ocean and Sandy Hook Bay, miles of hiking trails, the oldest lighthouse in America, and offers hour upon hour of fun year-round for surf hounds. It's also part of Gateway National Recreation Area that covers much of the shoreline surrounding Lower New York Harbor in New Jersey, Brooklyn, and Staten Island.

Not only is Sandy Hook one of the most scenic places on the Jersey shore, but it is also rich in history. Within the park is Fort Hancock, built during the

War of 1812, and Sandy Hook Lighthouse, America's oldest beacon, built in 1764. The Little Red Lighthouse of storybook fame was also once part of this site. From the Atlantic side of the park, there are great views of New York Harbor—the best are from the North Beach Observation Deck.

If you want to hit the trail, there are some short paths at the northern tip of the peninsula near Fort Hancock and also in the center of the park at the fishing beach area. But mostly we stick to the wide, open beaches and blaze our own elusive trail in the sand. Surf's up!

Dogs need to be leashed in all national parks and are not permitted on the ocean side of the peninsula March 15–Labor Day to protect nesting shorebirds. From June through Labor Day, a $10 entrance fee is charged until 4 P.M. A good first stop for maps and information is the Sandy Hook Visitor Center located in the center of the park. From the Garden State Parkway, take Exit 117 to Rte. 36 east for 12 miles over the Navesink River. Turn left onto Atlantic Drive into the park. Open sunrise–sunset. 732/872-5970.

Nature Hikes and Urban Walks

Twin Lights State Historic Site: After a wet and wild time at the beaches of Sandy Hook you need a place to shake that sand out. A climb up to the Navesink Highlands and the Twin Lights Lighthouse should dry you out while offering impressive views of Sandy Hook and the northern section of the Jersey Shore. The grounds are small, but the breezes and vistas are great. The lighthouse was built in 1828 and sits 200 feet above sea level.

Dogs need to be leashed on all state park property and are not permitted inside the lighthouse itself. The lighthouse is located off of Rte. 36 just east of the Gateway National Recreation Area and the Navesink River. The grounds are open 9 A.M.–sunset. The lighthouse is open 10 A.M.–5 P.M. 732/872-1814.

SECAUCUS

Places to Stay

Radisson Suite Hotel Meadowlands: Many of the 151 suites in this full-service hotel have a view of the New York skyline and you can also enjoy an indoor heated pool and health club. Rates range are $89–140. Guests with pets are asked to sigh the hotel's pet policy release form. 350 Route 3 West Mill Creek Drive, Secaucus, NJ 07094; 201/863-8700 or 800/333-3333; website: www.radisson.com.

Red Roof Inn: This motel offers easy access to the Lincoln Tunnel and New York City and even has a marina and boat ramp. One small pet per room is welcome. Rates are $65–90. 15 Meadowlands Parkway, Secaucus, NJ 07094; 201/319-1000 or 800/RED-ROOF (800/733-7663); website: www.redroof.com.

SOMERSET

Parks, Beaches, and Recreation Areas

28 Colonial Park 🐾 🐾 🐾 🐕

George and Inu make pilgrimages to the dog run at Colonial Park the way baseball traditionalists take trips to Chicago's Wrigley Field and Boston's Fenway Park. The hilltop dog run is the biggest we've ever seen (and we've seen a lot) and is a mecca for dogs all over northern New Jersey.

The run is about two acres in size, large enough to hold the above-mentioned baseball parks with room left over for some frenzied fans doing the Wave in the lower decks. And it is, naturally, almost always filled with happy dogs doing their own version of the Wave. There are a few trees, poop bags, and trash cans; it is completely covered with grass; and it is fully enclosed with a wood-and-wire snow fence that should be able to hold most dogs. There isn't any water at the run, but there are faucets nearby in the rest of the park. Most people bring their own water during the summer months.

The rest of Colonial Park also attracts a number of visitors, but things are a little more dignified away from the run. The lawns are cut and the trees are trimmed in just the right configuration; there are flowering gardens, meandering bike paths, and shimmering duck ponds throughout the park. The green space is shared with the adjacent Spooky Brook Golf Course so you really do get the impression of walking on estate grounds.

Except for the run, dogs need to be leashed. From I-287, take Exit 12 to Weston Canal Road (County Road 623) and proceed south for a mile. Turn left on Randolph Road and proceed for a mile. Turn right onto Schoolhouse Road for about 0.5 miles. Finally, turn left onto Mettler's Road and proceed for about 0.5 miles. The park and run are on your left. Open from 7 A.M. to a half hour after sunset. 732/873-2695.

SPRINGFIELD/CRANFORD

Parks, Beaches, and Recreation Areas

29 Lenape Park and Nomahegan Park 🐾 🐾

These two parks, along with adjacent Echo Lake Park in Mountainside (see listing under Mountainside) make up a trio of connecting Union County parks in the Rahway River basin.

Both parks are well maintained with plenty of grassy lawns and wooded areas. Nomahegan Park is more popular with two-legged folk because of its bike paths, playgrounds, ball fields, and duck ponds. For dogs, the bike paths and the few trails of Nomahegan make for an easy walk with plenty of pats by local walkers. Despite the free pats, however, George and Inu prefer the more open and relaxed atmosphere of Lenape Park just across

Kenilworth Boulevard. There are limited amenities here, but the main trail that starts in Nomahegan extends into Lenape through meadows following an aqueduct and a branch of the Rahway River. It eventually connects with Echo Lake Park.

Separately, the two parks are not much to shake a stick at but put them all together and they make for a good hike of over 2.5 miles.

Dogs need to be leashed in all Union County parks. From I-78, take Exit 49 to Springfield Avenue and proceed south for 1.5 miles through Mountainside and into Cranford. At the intersection with Kenilworth Boulevard, Lenape Park is on the left and Nomahegan Park is on the right. Open 6 A.M.–9 P.M. 908/527-4900.

Restaurants

Sam's Farm: It's hard to eat right when you are an on-the-go type, but this farm stand makes it easy to be healthy. Enjoy a fresh salad bar, cut fruit bowls, and plenty of whole fruit too. Get it to go and don't forget to pick up some of those famous Jersey tomatoes and corn. 831 South Springfield Avenue; 973/379-2916.

Places to Stay

Holiday Inn: This 190-room hotel also offers an indoor pool and fitness center. The rooms are clean and comfortable, and there is a restaurant on-site so you and your pup can order right in your room. Rates are $108–131. There is no additional fee for your pet. 304 Rte. 22 West, Springfield, NJ 07081; 973/376-9400; website: www.holiday-inn.com.

WEEHAWKEN

Parks, Beaches, and Recreation Areas

30 Hamilton Park 🐾 🐾 🐾

The cliff-top towns of Weehawken, West New York, and Guttenberg are dominated by the Lower Palisades and spectacular views of the Manhattan skyline just across the Hudson River. Along the cliffs and Kennedy Boulevard East are numerous parks and view points. By themselves most of the parks are not very interesting. They are small with a little grass and a few benches, but they all have great vistas and most of them are connected with a wide sidewalk along the cliffs.

Hamilton Park is located on the bluff where Alexander Hamilton was fatally wounded in his historic duel with his political rival, Vice-President Aaron Burr, on July 11, 1904. There is a commemorative plaque marking the duel that, in many ways, changed the course of New York City's future.

Dogs need to be leashed. The park is located on Kennedy Boulevard East at the intersection with Hudson Place. Open 24 hours a day. 201/319-6061.

Places to Stay

Sheraton Suites on the Hudson: With 10 floors and 347 suites, you are sure to find a room with a view of the Manhattan skyline to suit you. Each suite features a parlor with sleeper sofa, refrigerator, and microwave. Ferry service across the Hudson River leaves right from the hotel. There is a $75 pet fee per stay up to three weeks. Rates are $145–225. 500 Harbor Boulevard, Weehawken, NJ 07087; 201/617-5600 or 888/625-5144; website: www.starwood.com.

WEST MILFORD

Parks, Beaches, and Recreation Areas

31 Wawayanda State Park 🐾 🐾 🐾 🐾

Want to get away? Way, way yanda? Well, this is the place. Starting with a good drive from New York City and ending with 13,422 acres and over 40 miles of spectacular trails that you can just disappear into, we think this is a trip well worth taking. The wilderness terrain will also help to remove any lingering effects of the city. You can choose from ponds, swamps and Wawayanda Lake or thick hardwood forests, hilltop peaks and steep ravines. In fact, the only signs of civilization may be the remains of the ironworks that were prevalent in this area during the 18th century. The trails include 20 miles of the Appalachian Trail.

Dogs need to be leashed in all state parks. It's unlikely that you will see any, but there is a good black bear population in the park. So, hold on to that leash with your strong hand. Trail maps are available at the ranger station. From Memorial Day Weekend through Labor Day, there is a $5 weekday and $7 weekend and holiday entrance fee. A State Park Pass is available for $35 and is good for all state parks for a year. From Rte. 23, take Union Valley Road north for 8.5 miles. Turn left onto Warwick Turnpike and proceed for four miles. The park is on the left. Open during daylight hours. 973/853-4462.

WEST ORANGE

Parks, Beaches, and Recreation Areas

32 Eagle Rock Reservation 🐾 🐾 🐾

You will feel like you are in the catbird's seat when you catch the view from Eagle Rock. Part of the Watchung Mountain Range, this peak offers great vistas of the surrounding area and the New York City skyline. The park became a popular attraction at the turn of the century when a trolley line ran from Newark to the base of the mountain.

The lofty park is 408 acres in size and has 3.5 miles of hiking trails and bridle paths throughout the heavily wooded area of oaks and maples. Although it is not well marked, the Yellow Trail leads to Lookout Point, the highest point in the park and offering some of the best views. The farther north you go on the trails, the more you drop in elevation and the closer you get to the park's wetlands near the town of Verona. If hiking is not your thing, there are also a few open grassy fields and picnic areas.

Dogs need to be leashed in all Essex County parks and are not permitted at Highlawn Pavilion, the restaurant within the park. Plenty of parking is available. From I-280, take Prospect Avenue north for about 0.25 miles. Turn right onto Eagle Rock Avenue and proceed for about 0.25 miles. The park entrance is on the left. Open dawn–10 P.M. 973/268-3500.

33 South Mountain Reservation 🐾 🐾 🐾 🐾

By now, George and Inu have been to more parks than you can shake a stick at, and if there is one thing they have learned in all of their travels, it's that wherever you find the name "Olmsted" you find a great park. Frederick Law Olmsted (1822–1903) was the master of park design and the originator of landscape architecture in America. Central Park and Prospect Park in New York City, the series of parks called the Emerald Necklace in Boston, and the Capitol Grounds in Washington, D.C., are just some of the highlights of his brilliant work, but there are hundreds of parks around the world that were created by him or his partners. One of these companies, headed by Olmsted's stepson, created South Mountain Reservation.

This park is at the heart of the Watchung Mountain Range that runs through Essex and Union Counties and is a very popular park for New Jerseyites. Not because of its 4,067 acres of hills, woods, trails, and ponds that any dog would love, but because of the endless acres of manicured green lawns. And for any suburbanite who has tried to keep a lawn green, you know this is no easy task!

The rest of the park is just as spectacular. If you want views of the area including New York City, head for Crest Drive on the eastern end of the park off of Orange Avenue. This wooded, hilltop section is also good for walking and hiking. A number of trails cross through here, and the paved path along Crest Drive is closed to vehicles.

At the end of Crest Drive is Washington Rock, a Revolutionary War historic site. It was the location of a lookout station commissioned by General Washington to observe British troops.

In total, South Mountain has 19 miles of trails and 27 miles of carriage roads. Trailheads are throughout the park, but we like the woods around the southern end of the park near Diamond Mill Pond and Campbell's Pond. The Rahway River, which runs through the park, feeds the ponds and this "wet and wild" location is a great place for exploring the old mill and bridge at Campbell's Pond or Hemlock Falls, a 25-foot waterfall.

Dogs need to be leashed in all Essex County parks. Plenty of parking spaces throughout the park. From I-280, take Pleasant Valley Way south for a mile and enter the park on Cherry Lane, the park's main north-south route. If you continue for about 0.5 miles more, you will cross Orange Avenue, the park's main east-west route. Open dawn–10 P.M. 973/268-3500.

Places to Stay

Residence Inn: This extended-stay hotel just opened as we went to press. It offers 128 suites with separate living and sleeping areas and a fully-equipped kitchen. Dogs are allowed with a $100 deposit per stay. 107 Prospect Avenue, West Orange, NJ 07052; 973/669-4700 or 800/331-3131; website: www.residenceinn.com.

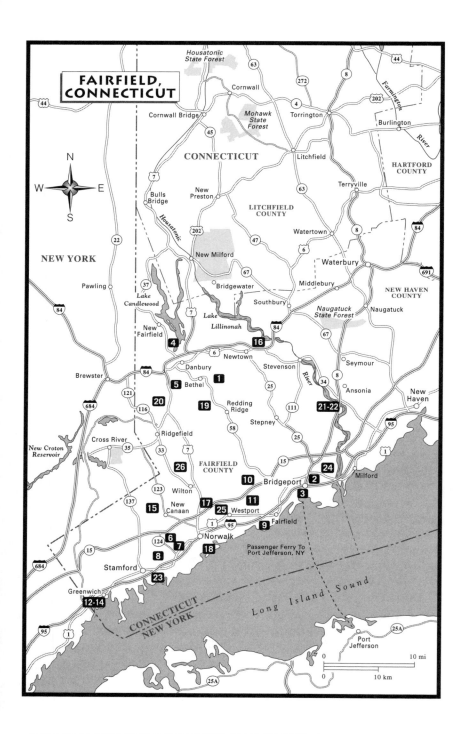

FAIRFIELD, CONNECTICUT

10 FAIRFIELD, CONNECTICUT

The truth is, friend, that dogs can read. Why else would they put those
signs on the doors of the post office? NO DOGS ALLOWED EXCEPT
SEEING-EYE DOGS. Do you catch my meaning? The man with the dog
can't see, so who else is left?

— From *Timbuktu*, by Paul Auster

Home to some of the wealthiest communities in the United States, the lovely
towns and villages in Fairfield County are a world unto themselves. Just a
short commute away from the heart of Manhattan, this county is often
thought of as a bedroom community of New York City (more like the Lincoln
Bedroom of New York City). Operating on the "commuter corridor," the
residents of these coastal towns along the Long Island Sound enjoy easy
access to the Big Apple, but we have a hunch most of them would be happy
to pull up the drawbridge when they return each night.

For when they named Fairfield County they sure weren't thinking of our
canine companions. Most of the fields here, not to mention the parks, beaches,
and recreation areas, are off limits to dogs and that's just not very fair. In fact,
many of the parks are only for town residents, making it very difficult to find
a fair field for Fido.

PICK OF THE LITTER–FAIRFIELD HIGHLIGHTS

Silvermine Tavern, Norwalk

Swanky Franks, Norwalk

Taylor Farm, Norwalk

Winslow Park, Westport

Woodies Roadhouse, Westport

Now we're not trying to depress you, or even discourage you from coming here. (All those "No Dogs Allowed" signs take care of that!) Because we don't give up easily and thanks to the noses of our trusty dogs, and a few good maps, we've sniffed out enough green spaces here in Connecticut that even a Yankee-loving dog can still find an escape.

BETHEL

Parks, Beaches, and Recreation Areas

🐾 Collis P. Huntington State Park 🐾 🐾 🐾

This 878-acre park, a gift of Archer and Anna Hyatt Huntington in memory of his stepfather Collis P. Huntington, is ideal for a quiet stroll through well-kept woods.

This lovely park is located off the beaten path, which maintains its favored park status with locals. None of the trails are marked, but the well-worn paths are fairly easy to follow. From the parking area, you can take the main loop trail, which runs for 5.5 miles through the entire park, passing by several wooden bridges, two ponds, several streams, and flowering trees in a hardwood forest. Take note of all the lovely statues here, the work of renowned sculptress, Anna Hyatt Huntington.

Dogs must be leashed. From Rte. 302, take Rte. 58 south for a mile. Bear left and then right onto Sunset Hill Road and proceed for two miles. Turn left onto Dodgingtown Road and enter the park. Open 8 A.M.–sunset. 860/424-3200.

BRIDGEPORT

Parks, Beaches, and Recreation Areas

🐾 Beardsley Park 🐾 🐾

Beardsley Park, the home of Beardsley Zoo, is a little like Rome—all roads lead to it. Resplendent in its Victorian detailing, this park is a popular and busy city centerpiece. Although dogs are prohibited from the zoo itself, you won't mind making do in the park surrounding the zoo. There is a wide paved path running throughout and if you can avoid the Canada geese who seem to be trying to become permanent fixtures, you'll enjoy your walk.

Of course beauty isn't everything. While dogs in the 19th century would have had the run of the park, their modern-day descendants are relegated to ho-hum leashed walks on the gravel path.

Dogs must be leashed. From U.S. 8, take U.S. 1 north for a mile, then turn left onto Nobel Avenue and proceed for about 0.5 miles. The park is on the left. Another entrance is off of East Main Street. Open 8 A.M.–sunset. 203/576-7233.

❸ Seaside Park 🐾 🐾

Established in 1865, this 370-acre park retains much of its Victorian feel, giving visitors a glimpse of life over 100 years ago, when seaside parks were *the* places to see and be seen.

Although the highlight is a Ferris wheel and other amusements dogs won't get too worked up over, a wide grassy path that runs alongside the no-dogs-allowed beach is considered fair game. The multi-use recreation path gets its fair share of paw prints as well.

Leashes are required, and with the many picnickers this park attracts, we actually wanted to keep our dogs close by. Inu tends to see picnics as a moveable feast spread out for his pleasure. From U.S. 1, take Park Avenue south for two miles to the intersection with Waldemere Road and the park entrance. Open 8 A.M.–sunset. 203/576-7233.

Restaurants

Auntie Babe's Ice Cream: We all wished we had an Auntie Babe like this when we were growing up—the ice cream and grilled food is heaven to a 10-year-old. Or a dog. Make that a corndog. There's a take-out window and benches. 4191 Main Street; 203/365-0294.

Places to Stay

Holiday Inn: Just across the street from the courthouse, this hotel is centrally located in town, but be wary of late night walks. There are 234 rooms, with rates in the $99–139 range. Small dogs under 20 pounds are welcome, and there is $50 refundable pet deposit. 1070 Main Street, Bridgeport, CT 06604. 203/334-1234; website: www.holiday-inn.com.

BROOKFIELD

Places to Stay

Twin Tree Inn: Well-behaved dogs are welcome at this 46-room country home. The deluxe suites have sliding glass doors that open onto the back lawn, making midnight walks a snap. Rates from $75, plus a $10 pet fee. 1030 Federal Road, Brookfield, CT 06804; 203/775-0220; website: www.travelhero.com.

DANBURY

Parks, Beaches, and Recreation Areas

4 Bear Mountain Park 🐾 🐾 🐾

The local federal correctional institution donated this land to Danbury to create the park, which has the distinction of being one of the few places where you start uphill and proceed down. Begin at the top of Bear Mountain, 888 feet above sea level; from here you can mosey down to Lake Candlewood and excellent views of the water.

Along the way you'll pass through a lovely wooded forest, but remember that although it's a fairly easy walk *down* the wooded trail, it'll be *uphill* on the way back with your leashed Lassie.

Dogs are not permitted to swim in the lake. From I-84, take Exit 6 to Rte. 37 and proceed north for 3.5 miles. Turn right onto Bear Mountain Road into the park. Some signs read Kennedy Trails—that is also Bear Mountain. Open dawn–dusk. 203/743-0546.

5 Tarrywile Park and Mansion 🐾 🐾 🐾 🐾

Our dogs love to tarry awhile in Tarrywile, a former private estate turned public park. Purchased by the city in 1985, there are currently 636 acres of woods and meadows to explore, but that number keeps going up as the city acquires more land.

Visitors can choose a short 1.5-mile hike, or spend a half-day exploring the longer trails. All in all, there are seven miles of trail choices, taking you through old orchards, gorgeous flowering trees, and to several ponds. The most popular destinations include Parks Pond and Tarrywile Lake or the picnic area in the fruit orchard. Maps are available at the mansion headquarters.

Leashed dogs are permitted in the park, but they are not allowed to swim here. From U.S. 7, take Wooster Heights east for a mile. Turn right on Southern Boulevard and proceed for a mile. The park and mansion entrance are on the right. Open sunrise–sunset. 203/744-3130.

Restaurants

Cor's: This place is open for breakfast and lunch every day, and everything is homemade. The menu specials rotate, but our dogs give the meatloaf and grinders a special paws up. You can take out, but there's no outdoor seating. 65 West Street; 203/792-9999.

J. K.'s Restaurant: J. K.'s serves up something called Original Texas Hot Wieners—short fat dogs, smothered with either chili or mustard. A Danbury institution for the past 75 years, one bite will tell you why. Our dogs wanted to be smothered with their dogs. They also have hamburgers and other grilled grub to go. No outdoor seating, but it's good enough to eat standing up. 126 South Street; 203/743-4004.

Places to Stay

Hilton and Towers: This 115-room full-service hotel welcomes dogs with a $10 pet fee. There is a restaurant on-site, and all the usual modern amenities. Rates are in the $99–185 range. 18 Old Ridgebury Road, Danbury, CT 06810; 203/794-0600 or 800/HILTONS (800/445-8667); website: www.hilton.com.

Holiday Inn: Don your bonnets, this Holiday Inn has a hat theme. Since Danbury was the home of the first American hat and is the center of the hat industry in the United States, this hotel celebrates it. The hotel prefers smaller dogs, and they'll do a quick security sweep after checkout. Rates $115–129. 80 Newtown Road, Danbury, CT 06810; 203/792-4000 or 888/452-4772; website: www.holiday-inn.com.

Ramada Inn: Dogs are welcome at this 180-room hotel, conveniently situated on the edge of town. Rates $59–125. 116 Newtown Road, Danbury, CT 06810; 203/792-3800 or 888/298-2054; website: www.ramada.com.

DARIEN

Darien parks are less than dog-friendly, especially if you are a dog from out of town. You must be a Darien resident to use the parks and even then, with the exception of one leash-free park, the town officials are not extremely happy to see dogs on their paths. Also, dogs are not allowed on any Darien beaches year round. It's enough to make us want to hightail it out of there (which is, we suspect, exactly the idea).

Parks, Beaches, and Recreation Areas

6 Cherry Lawn Park 🐾 🐾 🐾 🐕

This place is awesome, but you have to have a Darien permit to officially use the parking area. So unless you are willing to buy a house or befriend a resident, you can't set paw in this park. But, since it's the only leash-free park in the city, if you can find a way to get here, do.

The park has wide grassy areas that lead to a swimming pond. There's a mile-long trail that beats a flat wide path into the woods from the pond; local dogs gather here for regular romps, so your pooch is likely to spot a friend if you visit.

This park is also home to the Darien Nature Center, which is open year-round and hosts a number of guided walks in the park. From U.S. 1, take Brookside Road north for about 0.25 miles. The park and parking lot are on the right. The Darien Nature Center is open 9 A.M.–2 P.M. 203/655-7459. The park is open dawn–dusk; 203/656-7325.

❼ Tilley Pond Park 🐾 🐾

This park is a little on the small side, but it provides a great place to take a break from shopping in Darien. The park contains manicured grassy stretches and paved walks in the park and woods. Make sure to accessorize with a matching leash, as they are mandatory here. From U.S. 1, take Mansfield Street north one block to the park. Open dawn–dusk. 203/656-7325.

❽ Woodland Park Nature Preserve 🐾 🐾 🐾

Thanks to a resident, Walter Irving, who sold his land to Darien in 1959, this park has been a delight for 40 years. You are likely to catch sight of some unusual birds and lovely wildflowers. Local hounds haunt this park, so this is your chance to run with the home dogs.

There are just two miles of marked trails, but they offer a pleasant and beautiful woodsy walk. We recommend the one-mile White Trail or the 1.5-mile Yellow Trail. Both lead through the mature pine forest.

Dogs must remain leashed on all the trails. From U.S. 1, take Hollow Tree ridge Road north for about 0.5 miles. Turn left onto Middlesex Road and proceed for about 0.25 miles. The park is on the left. Open dawn–dusk. 203/656-7325.

Restaurants

Uncle's Deli: This place rocks for breakfast or lunch, and you can take your order to the outdoor picnic table. This green and white deli is practically a fixture in Darien. Our dogs love the roll-ups as much as the locals do. 1041 Post Road; 203/655-9701.

FAIRFIELD

Although there are city parks in Fairfield, none of them welcome you and your dog. Apparently in these parts, parks are to be seen, but not enjoyed. Not only are they for Fairfield residents only, but the dogs of this city are clearly not given resident status. However, there is a bright spot: land designated as Open Space and managed by the Conservation Department does allow dogs—even non-resident dogs—and for the most part, they don't require leashes.

Parks, Beaches, and Recreation Areas

🐾 Ash Creek Open Space 🐾 🐾 ◀🐾

The focus of this 25-acre park is the preservation of Fairfield's history and salt marshes. Once the site of the Penfield gristmills, today the park's short nature trails permit you to explore the salt marsh on a peninsula in Ash Creek, taking you through a wildflower meadow on its way. You can also get up close to the mill foundations and other remnants of this park's former life, all while overlooking Ash Creek.

Dogs must be leashed and are not permitted in the playground or picnic areas. From U.S. 1, take Old Post Road south for a block. Turn left onto Turney Road, and you'll find the parking area is directly on the left. Open dawn until one hour after sunset. 203/256-3071.

🔟 Brett Woods Conservation Area 🐾 🐾 🐕

This 185-acre stretch is one of the largest parks we've found in Fairfield. There are a few rough hiking trails that run through a variety of woodlands and streams and even some wetlands, but be careful of the ticks. A former town road leads into the woods from the lot, and several north-south spur trails run from it. If you go south, the trails lead through wooded terrain to the former Treasure Road and a secondary parking area. If you head north instead, you—and your dog—will run smack into Brett Woods Pond, where your dog can cool off with a dip.

Your dog can forgo the leash, if she obeys voice commands. From Merritt Parkway, take Black Rock Turnpike north for about 0.5 miles. Turn left onto Hemlock Road and proceed for about 0.25 miles. Turn right onto Burr Street and continue for another 0.25 miles. Finally, turn left onto North Street and continue for a mile to the park entrance. Open from dawn until one hour after sunset. 203/256-3071.

🔢 Lake Mohegan Open Space 🐾 🐾 🐾 🐕

Local dogs beg to be taken here, and we can see why. The 167 acres contain miles of wooded trails, but the locals come for the swimming. Lake Mohegan, Mill River, and North Pond are all options for a dip, and Inu was eager to try them all.

You can take a loop trail around most of the lake, and several spur trails lead along the river and into the woods. Two-legged folk may also swim at Lake Mohegan, so dogs need to stay away from the designated swimming holes. There are, however, plenty of other swimming options along its shores.

Dogs need to be under voice control. From the Merritt Parkway, take Black Rock Turnpike south for a mile. Turn left onto Tahmore Drive and continue for about 0.5 miles into the parking area. Open dawn until one hour past sunset. 203/256-3071.

Restaurants

Firehouse Deli: The blackboard is the cue to what's fresh and what's hot at this historic red firehouse-turned-deli. The outdoor tables fill up quickly at lunch, so get fired up, grab a sandwich and slide over to a perch at this great people watching place. 22 Reef Road; 203/255-5527.

Pizza Works: Pizza by the slice, an East Coast tradition, is alive and well here. On a nice day, there are plastic chairs lining the front of the store. Nothing fancy, but it's quick, cheap and good. 1512 Post Road; 203/255-0303.

GREENWICH

If you're a dog in Greenwich, you are relegated to leashed walks on your neighborhood sidewalk. If you're visiting here, don't even bother trying to find a place to walk your dog. It doesn't exist. After trying to get the park rules and regulations from city officials we were told firmly that although residents can walk your dog in some of the parks in Greenwich, they'd really rather *you* didn't. They didn't even want to appear in a book that "advertised" parks for dogs. So what can we say? The following parks "tolerate" your pet, but if city officials never saw a dog in a Greenwich park again, we feel certain they would be thrilled.

Parks, Beaches, and Recreation Areas

🖹 Grass Island 🐾 🐾

This is one of the two parks in the Greenwich inner harbor, and the main attraction here is the view. There are picnic tables, grass and, uh, did we mention the view? Look out over the harbor at all those yachts and just imagine how the other half lives. Inquiring dogs want to know. Dogs must be leashed. You must have a resident sticker to park here. The park is located off Shore Road in the village of Belle Haven. Open dawn–dusk. 203/622-7830.

🖹 Greenwich Point Park 🐾 🐾

The fee for this peninsula park on Tod's Point is steep: to get into the park during the summer, you have to buy a house in Greenwich. Or know somebody who can smuggle you in, as we did.

If you live in town, you'll find a beachfront, picnic areas, and walking and biking paths. Our dogs liked exploring the foundations of the old cannon turrets, remnants of the old fort that once stood its ground here. And when George fetched the newspaper, all he brought back was the real estate section. Hmm....

Dogs must be leashed. From I-95, take Exit 5 to Sound Beach Avenue and continue south for two miles. Turn right onto Shore Road to the end and a small parking area. Open dawn–dusk. 203/622-7830.

EARMARK YOUR CALENDAR–SUMMER

Connecticut has its fair share of outdoor summer concerts, open to human and canine alike.

And the Bands Played on... Have a howling good time every Wednesday, Thursday, and Sunday evening at 7 P.M. for a series of summer concerts on the Sherman Green throughout July and August. For performance schedules, call 203/256-3144.

Pups in the Park: Pop on down to hear a little night music at the open-air concert series by the Greenwich Pops, every Wednesday night at Baldwin Park. Both choral and symphonic concerts are featured at the Pappas Pavillion. The concerts run from 7:30 to 9 P.M. For performance schedules, call 203/622-7830.

Strings under the Stars: The summer brings music to the two-acre Norwalk Green. The city sponsors a couple of concerts a month, usually held from 3 to 5 P.M. on weekend days. Leashed, well-heeled pooches welcome. 203/854-7746.

Concerts on the Green: On Tuesday evenings in July and August, you can catch some catchy tunes in Trumbull. The fun begins at 7 P.M. every Tuesday on the Green in the center of Trumbull. Dogs welcome as long as they don't try to sing harmony. For more information, call 203/452-5060.

Wilton Courtyard Concerts: The Wilton Library holds a free summer concert series, where live bands do their level best to entertain the lunch crowd. No one shushes you here, despite the abundance of librarians in attendance. Bring your lunch and your dog to the steps of the courtyard at 137 Old Ridgefield Road. For more information, call 203/762-3950.

14 Roger Sherman Baldwin Park 🐾 🐾

Walk along the boardwalk here and breathe in the salt air. This small park does not have trails; the walk along the water and the view of the sound are pretty much it—but they are enough to lure us back. Although not a large space, there is a concert pavilion on the grounds, so stroll by on a summer evening for a little night music.

Dogs must be leashed. From U.S. 1, take Greenwich Avenue south for a mile. Turn right onto Arch Street. The park is on the left. Open dawn–10 P.M. 203/622-7830.

NEW CANAAN

Parks, Beaches, and Recreation Areas

15 New Canaan Nature Center 🐾 🐾 🐾

One visit here and you'll know you've arrived in the land of Canaan. Located on 40 gorgeous acres, you'll find two miles of criss-crossing paths covering meadows, two ponds, woodlands, dense thickets, an old orchard, and a cattail marsh. You can even walk across a marsh on a 350-foot boardwalk. Don't miss the northern corner of the park, where the butterfly field is located. It is really a ticket back to your childhood—or puppyhood, as the case may be. George gave up chasing his usual tennis ball in favor of hightailing after a butterfly.

Leashed dogs are permitted. No fee, but donations requested. From the center of New Canaan on Rte. 106, take Rte. 124 north for about 0.5 miles. The park is on the left. Grounds are open dawn–dusk. 203/966-9577.

NEWTOWN

Parks, Beaches, and Recreation Areas

16 Paugussett State Forest 🐾 🐾 🐾 🐾

You can take the high road or the low road in this 1,935-acre park, which is divided into two sections.

In the 794-acre "upper" section, we recommend the Lillinoah Trail. It is a six-mile loop through a pine forest and is part of the statewide Blue Trails system. Sections of this trail are closed from December 15–March 15, however, so as not to disturb wintering bald eagles who nest here.

The lower portion of this forest hugs the Housatonic River and is accessible via the Zoar Trail. This 6.5-mile loop trail runs through the forest and back along the banks of Lake Zoar. About a mile in, you will find a small beach—if your dog doesn't find it first. Doggy paddlers permitted. The remainder of the trail follows a series of ups and downs—climbs to lake overlooks, then back down and up again.

DIVERSION

Wine Not?: Family-owned **McLaughlin Vineyards,** on the Connecticut Wine Trail, is delightfully dog-friendly. Dogs are welcome on the grounds for hiking and picnicking on the estate, which slopes down to the Housatonic River. Even without the chance to sample some of the vine's finest, this place is worth a visit. Alberts Hill Road; 203/426-1533.

Dogs need to be leashed. The forest is open to hunting October–February. From the intersection of Rte.s 34 and 111, take Great Quarter Road north for 1.5 miles to a parking area turnaround. Open 8 A.M.–sunset. 860/424-3200.

Restaurants

Newtown General Store: For over 200 years, this store has served the needs of hungry travelers. It serves up breakfast, lunch, and ice cream. Judging by the crowd gathering for morning coffee, Newtown is still an early to bed, early to rise kind of place. 43 Main Street; 203/426-9901.

NORWALK

Parks, Beaches, and Recreation Areas

🖤 Cranbury Park 🐾 🐾

This 130-acre preserve has a variety of hiking and walking trails, and sadly, a leash restriction. But beggars can't be choosers because most of the parks in Norwalk don't allow dogs at all. This former estate still features the mansion, manicured lawns, and tended gardens. The trails meander through the property, along shade trees and open, grassy spaces. There is also a bike path and a concert pavilion here. From U.S. 7, take Kennsett Avenue east for about 0.5 miles to Gruman Avenue and the park. Open 7:30 A.M.–8 P.M. 203/854-7806.

🖤 Taylor Farm 🐾 🐾 🐾 🐾 🐕

This big strip of a leash-free park is the exception to the rule in Norwalk. One of the few parks that allows dogs at all, we think it's doggone civilized that it also happens to be a leash-free park. Since this is the obvious hot spot for the locals, you'll always meet up with a pack of happy canines on a visit here. Fortunately, the natives are friendly in these parts and will be eager to show you around.

In addition to the large play field, which is perfect for throwing balls, there are some short trails in the park for a more solitary stroll. The field is fenced, for those dogs who have wandering paws. From I-95, take Exit 16 to East Avenue south for about 0.25 miles. Bear left on Gregory Boulevard and continue for about 0.5 miles. Bear left onto Calf Pasture Beach Road and continue to the end. Finally, turn left onto Beach Road. Open 7:30 A.M.–8 P.M. 203/854-7806.

Restaurants

Swanky Franks: Well, you only need one restaurant listing when it's a place as famous as this one. Listed on every top-roadside-eatery list, this joint really knows how to put on the dog. Swanky doesn't mean lace tablecloths, but it does mean tasty grilled meat, sandwiches, and seafood. You can sit outside at the rainbow-colored picnic tables to enjoy your meal. Be prepared to wait on hot summer days. This place is one very popular doghouse! 182 Connecticut Avenue; 203/838-8969.

Places to Stay

Silvermine Tavern: This is paws-down George and Inu's favorite place to hang their leash in Connecticut. This historic landmark permits pets in the 12 rooms above the country store, and they are lovely and delightfully television-free. You and your pooch are welcome to pass the evening in front of the fireplace in the main building. Rates $80–120 per night. 194 Perry Avenue, Norwalk, CT 06854; 203/847-4558; website: www.silverminetavern.com.

REDDING

Parks, Beaches, and Recreation Areas

19 Putnam Memorial State Park 🐾 🐾 🐾

Connecticut residents think of Putnam Memorial State Park as their very own Valley Forge, for this is where General Israel Putnam spent the winter of 1778–1779 with his revolutionary war soldiers. Valley Forge was no picnic that winter, so just imagine how much colder and more brutal the winter was 250 miles north, here in Redding.

This is a perfect spot for those inclined to mix a history lesson with a walk in the park. In the eastern half of the 252-acre park, there is a road that winds past a number of memorial sites, including Putnam's encampment site, the cemetery, and the officers' barracks. Across the road in the western section of the park, there are more rustic trails and Lake Putnam to explore. Although you can't swim here, there is a scenic trail along the water.

Dogs must be leashed.

The park is just north of the intersection of Black Rock Turnpike and Putnam Park Road (Rte. 107) on Putnam Park Road, which divides the park. Parking is available on both sides of the road. Open 8 A.M.–sunset. 860/424-3200.

RIDGEFIELD

Parks, Beaches, and Recreation Areas

20 Seth Low Pierreport State Park Reserve 🐾 🐾 🐾

As Inu can attest, a wet dog is a happy dog, and boy, oh boy, was he happy here. The parking area for this park doubles as a boat launch, and dogs are free to swim here as long as they stay out of the way of the boats. So before starting our trek into the 300-acre woods, the dogs hopped into the clear clean lake for a dip.

Once you drag your dog away from the water, there's a great outlook and vista of Lake Naraneka below, reachable via a short hike up from the parking area. Several other short trails weave their way through this reserve, but there are no maps or markings to guide you.

Dogs must be leashed. From Rte. 35, take Rte. 116 north for three miles. Turn right onto Barlow Mountain Road and follow the boat launch signs to the parking area on the right. Open 8 A.M.–sunset. 860/454-3200.

Nature Hikes and Urban Walks

Walking Tour of Ridgefield: This exceedingly well-preserved New England town dates back to 1708 and features such famous past residents as Benedict Arnold and Eugene O'Neill. Main Street is located on a 750-foot high ridge where mansions, parks and restaurants share the stage with this unique geology. The Housatonic Valley Tourism Office on Main Street provides a brochure detailing the history of the town and the buildings. 203/743-0546.

Restaurants

Country Corners: This deli-bakery-general store combo is right on the corner of Rte.s 35 and 116, making it the perfect place to watch the world go by. Grab a sandwich or deli delight inside, then settle in at the outdoor plastic tables and chairs for prime viewing of the world. 622 Main Street; 203/438-8465.

SHELTON

Parks, Beaches, and Recreation Areas

21 Indian Well State Park 🐾 🐾 🐾 🐜

The trail system in this state park includes short, scenic hikes through forests and meadows, including one to a waterfall, and the longer—and even more scenic—Paugussett Trail. This trail runs along the very scenic Housatonic River all the way to Stevenson Dam, then on to the town of Monroe. The first three miles are the most scenic and certainly the most pleasant for walking; when we hit the 100-foot-high ledge that required us to climb straight up, the dogs looked at us as if to ask, "did we sign up for this?"

For a short walk to the scenic waterfalls, take the trail leading from the main parking area.

Dogs must be leashed in all state parks. From U.S. 8, take Rte. 110 north for 2.3 miles. The park is on the right. Continue north about one mile further for access to the Paugussett Trail. Open 8 A.M.–sunset. 203/924-5907.

22 Riverview Park 🐾 🐾

This tiny park is a lovely jewel with a name that describes its stunning view of the Housatonic River. Just a hop, skip, and a jump from Indian Well State Park, this much smaller cousin is more laid back and less crowded than its well-developed neighbor.

Dogs must be leashed. From U.S. 8, take Rte. 110 north one mile. The park is on the right. Open dawn–dusk. 203/925-8422.

Places to Stay

AmeriSuites: Chihuahuas only need apply; this hotel only accepts pets that are 10 pounds or under. If you make the cut, rates range $109–154 a night. 695 Bridgeport Avenue, Shelton, CT 06484; 203/925-5900; website: www.amerisuites.com.

Ramada Hotel: This newly-renovated Ramada welcomes you and your pup to its 155 rooms. Rates from $69 per room to $155 for the suites. 780 Bridgeport Avenue, Shelton, CT 06484; 203/929-1500 or 888/298-2054; website: www.ramada.com.

Residence Inn by Marriott: This is mainly an extended-stay hotel, and the rooms have small kitchenettes. At $20 per day, the pet fee is pretty steep. Room rates depend on length of stay, but start at $115 per night. 10001 Bridgeport Avenue, Shelton, CT 06484; 203/926-9000; website: www.marriott.com.

STAMFORD

Parks, Beaches, and Recreation Areas

23 Cove Island Park 🐾 🐾

This park is mostly about water—the Long Island Sound, to be exact. For Stamford residents, it's open year-round, but the park is off-limits to non-residents in the summer months from June through August. What you'll find when you visit are plenty of grassy areas and perfect picnic spots overlooking the sound.

Locals concerned about Long Island Sound sponsor occasional clean-up days, and leashed dogs are welcome. In fact, the last clean-up day resulted in a small mound of unclaimed tennis balls, to which happy canine helpers helped themselves. For more information, call 888/SAVE-LIS (888/728-3547).

A parking permit must be purchased at Terry Conners Ice Rink. From Boston Post Road, take Weed Avenue until it ends. The entrance is on the left. Open dawn–dusk. 203/977-5217.

Restaurants

Brasitas Restaurant: *Ole!* This place is not just for dogs south of the border, as our salsa dogs can attest. Take your pick of Latin specialties like Camarones al Ajillo, shrimp tossed with fresh tomatoes and garlic and chardonnay—all at the restaurant's outdoor seating. We washed it all down with tropical Latin fruit smoothies. 954 Main Street; 203/323-3176.

Planet Pizza: Dig into a dish of pizza and other updated Italian specialties available here. The outdoor tables are the perfect spot for dinner with your dalmatian. 920 Summer Street; 203/357-1101.

Pat's Hubba Hubba: The dog tails start wagging just as soon as we pull up to this hot-pink, retro 1950s-style diner in the middle of Stamford's downtown area. We get fries for the whole pack, and you can also order dogs (hot dogs, that is), burgers, and fried seafood dinners. 189 Bedford Street; 203/359-1718.

Places to Stay

Holiday Inn Select: 383 rooms are just waiting for you and your canine. There is a refundable deposit between $75 and $150 required, so make sure your pooch is on his best behavior. Rates $205–320. 700 Main Street, Stamford, CT 06901; 203/358-8400; website: www.holiday-inn.com.

STRATFORD

Parks, Beaches, and Recreation Areas

24 Boothe Memorial Park and Museum 🐾 🐾

This National Historic landmark makes an excellent backdrop for wedding photos, as we discovered on our last visit. We stumbled on a bridal party in full regalia. Inu, thrilled with the prospect of hors d'oeuvres, nearly jumped into the limo with the bride, where he was about as welcome as a muddy dog in church.

After dragging him away from the fun, we discovered why so many brides make this the backdrop of choice. This 32-acre homestead has a single path that leads through a charming rose garden, clock tower, barn, picnic areas, and icehouse. In other words, this is one pretty park, but not for dogs who have boundless energy.

Dogs must be leashed. From the Merritt Parkway, take Exit 53 to Rte. 110 south. Take an immediate left onto Main/Putney Street and continue for about 0.5 miles to the entrance on left. Open 7 A.M.–dusk. 203/381-2046.

TRUMBULL

Trumbull parks are lovely, but the parks and recreation department aren't so friendly. In fact they refused to give us any information about their parks and requested we not include any descriptions in this book. So what we can tell you is this: Trumbull parks are for Trumbull residents only; cars need a resident parking sticker—and officers do check. All parks require leashes and are open dawn–dusk. For residents, the parks with trails are: Old Mine Park, Indian Ledge Park, and Beach Memorial Park. If you would like directions or more information, you may call 203/452-5060. For the rest of us, we suggest you keep on moving to friendlier parts.

Restaurants

Trumbull Inside Scoop: This place beats the heat by dishing up some delicious ice cream. Oh, and they serve grilled food, as well. 926 White Plains Road; 203/459-4780.

EARMARK YOUR CALENDAR–SEPTEMBER

Dancing Dachshunds: The Trumbull Arts Festival kicks off the week after Labor Day each year, celebrating the arts, including music, dance, drama, and literature. Held on the Trumbull Green, it also celebrates the most delicious art of all—food! For more information, call 203/452-5065.

WESTPORT

Parks, Beaches, and Recreation Areas

🔲 Winslow Park 🐾 🐾 🐾 🐾 🐕

If George and Inu could create their own park, this place would most likely be it. Over 75 percent of the park is off-leash area, and the rolling hills, streams, poop bag dispensers, and park benches make this an inviting spot for everyone. Local owners have even supplied the park with a water bowl to refresh parched pooches. With a place this fabulous, you know the local dogs flock here, so a drop-in doggy play group always seems to be in full swing.

The off-leash area is in the back of the park, behind the split-log fence. You must keep your dog leashed until you get to the leash-free area. Behind the fence is acre after acre of open fields, wooded trails, and a stream just waiting to wallow in.

The park is at the intersection of Compo Beach Road (Rte. 136) and U.S. 1. Open dawn–dusk. 860/454-5188.

Restaurants

The Chefs Table: After tasting this chef's food, you will want to beg at his table. This place does gourmet everything, with homemade soups and good-for-you meals like fat-free turkey burritos. Order take-out and head for the back patio seating where your dog can join you. 42 Church Street; 203/226-3663.

Tacos or What: This yummy Mexican take-out place has the one thing all burrito-loving hounds look for: an outdoor table to get under and catch everything that drops. So take out your tacos, tamales, and quesadillas, and make your pooch a happy hound. 1550 Post Road; 203/254-1725.

Woodies Roadhouse: If ribs are your dog's delight, you'll want to make this a must-stop on your way into your pup's good graces. Formerly Swanky Franks (not to be confused with its sister store in Norwalk, although the ownership is the same) Woodies offers a smorgasbord of choices for breakfast, lunch, and dinner. Outdoor picnic tables in the summer months mean your dog can sit by your side as you tickle your ribs. 1050 East Post Road; 203/226-5355.

WILTON

Parks, Beaches, and Recreation Areas

🔲 Woodcock Nature Center 🐾 🐾 🐾

About half of this 146-acre preserve is wetlands, created by dams in the Spectacle Creek Watershed. The other half is scenic woodland and boulder-strewn trails—all perfect for an afternoon walk with your favorite four-legged pal.

There are four color-coded trails here, all named in honor of former directors of the Woodcock Nature Center. Your best bet is to start with the Yellow Trail, which takes you along the outer edges of the Preserve, passing through forests and overlooks—although the shrubs are a bit overgrown to see very far. The wetlands are best seen from the swamp boardwalk.

There is a map board to guide you and information is available at the center itself.

This is a not-for-profit center, and donations are welcome, but there is no fee to access the trails. From the intersection of Rte.s 116 and 102, take Rte. 102 and proceed west for 2.5 miles. Take a left onto Nod Road at the major fork in Rte. 102. Continue for 1.5 miles south until you see signs on the right. Turn right onto Deer Run Road, and follow it for approximately 1 mile to the entrance of the Woodcock Nature Center on the left. Go through the gates, and proceed to the small parking area. Open dawn–dusk. 203/762-7280.

Nature Hikes and Urban Walks

Weir Hill Farm National Historic Site: J. Alden Weir was an American Impressionist painter who had a summer home and studio here in Wilton. The buildings and grounds are immaculately preserved and are part of the Connecticut Impressionist Art Trail. No dogs are allowed in the buildings, but the grounds are open to visitors (canine and otherwise) year-round.

There are periodic guided walking tours of the estate that you are welcome to join. Leashes are required. The site is located on Old Branchville Road off Rte. 102. Grounds are open dawn–dusk. 203/834-1896, or Weir Farm Trust at 203/761-9945.

Restaurants

Inside Scoop: We have the inside scoop on the Inside Scoop. There's a menu of hot dogs and hamburgers, as well as some salads for hounds hankering for healthy. But best of all are the buckets of ice cream flavors. Convenient picnic tables surround this roadside eatery. 951 Danbury Road; 203/544-9677.

BEYOND THE SKYLINE

A door is what a dog is perpetually on the wrong side of.

—Ogden Nash

After you've checked out all the parks, restaurants, and hotels featured in the preceding chapters, not to mention those dog walks, festivals, and diversions, you and your pup are probably asking, "What else can there be?" Well, if you have the energy, desire, and hopefully a car, you and your faithful companion can explore beyond the New York metro area. Below are some of George and Inu's favorite picks beyond the skyline.

AUSTERLITZ, NEW YORK

Don't Let Any Moss Grow Under Your Feet: When your dog just has to get away, let her spend an exhilarating weekend in the country with dog trainer Alice Moss and her husband at their 30-acre home in Austerlitz, NY. Once a month, a group of very lucky dogs pile into Alice's van and head north for a weekend in the country.

The dogs are pre-selected for temperament, and once they arrive it's a dog-love-dog world. They play, they romp, they take long walks. They nap, they eat, they relax. In other words, your dog gets to enjoy all the things you like to do when you're on vacation. Alice keeps an eye on your pup, but also lets the dogs be dogs in a natural environment, away from the restrictions of city life. So, if you just have to be away from your dog for a weekend, spend it knowing your pal is in good hands at Alice's country retreat. Her personalized pet care services have been featured on *Good Morning, America* and PAX TV.

A two-day weekend is $125; longer weekends are $150. Alice provides most brands of food and dog toys. Reservations must be made well in advance. 212/228-7894; website: www.doggiediva.com.

HYDE PARK, NEW YORK

Hyde Park Trail: This 10-mile hiking trail is only a few hours north of New York City, but you and your dog will feel as if you've traveled much farther away. Running along the Hudson River and through estates like the Franklin D. Roosevelt National Historic Site, Val-Kill National Historic Site, Vanderbilt Mansion National Historic Site, Margaret Lewis Norrie State Park, and Ogden and Ruth Livingston Mills State Park, this trail covers territory once reserved for the very rich.

As you wander between the historical mansions, you'll experience beautiful views of the Hudson River and climb gentle hillsides that offer even more panoramic vantage points. Around the magnificent homes, the trail runs through gorgeous gardens and manicured lawns. Once out of sight of the buildings, you'll also meander through woodlands, swamps, streams, and rocky outcrops.

If tackling the whole 10 miles seems too much, you may wish to sample this lovely trail in sections. We suggest starting at the Vanderbilt Mansion and following the 2.5-mile Vanderbilt Loop, or taking the five-mile round trip between Roosevelt Mansion and Riverfront Park. The full trek between the Mills Mansion and Norrie Point is four miles, or you can just pick any of the sites and wander on the many carriage roads and trails on each property.

Maps are available at each historical site and state park. Leashed dogs are welcome on the trails and the grounds of the estates, but are not allowed inside any of the public buildings. The trail, historic sites, and parks are all accessible off Albany Post Road (Rte. 9).

You can obtain more information about the estates by contacting the National Parks Department at 914/229-9115. The Town of Hyde Park Recreation Department will also provide information on the trails at 914/229-8086.

LAKE PLACID, NEW YORK

Champagne Camping: When you need to get out of the city for a true retreat, look no further than the luxuriously "rustic" Lake Placid Lodge, an elegant 19th century resort created in the Great Camp tradition. With a private beach right on beautiful Lake Placid, beautiful handcrafted furniture in every cottage, feather beds, down comforters, fireplaces, marble bathrooms, Jacuzzis, and even a doggy goody bag provided on check-in, "ruffing" it never felt so good. Dogs are welcome in the Birch and Pine cottages, and there are plenty of trails at adjacent Adirondack Park where you and your leashed pup are welcome to roam. For a vacation that everyone in the family can enjoy, our dogs recommend this wonderful lodge every time. Rates are $200–450 per night. Whiteface Inn Road, P.O. Box 550, Lake Placid, New York 12946. 518/523-2700; 877/523-2700; website: www.lakeplacidlodge.com.

WOODSTOCK, NEW YORK

Weekends at Woofstock: Join Shelly Davis and her canine crew at her 40-acre farm in Woodstock, NY. She brings up to four or five lucky pooches with her each weekend for a three- to four-day retreat in the country. Open April–October, this "canine country club" offers your dog a chance to escape the concrete jungle, to provide you with a guilt-free weekend on those occasions when you just can't take your dog with you.

Those lucky dogs get to play, take walks in the woods, relax in a cageless environment, sleep on cushions, dog beds, sofas, and whatever else suits a vizsla on vacation. All your pup needs to pack is his favorite food. Be assured Shelly will treat your favorite companion as well as you do. This retreat is a true home away from home.

Four-day weekends cost $200. Dogs must be pre-approved to make sure each dog is suited for this special weekend away. As you can imagine, reservations are required well in advance. To book a spot for Spot, call 845/246-6340 or 212/475-6064 or visit website: www.bednbiscuit.com.

DELAWARE WATER GAP, NEW JERSEY

Welcome to the Eighth Wonder of the World!: You'll have to forgive us. It's just that when we find something good we really go all out, and the Delaware Water Gap is something we get very excited about. This spectacular 70,000-acre wilderness of mountains and water in the northwest corner of the state (and Pennsylvania) provides a plethora of parkland surrounding the Delaware River. The Water Gap refers to a 40-mile break, or gap, in the Appalachian Mountains created by the Delaware River as it cuts through the rock. Here you'll find a national recreation area, a national trail, two state forests, and two state parks. (Not to mention eons of history and a paradise of fishing, canoeing, and rafting.)

If you plan on visiting, however, recognize that this is not midtown Manhattan and that ticks, bears, and snakes do exist here—most of the time without incident. For real nature lovers, this is your best chance to experience true unfettered wilderness so close to such a dense urban area.

The best times to visit the Gap are in June when the mountain laurels bloom and again in October for the fall foliage.

Dogs need to be leashed.

The following is a list of the parks within the Delaware Water Gap with some highlights, regulations, and contact information.

Appalachian Trail: 73.4 miles of this Maine to Georgia national trail run through New Jersey and most of it is in the Delaware Water Gap. It is a great place for a hike and you don't have to worry about running out of trail. For more information on the trail, contact the New York–New Jersey Trail Conference at 201/512-9348; website: www.nynjtc.org.

High Point State Park: There are 14,193 acres here and the park is home to the highest point in New Jersey, the aptly named High Point at 1,803 feet. 973/875-4800.

Stokes State Forest: There are 15,735 acres in this state forest and most visitors head for Sunrise Mountain. The peak, at a height of 1,653 feet, offers breathtaking views. The summit is accessible via a number of hiking trails or by car on the park road. (973) 383-3820.

Swartswood State Park: This smallish state park encompasses 1,744 acres and much of it is swallowed up by Swartswood Lake. There are plenty of trails around the lake and even more spots to pause for a refreshing dip. (973) 383-5230.

Worthington State Forest: There are 6,200 acres here and most of it is mountainous and rugged. The park's easiest and most popular hiking areas are around Sunfish Pond and Dunnfield Creek. Both offer water spots for your dogs and scenic vistas for you. (908) 841-9575.

From Memorial Day through Labor Day, there is a $5 weekday and $7 weekend and holiday entrance fee at the two state parks. A State Park Pass is available for $35 and is good at all New Jersey state parks for a year. Maps, information, and park passes are available at the Kittatinny Point Visitor Center right off I-80 near Exit 1.

Most of the parks and trailheads are accessible from Old Mine Road, which is also off I-80 at Exit 1. All sections of the park are open sunrise–sunset, except the state forests, which are open 8 A.M.–8 P.M. 908/496-4458.

RESOURCES

TRANSPORTATION SERVICES

Manhattan

Hampton's Express: Dogs of all sizes are allowed in these vans, but they must be muzzled or in crates. We wouldn't receommend this on a busy Friday afternoon, but if you go in the off-peak hours and days, you might be okay. Dogs are an additional $10 each way. 212/861-6800.

Hampton Jitney: Dogs are allowed in carriers, but space is tight. If your dog is larger than a lap dog, you might want to travel with a transport company instead. $10 each way for your pup. 800/936-0440.

Madison Avenue Limousine: For dogs that demand nothing but the best, this luxury limousine company will take you and your pup anywhere you want to go. Whether you're on your way to the dog spa, personal trainer, or just a day of shopping, Madison Avenue is only a phone call away. 38 East 15th Street; 212/674-0060.

Paw Mobile: Canine chauffeurs transport pups of all sizes in the very special "Paw Mobile." This is something like the Bat Mobile without all the weird gadgets. Designed with a dog's needs in mind, you and your pampered pooch will ride in style wherever you wish to go in the five boroughs. 212/594-7087, 917/734-2779; website: www.pawmobile.com.

Pet Chauffeur: This car service will transport your pup anywhere in Manhattan (or in the country for that matter), with or without you along for the ride. They provide transportation for emergency services, are equipped with a pet stretcher and are familiar with all the emergency hospitals in the area. They are also authorized airline shippers. 135 East 32nd Street; 212/696-9744, 718/752-1767, or 866/PET-RIDE (866/738-7433); website: www.PetRide.com.

Petex, Inc.: Operating throughout the Tri-State area, the experts at Petex are happy to take your dog for a ride. Offering shuttles to the airport, around town, and trips out of town, this dog-friendly outfit welcomes pups with or without you along. 480 2nd Avenue; 212/685-1173.

Pet Taxi: This dog-friendly company will transport you and your pup anywhere in the Tri-State area. They also help with relocations and will arrange for your dog to travel on the airlines. 227 East 56th Street; 212/755-1757; website: www.epettaxi.com.

Pet Transportation: This airport shuttle service is happy to take dogs and their owners to and from all the major airports. For only $12 from Manhattan to La Guardia, $20 to and from JFK Airport, and $30 for a trip to Newark Airport, rest assured you won't miss a flight while you search for a cab. Pet Transportation is available for other trips in Manhattan as well. 212/929-2138.

Tommy's Taxi's: Tommy will transport you and your pup from New York City to the Fire Island Ferries for a mere $10 per dog. Ride in style in Tommy's van without all the usual hassle for those who want to get away for the weekend. Spaces get filled fast so reservations are required. Rates are $17–20 per person. 631/665-4800.

Queens
Animals Away: This pet taxi service operates throughout the New York City area and will pick up, deliver, or transport your pup wherever he or she (or you) may wish to go. Prices vary by location. 22-38 121st Avenue; 718/461-5684.

World Wide Pet Transport: This pet transportation company operates all over the Tri-State area. They will provide taxi service for your pet (with or without you along for the ride), pick up and deliver your pet to an appointment, and will even arrange for flight assistance if you need to ship your pet anywhere. 13-14 College Point Boulevard; 718/539-5543.

Long Island

Cross Sound Ferry: Operating across the Long Island Sound back and forth to Connecticut, pets must be leashed or in a carrier. Pets are also allowed in designated indoor areas or outside on the deck. 2 Ferry Street; 631/323-2525; website: www.longislandferry.com.

Fire Island Ferries: These seasonal ferries operate between Sayville, Patchogue, or Bay Shore from April to October. Leashed dogs are welcome on the outer decks. 631/665-3600; website: www.fireislandferries.com.

North Ferry Company: Operating from Shelter Island to Sag Harbor, dogs are allowed to ride with their owners either leashed on deck, or inside a car. 631/749-0139; website: www.northferry.com.

Orient Point Ferry: Operating from New London, Connecticut to Orient Point, leashed dogs are welcome on the outer decks. 860/443-5281; website: www.longislandferry.com.

Port Jefferson Ferry: Operating from Bridgeport, Connecticut to Port Jefferson, leashed dogs are allowed on the outer deck of the ferry. 631/473-0286; website: www.bpjferry.com.

South Ferry Company: Also operating from Shelter Island, leashed dogs are allowed on deck or in their owner's vehicles. 631/749-1200; website: www.southferry.com.

Viking Ferry Lines: This ferry operates between Block Island, Rhode Island to Montauk from May to October. Leashed dogs are allowed in designated passenger areas or on the outer decks. 631/668-5700.

24-HOUR EMERGENCY ANIMAL HOSPITALS

The last thing you need if your pet is having a real emergency is to be groping for the Yellow Pages, trying to locate the nearest emergency room. Our advice: know the location closest to you before you need it. We hope you never do, but here is a listing of the 24-hour animal hospitals in your area, just in case.

Manhattan/The Bronx

The Animal Medical Center
510 East 62nd Avenue
New York, NY 10021
212/838-8100

Park East Animal Hospital
52 East 64th Street
New York, NY 10021
212/832-8417

West Parc Veterinary Clinic
8 West 86th Street
New York, NY 10014
914/362-9100

Queens/Brooklyn

Crawford Far Rockaway
Animal Hospital

708 Beach 19th Street
Far Rockaway, NY 11691
718/327-0256

Staten Island

Northside Animal Hospital
773 Post Avenue
Staten Island, NY 10305
718/981-4445

South Shore Veterinary Medical Practice
125 New Dorp Lane
Staten Island, NY 10306
718/980-2600

Long Island

Central Veterinary Associates
Main Hospital
73 West Merrick Road

Valley Stream, NY 11580
516/825-3066

East Village Green Animal Hospital
4 East Village Green
Levittown, NY 11756
516/579-09

South Fork Animal Hospital
PO Box 1390, Montauk Highway
Wainscott, NY 11975
631/537-0035

Westchester County

Brewster Veterinary Hospital
3455 Danbury Road, Route 6
Brewster, NY 10509
914/279-5053

Mamaroneck Veterinary Hospital
649 West Boston Post Road
Mamaroneck, NY 10543
914/777-0398

Mount Kisco Veterinary Clinic
474 Lexington Avenue
Mount Kisco, NY 10549
914/241-3337

Veterinary Emergency Group
193 Tarrytown Road
White Plains, NY 10607
914/949-8779

Rockland County

County Animal Hospital, Inc.
49 Congers Road
New City, NY 10956
914/634-4607

Northern New Jersey

Animal Clinic & Hospital of
Jersey City P. A.
603 West Side Avenue
Jersey City, NJ 07304
201/435-6424

Bergenline Animal Hospital
7706 Bergenline Avenue
North Bergen, NJ 07047
201/854-7330

Emerson Animal Hospital P. A.
371 Kinderkamack Road
Emerson, NJ 07630
201/262-2950

Hoboken Animal Hospital P. A.
640 Washington Street
Hoboken, NJ 07030
201/963-3604

Red Bank Veterinary Hospital
210 Newman Springs Road
Red Bank, NJ 07001
732/747-3636

Fairfield County

Copps Hill Animal Hospital
30 Old Quarry Road
Ridgefield, CT 06877
203/438-8878

Veterinary Referral and
Emergency Center
123 West Cedar Street
Norwalk, CT 06854
203/854-9960

ACCOMMODATIONS INDEX

RESTAURANT INDEX

GENERAL INDEX

M

Macy's Thanksgiving Day Parade 74
Madison Square Park & James' Dog Run 43
Mahwah 253–254; accommodations 255;
    accommodations 255
Main Beach 158
Main Beach Surf and Sport 180
Mamaroneck 206
Manhattan 18–75
Manorville (Brookhaven Township) 170–171
Marcus Garvey Park 50
Marine Park 134
Marine Park (Brooklyn) 109–110
Marine Park (Red Bank) 265
Maryanne's Kayaks 180
Mastic Beach (Brookhaven Township)
    171–172; accommodations 172
Matawan/Old Bridge 255–256
McCarren Park & Dog Run 108
McLaughlin Vineyards 284
Mercer-Houston Dog Run 45
Mermaid Parade 104
Meschutt Beach County Park 168–169
Middle Island (Brookhaven Township) 172;
    accommodations 172
Middle Village 133
Midland Beach 141
Midtown East 40, 54–57; accommodations
    56–57; restaurants 55–56
Midtown West 58–62; accommodations
    59–62; restaurants 58–59
Miller Field 142
Mills Reservation 242–243
Monsignor McGolrick Park 110
Montauk (East Hampton Township)
    173–177; accommodations 175–177;
    restaurants 175
Montauk Point State Park 173–174
Montclair 256–257; restaurants 257
Morningside Heights 62–63; restaurants 63
Morningside Park 62–63
Morris Heights 79
Moss, Alice 293–294
Mott Haven 79
Mountain Lakes Camp 210
Mountainside 257–258
Mount Ivy 228–229
Mount Ivy County Park 228–229
Mount Loretto 142

Mount Loretto Conservation Area 142
Mount Pleasant 206–208
Murray Hill 133
Murray Playground & Dog Run 132
Mutts Marathon 243

N

Nassau Beach Park & Dog Run 170
Neighborhood Open Space Coalition 27
Nesconset (Smithtown Township) 177
Newark 259–260; accommodations 260;
    accommodations 260
New Canaan 284
New Canaan Nature Center 284
New City 230–231
New Dorp Beach 142–143; restaurants
    142–143
New Rochelle 208–209; accommodations
    209
Newtown 284–285; restaurants 285
New York Council of Dog Owner Groups
    (NYCDOG) 22
New York Dog Spa and Hotel Boutique 26
New York Pet Show 60
New York Waterway North Hudson
    Cruise 216
Nomahegan Park 269–270
North Bergen 260–261
North Castle 209
Northern New Jersey 240–273
North Hudson Park 260–261
North Salem 210; accommodations 210
North Shore Esplanade 144
Northside 110
Norwalk 285–286; accommodations 286;
    restaurants 285–286
Nyack 231–233; restaurants 232–233
Nyack Beach State Park 231

O

Oakland 261–262; restaurants 262
Oktoberfest, Bear Mountain Inn 224
Old Croton Aqueduct Trail 195, 215
Old Croton Trailway State Park 200
Old Westbury Gardens 177
Old Westbury (North Hempstead Township)
    177
Orangeburg 233
Orient Point Ferry 153

ABOUT THE AUTHORS

© JoAnna Downey & Christian J. Lau

George considers taking care of his person, JoAnna Downey, to be a very serious, full-time job. It's his duty to wake her up and ensure she gets plenty of exercise, sees the world in a different way, and makes new friends. He is also a very good listener and is quick to tell you he is available for a little free therapy whenever JoAnna looks like she might succumb to the person-eat-person world of New York City. George and his pal, Inu, authors of the books, *The Dog Lover's Companion to Boston* and *The Dog Lover's Companion to New England* came up with the idea of writing this book as a way to get their persons out of the house, on the road and into a better swing of things —all with one big swat of the paw.

George is a nine-year old "cannardly" (which means you can hardly tell what kind of dog he is), but people who insist on more limiting categories claim he must be a bearded collie, a Tibetan terrier, a puli, a Portuguese water dog—in other words, a cannardly. For the most part,

George shuns these labels and just considers himself a member of the species Canis familiaris (commonly known as "dog"). While residing at an animal shelter, he picked JoAnna out of the multitudes, decided she looked like the perfect meal ticket, and hitched a ride home. When he's not out sniffing trails and conducting research for his books, George likes to chase squirrels, teach JoAnna how to throw the ball in a straight arc and bark at weird people.

Inu is proud of his heritage and carries his golden retriever lineage with style. Although an enormously social animal, Inu loves the solitude of the Great Outdoors—a taste he developed while living in the Berkshires for the first three years of his life. Then, needing a home and deciding city life would provide the attention he so dearly loves, he adopted Chris Lau. Although Inu loves calling the city streets home, he still heeds the call of the wild and is ready to travel at a moment's notice. Inu, at twelve years old, is starting to slow down, but he never tires of looking for free pats, food, and adulation.

JoAnna and Chris have been friends and co-writers ever since George and Inu introduced them in the park over six years ago. When they aren't exploring the eastern seaboard with the dogs or disagreeing about the demise of baseball and whether or not the Brooklyn Dodgers should have ever left New York, JoAnna is a writing consultant and Chris works as a systems analyst and full-time dad to Connor, age five.

HUMANE SOCIETY OF NEW YORK

Animal Clinic / Adoption Center

I'm a Labrador Mix, big, yellow, a little klutzy. My old family liked me when I was small. But when I grew "too big" they said I had to go. They just didn't care anymore. If it hadn't been for the Humane Society of New York I don't know where I'd be now. The Society found me a "forever" home, with people who understand who I am and what I need. I love my new family...and I love the Society that helped me.

— Barney

More than 25 years ago the Humane Society of New York began programs supporting the emotional as well as physical needs of animals. We treat them with kindness, respect and, of course, expert professional care. It's an idea whose time has come. Today we are widely copied, and it pleases us to know that, near and far, animals' lives are the better for it. Each year 30,000 animals are helped at the Society. Currently, major programs include:

🐾 Our seven-day clinic, offering quality, comprehensive veterinary care at low cost.

🐾 Spay/Neuter services. Overpopulation is a major concern; without cutting the birth rate of unwanted animals, we cannot stop their suffering. The Society has always neutered all of its adoption animals, and we underwrite a variety of spay/neuter programs for city pet owners, including our Animal Mukti Free Spay/Neuter Program, our Outdoor Cat Spay/Neuter Project (the New York metro area's first trap-neuter-release effort), and ongoing free spay/neuter of pit bulls.

🐾 Our Vladimir Horowitz & Wanda Toscanini Horowitz Adoption Center is a safe haven — with no time limit — for rescued dogs and cats.

🐾 Exercise, training, grooming, top medical attention.

We excel at providing individualized care for each animal entrusted to the Society. We have been here for the animals since 1904. We make life-giving care a reality when there is no one else to help. The Society receives no government funds; our work is accomplished solely through private, voluntary donations.

To learn more, contact:

HUMANE SOCIETY OF NEW YORK,
306 E. 59th St., New York, NY 10022
t (212) 752-4842
f (212) 752-2803
www.humanesocietyny.org